SCIENCE
AND SPIRIT

SCIENCE
AND SPIRIT

Editor and Principal Author
Ravi Ravindra

An ICUS Book

PARAGON HOUSE
New York

Published in the United States by the
International Conference on the Unity of the Sciences
481 8th Avenue
New York, New York 10001

Distributed by Paragon House Publishers
90 Fifth Avenue
New York, New York 10011

An ICUS Book

The International Conference on the Unity of the Sciences (ICUS) con-
venes international, distinguished scientists and scholars from every field
of study to pursue academic discussion of theoretical and practical concerns. ICUS seeks an integrated world-view based on absolute values
generated through multi-disciplinary, academic dialogue.

Library of Congress Cataloging-in-Publication Data

Science and spirit / editor and principal author Ravi Ravindra
    400 p.   cm.
    "An ICUS book."
    Includes index.
    ISBN 0-89226-085-8
    ISBN 0-89226-082-3 (paperback)
    1. Religion and science—1946–   2. East and West   I. Title.
    BL241.R32   1990
    291.1'75—dc20   90-6962
                                                              CIP

To my Father
in whom the Spirit
supercedes everything else.

TABLE OF CONTENTS

PART FIVE: SCIENCE AND SPIRITUAL PATHS

ACKNOWLEDGMENTS

I am grateful to the International Conference on the Unity of the Sciences (ICUS) for inviting me to organize and chair a Committee on East-West Perspectives on Science and Spirit for their Seventeenth Conference held in Los Angeles, California, November 24–27, 1988. The sponsors also arranged a pre-ICUS conference in Delphi, Greece. Their generosity in both the conferences is much appreciated.

My wife, Sally Ravindra, was very helpful and supportive in looking after many organizational details of the meetings in Delphi with sensitivity.

Professors de Silva, Dy, Gooding, Murray, and Sharpe, whose contributions are represented in this volume, acted as co-chairs with me in different sessions during the ICUS meetings in Los Angeles.

Professor Priscilla Murray's editorial help in the selection of the papers and in the preparation of the manuscript is very gratefully acknowledged.

The papers gathered here were published or presented at conferences as acknowledged below. They are listed here in the order in which they appear in this volume.

Ravi Ravindra, "Physics and Religion," in *The Encyclopedia of Religion*, eds. Mircea Eliade *et al.*; Macmillan Publishing Co., New York, 1987, vol. 11, pp. 319–323.

Ravi Ravindra and Priscilla Murray, "The Indian View of Nature," presented at ICUS, Atlanta, 1987.

R. Balasubramanian, "The Hindu Attitude to Knowledge and Nature," presented at ICUS, Los Angeles, 1988.

Osman B. Bakar, "The Unity of Science and Spiritual Knowledge: The Islamic Experience," presented at ICUS, Los Angeles, 1988.

Manuel B. Dy, Jr., "Does the West Need the East?," presented at ICUS, Los Angeles, 1988.

Ravi Ravindra, "Experience and Experiment: A Critique of Modern Scientific Knowing," *Dalhousie Review*, vol. 55, 1975–76, pp. 655–674.

Ravi Ravindra, "Western Science and Technology and the

Indian Intellectual Tradition," *Manthan*, September, 1978, pp. 8–16.

Francis G. Nagasaka, "Between Physics and Natural History," presented at ICUS, Los Angeles, 1988.

Tor Ragnar Gerholm, "The Holy Nothing Versus the Quincunx of Knowledge: Is There a Reconciliation?," presented at ICUS, Los Angeles, 1988.

M.W. Padmasiri de Silva, "The Distance between the Laboratory and the Monastery," presented at ICUS, Los Angeles, 1988.

Alfredo Lagmay, "Science and Siddhartha," presented at ICUS, Los Angeles, 1988.

Ravi Ravindra, "Is Religion Psychotherapy?—An Indian View," *Religious Studies*, vol. 14, 1978, pp. 389–397.

Priscilla Murray, "Scientific Knowledge and Spiritual Understanding," presented at ICUS, Los Angeles, 1988.

Ravi Ravindra, "Yoga and Knowledge," presented at ICUS 1986.

Ravi Ravindra, "Perception in Yoga," *Re-Vision, Jour. Physics and Knowledge and Consciousness*, 3, 1980, 36–42.

Ravi Ravindra, "Science and the Mystery of Silence," *American Theosophist*, vol. 70, Nov. 1982, pp. 350–355.

Ravi Ravindra, "In the Beginning Is the Dance of Love," in *Origin and Evolution of the Universe: Evidence for Design?*, ed. J.M. Robson; McGill-Queen's University Press, Montreal, 1987, pp. 259–279.

Ravi Ravindra, "To the Dancer Belongs the Universe: Freedom and Bondage of Natural Law," presented at the Isthmus Institute, Dallas, in October, 1986.

Ravi Ravindra, "The Spiritual Quest," *American Theosophist*, vol. 73, June 1985, pp. 203–207.

Richard W. Sharpe, "Some Reflections on Science," excerpted from "Lost Science," presented at ICUS, Los Angeles, 1988.

Ravi Ravindra, "Where Are Religion and Science Complementary?" presented at ICUS, Boston, 1978. (Published in *The Re-evaluation of Existing Values and the Search for Absolute Values*, International Cultural Foundation, New York, 1979; pp. 395–399.)

E.C. George Sudarshan, "Science and Spirit: A Physicist's View," excerpted from "Is Modern Science Closer to Religion?," presented at ICUS, Los Angeles, 1988.

Ravi Ravindra, "Science as a Spiritual Path," *Journal of Religious Studies*, vol. 7, 1979, pp. 78–85.

David C. Gooding, "Michael Faraday's Apprenticeship: Science as a Spiritual Path," presented at ICUS, Los Angeles, 1988.

PART ONE:

INTRODUCTION AND THEME

ONE

INTRODUCTION

Ravi Ravindra

"It is no exaggeration to say," remarked A.N. Whitehead, "that the future course of history depends on the decision of this generation as to the relations between religion and science."

There is an increasing feeling among some people that an adequate view of life cannot be based solely on Western science and technology which are basically reductionist in their attitudes and methods, and that Eastern perspectives on nature, life, and Spirit may also contribute something of value to human welfare. It has been suggested that the various recent advances in the sciences themselves, in spite of the Western cultural assumptions in their procedures and foundations, may be revealing a view of reality which is hospitable to traditional Eastern spiritual perspectives. Also, in some quarters there is a growing disillusionment with the whole enterprise of science which is no longer regarded as being exclusively a force for the good.

The present global situation permits neither an isolation of the Eastern and Western values, nor the continuing military or economic domination of the West over the East. This situation has been brought about primarily by developments in science and technology, which are inevitably leading to the emergence of a planetary culture. If the intellectuals, both of the East and of the West, do not endeavor to forge a right synthesis of science and spirituality, of the Occident and the Orient, of modernity and tradition, this world-wide culture will be based on a very low common denominator, amounting essentially to a lack of ethical standards and of spiritual values. We can hardly over-estimate the difficulty of communication across cultures and disciplines, and also the urgent necessity for some understanding across these boundaries to be reached. We hope that this book can be of some help in the development of such an understanding.

Initially, some are likely to think that science simply means knowledge, as it does etymologically, and that any reasonable and systematic study of phenomena is science. It is easy to forget that there are certain basic presuppositions of scientific inquiry in the modern (post-sixteenth century) world, essentially derived from a particular stage in the European and Christian philosophical and religious history, which set modern science apart not only from the sciences of China and India but also from the ancient European sciences. These presuppositions involve the very essence of what makes any culture distinctive from another, namely issues dealing with the place and meaning of human beings in the cosmos, the nature and aim of knowledge, the relevance and importance of external experiments and internal experiences as providing data and evidence, the value and significance of faith in the development of science, and the like. Since the East—with all the immense variety derived from the ancient, vast and, at times, mighty cultures of Egypt, Persia, India, China, Korea, and Japan, and now comprising nearly three fifths of the human race—has several very different perspectives on all of these basic questions, it is not surprising that the Eastern views of science are also very different from the Western view, in spite of the fact there is something basically trans-national and trans-cultural about science. In part, it is an acknowledgment of the importance of science and technology in the modern world that there are different perspectives on them, for it is only on relatively unimportant matters that people can easily agree.

It is not very easy to come to an agreement on what a phenomenon is, and certainly not on what is reasonable, and therefore on what science is. For example, in a recent conference, there was a question repeatedly raised by some Eastern intellectuals whether a systematic internal investigation of various subtle energies in the human body is a scientific study. Is

Yoga a science? The hesitation of the Western intellectuals in agreeing with this is understandable, because science is not just any reasonable and systematic study of phenomenon, as one may be tempted to think. It is a particular kind of study requiring external evidence, independent of the level of spiritual development of the researcher, subject to repeatability, prediction, control, etc., based on identifiable philosophical assumptions and worldviews.

These considerations and difficulties, involving the nature of reason and the specific rationality underlying scientific procedures, are germane to the extremely important question of the relationship of science and Spirit. Of course, it is even more difficult to clearly define what Spirit is. Some of the papers collected here address these questions among others. However, one remark may be made here: traditional knowledge asserts that Spirit is higher than and prior to body-mind, sometimes for simplicity called only *body*. Even though the various spiritual traditions may express it differently, they can all understand and endorse the essence of '*In the beginning was the Spirit.*'

Two very closely related comments need to be made about the difference between the 'Eastern' and the 'Western' views, and between the 'spiritual' and the 'scientific' perspectives, keeping in mind the difficulties associated with such generalizations. (1) In general, the East thinks, as do all spiritual traditions, that "it is the spirit that has the body." On the other hand, from the scientific (Western?) point of view, if Spirit can be spoken of at all, it can only be that "*It is the body that has the spirit.*" Vast philosophic and cultural differences are implied in these expressions. (2) By and large, the scientific motivation for an inquiry into the relationship between science and Spirit seems to be "How can the spiritual energy be utilized in doing better science which will lead to a more useful technology?" The spiritual point of view seems to be "How can science, or anything else, be of service to the Spirit?"

If these remarks are more or less representative, they indicate the vast gulf in the very starting points of the Eastern and Western intellectuals, and of the spiritual masters and the scientists. *But are these remarks true?* It was partly in order to attempt to answer this question, in addition to the major one of the relationship between science and Spirit, that a group of thoughtful people among them some scientists, philosophers, religionists, and historians was brought together.

The Editor was the organizer and chairman of the committee which met to discuss this issue under the aegis of the International Conference on the Unity of the Sciences in November, 1988. Nearly half of the articles gathered in this book were presented at that conference. Not all the conference papers could be included for a variety of reasons, but mainly because they seemed a little tangential to the theme of this book. The comments of the discussants have been included here along with the papers only in two cases where they seemed particularly helpful. The rest of the articles in this book have been authored by the Editor and published in various journals over the last fifteen years. Each paper is self-consistent and can be read independently of the others. A little editing would have eliminated the inevitable repetitions in the various papers of the Editor; but this would have resulted in the loss of self-consistency of the articles. Clearly, there are arguments to be made on both sides; but on balance it was decided to leave most of the articles as they were initially published. The papers have been grouped together in thematic categories which are self-explanatory. Many of the papers included in this volume, especially those which were published a few years ago, do not use gender-neutral language. However, it is clearly the intention of the authors to use "man" and related pronouns generically rather than exclusively as referring to the male of the species.

The diacritical marks in the non-English words have been added only where they were originally included in the papers. A few of the papers were published in less academic journals, and do not carry diacritical marks; instead, some words have been written in a more anglicized form.

Here are some of the questions which were raised by the Editor for the participants in the conference to consider:

Origins and Context of Modern Science

1. Was the rise of modern science because of Christianity or in spite of it? This question can be raised both historically as well as theologically.

2. Was modern science, perhaps along with Humanism and maybe Protestantism, essentially an attempt to rescue Western culture in the face of decay in the heart of the Christian Church in Europe?

3. Is modern science anti-spiritual in its attitudes, procedures, and consequences? It is often assumed that science and technology have resulted in an exploitation of Nature and a desacralization of the whole Cosmos. Is it true? If yes, how has science come to be an agent of the Devil rather than a search for Truth as the greatest scientists have believed?

4. Is the distinction between 'science' and 'technology' tenable from the point of view of their underlying attitudes and methods? Is there not a seamless garment here? Can there be much technology now without science? And can science be funded without the expectation of a technological spin off? Is it not true that what the poor countries want is technology and that some of them realize that they cannot advance technologically without developing a scientific base?

5. Is it true that a vast majority of physical scientists, including physicists, chemists, engineers, and the like, throughout the world work for the military-industrial complex? If true, does this not mean that scientists end up supporting a social fabric based largely on fear and greed?

6. Is it true that the driving dynamo of technology, and by association of science, is power, which in turn is fueled by fear and gratification of pleasures? From the scientific point of view, *is understanding Nature tantamount to having power over Nature?*

7. Is there a relationship between the development of science-technology, and industrial-military power in the nations of the world since the sixteenth century? Is there a direct numerical correlation between the number of Nobel laureates in science and the mega weapons of destruction in a country?

8. Are technology and industrialization, with their built-in logic of expansion, innovation, and consumption, deeply dehumanizing and contrary to traditional and spiritual values?

9. Is it true, as Simone Weil had suggested, that given the exploitation and control built right into the fundamental assumptions, procedures, and methods of modern science, an Auschwitz must inevitably follow a Galileo?

Western Science and Non-Western Cultures

1. It is true that non-Christian cultures such as India and China did not produce modern science, but could they have? Are the relevant factors theological and philosophical or economic? Is it true that science can not really flourish in non-Christian countries? Do non-Christian cultures have to accept Christian theology in order to make scientific progress?

2. Is it true that a spiritual, moral, and ecological devastation has been brought about in the West by science and technology? Is there any reason to believe that other cultures such as India and China, and the cultures influenced by them, will escape such decay? Are the forces responsible for the corruption of the West peculiarly Western?

3. Is there any evidence to indicate that China, India, Japan, (or Persia or Egypt) have had a better record of ecological or spiritual sanity than the West since their independence from the Western powers? Or even historically, before the Western influence?

4. Are there fundamental differences in the Eastern and Western attitudes to Nature and knowledge? What are they? Are they bound to, or likely to, lead to different kinds of 'sciences'? Can they be reconciled in a higher synthesis or does one mode have to be set aside?

5. Does modern (Western) science essentially marginalize epistemologies based in other cultures and render them merely exotic and quaint, and of antiquarian interest?

6. Does the West need the East? It is sometimes said that the West is turning to the East for spiritual values. Is it mostly a thirst for something exotic? What is missing in the West that is not provided by Western religions or science and technology? Is it partly a sense of collective guilt, felt by some Westerners about their past colonial exploitation, which leads to the concession that the East should be allowed a say in world affairs?

7. Is it not equally, or even more, true that many intelligent,

energetic and sensitive people from the East are turning to the West, not only for scientific knowledge but also for liberal, humane, and spiritual values and human dignity? Is the reason why so many Easterners choose to stay in the Western countries—the reverse does not happen very often—exclusively to do with material comforts? Or are there social, intellectual, and spiritual factors also involved?

8. Does the world need Eastern wisdom? Does the East really have something of absolute value to contribute to human welfare? Or, can the Easterners be kept well-fed by Western science and technology, philosophically Westernized and be essentially marginalized in a world-culture, while being encouraged to engage in their songs and dances?

9. Does not Japan place a bold question mark in front of all the assertions about the East and the West? Is the rise of Japan in wealth, industry, and power, owing to its philosophy, spirituality, or wisdom?

New Science and the Contemporary Situation

1. Have the developments in transportation and communication technologies been the most important contributors to the present world situation? Are there factors other than these which have brought various cultures into a closer juxtaposition with each other?

2. Is it a consequence of the political developments since the World War II that colonialism is discredited so that the major cultures are no longer related to one another as either victors or vanquished? On the other hand, have the spheres of domination now shifted to economics and ideology? Are science and technology the major contributors to that domination?

3. Is there a new global philosophical situation since World War II which requires that the distinct philosophies, religions, and arts of the non-Western cultures be considered as valid as those of the West? What about the distinct 'sciences'—especially manifest in their systems of medicine and physical culture and psychotherapies—in these non-Western cultures? Are they as valid as Western science?

4. Is contemporary science philosophically and religiously different from modern science? From the point of view of the

attitude to spirituality, do the twentieth-century developments in science offer a radical departure? Is science now more in harmony with Eastern metaphysics? What happened to the Christian metaphysics from which the modern science supposedly sprang?

5. If contemporary science is somehow closer to the 'wisdom of the East,' does it follow that the contemporary scientists are wiser than the nineteenth-century scientists? Does science in fact have anything to do with wisdom?

6. It is sometimes suggested that contemporary physics is 'holistic' and has demonstrated the interconnectedness of everything. Is it true? What does this mean? Should it be assumed that the Nobel Prize winner in physics next year would be more whole and more in harmony with nature than was Kepler or Pythagoras?

7. If contemporary science is now saying what the Buddha or the Vedic and the Taoist sages said, as is asserted in many very popular books, should we assume that a few hundred years from now, when science has progressed further, the scientists would be wiser and closer to the Truth than the Buddha or Lao-Tze were?

8. Does science need the Eastern perspective? For what?

9. Does the East need science? For what?

Science and Spirit

1. Would spiritual life be affected for the worse if science is ignored? Why is it that for spiritual nourishment one so often looks to those cultures which have rather neglected science? Does science hinder spiritual life?

2. Would science be adversely affected if spirituality is ignored? It can be said that the essence of spiritual life is freedom from the ego or from selfishness, and that this freedom naturally expresses itself in love and compassion. What has all this do with scientific activity? Do great scientists manifest exemplary compassion?

3. What are the fundamental differences between the Eastern and Western perspectives on the relationship between science and Spirit?

4. William Blake regarded all systems and abstractions as

satanic. Is the degradation and devaluation of the unique and the individual essentially different if it is brought about by the abstractions of science or by the metaphysical abstractions of theology and spirituality? For example, in an analogy to be found in the *Chāndogya Upaniṣad* (6.1.4), and much quoted and admired by the Vedantists, it is said that clay alone is real, while its modifications are only names arising from speech. However true this statement may be at the mountain peak of consciousness, a vantage point vouchsafed to very few persons in human history, is it not here below a facile and destructive dismissal of all art, uniqueness, and individuality? Is an exquisite Chinese vase the same as a lump of clay? One may wonder if there is a relationship between the decline of the arts and the sciences in India and the triumph of Shankara, the great Vedantist philosopher.

5. Is it not true that only extremely rare human beings have the highest vision in which everything is seen both in its oneness and in its uniqueness at the same time? Is it not to be expected that any theorizing based on the words articulated in the peak vision by spiritual masters, but elaborated by those who do not have the comprehensiveness of the whole vision, cannot but be a further spinning of the webs of illusion and confusion? Does it not follow that in general the metaphysical philosophers add only confusion by their theorizing, and thus are as unhelpful in the real practice of spirituality as in that of science? One wonders if this is why Newton said, 'Hypothesis non fingo,' and the Buddha said, 'The Tathagata has no theories'?

6. Is it true that science, or reason in general, can be interpreted in the service of any system or doctrine—such as Christianity, Marxism, Democracy, Buddhism, or Taoism—as long as the interpreter has sufficient ingenuity and is able to ignore what does not fit into his scheme? One wonders if Einstein was right in suggesting that there is something reprehensible about such ideological, theological, and philosophical applications of science.

7. Can science itself be a spiritual path? Is one forced to make a clear distinction between a scientist and his attitude to science, and the science he produces? Have there been any scientists for whom science was a spiritual path?

8. Are there different levels of the mind and the corresponding levels of knowing? If knowledge is state-specific, depending on the state of consciousness or level of the mind from which a phenomenon is known, what is the proper place of science in the light of mystical consciousness? Is the whole edifice of science worth a single vision and the corresponding edifying enunciation of the Buddha or of the Christ?

Not all of these questions could be considered in the conference in detail for the simple reason that the subject is vast and complex. Some of the participants found a few of these questions rather irritating, and even irrelevant. Nevertheless, some general remarks can be made about the discussions which did take place and which are reflected in the papers collected in this book.

The Particularity of Modern Science

1. It does not seem to have been sufficiently appreciated in the meetings that modern (post-sixteenth century) science is truly distinct in its assumptions, procedures, goals, and methods from the earlier sciences within the Western world, and from other sciences, for example, those in India and China. One of the major features of modern science—and the reason why Galileo is justly regarded as the father of modern science—is a very subtle and peculiar combination of reason and experiment, theory and observation, contemplation and utility, mathematics and measurement, individual imaginative creativity and publicly repeatable verification. The success of this novel feature of the scientific enterprise was striking enough that it defined for subsequent generations a new rationality. This peculiarity is particularly evident in physics. No doubt this is the reason why since the sixteenth century physics has been the model for all other sciences to emulate.

2. One aspect of the above feature is a merger of some Platonic and Aristotelian tendencies in the metaphysics underlying modern science: the real world is the ideal world of mathematical forms which lies behind or underneath the actual world; but observations of the actual world, and not reason alone nor revelation, can and do inform us about reality. Now

we may wish to say, as was suggested by Dr. Gerholm, and also perhaps as a corollary of what Immanuel Kant said, that even our mathematical forms are projections of our own mind and do not and cannot lead to what is Real and independent of us. It is possible that the founding fathers of modern science embarked on a philosophical *cul de sac* as far as finding Objective Reality is concerned and that only in the post-quantum mechanics era do we appreciate the limitations of the project. However, it cannot be denied that it would be difficult for scientists, now as well as earlier, to put forth their best and most creative work were it not for the conviction, which might be wrongly founded, that their work is about the Real.

3. It is an important feature of modern science that the theoretical and the practical spheres are brought into one whole. This means, in the language of the scholastics preferred by some metaphysically oriented philosophers, as Dr. Bakar in this collection, that modern science fuses the intellectual and the moral orders. Therefore any comments which are applicable to science are also essentially applicable to technology, as far as their underlying metaphysical basis and ethos are concerned.

4. It is hard to deny the intimate connection between science and technology either philosophically or historically, in spite of some strenuous efforts. Useful distinctions can, of course, be made for administrative and other purposes; after all, even within the same science department researchers are often hired in one distinct sub-specialty or another without denying the general continuity of the fabric of science. Can scientists claim moral impunity for their science and blame all the ills on technology? The fact is that science and power—by which is meant not spiritual or moral or aesthetic power, but sheer brute physical power—are thoroughly intertwined. Many a Nobel prize in pure physics was won for the work done during the Manhattan Project to develop the atomic bomb and in its follow up projects. Conversely, the Manhattan Project would not have been inaugurated without the urging and pressure of *pure physicists*, and certainly would not have succeeded without them. The public holds scientists, especially physicists, in awe and gives them glory and funds their conferences because of the power associated with their work; pure poets are not so funded.

The wealthy swains of the military, government, and industry, are interested in courting even 'pure' scientists because they have been known to let their guards of purity down!

Spirituality

1. It was happily and rightly agreed among the participants that spirituality is universal, non-sectarian, and not restricted to the East or the West. Spirituality is not limited by geographical, historical, or sectarian divisions. It was also either assumed or realized by the participants that spirituality does not have much to do with a belief system or doctrine, theological arguments and proofs, or enthusiastic evangelism. It is primarily a quality of being, reflected in bodily stillness, in emotional generosity and compassion, no less than in mental clarity and serenity, a quality that represents a further evolution of the human being. Spirituality has to do with a new birth, transformation of consciousness, or a raising of the level of awareness—all this leading to a different person who is born into and manifests a new mode of being, almost a different species. In every aspect of a human being there is a wide range of variation of quality: in the sphere of intellectual capacity, there is a range from being a moron to being a genius; and from a sickly person to an athlete in the realm of physical strength and flexibility. In the sphere of spirituality, the variations are more subtle and more profound, touching the very core of a person and his destiny and significance. Spiritual profundity is not a matter of a particular accomplishment; it is concerned with the quality of the whole of the person and with his nearness to the Spirit.

2. In the light of the above, it is not surprising that the sages, saints, and mystics should have a great deal of difficulty in communicating with other human beings about their spiritual experiences. These are no more than the expected difficulties of what amounts to practically an inter-species communication. However, as is maintained in virtually all spiritual traditions, it may be possible that all homo sapiens by virtue of their form have the potentiality in principle of being in touch with the faculties which are specifically spiritual (as distinct from mental, emotional, or physical), and these faculties even when undeveloped do in some measure respond to the utterances of the

sages. Therefore, even when we do not quite understand what they are saying, we find it difficult to wholly ignore them; something subtle whispers in our ears, sometimes quite in spite of ourselves.

3. In order to understand the sages and scriptures *spiritually* we need to undergo a change of being or a rebirth or a cleansing of our perceptions on our part. This is also an implication of the remarks of Professors Murray and de Silva. An intellectual and physical (i.e., scientific) understanding neither requires any transformation of our being nor can it lead to such a transformation. Can we understand something of the process of spiritual transformation in the work which Dr. Lagmay has been doing? Neither scientific knowledge about people who have spiritual knowledge nor theoretical knowledge about the Spirit makes one a sage.

4. If the notion of the spiritual and the corresponding possibilities of enlightenment, freedom, or salvation are taken seriously, then what is spiritual is almost by definition, and also by universal consensus, higher than what is intellectual. The intellect is contained in being, as a part in the whole, and not the other way around. The point made by some, expressing a certain impatience and annoyance with the people who talk about 'higher knowledge' without being able to solve a differential equation, although a useful corrective against glib and superior sounding talk, cannot really be taken seriously on its face value. The Buddha or the Christ are not necessarily expected to know how to devise a better mousetrap or how to repair a television set. Does that mean that the Buddha was not enlightened or the Christ was not related to God?

5. In particular, Dr. Balasubramanian specifically brought out the issue of higher and lower knowledge. If science is lower knowledge by definition, presumably any modification of science (classical, modern, or future science) will always remain a part of the lower knowledge. Was it different for the 'lost science' for which Dr. Sharpe has some nostalgia? Some questions which arise are: 'Is there any connection between higher knowledge and lower knowledge? Even though traditionally the movement is always understood to be from higher knowledge, to lower knowledge, is it possible that the lower

knowledge which surely includes not only science but also philosophy, theology, and the arts, can lead to higher knowledge? Or does one have to transcend, quiet, deny, sacrifice, or kill the mind—all expressions to be found in standard religious literature—to come to what is higher?'

Science as a Spiritual Path

1. In the light of the questions raised above, in what sense can science be a spiritual path?

2. If it is true, as Dr. Gooding says, that for Faraday science was a spiritual path, do we conclude this by correlating some of his sayings or behavior with his scientific activities? Did his science make him spiritual? Or was he a certain kind of person, whom we could happily call 'spiritual,' who happened to be interested in doing science? Could we say that perhaps he remained spiritual in spite of doing science? Did he do a different kind of science in procedure or in results because he was religious? Is being *religious* the same as being *spiritual*?

3. Do those who practice *Yoga, Zen,* or any other sort of spiritual discipline produce a different kind of science than those who are not following a spiritual path? Or is the difference largely in their attitude to scientific activity? We can wonder why it is the case that although there have been great yogis or Zen masters who have been poets, artists, musicians, philosophers, warriors, or social workers, there do not seem to have been many scientists among them.

Science and Non-Western Cultures

1. In the light of the particularity of modern science, as mentioned above, the questions about the incompatibility or otherwise of the modern scientific worldview with the traditional spiritual perspective is as germane to the pre-modern Western world as it is to those cultures, such as China and India or the Islamic world, where other worldviews and attitudes (pre-modern or extra-scientific) are still considered desirable and an integral part of the indigenous culture. The fact that some Easterners can do world-class science does not prove the compatibility of the Eastern cultures with modern science, as was being suggested by some, any more than a few outstanding

examples of Western exponents of Bharat Natyam make it other than an Indian dance form.

2. Nevertheless, even with Bharat Natyam there are trans-Indian universal aesthetic elements and principles of movement which permit it to be practiced and appreciated by some non-Indians. Similarly, perhaps even more so, there are no doubt trans-Western universal intellectual principles in modern science which would be helpful to bring out. Otherwise, there is bound to be an imposition of the Western philosophical notions along with the sciences and the accompanying technology as was the case with the idea of 'nature' in Japan, as pointed out by Dr. Nagasaka.

3. The main imposition is likely to be at a very broad and subtle level, in the very notions of nature, causality, knowledge, reason, explanation, purpose, etc. Even though these notions are at the root of scientific inquiry and guide it along certain channels, they do not specifically enter into any particular scientific theory as opposed to another, thereby giving the impression that science is universal. This universality, however, resides in the structures which themselves are erected only on a specific sort of philosophy. For example, as Dr. Balasubramanian emphasized, one must ask about the purpose of the knowledge in question. If that knowledge does not lead to liberation, then it is not higher knowledge. Is there not an implication—although almost everyone is hesitant to acknowledge this—that lower knowledge, of which science is an example, is not really worthy of a person who is serious about ultimate things? It may be necessary for the economic or military development of the country, one may be addicted to it intellectually, but is it not the case that sooner or later one would see the light and undertake higher knowledge which alone matters?

4. It is possible that this metaphysical standpoint—which insists that the Ultimate Truth is beyond physics in the broadest possible sense—constitutes the main distinction between the mentality of present-day East and that of the West. Speaking very generally, in the past, a similar metaphysical attitude existed everywhere; now it persists only among the older intelligentsia in the East, perhaps as a part of their wisdom or spirituality or superstition. But in the West it has been pushed

into the non-rational sphere of faith and belief, so that the intellectuals can get on with science, and other forms of *lower knowledge*, quite unhindered by any sense that the intellect itself needs to submit to something higher. *Prayer* in the *West*, unlike *meditation* in the *East*, may strengthen one's faith but is not expected by anybody, intellectuals or others, to lead to any sort of *higher knowledge*.

5. The metaphysical standpoint is rapidly losing ground in the East as well, often as a consequence of national programs undertaken in order to create the infrastructure which will make the culture more hospitable to modern science and technology. To take an example from India: more than a hundred years ago as learned a man as Raja Ram Mohan Roy made submissions to an official British commission, charged with the introduction of modern education in India, in which he explicitly requested that the universities be set up to teach European science, philosophy, and literature and not Indian classical philosophy or Sanskrit which he felt had led over the centuries only to philosophical hair-splitting and disputation. The commissioners were happy to oblige; and they could rightly boast that the new education system would produce gentlemen who would be Indian in color but English in their soul. This is what in its turn brings about the sort of social changes that Dr. Dy discusses in his paper. It is puzzling that some participants from India insisted that cultural change is not necessary for science and technology to take root in the East. One wonders if the major difficulty lies in what one understands by *culture*.

The authors included in this volume approach the subject from a variety of points of view; that is a part of the value of this book. Since so many of the papers are by the Editor, it is worth remarking about the common perspective in them which is quite distinct from those adopted in most other books and papers on this and related subjects. The Editor wishes to remain true to the universal insight and assertion of the mystics and other spiritual masters that Spirit is above the mind. Of course, many other words have been used, in addition to Spirit, to indicate Higher Reality, such as God, Brahman, the One, Tao, the Buddha Mind, and the like. Furthermore, it has been universally said that in order to come to know this Higher Reality in truth, a transformation of the whole being of the seeker is needed for the purpose of yoking and quietening of the mind so that it may reflect what is, without any distortions, brought about by fear and fantasy.

Paraphrasing St. Paul, it can be said that the things of the mind can be understood by the mind, but those of the Spirit can be understood only by the spirit. It is this spiritual part in a person which needs to be cultivated for the sake of spiritual knowledge. In some traditions, this part, which like a magnetic compass always tries to orient itself to the north pole of the Spirit, is called *soul*. This part alone, when properly cultivated, can comprehend and correspond to the supra-personal and universal Spirit. Any other kind of knowledge can be about the Spirit but cannot be called knowing the Spirit. If a label were needed for the approach taken in these papers, it is not *philosophical* or *historical* or *scientific*; it is above all *spiritual*—with all the attendant vagueness and need for clarification—in which Spirit is given priority. In this perspective, the question cannot be 'How can I appropriate the Spirit?' The only real and worthy question is 'How can I—and along with myself, my science— be appropriated by the Spirit?' Such an attitude of spiritual humility is not wholly alien to all the scientists; for some of the greatest among them, science itself has been a spiritual path, a way—as Einstein said—of finding the secrets of the Old One.

TWO

PHYSICS And RELIGION

Ravi Ravindra

"Physics really began," said Albert Einstein, "with the invention of mass, force, and an inertial system. These concepts are all free inventions." The first modern approach toward precise definitions and use of these and other related concepts was made by Galileo Galilei (1564–1642), the father of modern physics. He initiated a distinct and new approach to the study of nature, with a characteristic integration of mathematical reasoning and experimental observation.

The Scientific Revolution

The essential philosophical basis of modern science was established during the great scientific revolution in Europe during the sixteenth and seventeenth centuries that culminated in the grand synthesis of Isaac Newton (1642–1727). All the major scientists participating in this revolution were Christians. Some of them were quite devout and some also very learned in the scriptures. Some had strong mystical tendencies; others were theologically oriented. Scientific works of several of them—for example, Copernicus, Galileo, and Descartes—were severely censured by the religious authorities; many others, including Kepler and Newton, held views out of keeping with the religious orthodoxy of their denominations. However, none of these savants, not even those who were persecuted for it, ceased being Christians or believers as a consequence of their scientific work. To be sure, given the times, any public exposure of loss of faith would have had serious consequences for them. Their religious views seem to have been much less, if at all, influenced by their scientific work than by their psychological makeup and the historical and sociological forces acting upon them. On the other hand, it is difficult to see how their scientific work was affected by their religious beliefs. It is sometimes said that the Judeo-Christian theology provided a hospitable ground for the rise of modern science, but it is also possible to say that progress in science was made in spite of, rather than because of, the distinctly biblical component of the Western mind. What the biblical stream did contribute to modern science was an ethos that facilitated the control and mastery of nature and permitted its technological exploitation. This, in turn, made possible the later Western domination of the globe.

During the revolution itself, two major attitudes toward science and religion prevailed among scientists. One was exemplified by Galileo, who, quoting a remark made originally by Cardinal Césare Baronio, said that "the Bible tells us how to go to Heaven, not how the heavens go." The concerns of the scriptures were different from those of the book of nature, and the Bible, according to this point of view, was not declaring truths of natural philosophy. The book of nature has its own principles and is written in the language of mathematics; the questions of natural philosophy should not and cannot be decided by appeal to theological authority. The second attitude was adopted by, among others, Kepler and Newton, who regarded themselves as the priests of God in the temple of nature. While they certainly endorsed the Galilean point of view regarding the distinction between the book of revelation and the book of nature, they considered their work in natural philosophy to be a hymn of praise. Their science was a celebration of the works of God, "to discourse of whom from the appearance of things," said Newton, "does certainly belong to natural philosophy." On another occasion he said, "When I wrote my treatise about our system, I had an eye upon such principles as might work with considering men for the belief of a Deity; and nothing can rejoice me more than to find it useful for that purpose. But if I have done the public any service this way, it is due to nothing but industry and patient thought."

One major change was obvious. Before the scientific revolution, and during its early phases, truths of natural philosophy were subject to theological, particularly biblical, authority. By the end of the revolution, theological and biblical pronouncements had no bearing on the propositions of natural philosophy. It has been suggested that the intellectual climate in Europe's Protestant countries was much more conducive to the growth of science than that in Roman Catholic countries. But, in neither case, from the eighteenth century onward, did the church or theological authorities have any moral, philosophical, or temporal power to influence either the theory or the practice of natural philosophy. Theology was on the retreat, trying to bolster itself by appropriating for its own purposes some theory or another in physics that might lend itself to such manipulation.

Many scientists themselves indulged in this theological service of proving the existence of God from the intricate and ingenious designs of His works. Newton provided perhaps the prime example of such activity, even though all his natural theology did not, in practice, lead him to a religious and wise life: the greatest of all scientists is said to have been a vindictive, jealous, suspicious, vain, and small-souled man. All his and other scientists' theologizing remained essentially theoretical and without influence on the actual conduct of their lives. Even as theory, theology had less and less connection with natural philosophy; within a hundred years of Newton's death. Pierre-Simon de Laplace—hailed as the Newton of France— confidently banished the hypothesis of God from the new scientific system of the world.

Assumptions of Physical Science

In general, the new science and the accompanying view of reality, of man and his place in the cosmos, and the purpose and nature of knowledge, led, as if with inexorable necessity, to a complete mechanization of the world and the accompanying despiritualization of both nature and human beings. All the other natural sciences, social sciences, and even humanities in the last three centuries have been attempting to imitate physics in its style, methods, and principles, owing largely to its precise, quantitative formulations of the laws of nature and to the remarkable success physicists have had in controlling and predicting natural phenomena. It is therefore useful for us to recall some of the fundamental assumptions of research in physics, because the age of science has been, in essential principles, the age of physics.

Essential Deadness of Matter

One fundamental assumption is that everything in nature is essentially dead: it has no *interiority*—no consciousness, purpose, or intention of its own. Whether one is dealing with an electron, a frog, a human being, or a culture, the assumption is that the entire existence and behavior of the object of investigation can be understood and explained in terms of its interactions and external forces, which, in turn, are themselves purposeless. An obvious aim of physical theory is taken to be the ultimate explanation of all of nature in terms of dead matter in motion. Objects do not have their own initiative; they can only react to external forces. In scientific psychology, this principle leads to behaviorism, with its emphasis on stimulus and response.

Hostility of Nature

A second fundamental assumption of physics is that the universe is hostile or at least indifferent (not intentionally but mechanically) to human purposes and aspirations. Therefore, it needs to be fought and conquered. The otherness of nature is an essential presupposition of the scientific attitude: this is what allows man to exploit nature.

Body-Mind Duality

Closely related to these two presuppositions is another, according to which, nature inside man is wholly different from nature outside. This is related to Descartes' well-known and sharp division between the *res extensa* (realm of extension) and *res cogitans* (realm of thinking). The former is the realm of the body; it is the material domain of nature. The latter is the realm of soul, which for Descartes is the same as the mind. Nature is only material and external. What is internal is merely subjective—in the sense of being personal, private, shifting, and unreliable. Only what is external can be objective and real. Even in the external realm a further division is made between what are called *primary* and *secondary* qualities. This division is necessitated by the demand for an unambiguous inter-subjective agreement about the external characteristics of an object. Only those characteristics are regarded as primary that can be quantified and measured and can thus be divorced form any consideration of the individual observer's relative quality of attention, clarity of perception, or level of being. A well-known twentieth-century statement about the importance of measurement, by the famous physicist Max Planck, is "That which cannot be measured is not real." Reality is thus, by assumption, divested of higher feelings or of sensations requiring purified perceptions; it is reduced to those characteristics that can be mechanically quantified, such as size, mass, and so on. "Just as the eye was made to see colors, and the ear to hear sounds," wrote Kepler, "so the human mind was made not to understand whatever you please, but quantity."

Reality as a Mathematical Construct

In physics, an abstract and purely rational and mathematical construct is assumed to underlie the perceived reality. What is experienced is then called "appearance," while the mental construct is called "reality." The scientific pursuit, then is to speculate about the imagined reality and to put these speculations to experimental tests involving only certain limited perceptions. The so-called objective reality of scientific concern is in fact a conjecture—perhaps one of the many that may be possible. However—and this is where the importance and glory of science lie—these subjective projections are confirmed (or falsified) by intersubjective experimental procedures. Nevertheless, the testing procedures are not wholly independent of the theoretical framework. Whether an experimental observation is taken to be a confirmation of a given conjecture is, as scientific experiments become more and more elaborate, increasingly a matter of interpretation.

Experiment versus Experience

It is partly a consequence of what has been said above about the various presuppositions of scientific inquiry that, although the modern natural sciences are thoroughly *experimental* in character, they are in fact determinedly counterexperiential, in the sense that scientists must not include in their data any observations that involve them personally in the immediacy of perception. It is important to distinguish clearly between *experience* and *experiment*, which have been used in quite different senses in the English language in the last three hundred years. What scientists do in their laboratories is to experiment with or on things; they make measurements based on those experiments. But it is wholly erroneous to say that they experience those things. Given enough research grants and ingenuity, good scientists can arrange their experiments, whether in physics or experimental psychology, so that they can be completely absent from their laboratories when the experimental data are being collected. Leaving out the immediacy of perception or the "minute particulars" (Blake) of reality and the secondary qualities in the collection of scientific data, one ignores most of what the arts and the spiritual disciplines have been traditionally concerned with, such as colors, sounds, tastes, feelings, sensations, purpose, and beauty. Whatever functions poetry, dance, music, or the various spiritual paths may serve, when it comes to the serious business of truth and knowledge, as understood by the modern natural philosophers, all these activities are essentially frivolous.

Herein lie the seeds of fragmentation of our sensibilities: arts and religion cannot lead to knowledge and science cannot lead to values. The resultant dichotomy between knowledge and faith, or between reason and feeling, particularly apparent in scientifically advanced Western culture, tends to be destructive of human wholeness. It is a fact of Western intellectual history that since Newton put modern natural science on a firm footing practically every major artist or poet has felt uneasy about the assumptions, procedures, or results of scientific enterprise. However, perhaps because of the separation among the domains of truth, beauty, and goodness that prevails in the mind of modern people, science has moved on, wholly indifferent to these critics, like a large iceberg unaffected by the thrashing of small fish. No matter that these small fish carried names like those of Goethe, Blake, Wordsworth, and Keats, who were all convinced that, in Blake's phrase, "Reason and Newton, they are quite two things."

The Rift Between Reason and Faith

Within the Christian religious tradition the essence of religion is often identified with faith. Although religious people are not likely, unless cornered by philosophers, to equate faith with belief in a set of propositions, they themselves seem to have taken their stand in the realm of faith as distinct from the realm of knowledge. Since knowledge which in the modern West has become more or less synonymous with science, is allied with reason, the relationship between faith and reason has become quite problematic. Faith is not always regarded as opposed to knowledge and reason, although there are some among both the opponents and the supporters of faith who think so, and who correspondingly recommend leaps of reason or leaps of faith, guarding against contamination from one or the other. More often than not, faith and knowledge are considered somewhat tangential to each other. However, if faith is regarded as having no connection with reason, because faith is radically transcendent or superrational, reasonable people tend to become indifferent to it—as in most scientific laboratories in the Western world. The sharp discontinuity introduced by Immanuel Kant between *phenomenon* and *noumenon*, the former the concern of reason and the latter of faith, is an illustration. This attempt to save faith from the onslaught of reason crystallized the separation of the two, gradually resulting in a rationality without significance and a faith without foundation. Then followed an inevitable inversion: faith that was removed from the scrutiny of philosophical analysis by Kant as superrational *noumenon* came in later for psychological analysis by Freud as sub-rational *neurosis*.

In the most fundamental manner, the scientific cosmology is materialistic—that is, it takes matter to be both temporally and ontologically prior to intelligence and spirit, and it therefore attempts, wherever and as far as possible, to explain all phenomena (including higher spiritual functions) in terms of dead matter in motion reacting to purposeless external forces. The fact that such explanation has not been possible does not alter the basic wish and tendency. Traditional religious cosmologies proceed in the reverse direction: from above downward, from spirit to matter. In this century, Aurobindo Ghose in India and Pierre Teilhard de Chardin in Europe have made the most outstanding philosophical efforts to reconcile the two opposed cosmological tendencies: that of the traditional religions, in which the spirit creates and descends into matter, and that of modern science, in which matter subject to accidental external forces evolves into higher intelligence and spirit. Among physicists themselves, but only among those who are concerned about the philosophical and religious underpinnings of their scientific work, the general feeling has shifted from the biblical, personal God to a philosophical intelligence, the source of truth, order, and beauty, Pascal's God. "God of Abraham, Isaac, and Jacob—not of the philosophers and scholars," was already creating trouble for Newton and his mechanical world system based on universal laws—a system that made room for God rather in the guise of a retired engineer only. Most contemporary physicists, if they describe themselves as having religious feelings at all, would accept Einstein's description of those feelings as "the rapturous amazement at the harmony of natural law, which reveals an intelligence of such superiority that, compared with it, all the systematic thinking and acting of human beings is an utterly insignificant reflection."

Religion and Twentieth-Century Physics

None of the presuppositions of modern natural philosophy or the attitudes associated with them, as mentioned above, has been in any significant manner altered by the revolutionary theories in physics introduced in the twentieth century, namely, the theories of relativity and quantum mechanics, both of which were essentially brought to their present form before the 1930s. However great the revolution in twentieth-century physics has been, it remains a revolution within science and does not compare in philosophical importance with the great revolution of the sixteenth and seventeenth centuries, which initiated an altogether new and distinct mode of inquiry into nature. That the present physics is basically of one piece with Galilean physics can easily be seen by the applicability of the heuristic principle in physics called the "correspondence principle," which states that all newer, more comprehensive theories must include, and reduce to, earlier theories under the appropriate limiting conditions. But this principle is not extended to the pre-Galilean natural philosophy. By this principle, both quantum mechanics and relativistic mechanics must, and do, yield the standard Newtonian mechanics as a limiting case.

Relativity

The special theory of relativity led to the very important formal $E = mc^2$, relating energy and matter in such a way that what was said above about the priority of matter in scientific cosmology may now need to be modified to the priority of matter-energy (sometimes labeled simple as mater or simply as energy inclusively, but in no way involving the difference in the emotional overtones in the two words, as it exists in the popular mind). According to this theory, time and space intervals do not have an operational meaning independent of each other because the simultaneity of two events depends not only on their relative position but also on their relative linear motion with respect to each other. Far from making everything relative, as is often said or implied in popular accounts, the attempt in this theory is to remove the ambiguity created by the relativity of motion by defining invariants, such as "proper time" (which includes a component of space) or "proper mass" (which includes a component of energy), that are independent of the state of motion or of rest of the observer. Einstein's general theory of relativity, which has been called "perhaps the greatest achievement in the history of thought" (J.J. Thompson), extends the results of the special theory to the case of accelerated motion and gravitation and shows how the presence of matter affects the geometry of space and time around it. These theories have often been pressed into the service of various theological, philosophical, or even political views, by those seeking support from the sciences. In general, such applications are based on unwarranted extrapolations and interpretations, none of which was ever encouraged by Einstein himself. He, more than anyone else, seems to have been aware of the limited domain of these theories, however marvelously exciting and revolutionary they have been in natural philosophy.

Quantum Theory

The theory of quantum mechanics has created considerable theological and philosophical excitement, far more than the theory of relativity. It has revealed a deep-seated discontinuity in natural processes and entities like time and energy, so that the laws of nature yield only statistical probabilities of certain events taking place. Individual particles are determinable only up to accuracies theoretically limited by Heisenberg's uncertainty principle as it is applicable to conjugate variables. That is, if the time is determined up to a certain accuracy, there is a calculable degree of uncertainty in the determination of energy; similarly for position and momentum and other appropriate pairs. Laws of nature still apply in a perfectly determinate and causal manner to ensembles of particles. The limitation on the precise predictability for a single particle has led many to discover a place for human free will in an otherwise completely determinate universe. This and other such attempts to find theological or mystical comfort in the latest findings of physics largely indicate a very mental, one-dimensional view of religion—concerned mainly with some propositions of belief—that is gradually being abandoned. Here and there, in some bold quarters, questions are being raised about the proper place of physics and other sciences in the light of many higher levels of consciousness—and the accompanying levels of wisdom and feeling—possible for human beings.

Bibliography

The classic study of the philosophical revolution brought about by the great scientific revolution of the sixteenth and seventeenth centuries is Edward Arthur Burtt's *The Metaphysical Foundations of Modern Physical Science* (1925; rev. ed., New York, 1932). How this new method in natural philosophy led to the superstructure of western domination throughout the world has been discussed by a well-known contemporary physicist, Kurt Mendelssohn, in his *Science and Western Domination* (London, 1976). Another useful book, written from a feminist perspective, is Carolyn Merchant's *The Death of Nature: Women, Ecology and the Scientific Revolution* (San Francisco, 1980). Of special importance are the following books, which also treat of the relation between science and religion: Reijer Hooykaas, *Religion and the Rise of Modern Science* (Grand Rapids, Mich., 1972); David C. Goodman, comp., *Science and Religious Belief: 1600–1900* (Bristol, 1973); and Colin Archibald Russell, comp., *Science and Religious Belief: A Selection of Recent Historical Studies* (London, 1973).

Useful supplementary material can be found in Newton's *Philosophy of Nature: Selections from His Writings*, edited and arranged by H.S. Thayer (New York, 1953), in *The Mechanization of the World Picture* (Oxford, 1961) by Edvard Jan Dijksterhuis, and in *The Religion of Isaac Newton* (Oxford, 1974) by Frank E. Manuel.

Ian G. Barbour's *Issues in Science and Religion* (Englewood Cliffs, N.J., 1966) and Stanley L. Jaki's *The Relevance of Physics* (Chicago, 1966) extend the discussion of the relation between religion and physics into the twentieth century. For a discussion of developments in physical theory, see Albert Einstein and Leopold Infeld's *The Evolution of Physics: The Growth of Ideas from Early Concepts to Relativity and Quanta* (New York, 1938). For a discussion of the philosophical problems raised by twentieth-century physics, see Henry Margenau's *The Nature of Physical Reality* (New York, 1950). The rise in the prestige and power of physicists in the United States is detailed by Daniel J. Kevles in *The Physicists: The History of a Scientific Community in Modern America* (New York, 1978). For Albert Einstein's views on science and religion and other social and cultural issues, see his *Out of My Later Years* (New York, 1950). Current discussions of the relationship between modern physics and Asian religious traditions can be found in Fritjof Capra's *The Tao of Physics* (Berkeley, 1975) and in my article "Perception in Physics and Yoga," *Re-Vision* 3 (1980): 36–42. [Reprinted in this volume; chapt.16.] This relationship is also the topic of two transcribed conversations: "The Physicist and the Mystic—Is a Dialogue Between Them Possible?" is a conversation with David Bohm conducted by Renée Weber and edited by Emily Sellon, *Re-Vision* 4

(1981): 22–35 and "Reflections on the New-age Paradigm" is an interview with Ken Wilber, *Re-Vision* 4 (1981): 53–74. Writings on religion by the major physicists of the twentieth century have been edited and given a useful introduction by Ken Wilber in *Quantum Questions* (Boulder, 1984).

PART TWO:

SOME TRADITIONAL VIEWS

THREE

The INDIAN
VIEW Of NATURE

Ravi Ravindra and Priscilla Murray

In the vast corpus of the thought of India there are many
views about *Nature*, and not a single consistent and invariable
one which could be regarded as the *Indian view*. Nevertheless,
there are some features common to most of the views about
Nature which have been influential in India. Furthermore,
some of these features are not shared by the mainstreams of
one or the other of the two major non-Indian world-views and
zones of thought, namely, the Western (European and American)
and Sineatic (Chinese, Korean, and Japanese). It can hardly be
over-emphasized that there is a great deal of variety in the views
about Nature within each one of the major cultures; and almost
all views can be found in each. Still, there are distinctive features
of the views about Nature which are noteworthy; they contribute one of the major ingredients in what makes any culture
distinct from the others.

Our main interest here is to point out some of the common
features of the Indian views about Nature; only secondarily do
we compare and contrast these features with the non-Indian
views. However, one general remark may be made regarding
the divergence of the major world-views about Nature.

Three Views of Nature

In the West, Nature is almost always viewed as alien to human beings. This alien is hostile and needs to be conquered, subdued, and reduced. In fact, for many a century the Westerners have not referred to Nature as *she*; she has been reduced to an *it*. There is a hostility, or at least a competition: it is Man versus Nature. Man is right and nature is wrong. This in its turn reflects another duality: that between God and Man. God is right and Man is wrong. In each of these dualities the lower aspect needs to be controlled and subdued. This needs action: technology (based on the scientific laws) to control external nature and religion (based on the Law of God, Torah) to control human will, the inner nature. Nature must be bent to the will, benefit, and use of man; and men to those of God. In either case, the unruly and wild nature needs to be tamed for some utilitarian purpose.[1] Post-Renaissance science and technology offer the paradigmatic case of the Western attitude to Nature. There is something very deeply anthropocentric in this attitude: Man separated from nature, hostile to it, and determined to conquer it. And nature exists for the use and benefit of Man—an attitude with a discernible continuity from the *Genesis* story to the so-called *Anthropic Principle* in contemporary physical cosmology.

Control is the main feature of the Western man's relationship with Nature; and it is almost always mental. Whenever this rational control is called into question, the relational pendulum swings to the sentimental. In general, the *developers* and the *conservationists* subscribe to the same level of spirituality, even though at that level their actions and the consequences of these actions are different and call for appropriate choices.

In the cultures influenced by the Chinese worldview, as one can see especially in Japan, Nature is not 'true' or 'natural' as she is. She must be molded or assisted to become 'natural,' which is an ideal form of her; then she is truly beautiful and perfect. This ideal form, which results from a transformation of Nature, is given material and visual expression, and does not exist only in the mind, as is the case with Plato's ideas. Nature must be transformed to be loved. It is perhaps not an exaggeration to suggest that the Japanese love not flowers but flower arrangements! Nature to be contemplated is not what she is, untransformed, but what she ought to be, ideally. If Nature is exploited in America, she is reformed and decorated in Japan! For example, the gardens in Japan are not *natural* in any ordinary sense of that word; something artificial and artifacted is drastically imposed on them, an unnatural order. Whenever this imposed order transcends the merely mental and emotional, as in some exquisite Zen gardens (as rarely happens in a Western garden, however pleasing to the mind and the senses it might be), there is present an unearthly—might we say supernatural—beauty and quality.

Formalization of Nature is based on a rejection of Nature in the raw. If the West imposes a grid of mathematics on Nature, Japan imposes a formal aesthetic sensitivity, yielding not abstract mathematical laws but hidden deep formal structures and arrangements. If the Western natural philosopher calculates and measures, the Chinese one contemplates and draws. In the one case, there is a technological control and manipulation, in the other there is an aesthetic awe and adjustment. In both cases, the attempt is to find what is hidden in Nature, below the surface. And in both cases a Man-Nature duality remains, although the nature of the relationship between the two in the duality is different. Rather than being hostile, Man is a part of Nature in the Sineatic view; Man has his place in Nature, as he has in the social relations—albeit ritualized and formal. In no case is Man only for himself, atomistically separated from other beings—in society or in Nature on the large—concerned only for his own advancement or convenience; a human being is always a part of a group or of a whole larger than himself. The new science of ecology is likely to find much more kinship with the philosophical traditions of China than with any other.

Moving to India, one moves away from the gardens altogether—whether they be French, English or Zen. The great Mughal gardens of India are not indigenous to the Indian sensibility, which is at home not as much in the garden as in the forest. No man-made order, mathematical or aesthetic, can be imposed on the forest, without reducing it in some way. The whole of Nature is like a giant forest: wild, mysterious, awesome. She is what she is: she cannot be tamed or controlled. She must be accepted as she is. There is a deep-seated acceptance in the Indian attitude towards Nature, and towards everything else. Nothing needs to be controlled or altered or transformed—except oneself. What needs to be changed is the level of one's vision. If one sees from the perspective of the Vastness (which is what *Brahman*, the highest Reality in Indian thought, means literally), one sees rightly and knows the true order in which everything has its right place. Nature does not need to be improved or corrected; it is one's vision which needs to be cleansed. The true order is not something to be imposed on Nature by Man, mathematically or aesthetically, by eliminating the surface. Nature does not need to be controlled or transformed or decorated; she needs to be accepted in her entirety as a whole—in depth as well as on the surface; and the depths cannot exist without the surface. She can be loved and celebrated as she is; or if one finds her too much of an enchantress she can be rejected as a whole. But she is alive and must not be diminished or reduced.

The most fundamental principle of a true philosopher in India is non-violation (*ahiṃsā*). Nature is right as she is, as is Man—deep down, essentially. There cannot be a conflict between what is and what ought to be. If one would see deeply, in reality, and not be stopped by the surface appearances, one would see the basic rightness of all there is. 'All this is Brahman,' says one of the *Upaniṣads*. There is no duality between Man and Nature, any more than there is between God and Man. No one needs to be subdued or controlled. Strictly speaking, viewed from the highest level of insight, which is by definition the most comprehensive and the clearest vision, there are no others; there is an essential underlying unity of all that exists. To be sure, if one's attention is co-opted by the surface of things then Nature, rather than being a revelation of the essence, becomes a veil. Nature is *māyā*, which means both the creative power of Brahman, as well as the magical illusion hiding Brahman. There is this persistent tension in Indian thought: between Nature as revelation of Divinity and Nature as illusion.

At root, the Indian attitude to Nature is metanatural: Nature does not exist by herself or for herself; she is dependent on the

Divine Energy and exists for Its sake. In this it parallels India's metasocial attitude to society: society does not exist for its own sake, no more than a human being does for his own. All small and large arrangements, organisms and constellations exist as varied manifestations of the Divine, and for the sake of Divinity. Ultimately, all forms derive their existence from and have their meaning in what is eternally beyond form. Truth, with a capital T, is not in forms; they are true to the extent they participate in the Truth. Truth, Freedom, and Brahman for the Indian are radically beyond the pale—the pale of society, language, thought, and time. At his best, the Indian is a complete supra-formal maverick, bound by no form or convention or law, responding only to the whispers from the Other Shore. Only the Buddha could have said, "I wander alone in the world like a wild rhinoceros." Perhaps not he alone: Yajnavalkya could have said that, as could have Mahavira, Patanjali, Shankara, Ramana, or Krishnamurti. But not Confucius, nor Aristotle.

That which is 'outside the square *(fang-wai)*' would be outside his concern, once declared Confucius, the master of Li. Li, the unnatural order of social norms and ceremonial rites created by man to govern his behavior and emotions, is operational only when it has the four walls as its reference of relevancy.[2] The only worthy concern of a serious person in India is that which is 'outside the square,' any square: only with respect to that can what is inside the square have any significance. At any level of perception, there is the pull of the visible and there is the ability to see beyond. Indian sages seem to have consistently sacrificed the visible for the power to see clearly. In that clarity, as the *Yoga Sutras* (1:48) of Patanjali says, 'the insight is truth-bearing.'

However, all great insights are bound to be understood at a lower and degenerate level when the requisite tension of the clear vision of the moment is dispersed in concepts and sentiments. It cannot be said that India (or for that matter China) has had a particularly praiseworthy record of care for the environment or natural resources, either in the modern times or the ancient. It may be that the strong pull of the transcendent concerns in India has almost always led to a lack of concern for the visible world, and the consequent devaluation of

Nature—space, time, materiality and causality. This is especially striking in the Vedanta and Madhyamika schools of thought which display nothing of the exuberant love and celebration of Nature and earthly life so characteristic of the Vedas.

In summary, remembering that a great deal needs to be elaborated and qualified in such large-scale generalizations; the Western attitude to Nature is predominantly scientific and technological, centered on Man; the Sineatic attitude is aesthetic and poetic, patterned on the relationships in the Society; whereas the Indian attitude is mystical and metaphysical, focused on Brahman. Clearly, these attitudes overlap each other and are only rarely met in extreme purity. None of these cultures has a monopoly either of wisdom or of stupidity; their perspectives can be understood at a high level of clarity and sensitivity or at a low one. Within each major culture, for it to have survived long, all variety of human responses are met.

However, each culture has its own peculiar genius and unique emphasis; each one presents a distinct cluster of attitudes towards Nature.[3] Also, it is worth noticing that when one speaks of the Western attitude, one is speaking of something which has developed largely in the modern times, although with a discernible continuity with its own past; but in speaking of China or India attention is focused on the classical periods, perhaps with some continuity into the present.

This is understandable historically: the impulse for major intellectual, economic, or military initiatives in the last few centuries has started in the West, and the modern epoch has been dominated by the West. The only insights and practices in the non-Western world which have not been swamped by the Western influence are pre-modern ones; they alone present possibilities of distinct contributions to the emerging global culture.

Main Features of The Indian View of Nature

The following attitudes and assumptions, some of which are implicit in what has been already said above, are more or less shared by practically all schools which have originated from India, including the Hindu, Buddhist, and Jain, although some of the terms used are different in different systems. Of course, there are many fine distinctions, or varied emphases and nuances, among different schools; but these details cannot be discussed here.

Unity of All There Is

There is One Energy which permeates the entire cosmos, visible and invisible, gross and subtle, but It manifests Itself at different levels of being and of consciousness. At the highest level is pure awareness without materiality, and at the lowest level is total materiality without awareness. These limits are like the theoretical limits in mathematics and are not to be met within the realm of *manifestation* which is the realm of Nature. This One Energy has been variously called *Brahman, Prāna, Om, Śunyatā*, and the like. It is worth remarking that there are schools, for example the Advaita Vedanta, which can be and have been interpreted as saying that the highest level is the only one which is real and is *Brahman*, with a radical discontinuity from all manifestation. However, it is also possible to understand this as an assertion that all levels are real because all of them are different manifestations of the same One Energy.

This perspective of One Energy needs to be distinguished from an apparently similar idea in modern science. It is an assumption in science that various forms of energy are interconvertible. The law of conservation of energy-momentum in a closed system presupposes this interconvertability. Therefore, we could quite rightly speak, from the scientific point of view, of one energy pervading the entire cosmos. However, in science, although there are many *forms* of energy, we cannot legitimately speak of many *levels* of energy. The notion of *levels*, although extremely difficult to pin down rigorously, is crucially important in understanding any of the traditional systems of thought.

Imagine making any sense of Dante without some notion of differences in levels! Confining our attention to the Indian thought at present, the Energy is One but is manifested at different levels, which have different degrees of consciousness, not only quantitatively but also qualitatively. The idea of *consciousness* is inherent in the notion of *levels* and *vice versa*.

Energies—or beings, when we speak theologically or *personistic-ally* (God, angels, humans) rather than cosmologically, each mode having its special advantage and flavor—at a higher level have higher consciousness than those at a lower level. There is a *verticality* in all traditional spiritual thought which is absent in modern science.

It may be remarked here somewhat parenthetically that this absence of levels of being in science is intimately connected with one of the fundamental assumptions of scientific inquiry that the level of being of a scientist—in terms of his quality of goodness, compassion, freedom from selfishness, largeness of vision; in short, the kind of person he is—has nothing to do with the kind of science he produces. He may be the humblest of human beings or the most insecure and arrogant, his science is independent of the level of his being. Conversely, therefore, whatever scientific knowledge one may possess, it cannot affect one's level of being. On the other hand, this vertical change in the level of being of a person is the only *raison d'être* of any spiritual tradition and discipline, making them in principle orthogonal to the scientific enterprise.[4]

Reverting to the unity of Nature, the notion of the unity of Spirit and matter is included in it, for *Spirit* is at the totally conscious end of the spectrum of One Energy, whereas matter constitutes some of the other levels depending on whether we are speaking about only the physical matter or biologically alive organic matter, or physically capable mental stuff (or grey matter). It seems to us obvious that spiritual, psychic and ma-terial (biological and physical) phenomena exist, even though sometimes prior philosophical commitments make it difficult for people to acknowledge one or the other. Also, a relationship between Spirit and matter is hardly in question: no spiritual or mental—which is different from spiritual—phenomenon can be studied without some mind and body experiencing it and interacting with it; otherwise we cannot know that such a phenomenon exists. The important question is: Are mind and spirit results of more and more complex organization of mat-ter—as is the general view of science, inherent in its notion of evolution[5]—or do different levels of matter result from differ-entiation or crystallization (or grossification) of the spiritual energy? The latter is more or less the universal view of spiritual-religious traditions. Does spirit produce matter or does matter give rise to spirit? The classical Indian tradition unequivocally affirms the former.

Higher and Lower Nature

It is a consequence of the unity of Nature that the entire human being is a part and parcel of Nature. To be sure, he has not only biological and physical aspects, he also has psychic and spiritual aspects. But there is a continuity among these various aspects and levels of being (or materiality), and not an opposition or a duality. There is not a mind-body dualism as there often is in Western philosophy, nor the soul-body dichotomy of Christian theology. There are subtle bodies (for example, *liṅga śarīra* of the Sāṅkhya School or *saṁbhoga kāyā* or *dharma kāyā* of Tibetan Buddhism) which can be formed and nourished by spiritual efforts in this very body and which can survive physical death. The spiritual aspects are also a part of Nature; they may be distinguished from other levels by being labelled *higher* or *inner,* as contrasted with *lower* and *outer,* but they are not super nature.

Krishna, the God incarnate, says in the Bhagavad Gītā (7:4–10, 12):

> My nature has eight aspects:
> earth, water, fire, wind, space, mind,
> understanding and individuality.
>
> This is my lower nature.
> Know my higher nature too,
> the life-force that sustains this universe.
>
> Learn that this is the womb of all creatures;
> I am the source of all the universe,
> just as I am its dissolution.
>
> Nothing is higher than I am, Arjuna.
> All that exists is strung on me,
> like many pearls on a thread.
>
> I am the taste in water, Arjuna, the light in
> the moon and sun, the sacred syllable in all
> the Vedas, the sound in space, valour in man.

Know me, Arjuna, as every being's eternal seed,
I am the intelligence of the intelligent,
Majesty of the majestic am I.

Know that nature's qualities come from me—
lucidity, passion, and dark inertia;
I am not in them, they are in me.

Subtle and Gross Nature

Clearly, we do not know all there is to know about Nature. Given the incredible amount of knowledge gathered about Nature in the last four centuries, we can easily imagine that the next four centuries or forty would reveal a great deal more about Nature.[6] What we know about Nature is not all there is. There are hidden aspects of Nature, hidden from us so far. With appropriate procedures and instruments, more will be revealed. There is a general principle in Indian thought according to which knowledge is state-specific, that is to say, what one knows and can know depend on the state and level of consciousness of the knower. A person at a higher level of consciousness can know more subtle aspects of nature which may be hidden from those at the ordinary level.

An important question is this: Do the successive discoveries of science based on an extension of our sense organs (including the rational mind [*manas* in Sanskrit] which is included among the senses in much of Indian thought) remain at the same level of consciousness? Does a telescope change what one sees or does it change the eyes with which one sees, and therefore changes how one sees anything? It is the latter which is the concern of the spiritual paths. The quantitative extension of observations in science reveals new sights for us to see, but it does not change our eyes.[7]

On the other hand, a major new theory in science, for example, the theory of quantum mechanics, does alter the way we look at Nature and what sorts of questions we ask of her. However, these new questions are also posed, and the answers are acceptable, within the mental-sensual sphere as before. This does not yet constitute a new level of consciousness as spiritual masters speak of it; so that new questions arise from a transformed questioner, and the answers are sought in a different domain.

There are phenomena, a whole class of them constituting a separate level, which are *personistic* in the sense that they always involve a person in the interaction, either person-to-person or person-to-object. Such phenomena—including all the extra-sensory and psychic phenomena which may well be simply an extension of the more usual psychological phenomena—cannot be measured and studied without a person being one of the necessary components of the experimental arrangement.

It is worth noting that this *personist* interaction is not necessary in the quantum mechanical phenomena in spite of the fact that a great deal has been written about the necessity of including the subject or the knower in what is sometimes described as the *interactive universe* of quantum mechanics. In all experiments dealing with the quantum phenomena, the scientist and every other person can go home to lunch while the data are gathered by a computer. This personist level of Nature, if it is hidden from us, is hidden in a different way than the many unknown things, for example the mechanism of super conductivity at high temperatures. The personist level is designated as *subtle Nature*, and the (occult) knowledge of it is in general said to require a cultivation of some capacity or faculty of the person in question. These capacities include attention, will, creative imagination and openness (or receptivity)—all the interior qualities which define the very essence of a person and determine his level of consciousness. It should also be said that there are many examples of people who have had special occult knowledge, and the corresponding powers, without any particular training. It is possible that these powers are quite natural, as in seeing and hearing, and that most of us lose them in the process of wrong education, or that different people are born with different degrees of these occult abilities, just as is the case with other abilities.

It is clear that the phenomena pertaining to Qi belong to the personist class, and require a cultivation of special faculties by those who would experience them. No doubt, some people are born with especially sensitive psyches and are able to relate with and manifest Qi more easily than others. However, what needs to be emphasized is that these subtle phenomena are not super-nature, they are very much a part of Nature—subtle

Nature perhaps, requiring procedures and methods other than those available in present science. There may be a fundamental difficulty here: as long as science proceeds basically from matter without any consciousness, however rudimentary, it is extremely difficult if not impossible to understand the personist phenomena which necessarily involves consciousness.

Perhaps we may be allowed to make a prediction of the mega trend in science: In the last four centuries science has been engaged with the fundamental project (Western project?) of understanding the whole of the cosmos, including life, mind, spirit and consciousness ultimately in terms of dead matter in motion. And there has been an amazing record of success in this project, and an astounding degree of control over nature. But inherent in this project has been a desacralization of Nature as well as of Man. Over the next few centuries—or decades, since everything is rather accelerated now—there will likely develop a science with a basic project (Eastern? Likely, global) in which the cosmos, including matter, will be understood in terms of movement of consciousness.

The attempts to scientifically understand and explore the material effects of *Qi* are a part of this project. It is important, however, not to lose the significance of the whole enterprise: it is not only *Qi*, or *Prāna*, which is in question in the judgment hall of science, but also science is in question as an exclusive approach to the truth about Nature. It may be tragic if *Qi* is subjected to the same sort of impoverishment by science as soul was in the nineteenth-century West, in attempting to prove its existence by measurements of its physical weight. It is partly a consequence of these misconceived attempts, which do not allow a difference in levels and the obvious necessity of bringing criteria from appropriate levels—St. Paul said in vain that the things of the spirit can be understood only by the spirit—that scientists, and Westerners generally, now either blindly believe in the spirit or the soul, or just dismiss them equally blindly. What gets lost is the idea that a different kind of mind—St. Paul called it the 'right mind'—can be and needs to be cultivated in order to understand spiritual phenomena.

If scientists themselves do not feel the need for something higher, well and good; after all, most people do not feel any need for poetry or philosophy or subtle feeling. Why give into the imperialism of an impoverished science in which Dante's 'the love that moves the sun and the other stars' (*Divine Comedy, Canto* 33:145) becomes merely the 'physical attraction between particles of matter,' labeled *gravitation* in *The Principia* by Newton? The scientific reductionism has been the chief force of desacralization of the West; that is why so many Westerners are looking to the East for something they do not find in their own culture. If *Qi* is completely scientized, without challenging the assumptions and procedures of science, there will be no East left to contribute anything distinctive.

Be that as it may, the point to be made here is that according to the Indian views of Nature, the extra-sensory phenomena may be extra-science, but they are not super-natural.

Fundamental Lawfulness of Nature

All levels of Nature, subtle or hidden or visible, are subject to laws. Even the *devas* or gods of Indian mythology are not above the laws; they may, however, know more subtle aspects of Nature which are hidden to the ordinary human level of consciousness and may thus possess powers which strike us as miraculous. But the cosmos is orderly and based on laws. This fundamental lawfulness of the cosmos at all levels is one of the most significant features of traditional Indian thought from the point of view of a *rapprochement* with modern science, and which sets it apart from the mainstream of the Judeo-Christian tradition and the concomitant conflict between science and religion which has been practically axiomatic in the Western world. (It is incredible how many scholars of otherwise fairly sound judgment—such as A.N. Whitehead, Albert Schweitzer, Paul Tillich, Teilhard de Chardin, to name only a few well-known representatives of different brands of Christian thinking—have misunderstood, not always innocently, this basic feature of Eastern thought!) Natural laws cannot be set aside, however fervent the prayers asking for this; but they can be overcome by the application of higher laws. One does not take off for the stars by repealing the law of gravity!

God Not Apart from Nature

Even the highest level of the One Energy, notwithstanding the designation Brahman, Spirit, or God, is not completely apart from the cosmos. (In the systems in which *Brahman* is totally apart from nature, the latter is completely an illusion and does not truly exist. Another way of viewing this is that whatever exists is *Brahman*, and is therefore divine.) The cosmos is frequently called *brahmāṇḍa* which literally means the egg of *Brahama*. That is why, strictly speaking, there are no creation myths in India. There are, rather emanation myths. A typical metaphor is that the cosmos arose from Brahman as a web emanates from a spider. "As a spider sends forth and draws in its thread, as herbs grow on the earth, as the hair grows on the head and the body of a living person, so from the Imperishable arises here the universe" (*Muṇḍaka Upaniṣad* I.i.7). Or, as Krishna says, quoted above: "All that exists is strung on me, like many pearls on a thread." Again, "I am the taste in water, Arjuna, the light in the moon and sun...." One of the contemporary sages of Bengal, Sri Anirvan, told us not long before he died: "You will know something true when you understand that God is dog and dog is God."

Sacredness of All There Is

Since everything emanates from *Brahman*, is the very egg of *Brahman*, is *Brahman*, everything in the whole cosmos is sacred. Nothing is profane — except perhaps that which is out of its proper place in the cosmic order (*ṛtā*). Lack of order is the mark of profanity. No particular activity is profane; all levels of manifestation, in their proper place, are needed for the maintenance of the cosmos. All these creatures, at all levels and manifestations, need not only to be tolerated or respected, but also to be celebrated. An Indian may confidently answer Blake's query in his little poem *Tiger, Tiger, Burning Bright*. Yes, it is the same hand that fashioned the Lamb which made the tiger of fearful symmetry; not only that, but the Lamb and the tiger are one.

Since all Being is one, which is to say that all levels of being are manifestations of the same One Energy, there is not a radical discontinuity between contiguous levels of being, from animals to humans, or from the humans to the *devas*. Further-more, in accordance with the Law of Karma, one may move up or down the scale of being. The Law of Karma posits a strong relationship between doing (including thinking, feeling) and being: one acts as one is, and one is as one acts. It simultaneous-ly sets a constraint on the permissible human action—some constraint is inherent in the very notion of lawfulness—and also allows a way for overcoming the limitations of a given level. Thus the Law of Karma is a law of responsibility, inviting each person to choose and strive for the level of being which he wishes to occupy. But, in order to be free, one must live according to the law.[8]

Compassion for All Beings

Not only other human beings, but all creatures participate in the same sacred One Energy and need to be accepted and respected. This feeling of compassion, along with joy and love, is a natural accompaniment of a life lived in accordance with the right cosmic order (*ṛtā*). It is not like a separate virtue to be practiced strenuously, it follows by itself from the clear vision in which one sees the interdependence, relatedness, and one-ness (also uniqueness, although there is no time to develop this point here) of all there is.

Thus the first and the most important principle of ecology is the cultivation of oneself so that one sees clearly and compre-hensively and lives in accordance with *ṛtā*. Otherwise, one is sure to impose on Nature some mental or emotional notion of what is good for her, later regretting some results of the law of the unintended consequences. There is a tension here: between a deep acceptance of Nature as she is and a sound management of her. Often, the Indian acceptance and non-violation of Nature have resulted in non-interference and neglect.

Unique Human Responsibility

Human beings are so structured that they can potentially perfect themselves or complete themselves, with the aid of the very faculties which make us essentially persons, namely, at-tention, effort, will, openness and creative imagination. A com-pleted person, who is *saṇskṛta* (cultivated, cultured, well-made), and not an ordinary human being, who is *prākṛta*, (common, vulgar, uneducated), is like a macrocosmos mirroring in all essentials the Vast Cosmos. For such a person the Nature inside him is the same as the Nature outside, and he contains within him all levels of the cosmos—in the sense that all levels of being have their counterpart in him, from the most spiritual to the most material. In such a person, *Prāna* resides in all its levels, whereas in an ordinary person, *Prāna* is the animal life-force, manifesting as breath. According to these ideas, even when apparently the same air is breathed by people of different levels of consciousness the subtle substances (or energies) which they take in are different, as are the substances which they breathe out.

The Continuum of Spirit-Matter

There is no radical discontinuity between Spirit and matter, or psyche (soul) and body, or other levels of being. (As has already been remarked that in the systems in which there is a radical discontinuity, there is no real existence of matter or Nature; such systems are more thoroughly monistic.) They affect each other, and no spiritual discipline is without a physical component. Yoga is a particularly good example of this. It is said in the *Haṭhayogapradīpikā* (2:76) that "One cannot attain perfection in Rāja-yoga [spiritual meditation, in this context] without Haṭha-yoga [physical postures and breath control], nor in Haṭha-yoga without Rāja-yoga. So both should be practiced till perfection is attained." Higher consciousness, or insight, affects the body chemically—although it may be better to say that the effects are *alchemical*, owing both to their subtlety and their transformational character. Conversely, a new body is needed for a higher consciousness to be able to manifest itself. It may be worth remarking that in this essentially spiritual perspective the driving thrust of the process of evolution is from above downwards, the Spirit demanding and forging more and more complex material organization in order to be able to manifest Itself in body. A more sensitive (human) body will be required for a superior manifestation of the Spirit on the earth.

Knowledge of Nature

Nature cannot be known truly by studying her only as an "it"—without consciousness and purpose. Furthermore, she cannot be understood comprehensively by studying her externally without at the same time studying oneself—that is to say, one's internal Nature. Unfortunately, all too often *objective* and *subjective* are used synonymously with *external* and *internal*; whereas one can study external phenomena subjectively, just as one can study internal phenomena objectively. A comprehensive and objective knowledge of Nature requires a study of both the external and the internal Nature so that the mind does not subjectively interfere with true knowledge of reality and lets the object reveal itself, both in its interiority and exteriority.[9]

Based on these general principles of Nature, a great deal of sound wisdom and right attitude to Nature, to ecology and conservation, can be gathered, resulting in respect for and celebration of all life. The key lies in the understanding that there is One Energy (*Prāna*, *Qi*) which underlies, manifests in and delights in all creation. However, India's own record in these matters is not enviable, and one may rightly wonder if great and wonderful ideas have any practical effect at all. The main energy and the major insights of India all seem to have been occupied for centuries with the transcendent Truth. The more mundane and here-and-now concerns somehow get neglected. And the few—there can only be a few—who have won the kingdom of the Other Shore, like the great Buddha, do not seem to be interested in ruling the kingdom of this shore.

It may be that the right attitude needs a proper mix of the transcendent insight of India, the relational this-worldly wisdom of China and the practical no-nonsense knowledge of the West. Our times may be uniquely situated in a historical moment where a new global culture is emerging, and we might become as much the heirs of Plato and Aristotle, as of Lao Tze and Confucius, and of the Buddha and Krishna.

Notes

1. In this connection see R. Ravindra, "Physics and Religion," in the *Encyclopedia of Religion*, eds. Mircea Eliade *et. al.*; Macmillan Publishing Co., New York, 1987, Vol. 11, pp. 319–323. [Chapt. 2, this volume.]

2. See Nelson I. Wu, *Chinese and Indian Architecture* (New York: George Braziller, 1963), 45–46.

3. For some of the differences between the spiritual and religious traditions of the East and West, and some similarities, please see R. Ravindra, *Whispers from the Other Shore: Spiritual Search—East and West* (Wheaton: Quest Books, 1984), especially chapters 1, 5 and 6.

4. In this connection, see R. Ravindra, "Experience and Experiment: A Critique of Modern Scientific Knowing," *Dalhousie Review*, Vol. 55, 1975–76, pp. 655–674. [Chapt. 7, this volume.]

5. All that can legitimately be spoken about in science is *change*, without the emotional overlay of *progress* involved in the notion of *evolution*. In this connection, see R. Ravindra, "In the Beginning Is the Dance of Love," in *Origin and Evolution of the Universe: Evidence for Design?*, ed. J.M. Robson; McGill-Queen's Univ. Press, Montreal, 1987, pp. 259–279. [Chapt. 18, this volume.]

6. Of course, one cannot be unmindful of the fact that to speak about any long-term future of knowledge in the midst of the infernal nuclear weapons in the hands of the frightened and chauvinistic people shows either a dangerous ignorance of knowledge of the facts or an innocent faith in the miraculous.

7. In this connection see R. Ravindra, "Perception in Physics and Yoga," *Re-Vision*, vol. 3, 1980, 36–42. [Chapt. 16, this volume.]

8. See R. Ravindra, "To the Dancer Belongs the Universe: Freedom and Bondage of Natural Law," Chapt. 19 of the present volume.

9. See R. Ravindra, "Yoga and Knowledge," Chapt. 15, this volume.

FOUR

The HINDU ATTITUDE To KNOWLEDGE And NATURE

R. Balasubramanian

Hinduism: Both Philosophy and Religion

Though the Indian tradition distinguishes philosophy and religion, it never separates them by placing them in water-tight compartments. Even a casual study of Hinduism will reveal this salient feature. It is, therefore, difficult to say where philosophy ends and religion begins in the case of Hinduism. If so, it is not inappropriate to speak of Hinduism as both philosophy and religion. This is equally true of Jainism and Buddhism, which are two other major schools of the Indian tradition.

Hinduism as Philosophy

The conception of philosophy in the Indian tradition is broad enough to justify the unity of philosophy and religion. The word "philosophy" etymologically means love of wisdom. One who loves or cares for wisdom as worthy of attainment must pursue it through inquiry; and the inquiry must consummate in the vision or seeing of reality. In the Indian tradition, inquiry is called *vicāra*, and seeing is called *darśana*, the two being related as means and end. If the focus is on inquiry into the nature of reality through the different methods of reasoning, it is called *tattva-vicāra*; and if the focus is on the vision or the seeing of reality, it is known as *tattva-darśana*. So every philosophical tradition in India speaks of inquiry (*vicāra*) and vision (*darśana*), the former paving the way for the latter.

A brief elucidation will be helpful in this connection. For example, Jainism speaks of right seeing (*samyag-darśana*), right knowledge (*samyag-jñāna*), and right conduct (*samyak-cāritra*) as the "three jewels" (*triratna*), of which the last through the second leads to the first. What is laid down here is that the practice of ethical and spiritual discipline leads to right knowledge, and right knowledge in its turn to right vision.

In the case of Buddhism what is known as right concentration (*samyag-samādhi*), which is the last step in the eightfold noble path (*aṣṭāṅgika-mārga*), comprises *inter alia* reasoning (*vitarka*) and investigation (*vicāra*), which produce the joy of pure thinking. This is also true in the case of the Hindu tradition right from the Vedic times. The *Taittirīya Upaniṣad*, for example, says that Bhṛgu practised inquiry for knowing the supreme reality which is the source, support, and end of all beings.[1] Śaṅkara emphasizes the importance of inquiry through reasoning as a preliminary to the understanding of the import of the scriptural text. He observes that inquiry into Brahman leads to experience (*anubhava*) and that anything that is accepted without inquiry will not be conducive to the good.[2] Ramana Maharishi, a contemporary exemplar of the Advaita tradition, has advocated the path of inquiry (*vicāra-mārga*) for the realization of the ultimate. So inquiry into both knowledge and reality is absolutely necessary for seeing or realizing reality.

It may be mentioned here that of the two kinds of inquiry, inquiry into knowledge and inquiry into reality, the former has precedence over the latter in the Indian tradition. Inquiry into knowledge and the means thereto is called *pramāṇa-vicāra*, while inquiry into reality which is the object of knowledge is called *prameya-vicāra*. A systematic exposition of Hinduism, as also of Jainism and Buddhism, starts with epistemology before proceeding to metaphysics. Inasmuch as epistemology and metaphysics are integral to it, it is treated as philosophy.

Hinduism as Religion

Hinduism is more than philosophy; it is also religion. Religion, according to Paul Tillich, is the ultimate concern of man about what is experienced as ultimate. The ultimate is inclusive of everything—man, world, and God. It means that no aspect of man can be excluded, that no part of the world can be set aside, and that no dimension of God can be ignored from our conception of the ultimate. It follows that God, man, and the world will be, as in the case of philosophy, the subject matter of religion. But what distinguishes religion from philosophy is the practical side. The ultimate concern of man, which is unconditional, is a commitment; it is a way of life. Unlike philosophy, which is usually understood as merely theoretical, religion calls for a *total* response, cognitive, affective, and conative, of the *whole* man to the ultimate. Since philosophy as traditionally understood in India includes the practical side, there is justification for saying that Hinduism is also religion. According to the Indian tradition, inquiry into knowledge and reality to be fruitful calls for the right frame of mind; and the right frame of mind, what is usually called the "mental set" necessary for philosophical inquiry, requires training, both moral and spiritual. It is not, therefore, surprising that some kind of a preliminary moral and spiritual discipline has been insisted upon as the prerequisite for inquiry in the Hindu as well as Jaina and Buddhist traditions.[3] And this discipline in a more intensified form will continue till one attains the vision or the seeing of reality. It follows that in the Indian tradition philosophy is not only theory, but also practice, not only a view of life, but also a way of life. In other words, philosophy and religion are inseparable, though distinguishable. It is the combination of theory and practice that confers upon Hinduism the philosophical-religious character. It should be borne in mind that there is a variety of schools of Hinduism, each formulating its epistemology and metaphysics. These schools have interacted with one another in the discussion of epistemological and metaphysical issues, sometime agreeing on certain issues and differing on certain others. The sophisticated analysis of the issues in these two areas is comparable to that in the different schools of Western philosophy.

Realistic Epistemology

Subject-Object Relation

There are two important metaphysical trends in Hinduism—theistic and trans-theistic. The latter is also called absolutistic or monistic. The expression "trans-theistic" is helpful as it suggests that the metaphysics which is labeled trans-theistic is not opposed to theism, but transcends theism. Irrespective of the metaphysical position which may be theistic or trans-theistic, Hinduism follows realistic epistemology. The minimum that is claimed in realistic epistemology is the admission that there is such a thing called "knowledge." With the admission of knowledge, one will be required to admit the existence of both subject and object. There is no such thing as knowledge in abstraction. Knowledge as ordinarily understood belongs to someone, and is about something. It means that knowledge is relational, requiring a subject who knows and an object which is known. There is no epistemology without the subject-object distinction.

The question how the subject-object or knower-known distinction arises need not be considered here. However, the question of the relation of knowledge to the object, on the one hand, and its relation to the subject on the other, has to be considered at this point. Knowledge by its very nature is revelatory of the object: that is to say, it reveals the object to the subject. Knowledge, or the language through which it is expressed, is a picture of the object as the early Wittgenstein would put it. If knowledge is capable of revealing the object as it is, it is because of the fact that it is dependent on the object (*vastu-tantra*). "As the object, so is our knowledge." There is no knowledge in the absence of the object. Though it is related to the subject, it is not dependent on the subject for what it is. The person concerned does not have any choice in respect of it, as it is bound to arise, given the object and the necessary conditions for the origination of knowledge. No one imagines knowledge, and what is imagined cannot be knowledge.[4] Though knowledge is knowledge of someone, it is not what it is because of the personal factors such as imagination, wish, desire, and so on of the person concerned. The person concerned has no part to play with regard to the origination or non-origination of knowledge; nor could he alter it from being what it is. Knowledge, therefore, is not person-dependent (*puruṣa-tantra*) in whatever way its relation to the knowing subject is thought of—as a specific quality of the self, or as an activity of the self, or as a manifestation of the intrinsic sentient nature of the self.

Intrinsic Validity of Knowledge

Knowledge as it arises is accepted to be valid. Its claim to validity is doubted or denied only when there are grounds for doubt or disbelief. When I perceive a thing, say a tree, and claim that it is a tree on the basis of my perceptual knowledge, I believe in it as soon as knowledge arises in me; and the fact that such knowledge leads to successful activity confirms that my knowledge is valid. Whatever I claim about the object—that it is tall, that it has many branches, and so on—is based on my knowledge of it; and I believe in everything that I say about the object on the basis of my knowledge, unless there are reasons to show that I am wrong in my claim. Normally we carry on our day-to-day life on the assumption, "As our knowledge, so is the object." It means that knowledge is intrinsically valid, and that it is also believed to be valid, whatever be the source—perception, inference, or verbal testimony—through which it is obtained.[5]

Pragmatic View of Knowledge

Though the validity of knowledge is not dependent on its utility, Indian thinkers generally take a pragmatic view of knowledge. Knowledge is the basis of all life's activities. Whatever a person does in his daily life is based on his knowledge of things. Practical activity to which knowledge leads is a consequence of it. But it does not follow from this that every case of knowledge leads to practical activity. It may or may not, depending on the presence or absence of *motive*, which is the link between knowledge and practical activity. Knowledge *per se* does not lead to practical activity unless there is a motive operating subsequently to the knowledge of anything. If a person, after cognizing something, thinks of it as useful, then he desires to attain it; if, on the contrary, he thinks of it as something harmful, then he dislikes and avoids it; consequently, his engagement in appropriate action will be in accordance with his desire or aversion. So the motivation to attain what one likes and to avoid what one dislikes on the basis of pragmatic considerations of good and bad respectively should arise subsequent to knowledge. In the absence of such motivation mere knowledge does not lead to practical activity.

The Distinctive Nature of Human Being

Human life is purposeful. The Hindu mind never thought of knowledge as an end in itself. Pursuit of knowledge for the sake of knowledge has never been the Hindu ideal. A celebrated Vaiṣṇava teacher, Vedāntadeśika, observes that the knowledge which man possesses is to help him secure the goals of life and for adopting the appropriate means to secure these goals.[6] The goals of life at which man aims must be fully reflective of his nature. Otherwise there will not be any difference between man and animals. The life-activity of man should not be confined to the cultivation of the senses, which has already been achieved at the animal level. Man cannot be considered to be "human" unless his senses have become "human" or refined. His senses should not be subservient to the basic needs alone such as hunger, sleep, and sex. The *Hitopadeśa* says: "Hunger, sleep, fear, and sex are common to man and beasts. It is *jñāna* (i.e., reflective awareness) that socially characterizes man."

Śaṅkara maintains that man is preeminent among all creatures on the ground that he alone is eligible for the pursuit of knowledge and the practice of religious duties (*karma-jñāna-adhikāraḥ*).[7] He justifies this speciality of man which lifts him above the animal level on three grounds. First of all, man has the ability for acquiring knowledge not only of the things of the world, but also of the supreme reality, which is the source and support of all beings, since he is equipped with mind which, being inspired by the self, is capable of comprehending everything, including the highest reality. Unlike other creatures, man has the ability to understand scripture and follow it; and scripture is the authority for the performance of religious duty as well as for our knowledge of the highest reality. Second, he has the distinctive quality of desiring certain ends as a result of discrimination, deliberation, and choice. He cognizes something, desires it, and is engaged in activity with a view to fulfill his desire. The sequence of cognition, desire, and action, i.e., cognition followed by desire, and desire leading to action, is characteristic of man's goal-seeking activity. Third, when man exercises his choice on the basis of the knowledge of the object presented to him, he is not indifferent to the object of his choice. On the contrary, he is earnest about it. He is in search of the right means to realize the end chosen by him. So the life-activity of man which is fully reflective of his knowledge, desire, deliberation, and choice is directed towards the pursuit of worldly prosperity, happiness, and freedom. So the question, "What is knowledge for?" which underscores the pragmatic attitude of the Hindu mind, has to be answered with reference to the distinctive feature of the human being.

Knowledge and the Value System

Man leads his life at two levels—organic and hyper-organic. The value system of the Hindus, which takes note of man's life at organic and hyper-organic levels, provides the answer to the question about the utility of knowledge. The Hindu mind has reduced the entire range of values to four—wealth (*artha*), pleasure (*kāma*), duty (*dharma*), and liberation (*mokṣa*)—in a hierarchy. While the first two values belong to the organic level, the last two belong to the hyper-organic level. Bodily and economic values which contribute to material well-being and happiness have been emphasized right from the Vedic times. Prayers and sacrifices which we come across in the *Vedas* are for a happy, healthy, and full life of a hundred years. The spiritual side of man which is not satisfied merely with material prosperity and happiness is interested in other values as well. Intellectual, moral, aesthetic, and religious values which are higher values in comparison to bodily and economic values are pursued by man as a hyper-organic being in fulfillment of the mental and supra-mental dimensions in him. It may be noted that *dharma* is not only a value, but also a regulative principle which allows the pursuit of both wealth and pleasure without jeopardizing individual well-being and social welfare. So, if knowledge is cared for, it is because of its usefulness in the pursuit of the various values desired by man.

The Pleasant and the Good

According to Hinduism, the purposive character of knowledge has to be finally explained with reference to the existential problem of suffering which is bondage. When superficially viewed, it may appear that man has not only body, but also spirit, as if both of them constitute the nature of man. The truth, however, is that man is essentially spirit having association during empirical existence with a psycho-physical body which is external and accidental to it. If the source of suffering is to be identified, then it is necessary to distinguish the self or spirit from the psycho-physical organism which serves as its outfit. The self which is "soundless, touchless, colorless, undiminishing, tasteless, eternal, odorless, without beginning and without end,"[8] as the *Upaniṣad* would describe it, is by its very nature free, and no experience of any kind—cognitive, or affective, or conative—can be associated with it. If the self *per se* is totally free, i.e., free from everything including suffering, then the source of suffering in embodied existence must be the psycho-physical body.

But the body separated from the self can have no suffering, because when separated from the self it is in no way different from a piece of wood or stone. It is only the *sentient* body that has the experience of suffering; and the body becomes sentient only when the self is associated with it. Neither the disembodied spirit nor the dispirited matter can have the experience of suffering. On the contrary, it is only the embodied spirit that is subject to suffering. So there is the existential problem of suffering for man as the embodied self.

It is not enough if man attains bodily freedom, as it will not solve the problem of suffering. Bodily freedom is freedom for the body from economic, social, political, and other kinds of restraints. Though it is desirable, its attainment does not necessarily terminate suffering. Freedom from the manifold demands of the body becomes equally necessary in the course of one's spiritual development. Nothing short of spiritual freedom, i.e., freedom of the spirit, will satisfy one who is discerning and reflective. According to Hinduism, liberation of the spirit, which is called *mokṣa*, is the highest value. On the basis of the dichotomy between the good and the pleasant, the highest value is called the good (*śreyas*), whereas all other values are brought under the category of the pleasant (*preyas*).

Referring to this distinction the *Upaniṣad* says: "Both the good and the pleasant approach a man. The wise man, pondering over them, discriminates. The wise chooses the good in preference to the pleasant. The simple-minded, for the sake of worldly well-being, prefers the pleasant."[9] In the course of his commentary on this text, Śaṅkara points out that the two goals, *viz* liberation and worldly prosperity, are radically different in their nature, calling for different means for their attainment and that, though both the options are open to man, it is impossible for him to pursue both of them at the same time.[10] The choice of one means the rejection of the other, though there is no compulsion as to which one he should choose. However, the human being cannot escape from this predicament of value preference, as he has to choose one of them exercising his discrimination.

Higher Wisdom and Lower Knowledge
Axiological Approach

Hinduism divides knowledge into two kinds on the basis of axiological consideration. The distinction between the good and the pleasant involves a broad classification of knowledge into higher wisdom and lower knowledge. That which is conducive to the attainment of the good, i.e., liberation, is called higher wisdom (*parā-vidyā*), whereas the knowledge of the objects of the world, which is the means to the attainment of material prosperity and happiness, is called lower knowledge (*aparā-vidyā*). One who pursues values of various kinds belonging to the sphere of the pleasant is ignorant of the highest reality. Such a person, notwithstanding his knowledge of things empirical, is therefore said to be in the state of ignorance; and lower knowledge itself for this reason is called "ignorance" by Śaṅkara.[11] The terms "lower knowledge" and "ignorance" are not used in a derogatory sense. From the perspective of higher wisdom, it is called lower knowledge. Since the scope of lower knowledge does not extend to the highest reality, it is given the label "ignorance" with a view to emphasize what is and what is not comprehended by it.

The *Bhagavad Gītā* conveys this distinction by using the imagery of "day" and "night."[12] It speaks of the difference between the sage who is awakened to truth and others who are ignorant of it by saying that what is "night" to others is "day" to the sage who sees and that what is "day" to the sage is "night" to them. There is an explicit reference to two kinds of knowledge in the *Muṇḍaka Upaniṣad*. When Śaunaka requested Aṅgiras to teach him "that which having been known all this becomes known," the latter told him: "'There are two kinds of knowledge to be acquired—the higher and the lower'— this is what, as tradition goes, the knowers of Brahman say."[13]

After making such a distinction between higher and lower knowledge, the *Upaniṣad* proceeds to give an account of what is included in the lower knowledge vis-à-vis the content of the higher wisdom. It says: "Of these, the lower comprises the *Ṛg-veda*, *Yajur-veda*, *Sāma-veda*, *Atharva-veda*, the science of pronunciation, etc., the code of rituals, grammar, etymology, meter, and astrology. Then there is the higher knowledge by which is realized the Immutable."[14] The seventh chapter of the *Chāndogya Upaniṣad* presents the classic case of Nārada who was in sorrow notwithstanding his proficiency in all the disciplines dealing with things empirical: he was "the knower of words and not the knower of the Self."[15] Hence he sought instruction from Sanatkumāra for overcoming sorrow.

Ontological Approach

The twofold classification of knowledge arises not only from axiological, but also from ontological consideration. Just as there is the distinction between the good and pleasant, there is also the distinction between the Self and the not-Self. While the former distinction is axiological, the latter is ontological. While the supreme Self, the highest reality, is trans-empirical, everything other than the Self is empirical. That which is the highest value axiologically is also the highest reality ontologically. The Hindu tradition, therefore, identifies the good with the real. As in the case of the value system, so also in the ontological scheme there is a hierarchy comprising the empirical and the trans-empirical. Following a particular pattern, the senses, the sense-objects, the mind, the intellect, and so on, which are material and which constitute the empirical realm, are arranged in a hierarchy; and the Self, also called the *Puruṣa*, is said to be higher than the highest in the empirical.

Consider the following passage from the *Kaṭha Upaniṣad*: "The sense-objects are higher than the senses, and the mind is higher than the sense-objects; but the intellect is higher than the mind, the *Mahat* is higher than the intellect; *Avyakta* is higher than *Mahat*. *Puruṣa* is higher than *Avyakta*. There is nothing higher than *Puruṣa*, which is the end, the final goal."[16] Terms such as "*Mahat*," "*Avyakta*," and "*Puruṣa*" have been employed in the Sāṅkhya school. *Avyakta* is *Prakṛti*, the primordial material of the physical universe; and *Puruṣa*, or the Self which is totally different from the material *Prakṛti*, is said to be higher than it. So in the ontological hierarchy there is in the final analysis the dichotomy between the Self and the not-self, between *Puruṣa* and *Prakṛti*, between the trans-empirical and the empirical. Corresponding to this dichotomy, there is the twofold division of knowledge into higher and lower: the higher knowledge comprehending the Self or *Puruṣa*, and the lower knowledge comprehending *Prakṛti* and its products which are material and empirical.

Relation between Higher Wisdom and Lower Knowledge

It is necessary at this stage to consider the question of the connection between the two kinds of knowledge and of the order and mode of transition from the one to the other. This question cannot be considered to the exclusion of the objects of knowledge, as any discussion of knowledge carries a reference to its content. It should be noted first of all that according to the *Upaniṣad* both kinds of knowledge have to be acquired (*dve vidye veditavye*).[17] It does not say that only higher knowledge has to be acquired and not the lower one. In fact, the distinction between higher and lower knowledge can be spoken about only by one who has attained the higher knowledge, just as one who has climbed the peak can, on the basis of one's authentic experience, meaningfully talk about what is lower than the highest point which has been reached. That is why the *Upaniṣad* says that the knowers of Brahman (*brahmavidaḥ*, i.e., those who have realized the truth or the highest reality) make such a distinction.[18] The implication is that others cannot make such a distinction.

Second, nowhere does the Hindu tradition say that lower knowledge or things comprehended by lower knowledge are useless. There are *mantras* enjoining prayer and sacrifice for attaining intelligence and prosperity, which are necessary for a happy life in this world. Śaṅkara observes that, if intelligence and prosperity are enjoined in scripture, it is because of the fact that they are also indirectly helpful to the attainment of higher knowledge.[19] In another context, Śaṅkara points out that learning and teaching, socially good conduct, getting married and raising children, entertaining guests, and so on, which are enjoined in the *Vedas*, should not be neglected, because they are contributory to the attainment of human goals.[20] The different kinds of activities, secular and scriptural, connected with the empirical realm are characterized in the *Upaniṣad* as *satyam*, i.e., true or real, as they are unfailing in ensuring human goals. Studies relating to polity and society, mathematics, astronomy and medicine, erotica and dance, art and sculpture, and so on would not have found a place in the Hindu tradition if lower knowledge was considered useless.[21]

The list of subjects in which Nārada claims to be proficient is impressive as it covers the entire range of the empirical.[22] Nevertheless, he is unhappy because he has not realized the Self through higher knowledge. It should be borne in mind that even philosophy must be consigned to the category of lower knowledge if it fails to produce higher knowledge of the ultimate reality, because higher knowledge, the *Upaniṣad* says, is that by which "the wise realize everywhere that which cannot be perceived and grasped; which is without source and features, eyes and ears; which has neither hands nor feet; which is eternal, multiformed, all-pervasive, extremely subtle, and undiminishing; and which is the source of all."[23]

Third, the transition is from lower knowledge to higher knowledge and not the other way. The nature and scope of lower knowledge should be known, for detachment from objects of lower knowledge arises, so the tradition holds, only as a consequence of knowing its nature. That is why the *Upaniṣad* itself says that "only after examining the worlds acquired through works" that one should resort to renunciation for the pursuit of higher knowledge.[24] Śaṅkara in his commentary remarks that "one who is detached from the whole world of means and ends is competent for higher knowledge."

There are also other reasons to show why the transition is from lower to higher knowledge. That we proceed from the known to the unknown for the purpose of instruction is well known. Normally it will not be possible for one to understand the highest reality which is said to be acosmic (*niṣprapañca*), devoid of qualities and specifications (*nirguṇa* and *nirviśeṣa*), one only without a second (*ekameva advitīyam*) independently of the pluralistic universe which falls within the scope of lower knowledge.

So the normal procedure is from lower to higher knowledge, which is similar to the technique of pointing to a branch of a tree for the purpose of showing the moon. Also, it is easy to teach gross things first before teaching, step by step, subtle and more subtle things.[25] In the ontological hierarchy of things mentioned earlier in which the senses are placed at the bottom and *Puruṣa* at the top, what is subtle is rated higher than what is gross. The supreme Self or *Puruṣa*, declares Śaṅkara, is the highest, because it is the most subtle, the greatest, and the most inward of all things.[26]

If it is admitted that there is axiological choice or category preference, it follows that no one could be compelled to pursue the good instead of the pleasant, or the trans-empirical instead of the empirical. It may be that there is someone who is not inclined to have any axiological/ontological preference of values/categories thinking, to use the well-known aphorism of Bentham, that "push-pin is as good as poetry." But if someone with a discerning mind exercises his choice, it is because of the fact that a lower value does not satisfy his desire or that a lower category does not fully answer his metaphysical urge, and so he prefers the higher in the scale. It is this value/category preference on the basis of the intrinsic worth of things that was suggested by J.S. Mill when he said that it was better to be a human being dissatisfied than a pig satisfied. It is by following the criterion of intrinsic worth, of value preference that the *Upaniṣad* says that one should see the Self—through hearing, reasoning, and contemplation. The transition from the lower knowledge to the higher takes place for one who, equipped with discrimination, detachment, and dispassion, has a deep urge or longing for the latter. It may be noted that the transition is neither easy nor automatic. The higher is accessible only to one who has fulfilled the requirements therefor.

The distinction between higher wisdom and lower knowledge is not absent in the West, though it may be doubted whether it receives the same attention in the writings of the academic philosophers in the present century. After classifying knowledge into three kinds—theoretical, practical, and productive—according to whether it is pursued for its own sake, as a means to conduct, or as a means to making something useful or beautiful, Aristotle refers to "sensory knowledge," "memory," "experience," "art," and "wisdom," arranging them in a hierarchy in which the sensory knowledge is placed at the bottom and wisdom at the top.

"Wisdom," according to Aristotle, is the highest knowledge, because it is not limited to just practical and productive ends. He maintains that the knowledge of the first and final cause of all things must be called "wisdom" because (1) it is the most comprehensive; (2) it is the knowledge of the most difficult to know; (3) it is the most precise knowledge; (4) it is the most instructive; and (5) it is the most self-contained.[27] The knowledge of the first and final cause of all things mentioned by Aristotle is *parā vidyā* of the *Upaniṣads*. It is worthy of attainment, because it is the saving knowledge. The point to be emphasized here is that this knowledge of the One, the first and final cause of all things, should not be mediate but immediate. It is this immediate knowledge (*aparokṣa-jñāna*) that liberates one from suffering (*sā vidyā yā vimuktaye*).

Consciousness:
The Presupposition of All Knowledge

Advaita makes the distinction between consciousness and what is presented to consciousness as its object; and it is on the basis of this dichotomy that it explains knowledge of external objects as well as knowledge of subjective states. The senses and the mind are material. The senses by themselves cannot give us knowledge of external objects without the functioning of the mind and the Self. The mind or the intellect cannot give us knowledge of anything without the functioning of the Self. According to Advaita, the Self is consciousness, and in the absence of consciousness, no knowledge is possible. Śaṅkara speaks of two kinds of seeing: ordinary seeing and the seeing of consciousness (the seeing of the pure Self). In the words of Śankara: "Seeing is of two kinds. Ordinary seeing is a function of the mind as connected with the visual sense; it is an act, and as such it has a beginning and an end. But the seeing that belongs to the Self is like the heat and light of fire; being the very essence of the witness (Self), it has neither beginning nor end…. The ordinary seeing, however, is related to objects seen through the eye, and of course has a beginning…. The eternal seeing of the Self is metaphorically spoken of as the witness, and although eternally seeing, is spoken of as sometimes seeing, and sometimes not seeing."[28]

Like Husserl, Advaita holds that consciousness is the "principle of principles"; and that the evidence of consciousness is the only one that is certain and apodictic for any claim that we make—claim that we know something as well as the claim that we do not know something. Every source of knowledge is dependent on consciousness—be it perception, or inference, or scripture. Consciousness which is the presupposition of every kind of knowledge and of every source of knowledge cannot be validated by any other principle. Since both sensory perception and rational understanding depend on consciousness, the controversy of rationalism vs. empiricism dominant in the Western epistemology since the days of Descartes and Locke is absent in the Hindu tradition. Nor is there any justification for the Humean legacy that human knowledge is restricted to two spheres, ideas of relations (mathematical knowledge) and matters of fact (empirical knowledge).

The ultimate reality which is trans-empirical cannot be known through the senses and reason. Even though reason may help us to know that there is the ultimate reality which is the ground or the cause of the world, it can give us only *mediate* knowledge of this reality. The Hindu tradition holds that the trans-empirical reality can be known and realized only through scripture. It establishes the validity of scripture as a source of knowledge on the ground that what it teaches (1) cannot be contradicted by other sources of knowledge, and (2) is not a restatement of what is conveyed by other sources of knowledge.[29] There is demarcation between scripture and other sources of knowledge. While the authority of the former is restricted to the trans-empirical reality, that of the latter is restricted to things empirical. Hence, there is no scope for conflict between them, or duplication of work by them.

The Physical World/Nature

The Concept of Kṣetra

The human being is a complex entity consisting of spirit and matter. What is distinctive of the human being is the possession of "reason" and "will"—reason being the capacity for conceiving the perfection (i.e., liberation), and will being the capacity to action for the realization of the perfection. Śaṅkara speaks of this distinctive feature as the eligibility for knowledge and action. The functioning of both reason and will presupposes a physical medium which the human being possesses in the form of mind-sense-body aggregate. The mind-sense-body complex, which is material, helps the human being to have cognitive, affective, and conative experience during empirical existence.

It is not necessary here to consider the work of each of these three factors separately. All these three, individually and collectively, help the human being to be engaged in the various kinds of life-activity. There is also the external world of material objects for our enjoyment. Hinduism holds that the mind-sense-body aggregate, as well as the physical world, is necessary for the attainment of the pleasant and the good. It uses a common term "*kṣetra*" which denotes both the mind-sense-body aggregate and the physical world. Since everything other than the Self or spirit, which comes under the category of nature, is an object of knowledge to the Self, the latter is called the knower of nature.[30] The Sanskrit word "*kṣetra*" is very significant. The entire mind-sense-body complex is called *kṣetra*, because it protects the Self from the evil by being conducive to the origination of the saving knowledge (*jñānotpādanadvārā kṣatāt trāyata iti kṣetram*), or because it is destructible or changeable (*kṣiyate iti, kṣarati iti vā kṣetram*), or because it is like a "field" for the reaping of the fruits of action (*karmaphalānām asmin niṣpatteḥ kṣetram*).[31] Since the reasons for calling the mind-sense-body complex *kṣetra* are applicable to the external world, the latter is also called *kṣetra*. So, everything other than the Self or spirit, according to Hinduism, is material.

Source of the World: Eternal Atoms

Every object which is composite and limited, e.g., a pot or a table, is an effect originating from a material cause. If so, what is the cause of the material universe which is a conglomeration of objects which are composite and limited? Hinduism answers this question in two ways. Let us first consider the Vaiśeṣika answer to this question. Not everything in the universe is created according to the Vaiśeṣika. Making a distinction between eternal substances, viz four kinds of atoms, *ākāśa*, space, time, mind, and self on the one hand, and composite objects on the other, the Vaiśeṣika holds the view that all composite objects of the universe are the products of the eternal atoms which are simple, indivisible, and infinitesimal. There are, according to this school, four kinds of material atoms, viz atoms of air, fire, water, and earth; and all composite and therefore non-eternal objects are the aggregation of these atoms. The atomic theory of the Vaiśeṣika, it should be borne in mind, is not applicable to space, time, *ākāśa* (ether), mind, and self, since each one of these substances, being eternal, can neither be created nor destroyed. Since not all objects in the universe are products of material atoms, it is wrong to think of the Vaiśeṣika philosophy as materialistic. The Vaiśeṣika accounts for the combination and separation of atoms, which are called respectively creation and destruction of the universe, through the will of God who controls the atoms and makes the world a moral order, dispensing justice on the basis of the stock of merit and demerit (*adṛṣṭa*) of the individual souls. So the universe as conceived by the Vaiśeṣika consists of living beings and physical things, and of these some are eternal and some non-eternal. The processes of creation and dissolution are applicable only to the non-eternal composite objects.

Source of the World: Primordial Matter

According to the second answer given by theistic schools like Śaivism and Vaiṣṇvism, as well as by the trans-theistic school of Advaita, the entire manifested physical universe other than the Self must be traced to a primordial material stuff called by different names such as *prakṛti, māyā, avyakta,* and so on. Creation and dissolution of the world alternate like day and night. When the world manifests in a particular order from the primeval material stuff, it is called creation; and when it gets back to its source and remains in the unmanifest condition, it is called dissolution. Since the Self called *Puruṣa* or *Ātman* is eternal, it is not subject to the processes of creation and dissolution, though the psycho-physical organism which it is equipped with during its empirical journey is subject to these processes.

Like the Vaiśeṣika, these schools also admit the existence of God who is responsible for the change from the unmanifest to the manifest condition, and from the manifest back to the unmanifest condition, of the physical universe, as the primordial material stuff by itself cannot undergo these periodical changes. There is, however, an important point of difference between the theistic and the trans-theistic schools. While the former schools hold the view that the primordial material stuff, which is the source of the world, is eternal and coeval with God, according to the latter it is not eternal; and nothing is eternal excepting the non-dual Brahman which is the sole reality. Whether eternal or not, *māyā/prakṛti/avyakta* which is the primeval source cannot exist and function independently of God.

Some Implications of the Hindu View of the World

It is necessary at this stage to highlight some of the implications of the Hindu view of the physical world. One of the ways by which we try to understand the nature of the thing is by finding out its material cause. A pot made of clay is *essentially* clay; a table made of wood is *essentially* wood. If the physical world is a product of *māyā/prakṛti/avyakta*, it is essentially material, because its cause is material. When an object which is subject to modification undergoes change of state, it is called cause in one state, and effect in another state: that is to say, the difference between cause and effect is the difference in states of one and the same entity.

Hinduism does not think of cause and effect as two discrete unconnected entities. If that were the case, there would be the difficulty of accounting for their connection which confronted Hume. If cause and effect are distinct "configurations of matter" separated by space, there will be no way of overcoming the bifurcation between them, and Hume will remain unanswered. Hinduism emphasizes the inner tie between cause and effect by saying that the effect is non-different from its material cause (*kārya-kāraṇayoḥ ananyatvam*). There is the inner tie not only between the manifested world and its primordial source, but also between God and the primordial source. There is more than one explanation for the inner connection between God and *prakṛti/māyā/avyakta* in the Hindu tradition. While some view *māyā* as the power of the Lord, some others say that God is both the material and the efficient cause rolled into one to show that the material cause of the world is not separate from God.

Since everything other than the Self or spirit is material, there is no mind-body dualism in Hinduism. Mind and matter are not radically different substances as in the case of the Cartesian theory; and so Hinduism is free from the problem of reductionism—reducing matter to mind, or mind to matter. However, there is another kind of dualism in Hinduism—the dualism of spirit and matter, *Puruṣa* and *Prakṛti*. This dualism does not amount to a physical separation of the two entities, though there is the need to discriminate the one from the other. The relation between these two entities is sought to be explained in terms of the ground and the grounded, or in terms of the organic relation between soul and body. The concept of the *antaryāmin* (the inner controller) which has been elaborated in one of the *Upaniṣads* is relevant in the context.[32] The *Upaniṣad* speaks of the Self as the indwelling ruler of everything. It first of all says: "He who dwells in the earth, yet is within the earth, whom the earth does not know, whose body the earth is, who controls the earth from within, he is your Self, the inner controller, the immortal."[33]

Then it speaks of other elements and the various parts of the body, and says that the Self is the inner ruler of everything. Finally, it concludes by saying: "He is never seen, but is the seer; he is never heard, but is the hearer; he is never perceived, but is the perceiver; he is never thought, but is the thinker. There is no other seer but he; there is no other hearer but he...."[34] The *antaryāmin* section of the *Upaniṣad* admits of more than one interpretation. Whatever may be the interpretation, the highest reality, according to Hinduism, is not only ontologically immanent in everything, man and the world, but is also the inner ruler of everything. Admitting the distinction between spirit and matter both at the microcosmic and macrocosmic levels, Hinduism assigns different values as well as different ontological statuses to them. The body exists in order to subserve the purpose of the Self.

Spirituality and Religious Experience
Spiritual Disposition

Spirituality is a disposition, a disciplined way of life through which one can attain spiritual awakening. Usually, it is contrasted with the materialistic way of life. The *Bhagavad Gītā*, the most popular scriptural text of the Hindus, draws a sharp distinction between spiritual disposition and materialistic disposition. It speaks of them as *daivī-sampat*, i.e., divine nature, and *āsurī-sampat*, i.e., demoniac nature, respectively. It enumerates the following virtues as constituting spiritual or divine disposition: "Fearlessness, purity, steadfastness in knowledge and concentration, charity, self-restraint, worship, study of one's scriptures, austerity, uprightness, non-violence, truth, absence of anger, renunciation, serenity, absence of calumny, compassion, uncovetousness, gentleness, modesty, absence of fickleness, energy, forgiveness, fortitude, absence of hatred and absence of pride."[35]

It also gives a list of qualities such as "ostentation, arrogance, self-conceit, anger, insolence, and ignorance of what is right and wrong" as constituting materialistic or demoniac disposition.[36] It declares that a person of materialistic disposition does not know what should be done and what should not be done and cannot, therefore, do anything conducive to one's prosperity and social well-being.[37]

A few comments are relevant in this connection. First of all, it is not the intention of the *Bhagavad Gītā* to list all the qualities of each of these two ways of life. The list in both the cases is only suggestive. However, the contrast between these two dispositions has been highlighted in unmistakable terms. Second, everyone in this world, irrespective of religion, region, gender and caste, can be classified under one of these two categories, spiritualistic or materialistic. It is, therefore, wrong to speak in exclusive terms of the spirituality of the East and of the materialism of the West as if the East has the monopoly of spirituality and the West, the monopoly of materialism. Spirituality is universal; materialism too is universal. As a contemporary Hindu philosopher puts it, countries which produced men like St. Francis of Assisi, St. John of the Cross, Eckhart, Boehme, Pascal, John Bunyan and hundreds of others cannot be less spiritual than the homeland of Hinduism.[38]

Third, there is no suggestion, explicit or implicit, in the text of the *Gītā* that only some persons, e.g. a philosopher or a theologian, are capable of spiritual disposition, and not others. Anyone who cares for and cultivates the virtues which constitute spiritual nature—such a one may be a philosopher or a scientist, a ruler or a social worker—may lead a way of life which may be called spiritual. Though it is admitted that spiritual disposition can be developed by everyone, it does not, however, follow from this that there will not be any variation at the level of spiritual development. It may be that spirituality is more intense in one and less intense in another; and this kind of *difference in degree* in spirituality is bound to arise among the seekers of truth, whoever they may be, as there is *difference in kind* between one who is spiritually oriented and one who is not. That is why we are able to speak of some as more spiritual, or very highly evolved, and so on. Fourth, spiritual disposition itself is not spiritual awakening; it is only a means to the latter. How soon or how late it will lead to the attainment of the saving knowledge depends on its strength or intensity and other factors. So it should not be thought that a person who is of a spiritual nature is a liberated one.

Religious Experience

Spirituality should not be equated with religious experience. Though in some cases spirituality as a way of life may be part of religious experience, it does not in every case constitute religious experience. A brief explanation of the nature of religious experience will be helpful to see the distinction between them. There are psychologists and philosophers who hold the view that there is no such thing as religious experience and that what goes in the name of religious experience cannot be separated from general experience.

According to some others who are extremely conservative, religious experience should be identified with some historical form of religion. If spirituality and religious experience are identified, it will not be possible to accept the former as something universal on the basis of any of these three views which deny the genuineness, or separate identity, or universality, of religious experience.

There is, however, a fourth view according to which religious experience is not only genuine, but also can be identified by means of definite criteria.[39]

According to this view, religious experience, first of all, is a response to the ultimate reality. Response is *response to* something. Being of the nature of a response, religious experience is not merely subjective. The reality to which we respond, in the language of Whitehead, is "beyond, behind, and within, the passing flux of immediate things; something which is real, and yet waiting to be realized; something which is a remote possibility, and yet the greatest of present facts...."[40] This reality to which we respond is characterized in the *Upaniṣad* as "without an earlier and without a later, without an inside and without an outside."[41]

The second criterion of religious experience is that it is a total response of the total being to the ultimate reality. Religious experience is the total response involving reason, feeling, and will; and it is the response of the whole man with the whole of human life. The third criterion of religious experience is intensity, suggesting that it is the most powerful experience of which the human being is capable. The intensity of religious experience as revealed by the lives of the charismatic spiritual leaders of all religions is well-known. Religious experience, according to the fourth criterion, finds expression in action for the upliftment of others, for the regeneration of all beings. This kind of action which is free from the sense of "I" and "mine" is associated, for example, with the *jīvanmukta* (the liberated-in-life) of Hinduism and the *bodhisattva* of Mahāyāna Buddhism. These four criteria are necessary for identifying religious experience.

It should be borne in mind that religious experience which transcends the frontiers of established religions, which is not bound by the limits of space and time, gender, caste, and race, is universal. However, the universality of religious experience should not be interpreted to mean that there will be no difference in religious experience. Since it presupposes a capacity on the part of the human being to respond, there is bound to be variation in its manifestation in thought as well as in action, though the *core* of it must be the same. Ramana Maharishi, a contemporary mystic-saint of Hinduism, points out that, while there can be degrees or levels of experience, there cannot be degrees of reality.[42]

Spirituality as a disposition may or may not involve a belief system. Many a person may follow some of the virtues which constitute spiritual or divine disposition without following or accepting a set of religious beliefs about man, cosmos, and the ultimate reality. But religious experience is based on a belief system in the form of anthropology, cosmology, and theology. Spirituality as a way of life does involve moral and spiritual discipline. But this discipline itself is only a means and not the goal which is variously described as spiritual awakening, enlightenment, liberation, mystic or religious experience, higher wisdom, and so on. Without this religious experience or vision, human life, declares Whitehead, "is a flash of occasional enjoyment lighting up a mass of pain and misery, a bagatelle of transient experience."[43]

Indian Culture and Modern Science
Hindu Tradition: Continuity and Change

The question whether the great tradition of Hinduism, which has admitted the distinction between higher wisdom and lower knowledge and has raised the problem of value preference and of ontological priority between them, can accommodate modern science which is Western and survive retaining its identity, is worth considering here. The Hindu tradition which has come down to us from the Vedic times is very ancient, more than four thousand years old. It has faced many encounters and challenges. The philosophy of Hinduism was challenged by Jainism and Buddhism, which provided a totally different picture of man and the world. Especially, the no-self theory (*anātma-vāda*) of Buddhism was a formidable alternative to the Hindu doctrine of the self. The fact is that Hinduism survived the combined challenge of Jainism and Buddhism. Subsequently, it encountered severe opposition from two alien religions, first from Islam and later from Christianity, and survived preserving the "essentials" of the great tradition, notwithstanding the support and patronage received by its rivals from the rulers at that time. This, however, does not mean that the great tradition has remained the same all over and that it has not been influenced by Jainism and Buddhism, Islam and Christianity, Western education, civilization, and culture.

It should also be noted that the work of the Hindu reformers of the Brahmo Samaj and the Arya Samaj and of the spiritual leaders of the renaissance such as Ramakrishna Paramahamsa, Swami Vivekananda, and others in the modern period of Hinduism did produce a perceptible impact on the tradition. No tradition worth the name can continue without changes. It will be petrified, dead, and gone without changes in it. At the same time, change cannot be total; total change is destruction. Change will be meaningful only in the context of identity. What goes in the name of Indian culture today, of which the great tradition is the main stream, is a product of the interaction and fusion of several facets contributed by Hinduism, Jainism, Buddhism, Islam, and Christianity.

Hinduism, nevertheless, has retained its identity. If the Hindu tradition is a reality, it is because of, in the words of Whitehead, the spirit of change and the spirit of conservation inherent in it. Whitehead remarks: "There can be nothing real without both. Mere change without conservation is a passage from nothing to nothing. Its final integration yields mere transient non-entity. Mere conservation without change cannot conserve. For after all, there is a flux of circumstance, and the freshness of being evaporates under mere repetition."[44]

There cannot be a better and more authentic statement about the continuity and change in the Hindu tradition than the one given by Radhakrishnan: "Hindu thought whether or not we agree with its transcendental claims has survived the storms of the world for over three thousand years. It has seen empires come and go, has watched economic and political systems flourish and fade. It has seen these happen more than once. Recent events have ruffled but not diverted the march of India's history. The culture of India has changed a great deal and yet has remained the same for over three millennia. Fresh springs bubble up, fresh streams cut their own channels through the landscape, but sooner or later each rivulet, each stream merges into one of the great rivers which has been nourishing the Indian soil for centuries."[45]

Hinduism Compatible with Modern Science

Many factors such as renaissance, reformation, enlightenment, and secularization have contributed to the emergence of the modern world in the West of which modern science is a characteristic expression. Though modern science originated in the West, it has become a pan-world phenomenon transcending the geographical frontiers. Just as religion, irrespective of its origin, is universal, even so modern science is universal. What is puzzling to quite a few is how the great tradition in India is able to accommodate or withstand the modern scientific revolution. The problem appears to be a clash of values— values of tradition vs. values of modern science and technology, as Earl MacCormac would put it.[46] If one thinks of a conflict between Hinduism and modern science, it must be in respect of subject matter or method. On the basis of the distinction between the Self and the not-Self, *Puruṣa* and *Prakṛti*, the trans-empirical and the empirical, Hinduism both as philosophy and religion is mainly concerned with the knowledge of the Self or *Puruṣa* which is trans-empirical. The entire realm of the empirical, it is necessary to reiterate, is neither unimportant nor useless; and the this-worldliness of Hinduism can never be neglected. So there is, according to Hinduism, a clear demarcation in respect of the subject matter.

Though Hinduism admits several sources or methods of knowledge such as perception, inference, and scripture, it holds that the Self or *Puruṣa* can be known only through scripture. Things empirical do not fall within the scope of scripture. They have to be known only through perception and inference. We do not require the help of scripture to tell us that fire is hot and that ice is cold, because this can be known through perception. Nor can scripture tell us anything contrary to this. As Śaṅkara puts it, "Even a hundred scriptural texts, declaring fire to be cold or non-luminous, will not be authoritative."[47]

In the same way, perception and inference, which can give us knowledge of objects such as the tree and the table, the mountain, the ocean, and the planets, which can be known, cannot give us the knowledge of the Self or consciousness. It is scripture that helps us to know the Self, even though the latter is not an object of knowledge like stocks and stones. It is not necessary to go into the details as to how scripture "shows" the Self which can neither be described by words nor comprehended by the mind.

The method of science consists in setting up principles or hypotheses, making logical conclusions from these principles or hypotheses in order to derive observable facts about them, and experimental checking or verification of these observable facts. The method followed by science does not come into conflict with the method followed by Hinduism for the purpose of knowing the Self. The distinction between these two methods has been very well brought out by Thomas Aquinas.

There are two ways in which we can explain our belief in a statement. One reason for believing a statement is that it can be checked by observation. This is what science does. Or, we can believe a statement because it can be deduced from an intelligent, self-evident principle.[48] The Self or consciousness is the ultimate, self-evident principle in terms of which other principles and statements can be understood. Hinduism is in search of the ultimate, "the principle of principles," on the basis of axiological preference and ontological priority. So there is no conflict between Hinduism and modern science in respect of method either.

It is true that modern science and technology are a challenge to the great tradition of Hinduism. A creative response is necessary to meet this new challenge. There is bound to be cultural change as a result of the institutional changes in society brought about by science and technology. But this cultural change in order to be creative should be within the framework of the great tradition. "If Christianity, European medieval culture, theology, and philosophy could put up with science and technology and achieve a new culture, cannot India do the same?"[49] asks a contemporary Hindu philosopher.

Notes

1. See 3.1.1. The text reads: "He practised *tapas*." The word *"tapas"* in the context means inquiry according to Sureśvara. See Sureśvara's *Taittirīyopaniṣad-bhāṣya-vārtika* (Madras: University of Madras, 1974, Revised edition, 1984), III, verses 14–19.
2. See Śaṅkara's commentary on *Brahma-sūtra*, 2.1.4: *"anubhava-avasānam ca brahmavijñānam."* Also, his commentary on *Brahma-sūtra* 1.1.1: *"tatra avicārya yat kiñcit pratipadyamāno niḥśreyasāt pratihanyeta anarthañceyāt."*
3. For example, while Advaita speaks of the fourfold discipline (*sādhana catuṣṭaya*), Viśiṣṭādvaita mentions the sevenfold discipline (*sādhana saptaka*) as the prerequisite for inquiry into reality. Śaṅkara enumerates the following in the preliminary discipline: (1) discrimination between the ephemeral and the eternal, (2) renunciation of the fruits of action, here and hereafter, (3) possession of "six treasures" such as control of the mind, control of the senses, etc., (4) an intense longing for liberation. According to the *Vākyakāra* of the Viśiṣṭādvaita tradition, the following constitute the preliminary discipline for the practice of *bhakti*: (1) purification of the body; (2) purification of the mind; (3) continuous practice of the presence of the indwelling self; (4) performance of the fivefold duty; (5) practice of virtue; (6) freedom from despair, and (7) freedom from exhaltation.
4. Just as a scientist, as Newton declared, does not imagine a hypothesis (*hypothesis non fingo*), even so we do not "imagine knowledge."
5. This idea is conveyed as follows: *"prāmāṇyam svataḥ utpadyate; prāmāṇyam svataḥ jñāyate ca."*
6. See his *Śrīmad Rahasyatrayasāra*, translated into English with Introduction and Notes by M.R. Rajagopaa Ayyangar, published by Agnihotram Ramanuja Thathachariyar, Kumbakonam, 1956, 53.
7. See his commentary on the *Taittirīya Upaniṣad*, 2.1.1.
8. See *Kaṭha Upaniṣad*, 1.3.15.
9. *Ibid.*, 1.2.2.
10. *Ibid.*, also see Śaṅkara's commentary on 1.2.1.
11. See Śaṅkara's commentary on *Muṇḍaka Upaniṣad*, 1.1.4.
12. 2.69.
13. *Muṇḍaka Upaniṣad*, 1.1.4.
14. *Ibid.*, 1.1.5.
15. *"mantravideva asmi na ātmavit."*
16. *Kaṭha Upaniṣad*, 1.3.10–11.
17. *Muṇḍaka Upaniṣad*, 1.1.4.
18. *Ibid.*
19. See his commentary on *Taittirīya Upaniṣad*, 1.5.1–2: *"medhākāmasya srīkāmasya ca mantra anukrāntāḥ te ca pāramparyena vidyopayogārthā eva."*

20. See his commentary on *Taittirīya Upaniṣad*, 1.9.
21. See *Muṇḍaka Upaniṣad*, 1.2.1.
22. See *Chāndogya Upaniṣad*, 7.1.2.
23. See *Muṇḍaka Upaniṣad*, 1.1.6.
24. *Ibid.*, 1.2.12.
25. See Śaṅkara's commentary on *Chāndogya Upaniṣad*, 7.1.1.
26. See his commentary on *Kaṭha Upaniṣad*, 1.3.10.
27. See W.D. Ross, *Aristotle* (Meridian Books, 1961), 152.
28. Śaṅkara's commentary on *Bṛhadāraṇyaka Upaniṣad*, 3.4.2.
29. See R. Balasubramanian, The *Naiṣkarmyasiddhi of Sureśvara* (Madras: University of Madras, 1988), III, 35, p. 258.
30. See *Bhagavad-gītā*, 13.1.
31. *Ibid.*, see Śaṅkara's commentary.
32. See *Bṛhadāraṇyaka Upaniṣad*, 3.7.
33. *Ibid.*, 3.7.3.
34. *Ibid.*, 3.7.23.
35. *Bhagavad-gītā*, 16.1–3.
36. *Ibid.*, 16.4.
37. *Ibid.*, 16–7.
38. See K. Satchidananda Murty, *The Indian Spirit* (Waltair: Andhra University Press, 1965), 6.
39. See Joachim Wach, *The Comparative Study of Religions* (New York & London: Columbia University Press, 1961), 30–37.
40. A.N.Whitehead, *Science and the Modern World* (Cambridge: Cambridge University Press, 1953), 238.
41. *Bṛhadāraṇyaka Upaniṣad*, 2.5.19.
42. Arthur Osborne (ed.), *The Teachings of Bhagavan Sri Ramana Maharshi* (London: Rider & Company, 1971), 177.
43. *Science and the Modern Word*, 238.
44. *Ibid.*, 250.
45. S. Radhakrishnan, *The Brahma Sūtra* (London: George Allen & Unwin, 1960), preface, 7.
46. Earl R. MacCormac, *Myths of Science and Technology* (Madras: Radhakrishnan Institute for Advanced Study in Philosophy, University of Madras, 1986), 83.
47. See Śaṅkara's commentary on the *Bhagavad-gītā*, 18.66.
48. See Philip Frank, *Philosophy of Science* (New Jersey: Prentice-Hall, 1958), 16.
49. K. Satchidananda Murty, *The Indian Spirit*, 27.

FOUR a

COMMENTS On Balasubramanian's PAPER

Philip C. Novak

First of all, I want to thank Professor Balasubramanian for the mini-compendium of Hindu thought presented in the first five parts of his paper. I find such reviews helpful, and though I have a few questions concerning it, I will pass over them so as not to take us too far afield from the topic of our seminar, namely, East-West Perspectives on Spirit and Science.

It is in regard to this topic that I wish to call attention to the final page of Prof. Balasubramanian's paper in which he says: "It is true that modern science and technology are a challenge to the great tradition of Hinduism."

My central question to him is: How so?—since it seemed to me that virtually everything in the paper suggested that spirituality (here Hinduism) and science are complementary.

Prof. Balasubramanian argues their complementarity on the basis of Hinduism's traditional distinction between a lower and a higher knowledge and Hinduism's belief that these two knowledges are not mutually exclusive.

Parenthetically I should note that Prof. Balasubramanian's "justification" for this distinction between two kinds of knowledges begs the question, for it is based on an appeal to an equally questionable distinction between the organic and the hyperorganic nature of man. Later in the paper he argues that higher and lower knowledges are complementary because their different methods (empirical observation vs. deduction from first principles) are equally valid. This begs the question once again because "deduction from first principles" is hardly recognized as a universally valid method of knowing. I confess that I would be more comfortable if Prof. Balasubramanian couched his assertions in the form of "Scripture says that…" or "I believe that…," for indeed, many of us probabiy share some of his beliefs. To try to give such assertions, based on faith and authority, the appearance of rational justification seems counterproductive.

Now Prof. Balasubramanian reminds us that Śaṅkara himself suggests a complementarity between lower and higher knowledges when he indicates that lower "worldly" knowledge must not be neglected and that it may in fact be indirectly helpful to the attainment of higher knowledge. Soon after this, however, he cites Śaṅkara again, this time to the effect that only "one who was detached from the whole world of means and ends is competent for higher knowledge."

Śaṅkara seems to be contradicting himself here. But the contradiction disappears when we think existentially instead of purely logically. Certainly one can pursue so-called lower knowledge—that is, means-end rational knowledge—at one time in life and pursue higher knowledge at another time in life. In much the same way one can pursue *artha* and *kāma* at one time in life and pursue *mokṣa* at another. Nevertheless Śaṅkara's second statement—that only one who is detached from lower knowledge is competent for the higher—runs precisely counter to Prof. Balasubramanian's thesis since it points out that lower and higher knowledges, as existential pursuits, *are* mutually exclusive in the sense that *they cannot both be ultimate concerns at the same time*.

Therefore, I want to suggest that Prof. Balasubramanian's argument about the *theoretic* complementarity of lower and higher knowledges (granting Hindu assumptions), though sound, is somewhat ineffectual, for it *masks* the deeper existential problem that exists between "science" and "spirituality."

Before I get to that, let me add one more parenthesis: Prof.

Balasubramanian's argument seems analogous to Descartes' ill-fated attempt to separate reality into two domains, assigning one domain to the scientists and the other domain to the theologians, so that each group could pursue its inquiry without stepping on the others' toes.

But (as suggested, for instance, by Prof. Dy's paper in this volume) plenty of toes are getting stepped on. Less metaphorically: the real problem is that all traditional ideas and pursuits —including, for instance, the very idea of a higher and a lower knowledge—are in danger of becoming eroded, eclipsed, or overcome by the pervasive imperatives of the global economic-political system and the increasing monetarization and bureaucratization of everyday life (all of which we can, for the sake of argument, attribute to the indirect effects of "science," that it's due to the predominance of its instrumental thinking in the shaping of the modern world's values).

In simpler terms, though it is true that so-called higher and lower knowledges are, in the traditional view, logically distinct and complementary, it is increasingly likely that fewer and fewer people care about "higher knowledge," believe that such a thing exists, feel the lure of its high calling, or are willing or able to undergo the discipline necessary for its cultivation.

The problem for Hinduism and for all "spirituality" is not whether or not the higher and lower knowledges are complementary, but rather how to sustain the human openness to the existence of such a knowledge in a world that is increasingly pervaded by its implicit denial.

The more central (and more difficult) question for Hinduism and all "spirituality" is how to stop the tide of alienation that seems to stem from our entrancement with, and our application of, those intrinsically good things called science and technology.

FIVE

The UNITY Of SCIENCE And SPIRITUAL KNOWLEDGE

THE ISLAMIC EXPERIENCE

Osman B. Bakar

In this paper the term *science* is understood in the restricted sense of an organized, orderly, and objective knowledge of the natural order. Science understood in the above sense is not the product of the modern mind alone. Such forms of knowledge had also been extensively cultivated in pre-modern civilizations such as in the Chinese, Indian, and Islamic civilizations. These pre-modern sciences, however, differ from modern science with respect to goals, methodology, sources of inspiration, and their philosophical assumptions concerning man, knowledge, and the reality of the natural world.

Another major difference between pre-modern and modern sciences pertains to the place of science in relation to other kinds of knowledge. In pre-modern civilizations, science was never divorced from spiritual knowledge. On the contrary, one finds an organic unity of science and spiritual knowledge. The main aim of this paper is to explain how this unity was achieved in pre-modern times. My specific reference is to the Islamic scientific tradition. However, many of the features of Islamic science mentioned here equally apply to the other pre-modern sciences.

By *spiritual knowledge* I mean knowledge pertaining to the spiritual order. The essence of spiritual knowledge is knowledge of the world of the Spirit. In Islam, this knowledge refers to the knowledge of the One, of God and His Unity. The principle of Divine Unity (*al-tawḥīd*) constitutes the central message of Islam. In Muslim classifications of knowledge composed over the centuries, the knowledge of *tawḥīd* was always held to be the highest form of knowledge as well as the ultimate goal of all intellectual pursuits.

Spiritual knowledge is not confined solely to the world of the pure Spirit. It is also concerned with the manifestations of the Spirit in the different orders of reality that make up the whole universe.

A fundamental component of a Muslim's knowledge of God is the knowledge of the universe as an effect of the divine creative act. Knowledge of the relationship between God and the world, between Creator and creation, or between the Divine Principle and cosmic manifestation, constitutes the most fundamental basis of the unity of science and spiritual knowledge. In Islam, the most important sources of this type of knowledge are the Qur'an and prophetic *ḥadīths*. To understand the Islamic conception and experience of the unity of science and spiritual knowledge, it is necessary to refer to some of the key concepts and ideas embodied in this knowledge.

The Qur'an as Source of Both Science and Spiritual Knowledge

The Qur'an is the fountainhead of Islamic intellectuality and spirituality. It is the basis not only of religion and spiritual knowledge but of all kinds of knowledge. It is the main source of inspiration of the Muslim vision of the unity of science and spiritual knowledge. The idea of this unity is a consequence of the idea of the unity of all knowledge. The latter is in turn derived from the principle of Divine Unity applied to the domain of human knowledge.

Man gains knowledge from different kinds of sources and through various ways and means. But all knowledge ultimately comes from God who is the All-Knowing. In the Qur'anic view, man's knowledge of things corporeal as well as spiritual is possible because God had given him the necessary faculties of knowing. Many Muslim philosophers and scientists assert that in the act of thinking and knowing the human intellect is illuminated by the divine intellect.

The Qur'an is not a book of science. But it does provide knowledge of the principles of science, which it always relates to metaphysical and spiritual knowledge. The Qur'anic injunction to "read in the Name of Thy Lord" has been faithfully observed by every generation of Muslims. It has been understood to mean that the acquisition of knowledge, including scientific knowledge should be based on the foundation of our knowledge of God's Reality. Islam, in fact, gives legitimacy to a science only if it is organically related to the knowledge of God and of the world of the Spirit. Consequently, Islamic science possesses a religious and spiritual character. According to the famous Muslim scientist, Ibn Sina (Avicenna), that science is true science which relates knowledge of the world to the knowledge of the Divine Principle.[1]

Nature as Source of Scientific and Spiritual Knowledge

Nature is a source of many types of knowledge: mathematical, physical, and metaphysical; scientific and spiritual; qualitative and quantitative; practical and aesthetical. This is because, as a world and viewed in its totality, the reality of nature is comprised of many aspects. Each type of knowledge corresponds to a particular aspect of nature that is singled out for study. Modern science has chosen to study only some of these aspects. In conformity with its scientific conception of nature and its reductionistic and materialistic worldview, modern science ignores, belittles, or denies altogether the metaphysical, spiritual, qualitative, and aesthetical aspects of nature. Eddington and Whitehead have rightly asserted that modern science is a kind of subjectively selected knowledge since it deals only with those aspects of the reality of nature which the so-called scientific method is competent to study.[2]

In Islam, the unity of nature is regarded as an image of the unity of the Divine Principle. The goal of Islamic science is to demonstrate the unity of nature, that is the interrelatedness of all its parts and aspects. Consequently, Islamic science seeks to study all the different aspects of nature from a unified and integrated standpoint. For example, the fundamentality of the mathematical aspect of the universe is well recognized in Islamic science. According to the Ikhwān al-Ṣafāʾ (The Brethren of Purity), an eleventh-century brotherhood of Muslim scientists and philosophers, "the whole world is composed in conformity with arithmetical, geometrical and musical relations."[3] But this mathematical content of the universe was never studied in Islam from a quantitative point of view alone. Muslim mathematics was both a qualitative and a quantitative science.

Following the Pythagoreans, whose mathematical conception of the universe found easy acceptance into the Islamic world-view, many Muslim mathematicians speak of the "virtues" and "personalities" of various geometrical figures. One of their declared aims in studying geometry is to help prepare the human soul in its journey to the world of the spirits and eternal life.[4] Similarly, the science of numbers is seen to be related to spiritual knowledge. Numbers are not merely quantitative entities on which may be performed the arithmetical operations of addition, subtraction, multiplication, and division. Numbers are also qualitative entities. In its qualitative aspect, number is the spiritual image resulting in the human soul from the repetition of unity. Numbers are therefore regarded as the projection or as so many expressions of unity. Knowledge of the generation of numbers from the number one presents to the human mind a powerful illustration of the generation of all things from God. The Ikhwan al-Ṣafāʾ compared the creation of the world by God to the generation of numbers from the number One.[5] The number zero, whose historical origin may be traced to the metaphysical speculation of the Hindus, is said to symbolize the Divine Essence which is beyond all determinations including Being.

Mathematics as cultivated by the Muslims emerges as a primary link between the physical world and the spiritual or metaphysical world of the Platonic archetypes. Arithmetic and geometry, the foundation of the mathematical sciences, find their application in the domain of the physical sciences as well as in the domain of metaphysical knowledge of *tawḥīd*. Muslim philosopher-scientists like al-Fārābī, Ikhwān al-Ṣafā', and Quṭb al-Dīn al-Shīrāzī considered mathematical training indispensable to having a sound knowledge of spiritual truths.[6]

Nature is also a source of spiritual and metaphysical knowledge because it is not merely 'natural.' Nature also possesses a 'supernatural' aspect. In Islam, the natural and the spiritual are closely intertwined. Spiritual reality manifests itself in the natural world while remaining independent of the latter. The two orders are connected by means of a vertical, metaphysical relationship. The natural world is variously described in the different religious traditions as an effect, a manifestation, symbol, or reflection of the spiritual world. Conversely, the spiritual world is described as the cause, principle, root, or archetype of the natural world.

In the religious and intellectual history of the West, however, a sharp distinction has often been made between the natural and the spiritual in a manner which is not conducive to the realization of the unity of science and spiritual knowledge. The natural world is identified with the profane and the spiritual with the sacred. There was also a sharp line drawn between the natural and the supernatural or between nature and grace. In modern science, nature has lost its sacred character. The natural world has been emptied of its spiritual content. Consequently, nature is no longer seen as having a meaningful role in religious and spiritual life.

The fact that there is something of a spiritual order that resides in nature finds numerous expressions in Islamic philosophical and theological literature. In the language of the Qur'an, nature is said to bear within itself the imprints of God. The phenomena of nature, in the macrocosmic world as well as within the souls of men, are said to be the *āyāt* (signs) of God. The verses of the Qur'an are likewise called the *āyāt* of God. Nature is therefore regarded as a divine revelation, a counterpart of the Qur'an. It conveys to man its metaphysical and spiritual message of transcendence. In this religious and spiritual conception of nature lies the basis of unity of science and spiritual knowledge.

Nature is also said to be a book of symbols. According to al-Ghazzālī, everything that exists in the natural world is a symbol of something in the higher world.[7] Symbol in its traditional sense is to be distinguished from allegory. As traditionally understood in Islam, symbol is the "reflection" in a lower order of existence of a reality belonging to a higher ontological status. That higher world which is symbolized by the natural symbols is the spiritual world. For example, the sun symbolizes the Divine Intelligence; the empty vastness of space symbolizes the Divine All-Possibility and also the Divine Immutability; a bird symbolizes the soul; a tree symbolizes the grade of being; and water symbolizes knowledge and rain revelation. We can go on and on giving countless other examples.

There is an inner nexus between the symbol and the symbolized. This nexus is metaphysical and not physical in nature. Knowledge of the meaning of a symbol or of this inner nexus cannot be gained through logical or mathematical analysis or through empirical investigation. This knowledge belongs to that science traditionally called the science of symbolism, which is metaphysical in nature. The science of symbolism is of crucial importance to the quest for the unity of science and spiritual knowledge. For this reason, this science was cultivated in almost every pre-modern civilization. However, by its very nature, this science poses a certain difficulty to the modern scientific mind. This is because this science presupposes the acceptance of divine revelation and intellectual intuition as two fundamentally real sources of objective knowledge. It also presupposes the acceptance of other levels of existence than the physical and of the hierarchic reality of the universe. These presuppositions are found to be contrary to many of the basic assumptions of modern science.

The science of symbolism implies that natural objects are not to be regarded simply as facts as is done in modern science. Natural objects or phenomena that admit of empirical and mathematical study are also to be viewed as symbols. What this means is that the reality of a natural object is not exhausted by its scientific and mathematical content. Symbolic knowledge of natural objects is not only possible but also is no less real than the corresponding scientific or mathematical knowledge. Muslim scientists of past centuries had shown that symbolic and scientific knowledge of natural things are not contradictory or unrelated. In fact, symbolic knowledge of nature helps to reveal the metascientific or metaphysical significance of scientific facts, theories, and laws discovered through empirical study of the natural world. And in a number of known cases, it was that symbolic knowledge itself which inspired Muslim scientists to embark upon new areas of scientific study leading to original discoveries in those areas. A good example is of how Suhrawardi's twelfth-century metaphysics of light and cosmology based on light symbolism helped to bring about intense scientific activity in the field of optics in thirteenth-century Islam. Quṭb al-Dīn al-Shīrāzī and his student Kamāl al-Dīn al-Fārsī made important discoveries in this field.[8]

The harmonious relationship between scientific and symbolic knowledge of nature is well illustrated by Ibn Sīnā in his work known as *Oriental Philosophy*. In this work, scientific facts became transformed into symbols which were to act as guide posts for the traveler upon the path of spiritual perfection in his journey through and beyond the cosmos to the Divine Presence.[9] Ibn Sīnā had drawn the scientific facts in question from a wide range of sciences including mineralogy, biology, astronomy, physics, cosmology, sociology and anthropology as these sciences were known to the medieval world of his time. Physical and astronomical realities of the universe of which this scientific knowledge is a description were no longer seen in this work as external objects and phenomena to be scientifically analyzed and manipulated. Thanks to the symbolic knowledge of nature, Ibn Sina was able to see these realities as part of a cosmos of symbols through which his spiritual journey to God must pass. Scientific knowledge of the physical world can, therefore, play an important role in the formulation of the idea of a spiritual journey through the cosmos provided that the traditional knowledge of symbols is present and accepted.

Since nature is regarded as a divine revelation it is a source for gaining knowledge of God's wisdom. Muslim scientists firmly believe that God's wisdom is reflected in innumerable ways in His creation. They study such things as natural forms, forces, energies, laws, and rhythms not only to gain scientific knowledge as currently understood but also to arrive at a better knowledge of the divine wisdom. Let us take the example of zoology. Muslim zoological studies were pursued with diverse ends in view. There was first of all the scientific study of the anatomy and classification of animals. Muslim classifications of animals were based on numerous criteria such as the nature of their habitats and the way they organize their defense from external attacks.

Muslim interest in animals also arose out of practical concerns, the most important of which is the medical. Considerable attention was given to both veterinary medicine and pharmacological uses of animals. Then, there was the study of animal psychology and physiology. Another major concern displayed by Muslim zoologists was with the spiritual, symbolic, and moral significance of animals.

What is of great significance from the point of view of our present discussion is the fact that there existed many individual scientists and treatises in Islam which testify to the unity of scientific and spiritual knowledge in the domain of zoology. In al-Jāḥiẓ, the ninth-century author of *The Book of Animals*, the most famous Arabic work on zoology, scientific, literary, moral, and religious studies of animals are combined. According to him, the primary goal of the study of zoology is the demonstration of the existence of God and the wisdom inherent in His creation. Al-Jāḥiẓ treated zoology as a branch of religious studies.

In the fourteenth-century zoological work of Kamal al-Din al-Damīrī, entitled *The Great Book of the Life of Animals*,[10] we encounter another good example of the combining of spiritual, moral, religious and juridical, literary, scientific and medical perspectives in studying animals. Al-Damīrī even dealt with the significance of animals in the interpretation of dreams, a discipline which is inseparable from spiritual knowledge. The injunctions of the *Sharīʿah*, the sacred Law of Islam, concerning dietary prohibitions related to animal flesh, have inspired the study of animals from a religious and juridical point of view. Muslim concern with religious and juridical status of animals according to the Divine Law of Islam provides one of the main frameworks for the unity of science and spiritual knowledge in zoology. Many Muslim scientists were interested in discovering the scientific justification for these religious dietary prohibitions.

Careful observation was made of animal behavior and the inner qualities and the genius of a particular animal species with a view of deriving spiritual and moral lessons from that animal species. There is a metaphysical basis for the belief that animals have much to teach man concerning the divine wisdom and about his own inner nature. According to Islamic spiritual tradition, man is a total reflection of the divine names and qualities whereas the animals are only partial reflections. However, the reflections in animals are often more direct than those in man. Animals are symbols of cosmic qualities and of spiritual attitudes. By virtue of possessing both good and evil qualities, animals present themselves as moral teachers to man.

From the Islamic point of view, a true zoology or science of animals only emerges when all of these different aspects of animals are taken into consideration. There is unity of scientific and spiritual knowledge in this conception of zoology. The link between the two types of knowledge is preserved not only in zoological works but also in works of art. Muslim artists drew miniatures of various animal species, which successfully captured the inner qualities of these animals. By virtue of the link that exists between the inner qualities of animals and the spiritual world, these works of art serve a kind of spiritual function, namely to enable man to contemplate the visible world as a reflection of the spiritual world.

Nature as a Source of "Divine Laws"

One of the main features of modern science is its success in the discovery of more and more of what is called in Western intellectual history "laws of nature." The idea that the cosmos has its own laws is found in all civilizations. There is order and harmony in the universe. However, in modern science, the "laws of nature" have lost their spiritual and metaphysical significance. In fact, the "laws of nature" are seen by many people today as being opposed to the "laws of God" found in religion. This modern cleavage between the "laws of nature" and "the laws of God" has disastrous consequences for the unity of science and spiritual knowledge. If we wish to restore this unity in the modern world, then one of the possible avenues is through the reassertion of the metaphysical or spiritual status of the "laws of nature."

In Islam, there has never been any cleavage between the "laws of nature" and the "laws of God." The "laws of nature" too are divine Laws. All laws are reflections of the Divine Principle. God is the Law-Giver. He manifests His will both in the cosmos and in the human domain through laws. In the human domain, God had prescribed a Law (*Shari'ah*) for every people. The Islamic *Shari'ah* is only the last to be revealed. While there are many different Divine Laws revealed to mankind in its history, which are spoken of in Islam as *nawāmīs al-anbiyā'* (Laws of the prophets), there is only one Divine Law governing the whole of creation. This latter Law is called *nāmūs al-khilqah* (Law of creation).

Although we speak of a single Divine Law governing the whole cosmos, there are different sets of laws for different orders of creation. Even within the same order of creation, such as in the natural order, there exist different laws for different species of beings. The Qur'an itself speaks of each animal species as an *ummah* (religious community) implying that God has promulgated a law for each species of being. The Qur'an also speaks of each creature as possessing its own nature. The goal of Islamic science is to know the true nature of things as given by God. Islamic science also seeks to demonstrate the unity of the "laws of nature" as a reflection of the unity of the Divine Principle. To know the nature and law of each species of being is to know the *Islam* or *manner of submission* of that species to the Divine Will. This is the Qur'anic way of looking at the unity of the "laws of nature" and the revealed Law of religion. According to the Qur'an, all creatures other than the human species are necessarily Muslims, understood in this universal sense, since they cannot rebel against their own nature. In the human order, those people are Muslims who submitted to the Divine Law which God has promulgated for them. Man alone among the creatures is capable of revolting against God's laws and his own nature. From the metaphysical point of view then, there is no difference in nature between the "laws of nature" and the revealed laws of religion.

The laws governing the different orders of creation are not of the same degree of fundamentality or universality. Some laws are more fundamental and universal than others. There is an hierarchy of universality of laws of creation corresponding to the hierarchy of the created order. For example, biological laws are more fundamental and universal than physical or chemical laws since the former laws concern the biological domain which possesses a higher ontological reality than the physical domain which gives rise to the latter kind of laws. But the biological laws themselves are subject to a higher set of cosmic laws which are spiritual in nature. If the attempt to unify all the known existing laws in physics and biology is progressively pursued and in an objective manner, then a point is reached whereby the higher, nonphysical orders of reality would have to be seriously considered and examined. In other words, there is a limit to the universality of physical laws.

Cosmological Knowledge as Source of Conceptual Framework for the Unity of Science and Spiritual Knowledge

In the foregoing discussion, I have dealt with some of the most important teachings of Islam, which provide the necessary philosophical and religious justification for the unity of science and spiritual knowledge. I asserted that this unity is realized when each of the particular sciences is organically related to the supreme knowledge of *tawḥīd*. But what is meant by this "organic relation" and the concrete manner in which it could be achieved need further clarification.

The various natural and mathematical sciences are particular sciences in the sense that they deal with particular domains of reality. The supreme knowledge of *tawḥīd* is a metaphysical science. It is the most universal science since it deals with the Supreme Reality which contains all things. Between the supreme knowledge of *tawḥīd* and the particular sciences there lies a body of knowledge called cosmological knowledge.

By cosmology, I do not mean the modern discipline known by the same name. Traditional cosmology, whether in Islam or in other civilizations, refers to that science which deals with the structure of the cosmos and its qualitative content. Insofar as cosmology deals with the whole reality of the cosmos, it is a universal science. In his famous treatise on the classification of the sciences entitled *Iḥṣā' al-'ulūm* (Enumeration of the Sciences), al-Fārābī considers cosmology a branch of metaphysics. He also maintains that from cosmology may be derived the principles of the particular sciences. Indeed, in Islam, cosmology plays an important role as a bridge between pure metaphysics and the particular sciences. Cosmology is a source of conceptual framework for the unity of science and spiritual knowledge.

What is meant by science being organically related to the metaphysical knowledge of *tawḥīd* is that the former is conceptually integrated into the latter type of knowledge. The particular sciences may be conceptually integrated into the metaphysical science of *tawḥīd* because the Divine Principle is the metaphysical source of the world of multiplicity dealt with by the particular sciences. However, the necessary "conceptual tools" for that integration need to be derived from cosmology.

Cosmology is competent to supply these "tools of conceptual integration" because its goal is "to provide a science that displays the interrelation of all things and the relation of the levels of the cosmic hierarchy to each other and finally to the Supreme Principle. Thereby it provides a knowledge that permits the integration of multiplicity into Unity."[11]

Cosmologically speaking, the world of sense perception is only one of many levels of existence. Muslims develop many cosmological models, each of which having its basis on certain scriptural data. Each model may be identified with the use of one or more types of symbolism. For example, in the cosmological model of Muslim Pythagoreans, such as the Ikhwān al-Ṣafā', a combination of numerical, alphabetical, alchemical, and astrological symbolisms is used to depict the levels and qualities of cosmic reality.

The Peripatetic model, such as that of al-Fārābī and Ibn Sīnā, makes use of the symbolism inherent in the geocentric scheme of Ptolemaic astronomy. The model of Ishrāqī-philosophers employs the symbolism of light. The Sufi cosmological model of Ibn 'Arabī presents all cosmic qualities as reflections of the Divine names and qualities and each level of cosmic existence as a "Divine Presence." But regardless of the type of symbolism used, we may discern in all these models three fundamental levels of cosmic existence, namely the spiritual, the subtle, and the physical. This division of the cosmos is a qualitative or "vertical" one, for it refers to three different levels of qualities.

Cosmology provides us with knowledge of how the three worlds are related to each other. The spiritual world is a principle of the subtle world and the latter a principle of the physical world. Cosmology therefore demands that the physical world be treated not as an autonomous domain which is cut off from higher orders of reality. It insists on the relevance of spiritual and subtle entities in the study of the physical world. For example, the traditional "ether" is a non-physical, subtle entity. Knowledge of this "ether" is essential to the understanding of the origin of the physical cosmos.

Similarly, living forms studied in the biological sciences are essentially related to the spiritual and subtle worlds. The question of the origin of life on Earth cannot be resolved in terms of physical entities alone, no matter how deep we penetrate into the molecular world. Life is a non-physical entity. It is an animating principle or energy which has penetrated into the physical realm. Molecular activities associated with living forms are not the source of life. Rather, they are a particular manifestation of life on the physical plane. The Islamic cosmological principle, which is essential to the understanding of the mystery of life, is the idea of the Universal Soul (*al-nafs al-kullīyah*). The Universal Soul is the "soul" of the natural order. It is to the natural order what the human soul is to the human body.

The Universal Soul, an entity which animates the whole cosmos, is what generates life in plants and animals. Plant and animal souls with their numerous respective powers or faculties are considered as so many faculties of the Universal Soul. The Universal Soul is itself created by God. Knowledge of the cosmic function, powers, and qualities of the Universal Soul, especially in relation to the natural order, is indispensable for the integration of the biological sciences into the spiritual knowledge of *tawḥīd*.

It is beyond the scope of this essay to go into a discussion of all the relevant cosmological principles. The examples I have given are sufficient to demonstrate the importance of cosmology as a source of conceptual framework for the unity of science and spiritual knowledge.

Conclusion

There is a need to revive traditional cosmology in the modern world. This cosmology has an important role to play in any proposed project aimed at realizing the unity of science and spiritual knowledge. The revival of traditional cosmology does not call for the abandonment or neglect of the experimental method and the modern tools of scientific research and inquiry, which have proved so successful in the quantitative study of nature. But it does call for fundamental changes in the modern attitude toward reality and knowledge. The acceptance of traditional cosmology has profound methodological consequences. It means that the modern scientific method has to drop its claim of being the sole way of knowing things. Other possible avenues to knowledge of the universe need to be acknowledged.

Modern science must come to terms with the historical fact that there have been societies and civilizations which cultivated diverse ways of studying and knowing the natural world. This diversity of ways of knowing is not to be construed as a kind of "epistemological anarchy" as imagined by some contemporary philosophers of science. Such societies and civilizations have seen unity in this diversity, thanks to the traditional doctrine of the hierarchy and unity of modes of knowing.

The spirit of reductionism which has come to characterize modern science has impoverished the natural order. The revival of traditional sciences and the cosmological sciences on which they are based may help to bring about in modern man a consciousness of the richness of reality.

Notes

1. F. Brunner, *Science et réalité* (Paris, 1954), 13.
2. S.H. Nasr, *Man and Nature: The Spiritual Crisis of Modern Man* (London: Allen and Unwin, 1976), 28.
3. See S.H. Nasr, *An Introduction to Islamic Cosmological Doctrines* (Shambhala, Boulder, 1978), 45.
4. *Ibid.*, 49.
5. "Know, oh Brother (May God assist thee and us by the Spirit from Him) that God, Exalted Be His Praise, when He created all creatures and brought all things into being, arranged them and brought them into existence by a process similar to the process of generation of numbers from one, so that the multiplicity [of numbers] should be a witness to His Oneness, and their classification and order an indication of the perfection of His Wisdom in creation. And this would be a witness to the fact, too, that they [creatures] are related to Him who created them, in the same way as the numbers are related to the One which is prior to two, and which is the principle, origin and source of numbers, as we have shown in our treatise on arithmetic." Ikhwān al-Ṣafā',Rasā'il Arabiyah Press, Cairo, 1928, trans. by S.H. Nasr in his *Science and Civilization in Islam* (Kuala Lumpur: Dewan Pustaka Fajar, 1984), 155–6.
6. I have dealt with the views of al-Fārābī and Quṭb al-Dīn al-Shīrāzī on this question in my doctoral thesis, *Classification of the Sciences in Islamic Intellectual History: A Study in Islamic Philosophies of Science* (to be published).
7. See his *Mishkāt al-anwār*, transl. by W.H.T. Gairdner (Lahore: Muhammad Ashraf Publications), 121–5.
8. For a discussion of these discoveries, see E.S.Kennedy, "The Exact Sciences in Iran under the Seljuqs and Mongols," *Cambridge History of Iran*, vol. V, ed. by J.A. Boyle (Cambridge, 1968), 676.
9. See H. Corbin, *Avicenna and the Visionary Recitals*, trans. W.R. Trask (Texas: Spring Publications, 1980).
10. For a modern study of this work, see J. de Somogy, "'Ad-Damiri's Ḥayāt al-ḥayawān: An Arabic Zoological Lexicon," *Osiris*, vol. 9 (1950), 33–43.
11. See S.H. Nasr, "The Cosmos and the Natural Order," in *Islamic Spirituality: Foundation*, ed. S.H. Nasr, vol. 19 of *World Spirituality: An Encyclopedic History of the Religious Quest* (New York: Crossroad Publ. Co., 1987), 350.

SIX

DOES The WEST NEED The EAST?

Manuel B. Dy, Jr.

Does the West need the East? The question presumes a certain problem with Western thinking and acting, a deprivation of sort that perhaps the East can satisfy. That many Westerners are turning to the East does not seem to be simply a fascination for something exotic, something different, because this fascination is coupled with a serious attempt to come to understand the East that entails on the part of the Westerner a humility, a "dying to one's self." What is there in the traditional Eastern cultures that is valuable to the West? But can the East of today, which is more and more westernized, really provide for the needs of the West? Or is it not the case that what is happening in the East today precisely manifests the problematic of the West? Would this not suggest perhaps a common human dilemma that needs the integration of both perspectives?

This paper attempts to answer these questions with the aid of Jurgen Habermas's critical theory. Although Habermas addresses his sociological philosophy to Western societies, his interpretation of Max Weber's thought seems to be applicable to Eastern societies as well.

Western Rationality

It is often said that science arose from the West and not from the East. This is not to say that the East did not have any discoveries in science. Long before the West, China had already invented the mariner's compass, gunpowder, vaccinations, and the taximeter, but the Chinese did not develop these. And it is not until the nineteenth century that a marked difference in technological advancement is evident between the West and the East. Science and technology are not the monopoly of the West nor should the term "scientific" be limited simply to Western standards, for how do we account for the recent interest in Chinese and Indian traditional medicine (e.g. acupuncture, yoga)? The research into these areas may yield results that prove a different standard for being scientific. But it is only in the West that science had a *development*, an evolution, whereas in the East science had only to repeat itself. Western culture then is predominantly scientific, but what is it in the Western mind that propels it toward scientific and technological development?

Western cultures and societies admit of several paradigms of nature: the cosmological from the Greek introduction of *physis* or physical nature; the theological from the Latin notion of *natura* or nature; the systemic-mechanistic from the French *la nature* or the system of nature as a machine; and the systemic-organic from the German *die Nature* or the system of nature as an organism.[1]

The Greeks looked at nature as an ordered unfolding of the cosmos, that can therefore be revealed to reason as *logos* and to which Aristotle gave the name of *Physis*. Christian thought, though rooted in the Hebrew tradition, adapted this paradigm of the Greeks together with their sense of the limited and proportional but introduced the notion of *finite*. Nature was finite, created out of nothing by an infinite God. To conceive of nature as finite and therefore dependent on a creator, however, is also to posit the immanence of God in it, a sense of mystery and depth. Man as a creature *par excellence* of God created in His image and likeness is called upon to probe into the depths of nature with his reason. The third paradigm continued this effort of the theological; nature can best be probed into by conceiving of it as machine, a whole made up of parts that can be measured mathematically. The rise of the biological sciences later made the systemic-mechanistic model inadequate, and so a second version tried to look at nature as an organism that includes all forms of life.

What can be gleaned from the above brief description of the four paradigms of nature in Western thought is an attitude towards nature that is both *theoretical* and *systematic*. The theoretical attitude looks at nature from a distance, an object apart from man. Man though himself a part of nature can by his rationality transcend nature to conceptualize and analyze it. The systematic attitude views nature as an ordered whole made up of parts, each part being related to the whole and to each other. Both the theoretical and systematic point to a kind of rationality that differentiates, analyzes in terms of a logic that is linear, that is to say, in progressive steps, each one building upon the previous one.

Western science is built upon this kind of rationality, and it is not surprising that from a theoretical and systematic attitude a technological attitude follows. The technological attitude attempts to master nature, to grasp its inner workings so as to control and utilize it for man's ends. Nature is subject to the apprehension and taming by man.

What can be seen in Western culture is thus the development of science into technology. The Greek classical constellation of *theoria, praxis, techne* has been transformed into a concept of theory to ground scientific discoveries and a notion of practical that has meant the technical. Theory meant for the Greeks the contemplation of immutable objects of the *episteme* and practical meant the ethical and political action in the life of the polis. The technical was reserved for the crafts that must conform to the natural. Now, theory is reduced to scientific theory and praxis to the technical. Habermas attributes this reduction to the rise of positivism and to the continual adherence to the Enlightenment's emphasis on reason.[2] Positivism insists on the separation of facts and values; an objective study of natural and social phenomena must avoid value considerations. This is in line with the Enlightenment's abhorrence of ignorance, dogmatism, and superstition.

What has happened in Western societies is the absolutization and ideologization of the scientific technological rationality.[3] Science and technology have assumed the status of absolute values, dominating and repressing the other spheres of life. This phenomenon can best be understood if placed in the framework of Habermas's notion of the three basic human interests—the technical, the practical, and the emancipatory.[4]

The technical interest refers to man's drive for instrumental action to master and control nature. Instrumental action here is purposive-rational, a means-end rationality whose aim is the exploitation of the world. The empirical-analytical sciences correspond to this interest.

The practical interest refers to man's symbolic interaction in a cultural tradition, to man's necessity for interpersonal communication, whether horizontally, among members of a particular culture or society, or vertically between societal groups of different cultures. While technical interest is born from the necessity of man to work in order to survive in a material world, practical or communicative interest answers an equally important need to relate intersubjectively in ordinary language communication. Interaction here is governed by binding consensual norms, based on mutual understanding of intentions and secured by general recognition of obligation. The historical hermeneutic sciences or social sciences correspond to this interest.

The emancipatory interest criticizes the ideological tendencies of the first two interests, and as such the sciences that correspond to this sphere are the critical sciences, philosophy and psychoanalysis. Ideology here is understood in its negative sense, as a distortion of reality and its consequent dogmatism and domination. Emancipatory interest seeks to unmask the forces of domination, dogmatism, and repression lying behind the reproduction of labor and the institutionally secured forms of general and public communication. It wants to break the barriers to open communication among social groups and persons, raising self-consciousness to the level of critique. A society must first interpret what it considers as life, and this must likewise be evaluated in accordance with the ideas of the good life or the criterion of what a society intends for itself as the good life. This entails an open communication, for the notion of the ideal is not something fixed nor conventional but based on the symbolic interaction (practical interest) and material exchange with nature (technical interest).[5]

Both technical and practical interests can have ideological tendencies, "a tendency to submit reality to dreams," to develop an escapist isolationism which is virtually schizophrenic, a distortion into an inverted image, a systematic domination.[6] This is because labor (technical interest) and language (practical interest) are very much intertwined with power.

But for Habermas, the dominant ideology of our time in the West is the ideology of science and technology. Technology as the "scientifically rationalized control of objectified processes"[7] has indeed satisfied the material needs of society, but it has also given rise to what Gabriel Marcel calls "technocracy." In a technocracy, the person is reduced to an efficient mechanical tool, if not a number or a stage of production. Relationships of man and fellowman cease to be interpersonal and become functional; one is identified and objectified by his function in society. Instead of bringing human fulfillment, work becomes monotonous and depersonalizes man. Means become ends in themselves: while the industrial system must become and remain functional, and be further enhanced, the individual person is subjected to the enormous apparatus of production and distribution. The subsystem of instrumental action has now become a system itself, entering and dominating the sphere of communicative action such that the person is used and manipulated to keep the technological system going. This repression of the person can disappear from the consciousness of the populace by a kind of legitimation of the domination—"the constantly increasing production of nature which keeps individuals... living in increasing comfort."[8] The domination of nature by technology has led to the domination of man by man, of man by nature as can be shown in the ecological ills such as pollution and the imbalances of nature.

Even the ideological tendency of the practical sphere can be the result of the domination of technology on all spheres of culture. Here, the state legitimated itself on the basis of its management in material reproduction, resorting to a diffused mass loyalty by keeping the citizens oriented to career, leisure, and consumption. A formal democracy is instituted in the form of periodic plebiscites to give a semblance of legitimacy. In the international scene, the ideological tendency of this sphere takes the form of neo-colonialism, the dominant culture maintaining its influence on a former colony on the basis of its own technical economic interests. The creation of man has become his own god.

This totalization and ideologization of scientific technological rationality in the West has resulted in a crisis expressed in various ways by many Western philosophers as: "alienation," "loss of meaning," "forgetfulness of being," "the death of God," etc. Given this crisis of Western culture, what can the East have to offer?

Eastern Traditional Values

Although the East is gifted with a variety of cultures, we can acknowledge some common aspects and tendencies that may be referred to as values if only to emphasize their embeddedness in Oriental cultures before the advent of Western rationalism.

First is the value of integration and cohesion versus differentiation and cleavage. The Orientals value a holistic, total attitude towards anything. In the East, politics, economics, and religion are one. Thinking, feeling, speaking, and doing are one and ought to be integrated. This value for the holistic accounts for the often-repeated characteristic of the Asian mind as intuitive and synthetic. In intuitive thinking, the subject approaches the object as a totality and has an immediate grasp of the object; the subject and the object are one.

It is of no surprise then that Lily Abegg prefers the term "envelopment" rather than "development" when speaking of the Asian soul:[9]

Thought based on envelopment first sees the whole, and the parts only subsequently find their place in this whole. In this kind of thinking every part belonging to the whole, the whole being already comprehended, must quite automatically have its place or its function in it. It is not necessary to analyze the details, for they are indeed already seen in their interrelationship. The parts are allocated their respective places without analysis. It is thought of a synthetic kind.[10]

The second value is the value of the natural and the organic, similar to what Weber calls the cosmocentric attitude that characterizes the Oriental religions. Nature for the Oriental has its own rhythm of birth, growth, and decay, where each has its own time, giving rise to the transitory nature of things. Nature as all-encompassing is held sacred and not to be subjugated. This regard for the natural and organic accounts for the cyclic motion of time for the Oriental, giving the impression of an eternal rotation of past, present and future. In behavior, punctuality is not to be expected of a traditional Asian, for he would work or be at leisure depending on what is natural.[11] With regard to issues, the Oriental can *roughly* tell you what the issue is but he rarely knows *exactly* what it is.

True to the feeling for the whole and the respect for the natural and organic, the Oriental is patient, tolerant, and humble. Patience, tolerance, and humility are values that pertain to seeing an affair or event from all sides, and seeing it as part of the process of nature, biding one's time, letting things ride.[12]

Death and life are viewed as natural and inevitable, but what is of utmost importance is that they be impregnated with meaning. There must be something or someone that one lives and dies for. The Orientals have always concerned themselves with problems of meaning, rather than facts and reasoning.

This brings us to the third value: the concern and quest for human perfection, a humanism of a sort distinct from the Renaissance humanism. The striving for human perfection is readily seen in the Confucian ideal of the *ch'un tze* or the gentleman, in the Taoist quest for inner tranquility, in the Buddhist aspiration for buddhahood, the cessation of desires, in the Hindu's mastery of oneself. Different ways lead to the same destination: the attainment of maturity of the personality in an organic process, unforced but natural.[13] A sign of this maturity is a genuine simplicity of lifestyle, a life "from the center," constrained and unsullied by passion.[14] What matters is not so much the development of abilities and skills—although the perfection of these can help in the development of the personality and society—but the unfolding of the self, the purity of the soul. Work and skills count "only as an emanation of personality."[15] To work hard for a thing in such a manner as to neglect the maturing of self is ridiculous and immoral. A good painter or carpenter is good because he is at the same time a harmonious personality.

Much of Oriental learning is therefore a striving after perfection, not originality—a lot of imitation of previous models, the repetition and reliving of great thoughts. The most important source of instruction for the Oriental is man, not the textbook, and the teacher or "*sensei*" (in Chinese, literally meaning "one born earlier") provides the latest link between the old master and the pupil.[16]

This Oriental humanism, however, is quite different from the humanism of the Renaissance, for it is at the core communitarian. The value of the community runs through most, if not all, Oriental cultures. Man is never isolated but forms a community with the living and the dead. For the Asian, "the true concept of human greatness does not lie in individual distinction, but in adapting oneself to the community, and in such a capacity as to realize the most perfect form of such a community."[17] The communitarian spirit gives rise to a sense of interdependence. Freedom is seen in the light of responsibility and expectation.

Fourth, the Oriental emphasis on the family is the origin and symbol of this interdependence. The family is the source of security and, at the same time, forms an organic unity of the past, present, and future. The network of relationships in the family symbolizes the spirit of interdependence in the larger society, providing the individual member a sense of security. Moreover, it is not simply a means for the biological perpetuation of the human species but the seat of creative transmission of what is held as valuable and normative. This transmission of familial and societal values provides the Oriental with a sense of immortality.

In this regard, the legal has always played a minor or secondary role in Oriental behavior. What is more influential is the moral code emanating from the authoritative power of the head of the family. There is no power *per se*, and laws are abstract unless they spring from the concrete figure of the authority. The head of the family makes the decisions but he is accustomed to summon the family council, including the women.[18] An Oriental "will scarcely ever rely exclusively on his own judgment when making an important decision: he will always consult his family and his friends beforehand."[19]

This brings us to the fifth value: the spirit of authoritative democracy. The respect for authority is strong in the Asian spirit; the politeness accorded to the superior verges on the ritual and the ordinary. Confucius, for instance, compares the ruler to the wind and the populace to the grass that follows wherever the wind blows. But this authoritarianism is coupled with an eastern democratic sense. Authority is a trust given to him who is in power so he can bestow benefit upon the community. Democracy understood in the Oriental sense is not formal but material: it is based on the dignity of the other, no matter what his position in society may be. Man is equal to his fellowman not because of what he has but because of what he is. When a ruler ceases to be concerned with the common good, he loses the mandate of Heaven, which is tantamount to the mandate of the people. The history of ancient China is replete with revolutions, but seldom has it been a change of a type of government as a change of despotic rulers.

All the above Oriental values can be summed up in the spirit of undifferentiating harmony. The Oriental ideal of sagehood is the ideal of being-at-one with the world, with nature, his fellowman and God. It is then not surprising that in the East religion has played the civilizing factor of humanity, for such is the original meaning and task of religion—to bind, to integrate oneself with what transcends the self, be it nature, the family, community or society, or the Absolute.

Could this not perhaps be what the West is looking for in the East? An inner coherence in a culture where "the interesting has replaced the lasting, the controversial the true, the assertive the substantial?"[20]

But in the process of modernization and Westernization of the East, has not rationalization affected and absorbed these traditional Oriental values?

The Encounter of Rationalism and Eastern Cultures

Habermas agrees with Max Weber that the rationality that defines modernity is a purposive or means-ends rationality whose aim is the mastery of the world. The progress of Western societies is the ascendancy of purposive rationality, of technique and calculation, of organization and administration, in the final analysis, of the triumph of bureaucracy.[21] Purposive rationality does dissolve traditional superstitions, prejudices, and errors but does not really replace traditional worldviews with anything that could fulfill the functions of giving meaning and unity to life. Weber then did not believe modernization could ever come to Oriental societies because of their deeply embedded religious worldviews.

We know now that Weber's prediction of the impossibility of the modernization of Eastern societies has been proven wrong. But from the reformulation of Habermas, he could have been right in another sense—*the rationalization of Oriental societies is impossible without it also being ideological.* By "ideological" we mean here a systematic domination and repression verging on the pathological, a distortion of reality, resulting in escapism and alienation. We see this happening in terms of the five Oriental values mentioned above.

The total holistic attitude of the life world of Oriental societies is gradually disintegrating, becoming fragmentary and pluralistic. Increasingly, the economic and political systems, have become so complex that they have penetrated deeper into the communicative sphere of the life-world, subordinating it to systemic imperatives, creating roles of employee and consumer, citizen and client of the state. The moral-practical elements of the life world are driven out of the private and public spheres, and everyday life is increasingly "monetarized" and "bureaucratized."[22] This has also led to a kind of cultural impoverishment: the professionalization demanded of modernization has separated the development of cultures from the communicative structures of everyday life. Traditional art is relegated to the museum and the theater on special occasions, resulting in the drying up of nature-like traditions. Thus a cleavage exists between the processes of mutual understanding in everyday life and the cultural resources.[23]

Likewise with the Oriental cosmocentric view of nature. In its place, we have an instrumentalistic view of the material universe, the artificial and interventional becoming the natural thing to do to grow and progress. Nature is manipulated so much to serve material ends without respect for its internal rhythm, giving rise to problems of ecological imbalance, and a growing disparity of urban and rural cultures. On the level of interaction, whereas before mutual understanding and expectation was covered in advance by traditional religious norms, now the medium is that of money and position. The rat race for money and power has dominated the Oriental cities. The market system has penetrated the domain of communicative interactions, such that interrelationships have become functional and fragmentary, meanings lost in the maze of efficiency.

And yet, the subconscious search for meaning surfaces in the alarming rate of suicide in many of our urbanized Asian cities.

The value of communitarian self-realization is being subverted and made subservient to the competitive mastery of things. Witness the proliferation in learning institutions of courses aimed at achieving skills and the large number of students enrolling in them rather than in the liberal arts. Learning has become a tool to land a well-paying job. The students want instant shortcut results, and they find the study of their classical texts irrelevant. What is new must be good, and so the youth must keep up with the latest in fashion, gadgets, and music, imitating Western models.

At the root of this competitive mastery of things is of course Western capitalism. We see this happening in the modernization of China today—and in many developing countries of Asia too—where communitarian humanism is gradually being replaced by individualistic ethics. From individualism to the assertion of my rights over others, rather than my obligations, the step is not far.

The individualism of purposive rationalism has not spared the value of the family from its tentacles. The family too has become individualistic and possessive. Now, it is my family versus the others, with the economic and political security as the prime motive for competition. Witness the phenomenon of "cronyism" in many Asian countries.

Purposive rationalism has also questioned the validity of authority based on traditional religious worldviews and in its place has introduced a formal type of democracy. Formally democratic institutions and procedures ensure both a diffused mass loyalty and a requisite independence of administrative decision-making from the specific interest of the citizens. In other words, the public realm is structurally depoliticized, its function reduced to periodic plebiscites. As organized rationality spreads, the cultural traditions are undermined and weakened, and conflicts arise between those who stand for progress and those (the cultural minorities, for instance) who want to preserve their identity.

Given the intrusion of Western purposive rationalism into Oriental cultures, the conflicts and problems that arise are not simply in the areas of material reproduction, of social justice, but also of cultural reproduction, of the kind of life that integrates and keeps their identity as a people.

A Common Need for Both West and East

If the West needs the East, will it find what it is looking for, now that the East is not what it used to be? And will it be possible for the East to go back to its original spirit of undifferentiating harmony with the universe? It would seem that both the West and the East need a different kind of rationalization, different from the purposive action of the technical interest, a rationalization of communicative (symbolic) action of the practical interest or what Habermas calls the rationalization of the life-world.

For Habermas the rationalization of the life-world involves first of all, a "linguistification of the sacred." The sacred here refers to the religious root of tradition, and the linguistification of the sacred means the rationalization of worldviews. Because the moral authority of social norms has its roots in the sacred (Emile Durkheim), rationalization of the life-world entails rationalization of worldviews. In linguistifying the sacred, "the authority of tradition is increasingly open to discursive questioning; the range of applicability of norms expands while the latitude for reasoned justification increases."[24] Here "the 'pre-judgmental power' of the life-world progressively diminishes, in the sense that communicative actors increasingly owe their mutual understanding to their own interpretive accomplishments, to their own yes/no positions on critizable validity claims."[25] In other words, the dogmatism of norms from religion that once was accepted without question is now reflected upon, criticized, applied by the participants of a particular culture to their historical situation in dialogical understanding.

For instance, the Golden Rule is one moral principle that is found in almost all world religions. As rooted in religious belief, it is accepted without question. To linguistify the Golden Rule means to reinterpret this in the light of modern-day realities, where greater access to communication exists side by side with inequalities of the benefits and burden of production. Kant's categorical imperative (I ought to act in such a way that my relative maxim can be made into a universal law of nature) is a rationalized version of the Golden Rule for his time. Perhaps for our time, the socialized version of Habermas can serve as a rationalization of the Golden Rule: I put forth a rightness claim which can be validated insofar as it is generalizable, that is to say, anyone who enters into dialogue with me can agree that it is good for humanity.

Thus, the rationalization of the life-world calls for an enlightened criticism of traditional culture in the face of modernization. "The neglect of criticism and the mere affirmation and preservation of the past would be tantamount to annihilating one's own culture."[26] Such a critique would include necessarily a critique of ideology, for a regime or movement aspiring for power tends to legitimize itself by appealing to values unearthed from one's culture. A critique of ideology is an act of distancing oneself from one's culture, a self-criticism that leads to open communication.

Open communication is necessary to bridge the gap between the rich and the poor, the intellectual elite and the masses, the authority and the citizenry, the developed nation and the developing country. Culture, unlike material reproduction, cannot be administered, and so the rationalization proper to the life-world is the "expansion of the areas in which action is coordinated by the way of communicatively achieved agreement."[27] This entails the removal of restrictions on communication so that it becomes free from domination. Institutions have to be developed that would set limits to material reproduction and subordinate it to decisions arrived at in an unconstrained communication. Such institutions would protect the private and public spheres from the functionalistic and objectifying effects of scientific and technological advancement, provide feedback relations between a differentiated modern culture and a culturally and spiritually impoverished everyday practice. Moral issues of general interest can then be submitted for public discussion and decided on the basis of discursively achieved agreement.[28]

The rationality of the life-world is an expanded role of rationality aimed at reaching understanding and coordination. It is really in essence a substantive or participatory kind of democracy similar to the Greek polis, the origin, after all, of Western culture, but with the difference that those who enter into dialogue are free citizens of the world and have a claim as to how life should be lived. Needless to say, participation in practical moral discourse is the only other way out of violence.

In the rationalization of the life-world, the West and the East need each other, for only by communicating openly to each other can the original harmony with nature that has traversed to conflicts and confrontation be transformed into a consensus with nature as the medium, that we all belong to one planet earth. Only by understanding each other in dialogue can both West and East realize that they need a common attitude: "an attitude in which existing is more than taking, acting more than making, meaning more than function,"[29] an attitude of being rather than of having. Only the religious in man, whether Occidental or Oriental, can provide this.

Notes

1. Kenneth L. Schmitz, "Paradigms of Nature in Western Thought," unpublished paper.
2. Jurgen Habermas, *Knowledge and Human Interests* (Boston: Beacon Press, 1971).
3. Jurgen Habermas, *Towards a Rational Society* (Boston: Beacon Press, 1970).
4. Jurgen Habermas, *Knowledge and Human Interests*.
5. Thomas McCarthy, *The Critical Theory of Jurgen Habermas* (The MIT Press, 1978), 90–91.
6. Robert Sweeney, "Values and Ideology," in A.T. Tymieniecka and C.O. Schrag (eds.), *Analecta Husserliana*, vol. XV (Boston: D. Reidel Publishing Co., 1983), 395–396.
7. Jurgen Habermas, *Towards a Rational Society*, 57.
8. *Ibid.*, 83.
9. Lily Abegg, *The Mind of East Asia* (London: Thames and Hudson, 1952), 12–13.
10. *Ibid.*, 49.
11. *Ibid.*, 306–307.
12. *Ibid.*, 264–265.
13. *Ibid.*, 201.
14. *Ibid.*, 194.
15. *Ibid.*, 197.
16. *Ibid.*, 197–199.
17. *Ibid.*, 162.
18. *Ibid.*, 153–154.
19. *Ibid.*, 190.
20. Louis Dupre, "The Religious Crisis of Our Culture," in Anna-Teresa Tymieniecka (ed.), *The Crisis of Culture* (Boston: D. Reidel Publishing Co., 1976), 216.
21. Thomas McCarthy, "Introduction," in Jurgen Habermas, *The Theory of Communicative Action*, vol. I, *Reason and the Rationalization of Society* (Boston: Beacon Press, 1984), xviii.
22. *Ibid.*, xxxii.
23. *Ibid.*
24. *Ibid.*, xxii–xxiii.
25. *Ibid.*, xxv.
26. Hajime Nakamura, *Ways of Thinking of Eastern Peoples: India, China, Tibet, Japan* (Honolulu: University of Hawaii, 1974), 29.
27. Thomas McCarthy, *op. cit.*, xxxvii.
28. *Ibid.*, xxxvii.
29. Louis Dupre, *op. cit.*, 217.

PART THREE:

SCIENCE
IN QUESTION

SEVEN

EXPERIENCE And EXPERIMENT

A CRITIQUE OF MODERN SCIENTIFIC KNOWING

Ravi Ravindra

It is commonplace these days to attempt to render all intellectual activities scientific. This adjective is almost synonymous with reasonable, rigorous, systematic, and desirable. The classical, ideal of seeking the true, the beautiful, and the good amounts nowadays, at least in the universities, to being scientific. The force of the mystique and metaphysics of science becomes particularly apparent in philosophical, psychological, and religious studies where the scientific stick has been widely used to drive out a great deal of sensitive feeling and imaginative thought. One could use the etymological meaning of the word 'science' and then wonder how anyone could question the obvious desirability of 'knowledge.'

But to do this is to insist on using ancient meanings which are related to the present intellectual opinion by very thin threads indeed. Presumably, when people talk about the scientific study of something, they have an explicit or implicit model of the modern natural sciences in mind. It is obvious that these sciences operate from many fundamental assumptions about the nature of man, truth, and reality; most of these metaphysical presuppositions have been incorporated into the contemporary social sciences and the humanities to their detriment. Here I wish to point out some of these assumptions and to discuss their validity and limitations; what is proposed is a radical re-examination and re-evaluation of scientific knowledge.

My intention is not to suggest that the study of man is fundamentally different from the study of nature and therefore should be based on different principles. On the contrary, I hope to show that this sundering of man and nature is built right into the presuppositions of the modern sciences and is entirely questionable. If one is persuaded that scientific studies have not yielded any essential understanding of man, one need not be driven to the belief in the disunity of man and nature, and consequently of knowledge. It is possible that the procedures and methods of the natural sciences are no more impeccable and beyond question in studying nature than they are in studying man. It may be that in the latter case, some of the metaphysical restrictions and limitations of science become more apparent. In general, those who attempt to understand man seem either willing to leave nature to the scientists, as if man had nothing to do with nature, or to utilize scientific procedures which inevitably lead to the impoverishment of man, as of nature. If for us science-nurtured moderns, cosmology has become, as a matter of course, a branch of physics, then it should come as no surprise that man is merely an aggregate of material particles. The tragedy of the post-renaissance intellectual life is that there are very few individuals who have included nature, man, and divinity in a unified continuum of investigation based not only on speculative concepts but also on experience and perceptions.[1] This, I have come to believe, is the result of an inner fragmentation in which man and nature are separated from each other, as are poetry and physics. This fragmentation is embodied in the very structure of the modern sciences.

The central core of any theory of knowledge, including science, is constituted by the triad of the knower, reality, and the connection between them. Different theories and practices emphasize different aspects of man (reason, feeling, sensation) or of reality (quantity, quality, mechanism, purpose) or of the connection between these two (repeatability, uniqueness, intersubjectivity, involvement). No great theory wholly ignores any one of these several aspects; the difference lies largely in the emphasis and in the underlying faith about what is primary and irreducible, in terms of which everything else must be explained. (An example of this is the scientific faith that quantity is somehow basic and that all qualities whatsoever can and must be explained in quantitative terms.) Appreciable satisfaction and success afforded by a theory of knowledge—the measure of which depends on our valuation of its purpose and accomplishments—can easily lead to its being established as the way to truth, making doubters into heretics.

Perhaps the most important innovation of the great scientific revolution of the sixteenth and seventeenth centuries was a restructuring of the triad of knowledge, with its insistence that empirical observations can and do lead to truth which cannot be approached by reasoning alone. Having been conditioned by centuries of scientific success, our very notion of rationality is now based on the model of scientific procedures; it is now difficult for us to realize that whatever the scientific revolution was about, it was not universally considered a triumph of reason. Whitehead has correctly observed that "Science has never shaken off the impress of its origin in the historical revolt of the late Renaissance. It has remained predominantly an anti-rationalist movement, based on a naive faith."[2] It was clearly a necessary reaction to the rationalistic extravagance of the scholastics. However, perhaps like all revolutions, the scientific revolution was based on simplistic assumptions. It swept away much in earlier thought that was useful and wise and in harmony with reality. Also by accepting a limited criterion of truth, it guaranteed an inner fragmentation of man. In spite of later considerable upheavals within scientific theories, the basic attitudes and presuppositions of the modern sciences remain essentially the same as they emerged during the revolution. From these we derive most of our scientific outlook, even in the humanities.

On a large historical scale, the relatively recent appearance of the scientific attitude should itself be a reminder that humanity can exist without it; many presently widespread signs, particularly among the young, seem to suggest that unless the metaphysical basis of science is understood and broadened to include much that has been arbitrarily excluded, we shall be soon ushered into the post-scientific age. And this enlargement of the scientific base is likely to come about largely from within the scientific community. We cannot exclude the possibility of some useful contribution from the outside, but in general most non-scientists are awed and overwhelmed by science into wishful acquiescence or frightened hostility. What science needs is neither worship nor rejection, but critical self-understanding and change. The need for this has always been there; now it has become urgent. To the extent that science is an avenue to Truth—yes, with a capital T, something which most scientists tacitly believe, however unsophisticated it may appear in the modern age—scientists cannot but be interested in the kind of knowledge they produce. It was a master-scientist, Albert Einstein, who said:

> How does a normally talented research scientist come to concern himself with the theory of knowledge? Is there not more valuable work to be done in his field? I hear this from many of my professional colleagues; or rather, I sense in the case of many more of them that this is what they feel.

> I cannot share this opinion. When I think of the ablest students whom I have encountered in teaching—i.e., those who distinguish themselves by their independence of judgment, and not only by mere agility—I find that they had a lively concern for the theory of knowledge. They liked to start discussions concerning the aims and methods of the sciences, and showed unequivocally by the obstinacy with which they defended their views that this subject seemed important to them.

> This is really not astonishing. For when I turn to science not for some superficial reason such as money-making or ambition, and also not (or at least exclusively) for the pleasure of the sport, the delights of brain-athletics, then the following questions must burningly interest me as a disciple of this science: What goal will and can be reached by the science to which I am dedicating myself? To what extent are its general results 'true?' What is essential, and what is based only on the accidents of development?...

Concepts which have proved useful for ordering things easily assume so great an authority over us, that we forget their terrestrial origin and accept them as unalterable facts. They then become labelled as 'conceptual necessities,' 'a priori situations,' etc. The road of scientific progress is frequently blocked for long periods by such errors. It is therefore not just an idle game to exercise our ability to analyze familiar concepts, and to demonstrate the conditions on which their justification and usefulness depend, and the way in which these developed, little by little...[3]

Experiment and Experience

One of the most important reasons for the avowed success of the natural sciences in investigating nature has been a particular wedding of a restricted notion of man, namely that he is essentially a rational cognizer, and a limited class of experience, namely experiment. It was the coming together of these two, reason and experiment, in a mutually regenerative role that characterized the scientific revolution and all subsequent science. In the formation of the scientific attitude to nature, experiments play a large role, for they are what ultimately constitute the scientist's handle on reality. What I am including under experiment is anything connecting scientific perceptions and conceptions; in other words, all the means and procedures for collecting scientific data, including observations, tests, surveys. The central place of experiment in the sciences is beyond question. No scientist will question the statement of Richard Feynmann on the first page of a fairly recent and highly successful physics textbook that "The principle of science, the definition, almost, is the following: The test of all knowledge is experiment. Experiment is the sole judge of scientific 'truth.'"[4]

It is important to distinguish between experiment and experience, although these two terms are often used interchangeably in scientific and philosophical writings. There are significant differences in their connotations and applications in different endeavors. The sciences by no means have a monopoly on observational and empirical procedures; the vast realms of aesthetics and spirituality are nothing if not empirical. In the sciences, it is ultimately the external experiment which is the arbiter of the truth of one theory or hypothesis against another.

In the sphere of spiritual becoming, on the other hand, the

central focus is the inner experience of the aspirant. Without the corresponding experimental data, scientific speculation tends to become sterile and fruitless; similarly, without reference to experience, all theological talk remains empty—full of comfort and hope perhaps, but not charged with real understanding. To make bedfellows of Francis Bacon and St. Paul, one could say that neither scientific knowledge nor spiritual understanding is a matter of talk; in either case it is a matter of power. The nature of this power depends on where the criteria of truth and falsity are centered—in experiment or experience. Both mediate between human beings and reality but differently, and with quite divergent consequences.

The word experience is derived from the Latin word *experientia*, and experiment from the Latin *experimentum*. Their etymology reveals some interesting features. Both experiential and experimentum are derived from *experiens*, the present participle of *experiri*, which means to try thoroughly. *Experiri* is a conjunction of the prefix *ex*, meaning thoroughly, and *periri*, which means to go through or try and to risk. This latter *periri* is also related with the English word peril; thus peril is a trial which one passes through. The word fare, meaning travel, as in the word wayfarer, also derives from the same root. It seems that to experience something is to pass through it thoroughly, involving some personal risk; it is to participate in and partake of personally to undergo. The knowledge obtained by such a procedure is what we would call understanding or comprehension. Experience includes perceptions, feelings, sensing. The word experiment, on the other hand, although derived from the same root, has in the last three hundred years diverged in its implications from the word experience. One set of meanings of the verb experiment used to be this: to have experience of; to experience; to feel, suffer.

These meanings however are obsolete, and it appears that the word experiment has not been used in these senses since early in the eighteenth century. The verb experiment is used these days as an intransitive verb, and no longer transitively like experience. I can experience a flower, but I can only experiment with or on it. To experiment now is primarily to conduct an experiment which is a test made to demonstrate a known truth, to examine the validity of a hypothesis, or to determine the efficacy of something previously untried. The knowledge obtained by these procedures is what constitutes scientific knowledge.[5] Clearly, experimental sciences are not experiential in character; in fact, they are determinedly contra-experiential in their attitudes, implications, and tendencies.

It seems that Galileo was the first modern scientist clearly to differentiate between these two concepts; before him experiential and experimentum were more or less indiscriminately used. He says in his De Motu: "Those things which we have demonstrated...must be understood as referring to moving bodies which are free from all external resistance, but since it is perhaps impossible to find such bodies in the material world, anyone performing an experiment concerning these things should not be surprised if the (resulting) experience disappoints, and that a large sphere cannot be moved by a minimal force, even if in a horizontal plane."[6]

Presumably, experience for Galileo refers to what one actually sees, and experiment is the procedure of testing a hypothesis. His hypothesis pertains to a conjectured ideal and rational world in which one can imagine ideal bodies free from all external resistance. Because of their ideal and rational nature, they can be reasoned about mathematically; inferences of this reasoning process is what he subjects to experimental test. Whatever the nature of this abstract theoretical construction may be, the testing procedure does not depend on experience in the sense of personal, existential, involvement. Even a cursory reading of the *Dialogue Concerning the Two Chief World Systems* written by Galileo, the first major modern natural philosopher, is enough to persuade one that the experimental method of knowledge is empirical only in a special and limited sense, and that it is certainly not experiential. What is apprehended by us directly with our mind, feelings, and senses is not what we depend on for true scientific knowledge. Feelings and senses are particularly suspect. Galileo commended Copernicus and his followers who "have through sheer force of intellect done such violence to their own senses as to prefer what reason told them over that which sensible experience plainly showed them to the contrary."[7]

It would take too long to establish that such an attitude towards feelings and the senses is a hallmark of the scientific revolution; however, on this attitude depends the all-important distinction between primary and secondary qualities—crucial to the development of physics, and the scientific notion of objectivity. Exclusion of the immediacy of perceptions and feelings is central to the scientific procedure; what one does in scientific experiments is to measure, not experience, certain qualities of things. This measuring can be done indirectly without the scientist seeing or feeling what he is measuring, and indeed without his being involved at all in the actual event of observing and recording—which can, in principle, always be done automatically. A successful experimenter can arrange matters so that he does not have to be present in the laboratory when data are collected about the scattering of electrons or the overcrowding of rats or the contraction of the uterus in childbirth. The personal equation is something that a scientist must assiduously attempt to eliminate. Where he needs to come in is in interpreting and manipulating data, imagining new hypotheses, and devising new experiments. Obviously, none of these activities is easy or trivial; they call for a great deal of cleverness, ingenuity, and sometimes genius. Nevertheless, the fact remains that for the observations themselves, which provide the only direct scientific contact with reality, no human intervention is strictly speaking necessary; in any case, certainly not of the feelings and most of the senses.

Now, what kind of data can be gathered by ignoring so much of what makes us human? What is this reality that is revealed by observations which can be made by properly programmed automatons? What sort of theories can be tested or satisfied with such impoverished data? What significance can be claimed by knowledge based on such determinedly partial perceptions? These questions call for a detailed and careful investigation, particularly these days when most academics have raised science and scientific method to an intellectual orthodoxy. Obviously, this is a longterm project. All I hope to do here is to open this line of inquiry, and to suggest that perhaps we have been dazzled by the magical successes of science and technology into accepting unwarranted metaphysical assumptions about the nature of reality and of man and their relationship with each other. These assumptions are partial and they necessarily lead to a further fragmentation of our sensibilities, resulting in an attitude of inner violence towards the object of investigation. The procedures based on them are quite unlikely to lead to a sympathetic understanding of either nature or man. In particular, what is higher, within us or above us, cannot even be approached by the divided self that is an inevitable consequence of the scientific mentality.

Clearly, there are many metaphysical assumptions underlying the scientific enterprise. Most of these assumptions are now widely taken to be valid in the humanities also, indicating the wholesale capitulation of the intellectual community and the pervasive influence of science. This influence asserts itself through something labelled the scientific method which most non-scientific academic disciplines are especially anxious to get hold of. It is difficult to find examples in intellectual history where creative thinking proceeded from methodology to practice. Even Descartes, who made so much of method, wrote his *Discourse on Method* after the scientific essays to which it forms a preface, and not before. It is only in the contemporary social sciences that one finds so much faith in the efficacy of verbalized methodology. Among the natural sciences it is a rare department which offers a course on method. The method simply is, as I think was expressed by P.W. Bridgman, to do one's best with no holds barred. Nevertheless, there are basic assumptions underlying the scientific procedures; these assumptions are handed down by tradition and are in general acquired by students unconsciously.

Objectivity

The locus of scientific objectivity is not in the object under investigation, but in the subjects investigating the object. What we call objectivity in the sciences is inter-subjectivity; we would say that we have come to an objective description of something if most of the competent investigators—who are such precisely because they share the same assumptions and procedures agree with each other about this description. Whether the description actually describes the object is another matter; we do not even know how we might determine this unless we were to allow the possibility that the object knows itself and reveals itself. Such a concession of consciousness and intention to any object runs directly counter to the basic scientific conception of the cosmos as a huge machine in which, ultimately, everything has to be explained in terms of (unconscious and purposeless) matter in motion (without meaning). The object is assumed to be controlled wholly from the outside and is defined exclusively in terms of its external characteristics and relations.[8] This denial of any inner reality, however rudimentary, to a stone or a tree or an ape leads, with rigorous logical necessity, to the denial of such a reality—consisting of consciousness, purpose, intention, and conscience to man.[9] In the absence of self-knowledge and concurrence by the object, which could be a tree, a man or a culture, all we have are our inter-subjective conventions concerning procedures and criteria for determining the truth or falsity of our statements about the object.

Niels Bohr was right in saying, in his argument with Einstein, that "It is wrong to think that the task of Physics is to find out how nature is. Physics concerns what we can say about nature."[10] The conventions we adopt depend on their effectiveness in pursuing what we take to be the purpose and aim of the knowledge we gather. I will return to this point later; for the present, I wish to draw attention to the convention and subjectivity, albeit a general one, inherent in the much-acclaimed scientific objectivity.

There is another, closely related, point to be made: at the root of this necessity of substituting inter-subjective agreement for objectivity is the assumption that the knowing subject and the object of knowledge are inalienably distinct and separable from each other. It is an implicit assumption of the scientific revolution that man the cognizer is not a part of the nature he investigates; he is over and against nature, or in any case separate from it. This becomes more apparent when we do not consider nature in any large sense but confine our attention to a specific object of investigation, such as a molecule, a frog, or a star. Moreover, this separation is ensured by the experimental procedure. The assumption of the separability of the subject and the object, which is a corollary of the presupposition that our self or identity is essentially nuclear and localized in space-time, has a much longer history and wider base than modern science; one does not question it lightly.[11]

Nevertheless, it remains a fact that many artists, poets, mystics, and others have reported that in their deeper experiences, the subject-object distinction is not as obvious and meaningful as it usually appears to our ordinary consciousness. There is a qualitative change from the relationship of separateness to that of oneness which, whenever it occurs, is almost always claimed, by the person who experiences it, to be the result of perceptions which are clearer and more heightened than usual. Some would even say that taking the appearance of the knower-known dichotomy for reality is the very root of ignorance, and that any observation in which the observer is distinct from what is observed is incomplete. The suggestion is not that there is no distinction between the subject and the object at all, and that an undifferentiated chaos prevails. It is, rather, that whatever is essential to the object—a tree, a poem, or a person—is not comprehended as long as one stands completely apart from it, without participating in it, concerned only with the characteristics external to it. In any case, the rigidity of the object-subject distinction may not be immune to doubt, at least in some circumstances. If one gathered knowledge with a different purpose in view, one might see things differently; and the obviousness of our total separation from each other and the objects around us might well be like the obviousness of the sun's motion around the earth.

Abstraction

Underlying the perceived reality in science is posited an abstract and purely rational construct. What is experienced is then called appearance, while the mental construct is labelled reality. The scientific pursuit, then, is to speculate about the imagined reality and to put these speculations to the experimental test, involving only certain limited perceptions. The so-called objective reality of scientific concern is in fact a conjecture—perhaps one of the many which may be possible—of subjective reason. However, and this is where the importance and glory of science lie, these subjective projections are confirmed or falsified by inter-subjective experimental procedures.

Nevertheless, the testing procedures are not wholly independent of the theoretical framework, and what observations are taken to be a confirmation of a given conjecture is increasingly, as scientific experiments become more and more elaborate, a matter of interpretation. It is not possible to make a scientific observation without a prior theoretical system, as has been emphasized by Karl Popper.[12] In science, any theory is better than no theory. In order to get going, scientists are happy to have partial, incomplete, or wrong, theories rather than wait for a correct one; until a new theory is available, the old one is not abandoned however many problems it may have. Theorizing is fundamental to scientific activity; what we subject to experimental observations is not nature, but our conjectures about nature. The scientific revolution marks a shift not only from experience to experiment but also from seeking certain truth to theorizing about probable truths. In science, reality is theory.

This is true for all the sciences, not only for physics. Every experimental science is first of all a theoretical science, although the theoretical system may be more or less explicit. Here is an example from Sigmund Freud: "Our purpose is not merely to describe and classify phenomena, but to conceive them as brought about by the play of forces in the mind, as expressions of tendencies striving towards a goal, which work together or against one another. In the conception, the trends we merely infer are more prominent than the phenomena we perceive."[13]

In the experiential approach to reality, as in some artistic and spiritual disciplines, the attempt is not to abandon the real phenomena that we perceive, by some kind of leap of reason, but to widen and sharpen our perceptions, and to bring all our faculties to bear on what we experience. Theory is important here too, for obviously the reason which calculates and theorizes is also a perceiving faculty; but experience is more than theory, its significant features are immediacy, concreteness, and directness of perception. The point of the theory is to help a person experience directly and fully. The point of experiment, on the other hand, is to lead to theory or to decide between one theory and another. In science, experiment has no meaning without theory; but in life, theory has no sense without experience.[14] What we seek in science, via experiment, is abstract explanation of phenomena; whereas what we might seek in life, aided by any theory, is concrete and experiential understanding of what is.

Quantity

One important feature of any scientific description is that it attempts to be quantitative. Most of the major scientists contributing to the scientific revolution appear to have been self-consciously opposed to the earlier, more qualitative, science. According to Galileo, "Philosophy is written in this grand book, the universe, which stands continually open to our gaze. But the book cannot be understood unless one first learns to comprehend the language and read the letters in which it is composed. It is written in the language of mathematics, and its characters are triangles, circles, and other geometric figures without which it is humanly impossible to understand a single word of it; without these, one wanders about in a dark labyrinth."[15]

Similar enunciations can be found in Kepler, Boyle, and Newton. It is not at all obvious, or even true, that to be mathematical means to be quantitative. Even the most apparently quantitative of all mathematical entities, namely numbers, cannot be considered without quality. Unity, duality, and trinity have qualitative aspects which are not exhausted by numerical manipulations. Nevertheless, in general, mathematization in science has meant quantification. According to the fathers of modern science, quantity is the fundamental feature of things, prior to other categories; in the realm of knowledge, quantity is the sole feature of reality. "Just as the eye was made to see colors, and the ear to hear sounds," wrote Kepler, "so the human mind was made to understand, not whatever you please, but quantity."[16]

Qualities, except insofar as they can be quantified, do not belong to what is real, and cannot be avenues to truth. There was a great leap forward for exact science when Isaac Newton in his *Principia* defined motion in terms of quantity of motion—without regard to whether this motion was part of a sacred dance or a funeral march—and when he defined matter in terms of quantity of matter—without any consideration of where that matter belonged and what function it served. Unlike earlier natural philosophers, modern scientists do not consider qualitative aspects like place and function as being relevant to a precise definition of matter, motion, and other entities. One cannot escape the impression that the prevalent general leveling down of quality and the pernicious reign of quantity— which has been passionately described by, among others, Ortega y Gasset in his *Revolt of the Masses*—is intrinsically connected with the scientific assumption that reality is primarily quantitative, and can be approached mainly by quantitative procedures. Whatever functions painting, music, and dance may serve, when it comes to the serious business of truth and knowledge, as understood by modern natural philosophers, they are essentially frivolous. This is the seed of fragmentation of our sensibilities. Our gods of reason and truth admit physics in their temples, but not poetry and painting. The wisdom of such gods is questionable; it may well be, as William Blake said, that "Reason and Newton they are quite two things."

Perceptions

The scientific assumption about man is that he is essentially a rational cognizer, and that everything else about him is secondary and capable of explanation in terms of his basic rational nature. This view of man as primarily a passionless, disembodied mind, which would be recognized as the rigorously intellectual point of view, is shared by all who claim to be scientific in their professional work, from Descartes to the modern analytical philosophers. Other faculties of man—his feelings and sensations—are not considered capable of either producing or receiving real knowledge. Those aspects of reality which correspond to the non-rational faculties of perception— aspects such as color, smell, taste, beauty, purpose—are either completely ignored or are relegated to a secondary status. It is no doubt true that, as we are, our ordinary sensory and emotional experiences are limited and subjective. In science, an attempt is made to minimize the dependence on such perceptions by agreeing that the corresponding aspects of reality not be considered as objectively real, and by dealing with only those aspects where rational constructs can be applied. (It is entirely reasonable, for example, to think about and to measure the mass and charge of an electron—though neither property can be directly sensed—but it is faintly ludicrous to ask about the taste or color of it. If one were to ask about its purpose, one would be outside the scientific arena entirely.)

On the other hand, we might attempt to cleanse and deepen our perceptions so that we could see those aspects of reality which we ordinarily miss because we are oblivious to them, being preoccupied with our personal, subjective emotional existence with our fears and hopes, desires and wishes, likes and dislikes. This subjective preoccupation is the chief characteristic of the general state in which we ordinarily live. However, it is possible for man to move in a clearer, more objective realm of feeling; and then to engage this important aspect of himself in perception, rather than to systematically eliminate it out of a suspicion, by itself well-justified, that our ordinary emotions are largely subjective and unreliable guides to truth.

Here, indeed, is an instance of throwing the baby out with the bath water. It has been bemoaned often enough that scientific knowledge does not address itself to the issues of human purpose and aspiration, or the meaning of man's existence. All these concerns reside in feeling when it is a little freed from exclusively subjective preoccupations. Yet feeling is the one aspect of our wholeness rigorously ignored in the scientific methodology. It seems to have largely escaped modern epistemologists that feelings when developed and trained, can yield objective knowledge. On the other hand, it is precisely through feelings, integrated with other faculties, that we can approach objective understanding, for feeling is the faculty of relation with any object; it is the reconciling aspect of man. Reason, on the other hand, differentiates, making distinctions and comparisons. By comparing different subjective measurements, it can lead to inter-subjective knowledge, not necessarily agreed to by the object. If we make a fetish of detached rationality, we unnecessarily impoverish our perceptions.

Control

Another basic assumption is implicit in the procedures and purpose of modern science, as distinct from that of ancient or medieval sciences. What modern scientists aim at is the prediction, control, and manipulation of what they investigate. Here is a statement by a Yale biophysicist about his work; he is discussing the question of the adequacy of the laws of physics in explaining the behavior of living organisms: "The biophysicist approaches this problem by assuming that the laws of physics do work in the living cell and by putting together what information he has to try to predict how a given system should work. If the prediction proves correct, then presumably the present physical laws are adequate. If not, then perhaps new things will have to be found."

After noting some of the difficulties in investigating these matters, he adds that, "Eventually, of course, we'll surmount these obstacles, and then we'll know whether the cold laws of inanimate nature are enough to explain the nature of the living cell. If such should be the case, it will give us a control over the living cell which we have never had before."[17] Notice how easily words like prediction and control enter here as a matter of course. This is what doing means, the doing which is so intimately connected with scientific knowing—a point which has been well appreciated by the pragmatists, and above all by John Dewey.[18]

One question that immediately arises concerns the reductionism involved in studying living organisms, particularly human beings with the laws of physics. Yet what is more pertinent here is something different; namely, the deep-rooted anthropocentric view of modern science, a view which, in the light of its own discoveries, could be considered nothing but absurd. It is certainly questionable that man's relationship to the entire universe—in which we occupy a small place, on an ordinary planet of a third-rate and peripheral sun in an average galaxy—should be primarily one of control. The spatial shift in the center of the cosmos, brought about by the Copernican revolution, appears to have been accompanied by a reverse epistemological shift towards a collectivized egocentricity in which man becomes the measure and end of all things.

What does this insistence on control and manipulation amount to in knowing something? Does it not guarantee that we cannot know, by these methods, anything that is higher than us, anything more subtle or more intelligent than us, if such a thing, or being, or force is not susceptible to our control? If scientists speak of lacking evidence of anything higher than man, that is to be expected, for their procedures specifically preclude the possibility of such evidence.

It can be argued that even though the scientific approach might not be suitable for knowing anything higher than man it is nevertheless suitable for investigating nature. Even if this were the case, the arbitrary assumption clearly remains that nature is lower than man, that it neither encompasses us nor has any larger purposes which humanity also serves.[19] The tools used by science ensure the self-fulfillment of this assumption. This sundering of nature and man is very much a contribution of the scientific revolution, in particular of Descartes. It then becomes a matter of course that man should want to conquer nature; and a terminology of combat enters the scientific ethos without notice or comment.

Before proceeding further, let me illustrate some of what I have said so far by quoting from Immanuel Kant, who was both a scientist and a philosopher, and who anticipated much of what later philosophers have remarked about the scientific method and the nature of experimentation:

> When Galileo let balls of a particular weight, which he had determined himself, roll down an inclined plane, or Torricelli made the air carry a weight, which he had previously determined to be equal to that of a definite volume of water; or when, in later times, Stahl changed metal into lime, and lime again into metals, by withdrawing and restoring something, a new light flashed on all students of nature. They comprehended that reason has insight into that only which she produces on her own plan and that she must move forward with the principles of her judgments, according to fixed laws, and compel nature to answer her questions, but not let herself be led by nature, as it were in leading strings, because otherwise accidental observations, made on no previously fixed plan will never converge towards a necessary law, which is the only King that reason seeks and requires. Reason, holding in one hand its principles, according to which concordant phenomena alone can be

admitted as laws of nature, and in the other hand the experiment, which it has devised according to those principles, must approach nature, in order to be taught by it: but not in the character of a pupil, who agrees to everything the master likes, but as an appointed judge, who compels the witness to answer the questions which he himself proposes.[20]

Scientific knowledge acquired by the imposition of this metaphysical straight-jacket on reality is like a confession obtained from an adversary under duress. Whosoever objects to such procedures is suspected by the contemporary intellectual orthodoxy of sabotage or defection to the enemy camp of hopeless romanticism or irrational mysticism—opposed to reason and progress. Nevertheless, it is important to appreciate the magical spell of science for what it is. It would appear that whatever we can study from the scientific point of view of manipulation and control—whether it is universe, man, or divinity—has been produced, at least partly, according to our plans; it is something that can be compelled by us to yield answers to our questions. It cannot be higher than us; for that which is higher—in nature no less than in man—can neither be coerced nor violated by us. We can prepare ourselves for it and wait, actively making an effort of attention, observing without violence.[21]

It should be clear that any vision of reality or any view of human knowledge that, in its very principles, accepts distinct fragmentation into compartments—such as the aesthetic, the scientific, the spiritual—is, to say the least, incomplete and productive of inner conflict and disharmony, which in its turn results in external aggression and violence. The primary task of a sound theory of knowledge is to work towards principles and procedures which do not ignore any faculty of perception nor any aspect of experience, thus maintaining the integrity and the wholeness of the investigators. Only then is it possible to ensure that the object of investigation will be understood as it is, rather than in conformity with a distorted sense of control and manipulation. There is no reason why we must accept Kant's opinion that we behave like an appointed judge, compelling the witness to answer our questions, any more than a pupil who is passive and subservient. We could, for example, approach reality sympathetically, neither aggressively nor passively, attempting to understand with the attention of all our faculties instead of a coercive reasoning.

It appears, then, that the first principle of a theory of knowledge ought to be concerned not so much with the question of how we know something as with the concern how we are to be with respect to it. The primary question is of our being rather than knowing. If our assumptions and methods do not violate the integrity and wholeness of our own being, only then is it possible for us to understand something real about any object, without violence and distortion.

In mentioning such a first principle, we have moved very far from the concerns and preoccupations of the metaphysics of science and of scientific philosophy. No major Western philosopher since Thomas Aquinas—with the possible exception of the Cambridge Platonists in the seventeenth century—has considered the question of being as germane to the question of knowing. This is also the period of the rise and hegemony of the scientific mentality which, both in theory and practice, diminishes all other faculties and aspects of man other than his reasoning ability, and systematically ignores much of what makes us whole. Taking external experiment—devised according to this ignorance—to be the sole criterion of knowledge institutionalizes a fragmentation of our sensibilities. Such knowledge cannot but work counter to the enlarging of being or consciousness in man. Even in the disciplines where one might imagine that such questions have an obvious place, the scientific procedures prevail, giving them a narrowly rational turn. Thus, to the extent that philosophy and theology become scientific, God is reduced to a mental construct: either a hypothesis for deduction or an inference from induction; in either case a construct for or against which one can have proofs or arguments, but of which one can have no experience. Theology thus becomes a rational profession dealing with metaphysical systems, rather than a psycho-spiritual path for the transformation of the being of man.

Experimental knowing, owing to the estrangement of the knower, is sundered from being, and is concerned with a low order of doing, involving control and manipulation. Experiential knowing, which now appears to be a different kind of knowledge—akin to gnosis, wisdom, or understanding—involves all aspects of man and is intimately connected with his being. Some of the ancients understood this, and Parmenides went to the extent of saying that "to be and to know are one and the same."[22] This concern for being, whatever else it involves, is a concern for the wholeness and integration of man, calling for a harmonization of the various faculties of perception. Only then can our different parts come together and act as a unified whole, enabling us to perceive openly, fully, and directly. This inner harmony of the soul is what Plato considered necessary for just and beautiful action; and he regarded the knowledge leading to such harmony as wisdom.[23] Clearly, no such inner synthesis and composure is possible without including our feeling perceptions. Science by systematically ignoring this side of man, has created a basic opposition to mysticism, which Goethe rightly called the dialectic of feeling.

A philosophy which loses sight of any one of the three major concerns and necessities of man—namely of being, knowing, and doing—is bound to be partial and self-defeating. By ignoring any one of these, we achieve knowledgeable action without compassion, or compassionate action without knowledge, or else wisdom without action. The desirable alternative to the fragmentation and aggressiveness of science is not well-intentioned impotence or mystical passivity, but rather robust and integrated activity, without violence and without disassociation of our sensibilities. Providing a sound critical basis for such theory and practice is important and urgent; otherwise irrational romanticism, for or against science, holds sway. Scientific commitment and sensibility of wholeness are not inexorably opposed to each other; however, reconciliation is possible only when the partial finds its place in the whole, and reason its place in being. Only when we proceed from an inner reconciliation can we hope to understand nature—its workings and its purposes—and cooperate in serving what is higher. Such knowledge can speak to our deepest aspirations and our search for meaning while revealing the beauty and mystery all around us.

Acknowledgments

Some of the ideas in this essay arose in response to various remarks made by Professors Eugene P. Wigner, John A. Wheeler, Thomas S. Kuhn, and Walter Kaufman in seminars or private discussions when I was a Visiting Fellow at Princeton University in the Program for History and Philosophy of Science, on a Canada Council Post-Doctoral Fellowship in Philosophy in 1968–1969. Much of it was written during 1973–1974 at Columbia University where I was a Visiting Scholar in Religion on a Fellowship for Cross-Disciplinary Studies awarded by the Society for Religion in Higher Education. An earlier version of the essay was presented, in a considerably different form, at a meeting in Toronto of the Canadian Society for the Study of Religion in May, 1974. I have had the benefit of discussions with Professor W. Nicholls of the University of British Columbia, Mr. Arvind Sharma of Harvard University, and Professors Wilfred Cantwell Smith, A. Hilary Armstrong, and Robert H. March of Dalhousie University. My friend Robert L. McWhinney was very helpful in his editorial advice. However, none of these gentlemen is necessarily in agreement with what I have written above. A research grant from Dalhousie University is gratefully acknowledged.

Notes

1. Perhaps the single well-known exception is Goethe. His criticism of Newtonian science, unlike that of Blake or Wordsworth, has the merit of being reasoned and consistent, besides having a detailed theory and example of doing science with alternative and more unifying assumptions. However, his influence in the scientific circles has been negligible. (Newton's own theology and alchemy are fascinating but show little continuity with his science.)
2. A.N. Whitehead, *Science and the Modern World*, Chapter 1.
3. Quoted in Gerald Holton, *Thematic Origins of Scientific Thought* (Cambridge: Harvard University Press, 1973).
4. *The Feynmann Lectures in Physics*, Vol. 1.
5. One can, no doubt, conduct experiments with others' experiences or with one's own; and thus obtain (unexperienced) scientific knowledge about the characteristics, causes, and effects of a given type of experience. An example of this sort of experimentation is the introduction of measured doses of hallucinogenic drugs in a given subject, recording the accompanying experiences and making inferences. Also, one can, of course, have an experience of conducting experiments, as most scientists do.
6. Opere, ed. Naz. I, 300–301.
7. *Dialogue Concerning the Two Chief World Systems—Ptolemaic and Copernican*; Third Day; trans. Stillman Drake.
8. The evolution of a species, for example, has to be explained in terms of environmental adaption, or some other mechanism external to the species, rather than, say, as the evolutionary thrust of consciousness needing more complex organisms for manifestation.
9. Thus, any notion of the Spirit which is 'pure consciousness' or soul which bears 'will' and 'conscience' is, from a scientific point of view, unacceptable *ab initio*. One recourse from this materialization of man is to posit a sharp discontinuity between man, specifically his mind, from the rest of nature. This is the path which Descartes chose and many now follow. Such a sharp division appears to be, both from the philosophic and the scientific point of view, quite unnatural. If we proceed on the basis of a humanization (or spiritualization) of matter—as is being suggested here—we should expect different kinds of scientific theories.
10. Ruth Moore, *Neils Bohr* (New York: Alfred A. Knopf, 1966), 406.
11. This may well be the area of the greatest divergence between a rational and humanistic metaphysics on the one side and a mystical spiritual metaphysics on the other. For the former, what is essential about a person is his particularity and uniqueness, whereas for the latter these are secondary manifestations of a transpersonal reality. Since the somewhat unfortunate alliance of Descartes and Locke, the

Western psychology has been basically atomistic, believing that a human being is primarily an isolated ego afloat in a sea of interactions, undulating in reaction to purposeless external forces.

12. See his *Conjectures and Refutations*.

13. S. Freud, *A General Introduction to Psychoanalysis*, trans. Joan Riviere (Garden City, N.Y, 1943), 60.

14. This is as true of scientific theories as of metaphysical or theological ones; what is being called in question here is that tyranny of reason which makes theory superior to experience. For example, to theorize that behind the material world there is a spiritual reality is not essentially different from theorizing that behind the same material world there is a mathematical reality. Indeed, there are things which are mysterious; but the practical question is "How can I experience these?" rather than "What can I conjecture about them?"

15. *The Assayer*, trans. Stillman Drake in *Discoveries and Opinions of Galileo*.

16. Quoted in E.A. Burtt, *The Metaphysical Foundations of Modern Science* (Garden City, N.Y.: Doubleday, 1954), 68.

17. E.C. Pollard in *Yale Alumnus Magazine*, March 1955, 7.

18. See the essay on John Dewey in John Smith's *The Spirit of American Philosophy*.

19. If one succumbs to such an impoverished and partial view of nature, then one is forced to posit some notion of the supernatural to account for those manifestations, such as human will and purpose, which do not seem to be governed by completely unconscious mechanical laws. It is the high regard accorded to nature by thinkers like Spinoza and Goethe that got them into trouble with both the naturalistic scientists and the supernaturalistic clerics. (Not infrequently, both of these tendencies co-exist in the same person, as if a denigration of nature needs to be balanced by a deification of something extra-natural establishing rigid boundaries between various levels of being.)

20. Immanuel Kant, *Critique of Pure Reason*; preface to the second edition. (Italics added.) A similar appreciation of the scientific method is evident in the writings of Francis Bacon, the patron saint of the Royal Society. He writes, for example, "Nature should not only be studied 'free and at large (when she is left to her own course...)' but should be studied even more when 'under constraint,' when 'by art and the hand of man she is forced out of her natural state and squeezed and molded.'" (*Instauratio Magna*.) *The Works of Francis Bacon*, ed. J. Spedding, R.L. Ellis, and D. Herth (London, 1857–74), 14 volumes, Vol. V, 145.

21. This preparation and waiting for the revelation of the higher is not a passive affair, as it might seem. This is not the place to dwell on this theme; suffice it to say here that the activity involved in this state is of a sort quite different from the ordinary doing mentioned earlier.

22. Parmenides, *Diels*, Fr. 185. An exactly similar doctrine is found in

Plotinus (*Ennead* VI.9). On the basis of such a theory of knowledge, in order to know something higher, one will have to become higher. This I take to be the central purpose of any spiritual tradition. The result of the scientific mentality in the realm of the Spirit is to attempt to seize—as with drugs—higher consciousness. It is forgotten that if the Spirit refers to anything higher than our ordinary self, the question is not how we can appropriate the Spirit, but rather how can we prepare ourselves so that we may be appropriated by the Spirit.

23.   *The Republic*, 443.

EIGHT

WESTERN SCIENCE And TECHNOLOGY And The INDIAN INTELLECTUAL TRADITION

Ravi Ravindra

Every major culture develops, over a period of time, an internal integrity. Its major manifestations—arts, religions, philosophies, science-technology—are intimately related with each other. It is a mark of the vitality of the intellectual tradition of a country that these various manifestations interact, nourishing and challenging each other. Tensions and contradictions among these can be very creative and can lead to a synthesis at a higher level. On the other hand, it is possible that because of a lack of effort and fearlessness in facing these contradictions a culture can be satisfied with superficial reconciliations.

One important area of cultural contradiction in India at present is modern science-technology. There appears to be a widespread tendency in India, both among intellectuals and

well-intentioned laymen, to imagine that there is no contradiction between modern science-technology and the Indian
spiritual-intellectual tradition. It has even been suggested that
the Indian tradition, rightly understood, will naturally lead to
modern science. I have the strong impression that these sentiments are based more on a vague feeling that all good things
are inherently harmonious than on any close analysis of the
situation. It is possible to hope that modern science and ancient
spiritual traditions can be integrated in some higher synthesis.
I would even say that such a task is the most important of all
that can be undertaken by contemporary intellectuals, for on
such a synthesis depends not only the global survival of man
but also the creation of the right environment, right both
physically and metaphysically, for future generations. However, this is a very big challenge and cannot be met easily.
Perhaps the intellectual efforts of a whole generation will be
needed for the task. There are some signs now mostly in the
Western world, and in particular in the U.S.A., but hardly any
in India—that this task is beginning to be undertaken on
several fronts with a vigorous quality of thought and a lack of
sentimentalism. A necessary step is to try to understand clearly
the essential nature of modern science and technology.

Modern science and technology everywhere—East or West—
are essentially Western in character. Their fundamental procedures and attitudes were developed in Western Europe
during the great scientific revolution of the sixteenth and the
seventeenth centuries. The rise and development of modern
science are closely linked with the spread of certain humanistic
and secular socio-political ideas in the West. There are several
philosophical presuppositions, concerning the nature of reality, of man and of knowledge, which underlie modern science
and technology; and they all arise from Western religions and
philosophy. It is necessary to be aware of these, for it is likely
that the spread of modern science and technology—which are
different in their philosophical attitudes from ancient and
medieval sciences and technologies even in the West, and
certainly from those in India—will bring with it the same sort
of spiritual ruination in India as it has done in the West, unless
we can bring the requisite understanding and the will for a

higher cultural synthesis. Some of these philosophical presuppositions, and by no means all, are discussed below.

Everything Is Essentially Dead

It is a fundamental assumption of all scientific inquiry that what one is investigating is essentially dead, i.e., it has no interiority. Therefore, it, whether electron, frog, man, or culture, can be completely described in terms of external forces to which it reacts, helplessly. It has no consciousness, purpose, or intention of its own, and its entire existence and behavior can be explained by referring to interactions with outside forces which, in turn, are themselves purposeless. Reality, on a small scale or on the whole,[1] may be dynamic but it has no self-initiative. Thus, it is internally completely passive: it reacts to forces but it cannot respond.[2]

The model here, as everywhere else in modern science, is physics, which bases itself entirely on principles derived from a study of 'inanimate' objects, or, more accurately, on principles derived from a study of those objects which are assumed to be completely inanimate. One may think on the face of it, that the above comments do not apply to biology which after all deals with 'living' organisms. This is true only in the minimal sense that the objects studied by biology have a property called reproducibility. They, however, are allowed no more interiority than the dead objects of physics. So, monkeys, cats, frogs, have no 'rights,' which might mitigate against any sort of experimentation on them. The only relevant fact is that human beings can overpower these animals and therefore subject them to any treatment whatsoever. Theological and ethical considerations aside, which are in any case notorious for their impotence in the laboratories, there is no scientific principle which would stand in the way of any experimentation on the members of a subject race. Also, the basic thrust of the entire work in biophysics and biochemistry is to find explanations of 'living' organisms in terms of dead objects and purposeless forces, i.e., in terms of physical laws.

In an older terminology, one might say that biology deals with animals as if they had no 'soul' and were only bodies. This, of course, is an old and standard Christian idea. Only human beings have souls; man is different from other animals precisely in this. (The question has occasionally been raised whether slaves, blacks, or women have souls.) Descartes, who is regarded as the father of modern Western philosophy and who had an enormous influence on modern biology, regarded animals very much in this Christian light and considered them as 'engines without will.' Man, on the other hand, for Descartes was an engine with a will.

Modern psychology, as it became progressively more 'scientific,' naturally eliminated any considerations of interiority, treating man only as a machine reacting to external stimuli in a predictable manner. Most of experimental and behavioristic psychology is based on the assumption that human beings can, in principle, be completely characterized by their reactions to external forces, and that we need not entertain the idea of there being 'a ghost in the machine,' as it is said, which we can label as consciousness or soul and which may be said to have an intention or purpose. There is no principle of scientific epistemology that would permit a treatment of human beings as persons rather than as objects.[3]

It is precisely this attitude that permeates modern scientific medicine, namely the attitude that a human being is essentially a physico-chemical machine, which is somehow alive—a fact which itself is determined by some external or externalized physical characteristics. In this machine, different components (traditionally labeled 'organs') can, in principle, be replaced by 'alive' or artificial components with similar functions from elsewhere.

In short, a fundamental assumption of modern scientific inquiry is that the whole of reality, at whatever scale we take it as the whole universe—an animal, a tree, or a stone—is a machine. Whether it has any consciousness or not is quite irrelevant to scientific procedures or conclusions; therefore, for simplicity, one might as well proceed on the assumption that there is no consciousness. The whole of nature is assumed to be made up of dead matter in purposeless motion. In fact, nothing whatsoever has any purpose. Neither purpose nor anything equivalent is a scientific category at all. Any connotation of purpose in the idea of cause before the major scientific revolution of the sixteenth–seventeenth centuries has been systematically eliminated since then. Now, objects or creatures do not have purposes; they merely have functions.

Otherness of Nature

The universe is hostile or at least indifferent, not intentionally but mechanically, to human purposes and aspirations. Therefore, it needs to be fought and conquered. The otherness of nature is an essential presupposition of the scientific attitude. This is what allows man to exploit nature. The more advanced a society is scientifically and technologically, the more pronounced is the exploitation of nature in it. Modern technology is essentially of a piece with modern science in its fundamental procedures and attitudes. What distinguishes them is their stance towards the control of nature. In science, the control of nature is tantamount to understanding nature, and one engages in it for the sport of it, for the pleasure of overcoming an adversary. In technology, the advantage over nature is exploited for gratification of human desires usually in the guise of assuaging fears and fulfilling needs. This shift from utilizing natural resources for the fulfillment of legitimate human needs to the exploitation of nature for gratification of unbridled desires—as is now clearly the case in the U.S.A.—is made easy by the attitude, common to science and technology, which regards nature as an enemy to be vanquished.

Objectivity of Reality

Closely related with the above two presuppositions is another one, according to which 'nature' inside man is wholly different from the nature outside. This is related with Descartes' well-known sharp division between two realms: *res extensa* (realm of extension) and *res cogitans* (realm of thinking). The former is the realm of the body; it is the material domain of nature. The latter is the realm of the soul, which for Descartes is the same as the mind. Nature is only material and external. What is internal is merely subjective—in the sense of being personal, private, shifty, and unreliable. Only what is external can be objective and real.

Quantification of Reality

Even in the external realm there is a further division made between the so-called primary and secondary qualities. This division is necessitated by the demand of an unambiguous inter-subjective agreement about the external characteristics of an object. Only those characteristics are assumed primary which can be quantified and measured[4] and can thus be divorced from any consideration of the relative quality of attention, clarity of perception or the level of being of any person. What is assumed to be primarily real about anything excludes not only the distortions likely to be introduced by agitated or wishful thinking but also the more subtle aspects perceivable only by sensitive and refined minds. Reality is thus, by assumption, divested of feelings and sensations requiring cleansed perceptions such as some artists and mystics have and is reduced only to those characteristics which can be mechanically quantified[5] such as size, mass, etc., "just as the eye was made to see colors, and the ear to hear sounds," wrote Kepler, "So the human mind was made not to understand whatever you please, but quantity."[6]

The secondary qualities contain all the features of reality with which arts and religions have been traditionally concerned, such as colors, sounds, taste, beauty, purpose (for example, it is entirely reasonable to think about and measure the mass and charge of an electron, though neither property can be directly felt or sensed, but it is faintly ludicrous to ask about its taste or color. If one were to ask about the purpose of an electron or of anything else, one would be outside the scientific arena entirely!) Whatever functions poetry, music, dance, or spiritual disciplines may serve, when it comes to the serious business of truth and knowledge as understood by modern natural philosophers, all these activities are essentially frivolous. Herein lie the seeds of fragmentation of our sensibilities: arts and religion cannot lead to 'knowledge' and science cannot lead to 'values.'[7] The resultant dichotomy between 'knowledge' and 'faith' or between 'reason' and 'feeling,' particularly apparent in Western culture, tends to be destructive of human wholeness and leads to narrow single vision. If our modern gods of truth and reason admit physics to their temples but not poetry or music or spiritual search, the wisdom of such gods is questionable. It may well be, as William Blake said, that "Reason and Newton they are quite two things."

Reality Is a Mental Construct

Underlying the perceived reality in science is assumed an abstract and purely rational construct. What is experienced is then called appearance, while the mental construct is labeled reality. The scientific pursuit, then, is to speculate about the imagined reality and to put these speculations to experimental tests, which involve only certain limited perceptions. The so-called objective reality of scientific concern is in fact a conjecture—perhaps one of the many which may be possible. However, and this is where the importance and glory of science lie, these subjective projections are confirmed or falsified by inter-subjective experimental procedures. Nevertheless, the testing procedures are not wholly independent of the theoretical framework. Whether an observation is taken to be a confirmation of a given conjecture is increasingly a matter of interpretation as scientific experiments become more and more elaborate. It is not possible to make a scientific observation without a prior theoretical system, as has been emphasized by Karl Popper.[8] In science, any theory is better than no theory. In order to get going, scientists are happy to have partial, incomplete, or wrong, theories rather than wait for a correct one; until a new theory is available, the old one is not abandoned however many problems it may have. Theorizing is fundamental to scientific activity; what we subject to experimental observations is not nature, but our conjectures about nature. The scientific revolution marks a shift not only from experience to experiment[9] but also from seeking certain truth to theorizing about probable truths. In science, reality is theory.

This is true for all the sciences, not only for physics. Every experimental science is first of all a theoretical science, although its theoretical system may be more or less explicit. Here is an example from Sigmund Freud: "Our purpose is not merely to describe and classify phenomena but to conceive them as brought about by the play of forces in the mind, as expressions of tendencies striving towards a goal, which work together or against one another. In this conception, the trends we merely infer are more prominent than the phenomena we perceive."[10]

Reality discovered through science is not necessariy something that is given, which we try to perceive more and more clearly and comprehensively by deepening or cleansing our perceptions as one attempts, for example, in Yoga. It is something postulated on the basis of data gathered through our ordinary perceptions, or perceptions which have been quantitatively extended, but not qualitatively transformed, through scientific instruments. Reality of science is not substantial, available to an immediate experience of anybody whosoever; it is conjectural and inferential. Scientific knowledge is not of 'minute particulars'[11] which can be directly and immediately apprehended. On the contrary, scientific knowledge leads away from immediacy and the attendant certainty and yields abstract generalizations forever subject to reasoning and change.

Fabric of Reality

Time is primarily linear and uniform, space is essentially isotropic, and energy is basically of one quality.[12] Energy can be more or less in quantity but not more subtle or grosser in quality. It can in principle be converted from one form to another. In ancient and medieval science, different planets were considered to be made up of different types of matter, subject to different laws because they occupied different regions of space and were made for different purposes. According to modern science, place, and function (which is a mechanical replacement for the idea of purpose) of a thing are not inherent to it but are accidental. Therefore, nothing essential or primarily real in the object can depend on its place or function. According to earlier ideas, the earth—and man on it—was situated in a specific place suitable for an intentional interplay of purposive energies. Now, since intention and purpose are not parts of natural philosophy, no place has any special importance with respect to anything. The earth happens to be where it is by chance, following a concatenation of mechanical causes.

Consistent with the presuppositions mentioned earlier, particularly in the third section, time, space, and energy of natural philosophy are all only objectively (i.e., externally) real.

They are completely independent of the level or the state of the perceiving consciousness, and they cannot in principle, and by assumption, be affected by consciousness. If a miracle takes place, which cannot be explained away as a trick, in which 'mind' can affect objective reality (i.e., external time, space, and energy as measured by clocks and sticks, etc.) the attitude of modern science is either to ignore it or to regard the miracle as contrary to natural laws or even as supernatural, rather than to admit that the present view of nature is a very limited one.[13]

Matter Precedes Intelligence

There is a near-universal traditional belief that causes are at a higher level—of subtlety and intelligence—than their effects.[14] From this perspective, spirit precedes mind, which in turn precedes matter. In the natural philosophy of the sixteenth–seventeenth centuries in Europe, owing to an emphasis on principles derived from 'inanimate' nature, and because of an assumption denying levels of materiality (since all matter is dead, it is all at the same level). Causes were taken to be at the same level as effects. In physics, the fundamental notion of causality is that in saying that state A of matter causes state B we mean only that state A changes into state B under specific conditions and subject to physical laws. (How and whether we can give a complete description of any state of matter, as individual particles or ensembles of particles, are some of the questions which have become problematic with the development of quantum mechanics. However, these considerations are not relevant to our concerns here.) There is no suggestion whatever that states A and B are at different levels.

As we move into scientific biology, in the nineteenth-century theory of evolution, we find that causes are now taken to be at a level lower than the effects. Less intelligent organisms precede and give rise to more intelligent animals. Matter is, and precedes all forms of, intelligence, which is taken to be a manifestation of a complex organization of matter. The more and more complex material organization and the consequent higher intelligence may be completely accidental or partly in response to external environmental pressures. What is important from a scientific point of view is that everything, including apparently inner attributes accompanying intelligence, must be explained in terms of external forces and matter. The evolution of a species, for example, has to be explained in terms of environmental adaptation or some other mechanism external to the species, rather than, say, as the evolutionary thrust of consciousness needing more complex organisms for manifestation.

All of these philosophical presuppositions are radically at odds with the corresponding assumptions in the Indian tradition. To be sure, it is rare to find a great poet or a spiritual seeker even in the Western tradition (Goethe, Blake, Wordsworth, Yeats, T.S. Eliot) who has not been uneasy with the philosophical and cultural implications of modern science and technology. Much of the contemporary spiritual malaise of the West is intimately linked with the triumph of these assumptions, as is much of what is considered desirable in terms of liberal, democratic, social institutions. However, one cannot deny the hegemony of these assumptions, even though one or the other of these is being challenged here and there, in one particular science or another.[15] One can easily see this from a well-known and wholly unchallenged fact that for us—in the West or in the East—modern cosmology, which is supposed to be a study of all there is, has become a branch of physics which deals with dead matter in motion.

Now there are some signs of change. The world is in the midst of a great metaphysical revolution which will shake the foundations of all human thinking. This revolution, which does not yet seem to have engaged the intellectuals in India, is calling into question all our established notions of space, time, materiality, causality, and mind. An alternative and a much more comprehensive science than the present one is in the making. It is possible that traditional Eastern spiritual disciplines and philosophies may provide, if they are cleansed of inessential religious accretions, some necessary elements for the emerging alternative philosophy of nature on a global scale. If science and technology in India had had an internal, organic growth, rather than a surgical transplant from elsewhere as is the case now, it is likely that Indian science would be as different from the Western science as Indian music is from Western music. There would no doubt be some quite basic similarities, but there would be differences in their essential aspirations. Furthermore, this alternative science and technology would have been more integrated with the rest of the Indian culture.

Whether this Indian science and technology would be adequate for the needs and aspirations of the emerging global culture is an open question. Nevertheless it is important for India to be free of the unhealthy epistemological imperialism of the West, more pernicious because of its unrecognized character. India does not need to go back to ancient times; certainly no more than the West stayed ancient. But history forced an alien development of mind in India without a corresponding change of heart. The Indian situation now is, however, quite different from that of Europe of the sixteenth–seventeenth centuries, largely owing to Western science and technology themselves. The major difference is that the Indians have to take into account—unlike the Westerners then and largely even now—not only their own history, philosophy, science, and religion but also Western history, philosophy, science, and technology. India will ignore the West at her own peril; but if India ignores her own soul, there will be nothing left that needs guarding from any peril.

True to the spirit of Indian culture, one cannot depend ultimately on any institutional or technological blueprints. India's future depends on the depth of understanding and the greatness of being of her intellectual leaders. (Just to remind ourselves, *buddhi* has an intelligence greater than that of *manas* alone, and includes feeling as much as reason. Furthermore a fundamental assumption in the Indian tradition is that to come to great truth one must have a great being.) Only those people can truly help in the proper growth—which must be from the inside outward—who are reasonably conversant with Western thought, science, and technology, but who are not overwhelmed by them into a state in which no alternatives are seen.

Nor must they be hostile to Western values and ideas simply because they are alien. The West also has a ray of the limitless truth, as does India. The rays are different, perhaps with complementary colors, needing scope for enlargement and expression. The Indian tradition has always believed that truth can be approached in many ways; still one has to find and devote oneself, both on the individual and the cultural scale, to one's own distinctive way. It is only by being authentically ourselves that we can understand the general human situation and contribute to global welfare. Thus the intellectual leaders in India will have to be deeply in touch with the Indian tradition, aware of its distinctive mission, and in love with it not for its own sake, but for the sake of the Truth, which, of course, is no more Indian than it is Western. For India to ignore her own essential depth will be to truncate one luminous emanation of the universal Sun, which is no mere material ball of fire; but is in truth one of the Adityas, born from the union of Aditi (unlimited) and Kashyap (vision), constantly dispersing Daityas who, by contrast, are born from limited (Diti) vision.

Acknowledgments

A Senior Fellowship from the Shastri Indo-Canadian Institute and a Leave Fellowship from the Social Sciences and Humanities Research Council of Canada are gratefully acknowledged. I am also thankful for the hospitality extended by the Department of Religion, Punjabi University, Patiala, and the Indian Institute of Advanced Study, Simla. Prof. T.R.V. Murty was very generous with his time in Varanasi and very patient with my questions about the philosophies of India. (Naturally, he is not responsible for any opinions expressed in this paper.)

Notes

1. In cosmology, a study of all there is, philosophic difficulties arise about external-internal forces. However, modern 'cosmology' is based completely on physics, which investigates dead matter in motion in reaction to external forces.

2. It is clear that what is called the theory of stimulus-response in psychology is a misappropriation of words. This theory should more properly be called stimulus-reaction.

3. To be sure, other orientations in the field of psychology have arisen in the last couple of decades; for example, orientations labeled 'humanistic psychology' and 'existential psychology.' The most common charge against these psychologies is precisely that they are not sufficiently 'scientific.'

4. Max Planck, the famous tweentieth-century physicist who was the father of quantum mechanics, said: "That which cannot be measured is not real."

5. The analogue of this quantitative attitude in philosophy is to be found in the Anglo-American analytical philosophy, particularly from the mid-forties to mid-sixties, where the vast and subtle realm of truth is reduced only to propositions for which one can prepare so-called 'truth tables' determining whether a particular proposition is true or false.

6. Quoted in E.A. Burtt, *The Metaphysical Foundations of Modern Science* (Garden City, N.Y.: Doubleday, 1954), 68.

7. The proposition that science is value free is sometimes cited as a glorious feature of science. There is a related philosophical question concerning whether "is" can lead to "ought"?—as if science is concerned with the description of what is, without any purpose.

8. See his *Conjectures and Refutations.*

9. Please see Chapter 7 in the present volume for the distinction between experiment and experience and discussion of the relevance of this distinction to the nature of scientific inquiry.

10. S. Freud, *A General Introduction to Psychoanalysis*, trans. Joan Riviere (Garden City, N.Y., 1943), 60. (Italics added).

11. This phrase is William Blake's. There is no restriction of scale implied here; the 'minute particular' could refer to a whole constellation of stars, or to the earth, or to a person or a tree. To know something as a minute particular is to know it in its concrete—which does not mean material, it could be supersensuous —uniqueness essentially. The idea is similar to the Indian notion that everything— tree, river, the earth—has an indwelling spirit (abhimāni devatā) presiding over it.

12. These assumptions, particularly about the linearity and uniformity of time, become problematic when considering questions relating to

the origin of the entire universe. It should be mentioned that it is a consequence of these assumptions that the laws of physics are applicable for all time and throughout all space. Also, the laws of conservation of energy, momentum, and angular momentum are intimately connected with the assumed symmetrical properties of space and time.

13. St. Augustine, in harmony with the common traditional view in India on these matters, makes a useful distinction when he says that we must not regard wonders and signs as 'contrary to nature' but 'contrary to what is known of nature' (*de Civ. Dei*, BK. XXI, Ch. viii).

14. This is particularly clearly enunciated in the Sāṅkhya thought, as grosser manifestations emerge from more subtle ones, and ultimately from the unmanifest (avyakta).

15. One may be tempted to think that the major scientific changes in the twentieth century have affected the foregoing assumptions. This is not the case, although it will take too long to establish this point here. Nevertheless the fact that there is a general feeling that this is the case has helped in preparing an intellectual climate in which a radical re-evaluation of science becomes easier.

NINE

PHYSICS AND NATURAL HISTORY

Francis G. Nagasaka

Science and Pseudo-metaphysics

Some time ago, in an interview for a Japanese popular science magazine, James D. Watson made a remark to the effect that after twenty years there will be no biologists, only molecular biologists. Morphology will be reduced to the study of DNA.[1] Perhaps it is everyone's belief that in the coming twenty years, molecular biology, and accordingly, its applications in so many fields, will make stupendous progress.

Nevertheless, even in the future society, ethology and ecology will never fade away but probably will play even more important roles, notwithstanding the tremendous progress molecular biology might make. Therefore, what Watson meant was tantamount to the assertion that, even if those branches of biology continue to contribute very significantly to the welfare of the human race, the specialists in these fields will not be given prestigious positions in the scientific community, or those branches simply will not be regarded as really scientific disciplines, perhaps only auxiliary science at best. The situation is somewhat similar to that which existed between pure and applied mathematics and science and technology up to the earlier part of the twentieth century. Watson is not a philosopher of science and probably does not ask what qualifications are required for systematic intellectual activities to be called scientific.

So it is not fair to scrutinize Watson's more or less casual remark made in the course of an interview by a journalist, but I think at least this much can be asserted: Watson believes that, if the utility of those and other branches of biology should be admitted, molecular biology would be situated at their root namely, it will account for the findings in those branches and will direct what research and how it is to be carried out in the respective fields. Clearly Watson is not concerned about the practical effectiveness of these disciplines, but rather considers the matter from an epistemological viewpoint, tacitly assuming a distinction between basic principles and derived knowledge, which is similar to the Galilean distinction between primary and secondary qualities. It may not be so strong an assertion as it sounds, but only a sort of working hypothesis which is by no means uncommon in the process of scientific theory formation.

Nevertheless, it indicates a view which is quite pervasive in the modern mind. Because the remark is casual, all the more it reveals a candid image he has about the world and science. What really matters is this image. It matters because it is pervasive, and because that sort of working hypotheses is the commonest in contemporary science: the conception that macroscopic phenomena, for instance, could be accounted for by means of microscopic science entirely. Notice that there is no theory worked out which connects up the two kinds really satisfactorily. There is no quantum theory of macroscopic phenomena in general.[2] The so-called quantum mechanical effects on the macroscopic level are those anomalies for which theories of classical physics have failed to provide satisfactory explanations. So the working hypotheses are hypothetical in the sense that they do not belong to the theory concerned, but one has to note that they have often been extremely effective in the process of theory formation, though there are many which have come to be abandoned in later periods: we may cite the conception of ether in the formation of electro-magnetic theory as a most outstanding example. Any theory of science may be said to be hypothetical in the sense that it may be superseded by a certain better theory. But it is an important characteristic of scientific theory that it is well elucidated and articulated, while the so-called working hypothesis lacks this fundamental characteristic. Of course there have been all sorts of working hypotheses proposed; most of them are with quite limited scopes, but some are so basic that the feasibility of the whole theory may hinge on the validity of the working hypothesis in question. Clearly those examples referred to in the above belong to the latter class.

As will be expounded later, scientific theories are always constructed upon the basis of certain metaphysical presuppositions. But the distinction between the metaphysical presuppositions and working hypotheses of the second type is subtle, for both play essential roles in scientific theory formation, and yet neither belong to those theories. But there is a fundamental distinction between the two: we must distinguish between the concept of *ether* and that of *matter*; clearly the latter is more basic than the former, and even after the former concept was totally abandoned, we have never dispensed with the concept of matter, though certain drastic modifications had to be introduced to the concept. Thus, the important and theoretically basic working hypothesis has, more often than not, a characteristic of metaphysics. We may call this kind of working hypothesis "pseudo-metaphysics." But the most important distinction between metaphysics and pseudo-metaphysics is that, while the latter is concerned only with certain scientific theories, the former is expected to provide a universal foundation for the world. We may say metaphysics is open, whereas pseudo-metaphysics is closed.

What I would like to point out concerning Watson's remark is simply this: the distinction between metaphysics and pseudo-metaphysics is so subtle that the demarcation between the two has often been obliterated, and as a consequence, people have endowed, inadvertently, the status of metaphysics upon working hypotheses or pseudo-metaphysics so tacitly propounded. I think that casual as it was, this is exactly what Watson did by making the remark. The upshot of this is that metaphysics, upon which scientific theories have been constructed and which would make it possible to understand them from a more general viewpoint, would be destroyed and a certain sort of pseudo-metaphysics would take over. This would deprive people of a metaphysical approach.

Whitehead called perhaps the most outstanding case of this kind "Scientific materialism:"[3] "There persists...throughout the whole period the fixed scientific cosmology which presupposes the ultimate fact of an irreducible brute matter, or material, spread throughout space in a flux of configurations. In itself such a material is senseless, valueless, purposeless....It is this *assumption* that I call 'scientific materialism.'"[4] A pseudo-metaphysical notion is an assumption, since there is no factual evidence nor theoretical ground to support it. It is not metaphysics, for it is closed; it is neither well articulated nor are there arguments for defending the thesis. This is exactly the situation that the development of science brought forth to the modern mind. The pseudo-metaphysics goes beyond the scope of science itself: being metaphysical, naturally it tends to exclude other kinds of metaphysical thinking; and being scientific, it tends to create a more or less materialistic, namely, senseless, valueless, purposeless mentality.

But the pseudo-metaphysics does not necessarily lead to, say, spiritual anarchy: we cannot see things without feelings; we cannot live and act without sense of value and purpose. It is impossible that our daily experiences should be totally devoid of these elements. So, more often than not, pseudo-metaphysics is supplemented more or less by certain metaphysical conceptions, perhaps with a sacrifice of consistency, and thus the requirement for complete rationality has often to be abandoned. And as a consequence, trust in rationalism has been greatly dissipated. It seems that recent controversial arguments concerning the rationality of science is at least in part derived from this situation.[5] This is at least one aspect of the crisis we are now experiencing.[6] But is it really possible to stop and reverse the gradual shift to spiritual anarchism which, we observe, has become accelerated especially in the latter half of the twentieth century? So this is the nature of the scientific crisis which has induced the spiritual crisis of the twentieth century, and I think this is also the gist of what Husserl called "the crisis of sciences" which represents the life crisis of Europe.[7] Husserl asserts: "the whole worldview of modern men was exclusively determined by the positive science and left blinded by the 'prosperity' it brought about," and by that "exclusiveness" Husserl meant that men had been led to turn away indifferently from the problem which is vitally significant to the true humanity.[8] In the fifty-odd years after the first paper of the series was published, the crisis nevertheless has become more acute and pressing, and we are still searching for the remedy.

Physics and the Seventeenth-Century Scientific Revolution

The term "scientific revolution" was employed by Butterfield in the *Origins of Modern Science* and became commonly used subsequently,[9] though the idea itself had been forwarded by Whitehead much earlier.[10] But I think the expression "scientific revolution" is quite misleading. It was only in the latter part of the nineteenth century that such terms as "science" and "physics" came into common use in the meaning in which they are now used. Before that time "philosophy" was the term generally employed. But even though the term "chemical philosophy" was commonly used in the seventeenth century, we cannot find during that period any drastic progress in the field. Thus the sort of intellectual enterprises which are generally categorized as science mostly emerged in the course of the nineteenth century and acquired much wider scope and greater impact on the society only in the present century. The only exception is physics, whose beginning may be dated in 1687 when the first edition of *Philosophia naturalis principia mathematica* was published, though its revolutionary significance had not been appreciated until more than one hundred years after its publication. On the other hand, however, the interval of one hundred years which was required for the full acceptance of the *Principia* shows most eloquently the profound depth of the revolution resulting from the thought which was initiated by Newton.

Furthermore, if we take a glance at the history of investigations achieved in such fields as chemical process, biology, and medicine in the seventeenth and eighteenth centuries, we find at once the presence of mechanistic views in these fields. Whether they might be due to the Cartesian or the Newtonian

163

mechanistic view, it is quite apparent that the superiority of the Newtonian philosophy of nature inspired and prompted these investigations to gradually form scientific disciplines in later years. The influence of physics on other disciplines became more manifest as time developed. Including Watson's remark, we find here the source of all sorts of physicalism and their justification. I think at least this much can be asserted: every scientific discipline contains some elements of the method of physics in an essential way. Thus, if we are to understand the nature of the scientific crisis and to find some way not to fall into the pitfall of spiritual anarchism, it is at least necessary to understand the nature of physics and its philosophical implications, including both metaphysical presuppositions and pseudo-metaphysical assertions concerned.

Precursors of the Newtonian Revolution

Science, physics in particular, is a product of Western civilization, or more precisely of the European civilization. Like so many other things in Europe, physics emerged out of the legacy of the views and intellectual habits the ancient Greeks held which were transmitted to Christian Europe mainly by way of the Arabian civilization. But the integration of Greek thought and the Christian tradition was by no means easy. The first integration was attempted by the Church Fathers, in which Platonic and Neoplatonic understandings and interpretations of Christianity were predominant. But after the so-called 12th-century Renaissance, the Aristotelian conception gradually advanced. The conflict between the new and old schools was remarkably exhibited in the decree of Cardinal Etienne Tempier of 1277 and subsequent controversial disputes.[11]

Clearly the very root of the controversies lies in the difficulty of the synthesis of faith and reason, and thus, many syntheses were attempted, though not all of them were very successful. Nevertheless, many of them, though controversial, were indispensable preliminaries for the Newtonian revolution. First, we must note that *Principia* was a book of philosophy of nature, and that the concept of *nature* had been established beforehand,[12] though it was God's creation. Nature is the object which has its own laws and could be studied independently without the aid of Revelation. Though this conception was not new but had gradually been developed in the medieval period, it was the Paduan school Averroists that really fostered the conception. Being Averroists, they did not bother too much about the formidable problem of synthesis of faith and reason. Furthermore, unlike earlier Latin Averroists, they made critical studies of Aristotle. Perhaps due to their close association with Occamists they became interested in such problems as whether the "primary attribute" of substance is quantity rather than quality and whether the "cause" of natural motion is its "form" or "force" which is known as the Paduan disputes.[13] Concerning the second problem, Galileo adopted the latter view, while Kepler adopted the former view, but concerning the first problem they both chose the former position.

The difference of attitude toward the Paduan disputes between Kepler and Galileo is not only most interesting in itself but made both of them real precursors of Newton, since the Newtonian philosophy of nature involves in an essential way the synthesis of the two opposing positions.

Before discussing the significance of the Keplerian conception of nature, it may be necessary to touch briefly on the history of astronomy. Greek astronomy was born in the Pythagorean school in the fifth century B.C. It is believed that "the Pythagoreans were the first to call the world cosmos (implying that it is a well-ordered and harmonious system) and to say that the earth is round."[14] It was the conception of the universe ascribed to Philolaus which provided the solid ground for the later astronomy and cosmology to the time of Descartes and Newton: the earth is a sphere which is tiny in comparison with the dimension of the universe and of comparable size with the moon and the planets; the moon shines because it reflects light it received from the central fire (later from the sun); light of celestial region is of the same nature as we observe on the earth; no divine or supernatural intervention should be required to account for the celestial motion.

One must note that this conception was necessary not only for theory construction but for accurate observations, and thus for mathematical representations of the celestial phenomena. What we observe of stars is that we see the stars in such and such directions. Those directions are given interpretations such that they correspond to the positions of stars in motion only if we have such theories as orbits of stars together with the notion of spherical shape of earth, only then those directions have meaning and become data upon which astronomical theories are to be constructed. It was those theories that were called "phenomena."[15]

Plato and Aristotle differed in ascribing causes to the phenomena. Whereas Plato searched for mathematically ideal formulation, Aristotle was not satisfied only with the formal cause. Instead, he demanded physical explanation for the celestial motion. The expression "saving the phenomena" was coined in the Platonic vein, but later it lost its original significance and meant merely more accurate mathematical analysis of the phenomena which would make precise predictions of the location of stars possible. "It is the business of physical inquiry to consider the substance of the heaven and the stars, their force and quality, their coming into being and their destruction, nay, it is in a position even to prove the facts about their size, shape, and arrangement; astronomy, on the other hand, does not attempt to speak of anything of this kind, but proves the arrangement of the heavenly bodies by considerations based on the view that the heaven is a real *kosmos*, and further, it tells us of the shape and size and distances of the earth, sun, and moon, and of eclipses and conjunctions of the stars, as well as the quality and extent of their movements." This is a passage of Simplicius' *Commentary of Aristotle's Physics*, translated by T.L. Heath.[16] Thus astronomy was a branch of mathematics sharply distinguished from cosmology. So in astronomy any theory was regarded as a hypothesis and acceptable as long as it gave an accurate account of the phenomena.

Mathematically speaking, the geocentric and heliocentric systems are equivalent, and the problem itself lost its original significance after the Newtonian revolution with the supposition of endlessly extended universe. In this regard Copernicus did not accomplish anything significant, except that his theory gave a more simplified and coherent mathematical system. But he called himself a Pythagorean, and he wanted to transform astronomy from a mere instrument to save the phenomena to *cosmology* in the Pythagorean spirit. His *Revolutionibus* was written in the current of revival of Neoplatonism which contained a strong Pythagorean element.[17]

As is well known, Kepler was a devout Pythagorean; so was Galileo, though somewhat in a different sense. Both of them believed that the principles, or the essence, of the universe must be mathematical. They accepted Copernicus because they believed in his Pythagoreanism. This meant an emergence of new cosmology, which is totally different from the Aristotelian physics. Being a Pythagorean, Copernicus could not tolerate any incoherences which could be found in the Ptolemaic system, notably the infamous "punctum aequans." This is the restoration of astronomy to the original Platonic conception. Burtt stated: "The transformation of the new world view, for him, was nothing but a mathematical reduction, under the encouragement of the renewed Platonism of the day, of a complex geometrical labyrinth into a *beautifully simple* and harmonious system."[18]

Among Renaissance philosophers probably Nicholas of Cusa was the most prominent figure in this vein. As is well known, he asserted the conception of an infinite universe. Clearly without his contribution and the subsequent development of his thought the Newtonian philosophy would have been impossible. But Koyré pointed out "he never affirms the infinity of the world (as Descartes mistakenly assumed him to do) but always calls it 'interminate' and opposes its limitlessness to the positive infinity of God."[19] So, if Koyré is right, then it was Descartes who established the notion of "infinity" of the created world and introduced the notion into mathematics as positive entity. Kepler as well as St. Thomas would have rejected the idea.[20] Kepler, being Pythagorean, naturally defended the idea of *cosmos*, and Koyré asserts that the transition was "From Closed World to the Infinite Universe."[21]

There is no question that Galileo contributed to this transition decisively, not because he accepted the notion of infinite universe, but because he was a Platonist and believed that "the Great Book of Nature is written in the language of mathematics." Burtt commented on this famous passage: "Galileo is continually astonished at the marvelous manner in which natural happenings follow the principles of geometry, and his favorite answer to the objection that mathematical demonstrations are abstract and possess no necessary applicability to the physical world, is to proceed to further geometrical demonstrations, in the hope that they will become their own proof to all unprejudiced minds."[22] Galileo was a Platonist, but at the same time he was also an Aristotelian belonging to the Paduan school.

This somewhat contradictory attitude toward Nature was exactly what Burtt pointed out with abundant evidence in the *Discorsi* and the *Dialogo*. So Burtt made a further remark: "It is abundantly apparent, however, from the whole of Galileo's achievements and interests, that he never seriously entertained the possible extreme of this mathematical apriorism."[23] Galileo sought the forms of the facts he observed. Since the form is reality in the Platonic sense, the fact is its representation, so the latter has to obey the laws of mathematics.

This is a sort of mathematical apriorism, and I do not think Burtt was mistaken because of the qualification, "possible extreme." It is due to this kind of apriorism that Galileo could assert the possibility of linear, uniform motion in vacuum, though we shall never observe such motion on the earth.[24] Perhaps we should regard the Galilean conception of "New Science" as a development of the Paduan critical Aristotelism.[25] Thus Galileo made critical studies of problems raised by Aristotle such as natural (fall) and projectile motion. This is what Kepler never attempted. Furthermore, Galileo was not satisfied with the formal cause alone but the efficient cause of motion, namely force, was also considered. Unlike the cosmology of Copernicus and Kepler, Galileo's was basically physical. His attempt to explain the phenomena of tide by means of motion of the earth is a good illustration of the nature of his cosmology.

Thus his concept of motion was not limited to so-called locomotion, but motions in quantity and quality had to be considered. If the world should be expressed in the language of mathematics, and only such knowledge should be regarded as true, then the distinction between primary and secondary qualities had to be introduced, which would enable us to distinguish objective knowledge from subjective knowledge. This distinction is clearly a legacy of ancient Greek thought, distinctions between *episteme* and *doxa* and between *theory* and *practice*.

However, the Galilean interpretation of these conceptions was quite different from the original. The concept of Nature had been well established by this time: it is an object, great as it is, in contradistinction to human beings, while Greek "physis" never had the connotation of object; the latter had multiple meanings such as underlying principle, reality, and inherent cause which gives rise to all the mutations, but never meant "things generated by physis" nor "cosmos": "physis" was opposed as in Plato, to "nomos" and also, as in Aristotle, to "techne," and all these connotations of "physis" were transplanted in the Latin "natura" through Plato and Aristotle, and other ancient authors;[26] furthermore, in Christian Europe "natural" was opposed to "supernatural." The original complexity of the meaning of "natura" and its further development in the Renaissance and subsequent eras were all manifest in the writings of Galileo, Kepler, Descartes, and Newton. Thus I maintain that this conceptual development has a vital importance in the formation of the Newtonian philosophy of nature.

Characteristics of the Newtonian Revolution

The principal aim of the *Principia* was to derive Kepler's Laws from more fundamental principles in the manner that geometrical theorems are derived from the axioms and postulates together with definitions. Since Kepler's laws were expressed in mathematical terms and formulas, the Newtonian fundamental principles, i.e., laws of motion and the principles of universal gravitation, must assume mathematical forms. Throughout the First and Second Books of *Principia* Newton discussed only "motions of bodies" and not Nature. We find only in the Third Book discussions concerning celestial phenomena, but in the theorems 20, 24, 36, and 37, of the Book such terrestrial phenomena as tide were also discussed. So in Newton the distinction of sublunar and superlunar worlds was completely lifted. This is a clear articulation of the conception that the whole universe is subsumed under the same principles, which is a development and elucidation of the Galilean idea, namely, there is only one world, objective, mathematical, and mechanical.

Like Galileo, Newton was in the vein of the Aristotelian heritage. His problem was to discuss "motion" or "change" in the Aristotelian sense. He had to determine the cause of motion, but his principles which would make knowledge "episteme" were not limited to the immutable formal cause, but the causes which would make the motion possible. According to Aristotle, "Motion, we say, is the fulfillment of the movable in so far as it is movable. Each kind of motion, therefore, necessarily involves the presence of the things that are capable of that motion."[27]

What are movable in the Newtonian philosophy are bodies, which are substrata of the motion. The attributes of bodies are extension and quantity of matter, and the latter corresponds to the Artistotelian material cause which made the Newtonian philosophy radically different from the Cartesian metaphysics of *res extensa* and *res cogitans*. Clearly extension is the form of matter, so matter is also substance and it is the position of matter that changes. Thus the Newtonian conception of body is very much parallel to the Aristotelian hylomorphism, in spite of the fact that the difference is quite obvious: "position" is an accident in the Newtonian matter whose attribute is its density, so matter is measured by quantity. Thus "the quantity of matter is the measure of the same, arising from its density and bulk conjointly."[28]

Therefore, bodies of which the world consists are determined by the form and quantity of matter. Thus matter is the substance of the (material) bodies, or beings, and it is characterized by its quantity alone, and it is the immutable substratum of motion; though bodies may change their forms and positions, the total quantity of matter will remain constant; though it is movable in the sense of locomotion, its attributes are density and extension which are represented in terms of mathematical entities, i.e. figures and numbers, and no other qualities but mobility and impenetrability are ascribed to matter. Therefore the Newtonian matter is an *actual* entity in contradistinction to the Aristotelian (primary) matter which is pure potentiality. So matter is substance and substratum, it would not undergo any *motion* unless it is acted upon by external force, keeping its state of *motion* or *state of rest*.[29] So matter does not possess by nature the ability of motion. This passiveness of matter is one of the outstanding characteristics of the Newtonian philosophy of nature. Gravity which originally was the internal ability of motion (natural fall) had to be amended so that a falling body is acted on and "gravitated" by an external agent, and the agent is another body: the gravitating power inherent in matter is the feature of the Principle of Universal Gravitation.

On the other hand, however, Newton was cautious in making metaphysical commitment: "We know the properties of things from phenomena, and from the properties we infer that the things themselves exist but we do not have any more idea of substances than a blind man has of colors."[30] Here we may think Newton is a precursor of Kant. But Newton always tried to evade metaphysical questions. We find the famous passage of General Scholium of the Principia: "and I frame no hypothesis; for whatever is not deduced from the phenomena is to be called hypothesis, and hypotheses, whether metaphysical or physical, of occult qualities or mechanical, have no place in experimental philosophy. In this philosophy particular propositions are inferred from the phenomena and afterward rendered general by induction. Thus it was that the impenetrability, the mobility, and the impulsive force of bodies, and the laws of motion and of gravitation, were discovered. And to us it is enough that gravity does really exist and act according to the laws which have been explained, and abundantly serves to account for all the motions of the celestial bodies and of our sea."

Thus as the Newtonian philosophy superseded the Cartesian metaphysics, all the metaphysical presuppositions of the former on which those discoveries were based receded into oblivion and as a consequence *scientific* materialism emerged subsequently.

In the above and in the preceding section, I have tried to expound the extremely complex philosophical situations which contributed essentially to the emergence of the Newtonian philosophy: it was a great philosophical revolution, but it was founded upon and derived from the Western tradition which contained many philosophical ramifications; and the latter were so interwoven that, more or less, a dialectic evolution of thought took place in the history of the Western civilization. Mathematization of the world was possible only on the Pythagorean and Platonic conception, which established the idea that mathematics is the form or cause of the world, or cosmology. It was pointed out by Leclerc, "this (Newtonian) metaphysical conception of nature was new, but the ontology which it entailed was not; it was the Neoplatonic ontology which had been revived in the antecedent two centuries....It has been maintained in the Neoplatonism prior to the seventeenth century that soul alone is incomposite, and thus 'being'; nature or physical, on the contrary, as composite of soul and matter, is in becoming. In this respect the new doctrine of the seventeenth century is fundamentally divergent from the antecedent one. For matter, qua 'matter,' is incomposite, and thus in itself changeless, which meant matter had to be accepted as 'being' according to the Neoplatonic criterion."[31]

What Leclerc pointed out indicates another peculiar feature of the Newtonian revolution: numerous factors contributed essentially to its fermentation; those factors are not necessarily coherent, but often paradoxical, and thus could imply many types of cosmology. Therefore, the Newtonian philosophy is just one type, but an unprecedented peculiar type of cosmology, a mathematical world to which the Euclidean geometry is validly applied, and which is mechanical so that the laws of motion may hold exactly, and yet which contains incomposite matter as constituent of the world; it is thus changeless in itself, and no quality but only quantity is ascribed to it. The world is completely objective or theoretical in the Aristotelian sense of the word so that it has nothing to do with human practice and value; it lacks purpose, for everything should be determined by the initial conditions in the past, and though it was created by God, the existence of human beings is accidental. What I said in the above does not belong to Newton himself entirely, but from his philosophy one could draw these conclusions, unless it is supplemented by certain metaphysics which have the power to endow sense, value, and purpose. "Man, as *per se* soul or mind, is in nature by reason of the soul's connection with the body, but man is not of nature, with the body, i.e., man is not part of material nature."[32] This peculiarity has been unnoticed perhaps due to the great success of the Newtonian philosophy, and it has often been called a great synthesis. I readily admit it was a synthesis but not without some reservation: it was new, and contains many elements but, nevertheless, it was a unified system comparable to that of the Euclidean geometry.

And yet, I am inclined to say it has elements of syncretism which, we find, had not been uncommon in the history of Western philosophy and theology before Newton. The history of physics provides abundant evidence that the great synthesis is just a matter of appearance. I maintain that its greatness was in its potentiality for so many ramifications in the subsequent eras; thermodynamics, even with its statistical formulation, could not be subsumed under the Newtonian principles. Fluid mechanics and theories of metals would not constitute parts of one single system of the Newtonian mechanics; electromagnetism is a sort of an annex to it. The system of physics is a compound construction, which contains many elements, but nevertheless without the Newtonian philosophy of nature the great system of physics, though heterogeneous as it is, would never have existed.

Apparently Newton was not a metaphysician, and we should not expect to find or fabricate any coherent metaphysics which might be contained in his philosophy of nature. He was a religious person, and being a sort of Unitarian, he denounced at least implicitly traditional doctrines of the Anglican and Roman Catholic church. To him his cosmology and faith were sufficient to dispense with metaphysics. But when the Roman Catholic church canonized St. Thomas Aquinas and called him *doctor angelicus*, metaphysics was officially acknowledged as *ancilla theologiae*, i.e., indispensable learning, for the Catholic faith. So such philosophy as Newton's would not be conceived in the minds of those faithful to the doctrines of the Catholic church. Nevertheless, Newton admitted the constant, perpetual presence of the providence of God whose existence thus could be known through the philosophy of nature. In this regard Newton could be said to have inherited the Christian tradition ascribed to St. Augustine's "Book of Nature."

After physics emerged out of the Newtonian philosophy of nature, its basic concepts have undergone many changes in the last two hundred years. Nevertheless, its fundamental way of seeing the world has remained unaltered, and as a consequence this view has had great impacts on other fields of intellectual inquiries; therefore, the inherent pseudo-metaphysics strengthened and broadened the scope of the view immensely. In spite of the changes and modifications introduced into its basic concepts, such as mass and spatio-temporal framework, it continued to retain its most fundamental peculiarities: being mathematical, the category of quality has no place in physics. Second, it has been theoretical, that is, it is always a system in which all the results of observations must be deduced from the fundamental principles, though it happened that new principles were added and the scope of old principles was restricted, and the explanatory model of the *Principia*, i.e., by means of certain substrata, is still used. Third, it has always been thoroughly objective, and as a consequence, human existence could not play roles in an essential way in the theoretical system. Fourth, certain entities have been introduced to be immutable substrata in the processes concerned. Thus mathematically, the notions of invariance and conservation have come to play vital roles in the processes of theory formation. I contend that the permeation and domination of basic views of physics are the fundamental characteristics of modern science, and I maintain that the root of the modern scientific crisis is here.

Physics and Natural History

Probably the term "natural history" came to be commonly used in medieval Europe through the influence of Pliny the Elder's *Naturalis Historia*, for this encyclopedic work had been the greatest source of knowledge and one of the earliest classical works known in the medieval West until the learning transmitted by Arabian civilization was introduced in the twelfth century.

Even in the European tradition, natural history has had an entirely different path from the development process of physics. It consists of accumulation of knowledge of things which exist by their nature. It served as a bridge through which man could communicate with those things. In the Western tradition natural history has been regarded as a branch of science, and contemporary ecology, ethology, morphology, etc. have been taken as a kind of its ramifications. Clearly the world conceived by natural history is not senseless, valueless, nor purposeless, for things are taken in their entirety, and human presence is essential in that Nature; birth, growth, and death are not necessarily limited to living things. Nevertheless, in the West even natural history could not be exempted from the Greek tradition nor from physics and was tinted with elements of objectivism.

But when the Christian faith prevailed, the great universe was viewed with awe, and one felt the hand of God in everything therein. Pascal remarked in his *Pensées*, "The eternal silence of the universe makes me afraid." Pascal was by no means exceptional. In a Benedictine monastery, there was no conflict between studying and praying; both were acts of faith and devotion. The Romantic reaction of Wordsworth, as well as the Transcendentalism of Emerson, may be regarded as the remnants of the past era. "...*The narrow and efficient scheme of scientific concepts*...was the product of a mentality which found the Augustinian theology extremely congenial. Calvinism and Jansenism exhibited man as helpless to co-operate with Irresistible Grace: the contemporary scheme of science exhibited man as helpless to co-operate with the irresistible mechanism of nature."[33] The *narrowness* means lack of metaphysics and spirituality, and it is very paradoxical that this situation resulted from Neoplatonic rationalism and the doctrines of extreme piety and total submission to God's Will.

In the above I used "natural history" in the broadest sense of the word, and it is my contention that it consists of accumulation of our daily dealings with the natural world, and our comprehension of the natural world constitutes the natural history, which contains man and his experience in an essential way. Experience is not mere perception, but more human life itself, which does not contain even the distinction between subject and object, for it is a theoretical entity which was introduced in the process of theorization.

If natural history is understood this way, then a particular type of natural history, and also metaphysics and spirituality, will be found in every human culture, for as far as human beings are intellectual, it inevitably contains such elements as how to live in it and with it, and how to live together: thus human experiences are never deprived of sense, value, and purpose.

We have seen that the restoration of natural history is vital in avoiding the catastrophe of scientific crisis. But now the influence of science and technology permeates almost every culture, and their confrontation with the traditional metaphysics and spirituality seems unavoidable. As has been witnessed in Japan, any culture other than the West would be more vulnerable in a scientific crisis than the West itself, for science and technology emerged out of the Western tradition and the tie which connects the former with the latter is not entirely lost, while in other cultures such ties are not present at all. When Japan started to accept Western civilization some one hundred years ago, "Japanese mind, Western ingenuity" (*wagon yohsai*, in Japanese), was a very popular slogan but contrary to the expectation, so much of traditional culture has been lost, or mixed up with the Western elements in the past hundred years, and now most Japanese do not know which is which.

The concept of Nature may illustrate the point. The term "nature" was translated into Japanese perhaps in the 1880s or very early part of the Meiji period.[34] The translation was "*shizen.*" In translating "nature," Chinese characters which had been used by the Japanese were adopted, but with different pronunciations and completely different connotations since the 7th century or so. The Japanese learned these Chinese characters from Taoism literature (although Japanese learned Chinese philosophy mainly through Confucian literature) and it had been pronounced as "*jinen*" until the translation dispelled the traditional meanings; but it had been pronounced also as "*shizen*" even before it came to be used as a translation of "nature," but with a different connotation. Apparently the translators understood the meaning of nature coincides with that of "*jinen.*" Clearly they did not conceive Nature as something objective. Though the traditional meanings of "*jinen*" are quite diversified, most Japanese intellectuals of the time knew those diverse meanings quite well, for they were quite familiar with Chinese classics, including those of Buddhism, and numerous Japanese interpretations of this literature, and also an ancient conception which was also represented by the same Chinese characters. But the Japanese pronunciation of the term in the last meaning was *"onozukara"* which meant *by itself* or *of itself*, and this is the most basic meaning of the Japanese conception of nature. This word can be found in the oldest Japanese literature where the influence of Chinese philosophy was almost negligible but had some minor elements of Taoism.[35] The concept might be traced back at least to the fifth century, and associated with ancient Shintoism.[36]

This conception represents the attitude of ancient Japanese toward nature: it contained the conception of a whole in an essential way, where the separation of man and nature did not exist; one should not take it for a form of animism (though the animistic interpretation is always possible where any close association between nature and man exists); it is the conception of nature that everything grows of itself, and so does man, and thus to be *"onozukara"* was the norm and aim of human life, which includes everything man does and creates, that is, the whole culture. Naturally it had very significant influence on the interpretations of Chinese classics and Buddhism which came to be introduced into Japan in later periods, and the abundant evidence found in the Japanese classical literature shows the vastness and depth of influence. The conception provided the foundation for such original authors as Motoori Norinaga, Andoh Shoeki, and Ishida Baigan, later in the Edo period.

On the other hand, *"onozukara"* is very close to the Greek conception *physis*, which also has the connotation of 'of itself' and 'by itself,' and like *"onozukara,"* was always used as an adjective or an adverb. But *"onozukara"* does not imply the opposition between *physis* and *nomos*; since the notion of transcendental God was absent in Japanese tradition, naturally it did not contain the connotation of object, and one must note that it was an adjective or adverb which modifies some sort of *becoming*, and the concept of substance was entirely absent in Japanese philosophy of nature or metaphysics from which the world of immutable mass and empty space was totally alien.

Since every *natural* process was thought to occur naturally or "*onozukara*," it had somewhat a status of common and unifying principle. There is a striking similarity between Whitehead's and the ancient Japanese conception of nature, though naive and totally unsophisticated it was. There is no distinction between *techne* and *physis* either. "*Onozukara*" was an ideal that Japanese tried to achieve in arts, not only in fine arts but such arts as architecture, *Nō*-play, tea ceremony, and flower arrangement. We could find abundant evidence of its essential influence in the formation of the Japanese mind; in philosophy, in religion, in ethical and aesthetic thinking.

Unfortunately, there is not space to discuss the concept further. Last, but not least, I maintain that most contemporary Japanese do not know what "*jinen*" and "*onozukara*" used to mean and that only their remnants remain in Japanese thought, even among the most sophisticated circles. Similar situations exist with respect to other numerous conceptions: in the above I have touched upon the notion of religion in contemporary Japanese thought. I maintain that this kind of situation, which is perhaps unparalleled in other civilizations, makes it more difficult for Japanese to comprehend the meaning of the pressing but puzzling plight brought about by the scientific crisis, for they have not acquired the Western tradition in the real sense of the word, with its depth and scope. Thus the problem of East-West perspective is, I believe, a really serious issue Japanese have to cope with in the age of science and technology.

Notes

1. Watson, 1987, 17.
2. Attempts to integrate the hypotheses of this kind into the theories often, if not always, lead to contradictory conclusions, as is best exemplified by the quantum theory of measurement. See Nagasaka, 1983.
3. Whitehead, 1950, 25ff.
4. *Ibid.*, 25. Italics are mine.
5. This view coincides with that Husserl advocated in Husserl, 1954.
6. The rationality of scientific theories has been questioned, and criticized. See for example Kuhn, 1970 and Feyerabend, 1975.
7. Husserl, 1954, Chapter I.
8. *Ibid.*, 3. The translation is mine.
9. Butterfield, 1962.
10. Whitehead, 1950, especially Chapter I.
11. Concerning the issue and its relation with scientific thought, see for example Dijsterhuis, 1961, 160ff.
12. Nature is a translation of "physis," which was used only as adjective or adverb, but it has another meaning as the objective world. This dual meaning played an important role in the development of European thought.
13. See for example Randall, 1940.
14. Sarton, 1960, 287.
15. N.R. Hanson propounded an assertion that all observed data are theory laden (Hanson, 1958). If we see a shining object in certain directions, in order that we may say it is a star, it is necessary that the sameness of the shining object through time must have been established. But the sameness of the object is not enough for our seeing to constitute data of astronomy: many presuppositions and theories must have been established so that our observations may have certain meanings.
16. Cohen and Drabkin, 1958, 90.
17. See for example Burtt, 1932, 40ff.
18. Burtt, 1932, 44.
19. Koyré, 1965, 197.
20. *Ibid.*, 196.
21. Koyré, 1957.
22. Burtt, 1932, 64.
23. *Ibid.*, 66.
24. See for example Koyré, 1943.
25. See for example McMullin, 1967, 15.
26. See for example Plato, *Laws*, 889B; Aristotle, *Physics*, 192b ff.
27. Aristotle, *Physics*, 251a, 9f.
28. Newton, *Principia*, Definition I.

29. See Koyré, 1965, 9f.
30. Hall & Hall, 1962, 360. This passage is found in the MS. Add. 3965, a draft of the Scholium Generale of the *Principia*, though it is omitted in the published edition.
31. Leclerc, 1984, 20.
32. *Ibid.*, 5.
33. Whitehead, 1950, 10, 106.
34. Yanagibu, 1977, especially Chapters 1, 2, 3.
35. See for example Fukunaga, 1987.
36. Shintoism cannot adequately be classified as a *religion*. The latter concept had never existed in Japanese tradition until it was translated as *"shuhkyoh,"* which had a meaning somewhat similar to religious dogmas in English. However, now the *"shuhkyoh"* is a well-established word among Japanese, but the word involves inevitable ambiguities and vagueness, and this situation, I believe, has given rise to considerable confusion when religious matters are discussed. In the Christian tradition the term "religion" designated Christianity, and when this is used as a categorical term, it seems that it still retains the Christian element quite significantly; and I maintain that this situation makes understanding the Japanese tradition considerably difficult not only for non-Japanese, but for Japanese as well.

References

Burtt, E.A. *The Metaphysical Foundations of Modern Physical Science.* London: Routledge and Kegan Paul Limited, 1932.

Butterfield, H. *The Origins of Modern Science.* London: G. Bell and Sons Ltd., 1968.

Cohen, M.R. and Drabkin, I.E. *A Source Book in Greek Science.* Cambridge, MA: Harvard University Press, 1958.

Dijksterhuis, E.J. *The Mechanization of the World Picture.* Oxford: The Clarendon Press, 1961.

Feyerabend, P.K. *Against Method.* London: New Left Books, 1975.

Fukunaga, K. *Taoism and the Ancient Japan.* Kyoto: Jinmon Shoin, 1987. (In Japanese)

Hall, A.R. & Hall, M.B. *Unpublished Scientific Papers of Isaac Newton.* Cambridge: The University Press, 1962.

Hanson, N.R. *Patterns of Discovery.* Cambridge, MA: Harvard University Press, 1958.

Husserl, E. *Die Krisis der Europäischen Wissenschaften und die Transzendentale Phänomenologie*. Haag: Martinus Nijhoff, 1954.

Koyré, A. "Galilei and Platon." *Journal of History of Ideas* 4, No. 4 (1943).

From Closed World to the Infinite Universe. Baltimore: The John Hopkins Press, 1957.

Newtonian Studies. Chicago: The Chicago University Press, 1965.

Kuhn, T.S. *The Structure of Scientific Revolutions*. Chicago: The Chicago University Press, 1970.

Leclerc, I. *Whitehead's Philosophy between Rationalism and Empiricism*. Leuven: Center for Metaphysics and Philosophy of God, Institute of Philosophy, 1984.

McMullin, E. "Introduction." *Galileo, Man of Science*. E. McMullin ed. New York: Basic Books, Inc., 1967.

Nagasaka, F.G. "Quantum Theory of Measurement: A Non-quantum Mechanical Approach." *Physical Sciences and History of Physics*, R.S. Cohen & M.W. Wartofsky eds. Dordrecht: D. Reidel Publishing Co., 1983.

Randall, J.H. "Scientific Method in the Paduan School." *Journal of History of Ideas*, 1, No. 2 (1940).

Sarton, G. *A History of Science, Ancient Science through the Golden Age of Greece*, Vol. 1. Cambridge, MA: Harvard University Press, 1960.

Watson, J.D. "From the Revolution in Biology to the New Era of Bio-science." *Newton*, A Special Issue, "Biotechnology" (1987): 8. (In Japanese)

Whitehead, A.N. *Science and the Modern World, Lowell Lectures 1925*. New York: The MacMillan Co., 1950.

Yanagibu, A. *Translation*. Tokyo: Heibonsha, 1977, (in Japanese, *Honyaku no Shisoh*).

PART FOUR:

SCIENCE AND SPIRITUALITY

TEN

The HOLY NOTHING Versus The QUINCUNX Of KNOWLEDGE

IS THERE A RECONCILIATION?

Tor Ragnar Gerholm

It has been argued that "we need a wisdom that transcends science if we are to have a full view of nature" and that this wisdom may come from Eastern philosophies. It is also said that the mystical experience may help to restore the harmony between man and nature by providing supplementary modes of human knowledge. Moreover, it is suggested that the findings of modern physics "is internally consistent and in perfect harmony with the views of Eastern mysticism." The purpose of this paper is to examine the validity of these claims.

The problem is, says Seyyed Hossein Nasr in *The Encounter of Man and Nature*, that "the domain of nature has become a 'thing' devoid of meaning, and at the same time the void created by the disappearance of this vital aspect of human existence continues to live within the souls of men and to manifest itself in many ways, sometimes violently and desperately."[1]

The reason is the rise of modern science, says Nasr:

> In order for the modern sciences of nature to come into being, the substance of the cosmos had first to be emptied of its sacred character and become profane. The world view of modern science, especially as propagated through its vulgarization, itself contributed to this secularization of nature and of natural substances. The symbols in nature became facts, entities in themselves that are totally divorced from other orders of reality. The cosmos which had been transparent thus became opaque and spiritually meaningless—at least to those who were totally immersed in the scientific view of nature—even if individual scientists believed otherwise. The traditional sciences such as alchemy, which can be compared to the celebration of a cosmic mass, became reduced to a chemistry in which the substances had lost all their sacramental character. In the process, the sciences of nature lost their symbolic intelligibility, a fact that is most directly responsible for the crisis which the modern scientific world view and its applications have brought about.[2]

Many agree. "What must be immediately apparent is that physical science has abstracted certain measurable quantities from an altogether richer reality, and has concerned itself with these, and these alone, to the exclusion of everything else which is of interest."[3] "We need a wisdom that transcends science if we are to have a full view of nature."[4]

Today, it is often suggested that this wanted wisdom may come from Eastern philosophies and that mystical experience may help to restore the harmony between man and nature by providing supplementary modes of human knowledge.

Gary Zukav, for example, claims in his highly praised book *The Dancing Wu Li Masters*[5] that "we are approaching the end of science" which is supposed to mean "the coming of Western civilization, in its own time and in its own way, into higher dimensions of human experience." According to Zukav[6] "the philosophy of physics is becoming indistinguishable from the philosophy of Buddhism, which is the philosophy of enlightenment."

And indeed physicist Fritjof Capra writes in *The Tao of Modern Physics*—a bestseller—"that the principle theories and models of modern physics lead to a view of the world which is internally consistent and in perfect harmony with the views of Eastern mysticism."[7]

Another contemporary physicist, David Bohm, says in *Wholeness and the Implicate Order* that:

> It is clear that the different ways the two societies have developed fit in with their different attitudes to measure. Thus, in the West, society has mainly emphasized the development of science and technology (dependent on measure) while in the East, the main emphasis has gone to religion and philosophy (which are directed ultimately toward the immeasurable).
>
> If one considers this question carefully, one can see that in a certain sense the East was right to see the immeasurable as the primary reality. For, as has already been indicated, measure is an insight created by man. A reality that is beyond man and prior to him cannot depend on such insight. Indeed, the attempt to suppose that measure exists prior to man and independently of him leads, as has been seen, to the 'objectification' of man's insight, so that it becomes rigidified and unable to change, eventually bringing about fragmentation and general confusion in the way described in this chapter.
>
> One may speculate that perhaps in ancient times, the men who were wise enough to see that the immeasurable is the primary reality were also wise enough to see that measure is insight into a secondary and dependent but nonetheless necessary aspect of reality. Thus they may have agreed with the Greeks that insight into measure is capable of helping to bring about order and harmony in our lives, while at the same time, seeing perhaps more deeply, that it cannot be what is most fundamental in this regard.[8]

Referring to Bohm's quest for a new physics, Zukav suggests that it seems to require "new instruments of thought." But these may already be in existence within the "sophisticated psychologies...we commonly call Eastern religions."[9] "It is ironic," Zukav continues, "that while Bohm's theories are received with some skepticism by most professional physicists, they would find an immediately sympathetic reception among the thousands of people in our own culture who have turned their backs on science in their own quest for the ultimate nature of reality."

The *perennial philosophy* represents, according to Aldous

Huxley—a modern mystic—a great interconfessional mystical tradition. In Seyyed Hossein Nasr the perennial philosophy has found an eloquent spokesman. The central thesis of his book *The Encounter of Man and Nature* is summarized as follows:

> In as much as the loss of metaphysical knowledge is responsible for the loss of harmony between man and nature and of the role of the sciences of nature in the total scheme of knowledge, and by the fact that this knowledge has been nearly forgotten in the West while it has continued to survive in the traditions of the East, it is to these Oriental traditions that one must turn in order to rediscover the metaphysical significance of nature and to revive the metaphysical tradition within Christianity. If the East is learning by impulsion and necessity the Western techniques of domination over nature, it is from Oriental metaphysics that one must learn how to prevent this domination from becoming sheer self-annihilation.[10]

The purpose of this paper is to examine the validity of these claims. The analysis proceeds as follows:

1. Some aspects of the development in modern physics are briefly reviewed with a particular attention to the "Copenhagen interpretation" of quantum mechanics. It is argued that it has become necessary to reconsider some of the currently held notions about the nature of physical knowledge.

2. An attempt is made to define the mystical experience. It is argued that there is no doubt such an experience exists but that the content of the experience is ineffable.

3. Some of the similarities and differences between mysticism and science are reviewed with particular reference to the relation between reality and language, and finally,

4. Some conclusions of the preceding analysis are presented.

The Meaning of Experience in Science

Something philosophically significant *has* happened in modern science. (In this paper the word "science" is used as a synonym for physical science or simply physics. Large and important areas in the social, human and even natural sciences have deliberately been excluded in order to focus the interest on what I consider to be the essential points.) We are currently faced with "a very radical revision of the notion of what a physical theory is supposed to mean, a revision that in turn follows from the fundamental role Bohr assigns to the indivisibility of the quantum."[11]

When science is conceived of as a quest for truth, this is generally understood in a realistic sense. Science can somehow provide true knowledge of autonomously existing objects. Whether these objects of knowledge are material or immaterial is of secondary importance. Realism comes in different ways: perceptual (materialism) and conceptual (idealism). Modern science gallantly embraces them both with equal enthusiasm.

Consider, for instance, Newtonian mechanics generally taken to be the epitome of the materialistic view of the world. Yet, in the very beginning of *Principia* Newton defines absolute space and absolute time: "Absolute space, in its own nature, without regard to anything external, remains always similar and immovable," and "Absolute, true, and mathematical time, of itself, and from its own nature, flows equably without regard to anything external."

Obviously these two concepts of autonomous existence are of an immaterial nature and for precisely this reason they have no sensuous qualities whatsoever. They cannot be experienced, but they do make experience possible. Moreover, space logically precedes matter. We can conceive of space void of all material content but we cannot conceive of matter without having some space to contain it. In the same manner time precedes motion, since we can conceive of time without material motion but not the other way round. It is time that makes motion in space with time possible.

Matter is not the point, what matters is the autonomy of existence.

The other important point about science is its empiricism. In science sensate experience, and sensate experience only, is accepted as a source of knowledge. In the scientific community observation, preferably, but not always, under controlled experimental conditions is universally regarded as the ultimate arbiter in matters of scientific dispute.

The famous paper by Einstein, Podolsky, and Rosen (EPR) opened the debate on the completeness of quantum mechanics. At the very first page Einstein and his co-authors state:

The correctness of the theory is judged by the degree of agreement between the conclusions of the theory and human experience. This experience, which alone enables us to make inferences about reality, in physics takes the form of experiment and measurement.[12]

Bohr could not be in more complete agreement. In his reply he writes, also on the very first page:

The extent to which an unambiguous meaning can be attributed to such an expression as "physical reality" cannot of course be deduced from *a priori* philosophical conceptions, but—as the authors of the article cited (i.e. EPR, TRG's remark) themselves emphasize—must be founded on a direct appeal to experiments and measurements.[13]

The two points just mentioned imply that science rests on a very peculiar foundation of metaphysics. This foundation is a combination of ontologic realism and epistemic empiricism. It is generally known as *scientific realism*.

Several objections have been raised. It has been argued, for instance, that concepts which lack all sensuous qualities such as absolute space, absolute time, forces, fields, and elementary particles cannot qualify as autonomous objects of existence. Concepts of this nature merely serve as "constructs" simplifying our mapping of external reality like the geographers' latitudes and meridians. Since positivistic attempts to rid science of all nonobservables have miserably failed, the claim of scientific realism to provide true, theory independent, knowledge of an autonomous existence has been questioned.

There is, however, a much more fundamental, albeit subtle, objection. It may be argued that realism and empiricism cannot be simultaneously held. In other words, empirical observations may turn out to be incompatible with predictions based on realism! That this, in effect, is an unavoidable consequence of quantum mechanics was first pointed out by Einstein, Podolsky, and Rosen in the paper cited above, although the authors—as it turned out erroneously—concluded that their observation indicated a major defect in the quantum mechanical description of the physical reality.

Quantum mechanics appears to predict that under certain circumstances measurements performed in one "local reality"

(S1 say) instantaneously affects the situation in another "local reality" (S2) completely causally isolated from the first one. (With the theory of relativity the Newtonian concept of absolute time was abolished. The notion of an instantaneous, universal and omnipresent *now* could no longer be held. And since this is a *sine qua non* for all forms of perceptual realism the very idea of realism was seriously threatened. It found, however, a humble retreat: *local realism* which is the expression used here.)

According to the theory of relativity, cause and effect cannot couple faster than with the speed of light. Therefore anything causally connected with an occurrence at a given location must be present within a sphere centered at the point of the observed effect and with a radius which is equal to the velocity of light multiplied with the time lapsed between the cause and the effect. This sphere is the "local reality." Commenting on this Einstein concluded:

> One can escape from this conclusion (that quantum theory is incomplete) only by either assuming that the measurement of S1 (telepathically) changes the real situation of S2 or by denying independent real situations as such to things which are spatially separated from each other. Both alternatives appear to me entirely unacceptable.[14]

Bohr undauntedly responded that it makes no sense to speak about observables prior to observation.

For half a century the physicists remained in the fortunate position of being able to combine a pragmatic use of quantum mechanics with a realistic ontology.

But the situation became alarming when it was shown that the predictions obtained from local realism sometimes are different from those given by quantum mechanics. The experimental results now obtained from very careful studies[15] are incompatible with local realism. But the agreement with quantum mechanics is perfect!

Unless one is willing to accept some mysterious "spooky" action at a distance, there seems to be no way out, but to abandon realism altogether. The spook must be expected not only to act instantaneously, and in some unknown fashion, but it must, as the experiments have shown, also be thought of as endowed with precognition.

But according to what has become known as the Copenhagen interpretation of quantum mechanics the answer to the question: "with what does quantum mechanics actually deal?" is simply:

> It deals not with the properties of micro-objects as such but, rather, with nothing more than the relationships among the observable large-scale phenomena. The phenomena are, however, considered as indivisible wholes, which it would be wrong to analyze, even abstractly and conceptually, as made up approximately of different parts, consisting of various kinds of micro-objects. The role of the theory is then regarded as merely the calculation of the probability distributions for the various possible types of phenomena.[16]

Or to use Heisenberg's famous remark: "the mathematical formulae no longer portray nature, but rather our knowledge of nature."[17]

In conclusion we note that both Einstein and Bohr, and all other contemporary physicists with them, have accepted the experimental results as decisive. Neither Einstein nor Bohr were willing to accept instantaneous—"spooky"—action at a distance. Therefore there is no validity in the often heard claim that "the Einstein-Podolsky-Rosen effect indicates that information can be communicated at *superluminal* (faster than light) speeds contrary to the accepted ideas of physicists"[18] offering a possible scientific explanation for telepathy etc.

There is nothing mysterious about quantum mechanics unless we insist on retaining the weird notion that objects of our knowledge exist by themselves and by their own nature independent of, and as it were, prior to our knowledge of them. David Bohm says:

> The same concept (e.g., position and momentum) appear in both classical and quantum theories. In both theories, all concepts obtain their experimental content in essentially the same way, i.e., by their being related to a specific experimental set-up involving observable large-scale phenomena. The only difference between classical and quantum theories is that they involve the use of different kinds of laws to relate the concepts....
>
> As long as we restrict ourselves to computing the probabilities of pairs of events in this way, we will not obtain any paradoxes similar

to that described above. In such a computation the wave function should be regarded as just a mathematical symbol, which will help us to calculate the right relationships between classical events, provided that it is manipulated in accordance with a certain technique, but which has no other significance whatsoever.[19]

The Mystical Experience

Etymologically *mysticism* is supposed to come from an ancient Greek verb *myein*, which had two different but related meanings: to close the eyes and to close the mouth. If this is the case the very word mysticism comprises many of the staggering difficulties encountered when one tries to understand its true nature.

Is there a mystical experience? Is there *a* mystical experience rather than many different? How is it experienced? What (if anything) is actually experienced? Is it a religious experience? Is it typically Eastern?

It is sometimes said that the mystical experience (if it exists) can be explained in terms of neurophysiology. It has been suggested, for instance, that the mystic uses only the right half of his brain during the experience. Such "explanations" are entirely beside the point. There is no doubt a neurophysiological basis for *any* experience. The fact that an experience can be accounted for neurophysically has nothing to do with the fact that *something* has indeed been experienced.

Since "religion" has come to denote almost anything that seems supernatural or held to be of supreme importance it is no wonder that the mystical experience is generally accepted to be of "religious" nature. Yet there are among the mystics sufficiently many non-confessionals to suggest that the mystical experience is not necessarily a religious experience at least not if "religion" is to be understood in the conventional sense as a specific system of belief. However the experience is more likely to be accepted and acknowledged by religious people than by non-believers, who presumably are more likely to explain away what they have experienced or at least to keep silent about it, lest they should be considered—and perhaps even consider themselves—as having been temporarily in a state of mental aberration.

Nor is the mystical experience necessarily Eastern. There are many great mystics in the Western tradition, including several of our most outstanding scientists, but then not in their scientific capacity.

In trying to understand the nature of the mystical experience we are faced with a problem, the nature of which is perhaps most easily explained by a comparison with what was said about empiricism in the previous section. The point about empirical observation and experimental studies is not the alleged certainty of knowledge about an external "real" world thus derived. The point is that the experiment provides us with a means for checking the *communicability* of the words and sentences used in the scientific language.[20] By "experimental verification" we do not prove our results to be "true," but we do prove that they can be communicated, i.e. understood and repeated. Such—and only such—words and sentences are accepted as factual by the scientific community.

For obvious reasons, this method cannot be applied to the cognitive content of the mystical experience. Its intersubjectivity—or communicability—must be secured in some other way if the mystical knowledge is to be accepted on the same footing as what is being derived by conventional scientific means. Since we are left with nothing but the words and sentences used by the mystics the measure of communicability must be wrought out of the language itself.

This is a task which seems to present insurmountable difficulties. Not only because words are used in many different ways: literally, instructively, symbolically, evocatively, expressively, and inspirationally,[21] but also because these words and sentences have to be understood and interpreted. This requires a thorough knowledge of the language in which the mystic has expressed himself. In addition the hermeneutic means available for the interpretation of texts must be applied with particular skill and care. These requirements exclude most of the mystical texts available from interpretation be it for linguistic reasons, lack of authenticity, incompleteness, or absence of circumstantial knowledge.

Yet, in spite of the semantic difficulties mentioned, it seems obvious from the evidence at hand that people have had mystical experiences. There is a vast literature on the subject. Testimonies appear in quite different cultural contexts during the span of thousands of years. The experience is not uncommon even in today's secularized Western world. Some of the mystics are famous men and women recognized for outstanding achievements in literature, the arts and sciences, or in political matters.

Sarvepalli Radhakrishnan (1880–1975) was born in Madras, India. Professor at Oxford University, ambassador and President of India (1962–1967), he has written extensively on Western philosophy and on Eastern religion. Radhakrishnan concludes that "mystical experience is a genuine part of human nature and it assumes the same general forms wherever it is developed."[22]

If this is taken for granted it is obvious that this "genuine part of human nature" is of a non-sensuous quality. Plotinus tells us to "cut away everything"[23] the psychological meaning of which he explains as follows:

> To separate first, the man from the body—yourself, that is, from your body; next to put aside that soul which moulded the body, and, very earnestly, the system of sense with desires and impulses and every such futility, all setting definitely to the mortal; what is left is the phase of the Soul which we have declared to be an image of the Divine Intellect....
>
> The true getting-up is not bodily but from the body.[24]

Similar expressions abound. St. Teresa of Jesus complained that she had suffered much from not having been able to understand that it is possible to see with something else than our bodily eyes. Eckhart made the same distinction between the inner eye of the soul turned towards the essence of being and our outer eyes beholding creation.

But *what* is experienced? Eckhart tells us about the vision:

> All that man has here externally in multiplicity is intrinsically One. Here all blades of grass, wood and stone, all things are One. This is the deepest depth...
>
> ...we are not wholly blessed, even though we are looking at divine truth; for while we are still looking at it, we are not in it. As long as

a man has an object under consideration, he is not one with it. Where there is nothing but One, nothing but One is to be seen. Therefore, no man can see God except he be blind, nor know him except through ignorance, nor understand him except through folly.[25]

This "Western" experience is obviously very similar to Hindu *samadhi* which according to Radhakrishnan[26] implies that we have sense of immediate contact with ultimate reality, of the unification of the different sides of our nature. It is a state of pure apprehension, in which the whole being is welded into one.

To conclude: people have had—and they still have—mystical experiences. There are reasons to believe that these experiences are of a similar nature. It may therefore be possible to identify a singular mystical experience ascribing to it certain characteristics. This is in fact a necessary although not a sufficient condition for being able to talk about the mystical experience as something "supplementary to scientific knowledge."

There have been many attempts to achieve precisely this, but the nature of the subject seems to call for a definition in *negative* terms. In a recent study a Swedish scholar, Christer Norrman, has suggested the following definition:

> mystical experience = an experience characterized by the following properties: lack of 1) sensory perception, 2) sense of space, 3) sense of time, 4) relationship between subject and object, 5) thoughts.[27]

Implicit in this definition is what seems to be the most important aspect of the mystical experience: *its ineffability*.

Why ineffable? Norrman[28] has identified nine different theories of the mystical experience. Only in one of them, that of Stace in his later period, is it held that the mystical experience is *not* ineffable, in spite of what the mystics themselves have said. According to Stace the mystic merely confuses ineffability with the paradoxical nature of his experience. Against this Norrman[29] and others[30] have, in my opinion convincingly, argued that there have been many able philosophers among the mystics from St. Augustine to Martin Buber. It is unlikely that they have had difficulties with the language without knowing it.

Moreover there are many mystics, who do not express themselves paradoxically, but who nevertheless speak of the ineffability of the experience.

What Norrman has called "conceptual ineffability" is particularly interesting from a scientific point of view. According to this theory, due to Paul Henle,[31] the ineffability is only apparent. The concepts required to express the experience have not yet been developed. (In science this situation is well known. Consider, for instance, the central motion of planets prior to the Newtonian theory or the studies of heat before the second law of thermodynamics.) Henle has explained his theory by an analogy, which in a slightly modified form may be presented as follows. Suppose we express *identity* with the algebraic expression $1 + 2 = 2 + 1$. In this terminology it is impossible to account for the existence of negative numbers since $1 + (-2) \neq 2 + (-1)$. Negative numbers are, as it were, "ineffable" simply because our conceptual framework is inadequate.

According to Henle's theory it is conceivably possible to overcome the present ineffability by developing new concepts for dealing with the mystical experience. Until this has been accomplished (if it ever will) ineffability seems to be an integral part of the experience itself. This is, indeed, what the mystics and their interpreters repeatedly assure us of. To give just a few examples:

Radhakrishnan writes about *Brahman*:

> It is not the object of thought or the result of production. It forms an absolute contrast to, and is fundamentally different from, things that are, as it is in its way nothingness. It can be expressed only negatively or analogically.[32]

Martin Buber has expressed it as follows:

> Sobald sie sprachen, sobald sie—wie es der Rede Vorspiel zu sein pflegt—zu sich sprachen, waren sie schon an der Kette, in den Grenzen; der Unbegrenzte spricht auch nicht zu sich, in sich, weil auch in ihm keine Grenzen sind; keine Vielheit, keine Zweiheit, kein Du im Ich mehr. Sobald sie reden, sind sie schon der Sprache verfallen, die allem gewachsen ist, nur nicht dem Grund des Erlebens, der Einheit. Sobald sie sagen, sagen sie schon das Andere.[33]

[Translation: Whenever you speak, wherever you—as is usually the case in speaking—formulate the words for yourself, you are already enchained, within boundaries; the unlimited never speaks to itself, within itself, just as there are no boundaries in it, no multiplicity, no twofold, no more you in me. Whenever you speak, you are already fallen in the language, overshadowing everything but the foundation of existence, the Unity. Whenever you say something, you have already said the other.]

In *Arrow in the Blue* Arthur Koestler writes:

In the following sections the contemplative trend will play a quantitatively smaller part than the active trend. This is unavoidable because the "oceanic experience" to a large extent eludes verbal communication, and attempts to convey it (unless one has the gift of poetic expression, which I have not) tend to fall flat or take a maudlin turn.[34]

According to Plotinus: "we can and do state what it is not, while we are silent as to what it is."[35]

Reality and Language

If the mystical experience is considered to be inherently ineffable, impossible to account for in any language, what then becomes of the words and sentences actually used by the mystics?

Words may not necessarily have a *descriptive* function. They can be used by the mystic *instructively* and *inspirationally* to guide and encourage the disciple on the way to the mystical experience. In a sense this resembles the scientific use of language. Scientists describe how to set up and perform an experiment in order to arrive at a certain observation. The ultimate conscious sense impression thus obtained cannot be accounted for in any more fundamental terms: be it the smell of sulphur in a test tube, the click of a counter in a laboratory of nuclear physics, or the hazy impression of light on an astronomer's retina watching the sky through a telescope.

We maintained above that "sensate experience and sensate experience only…is accepted…as the ultimate arbiter in matters of scientific dispute." But this statement needs some additional qualifications. It may well be argued that a click of a G M counter, as a sensous impression, is just as ineffable as is the *samadhi* experience or for that matter the taste of bacon. But there is a subtle difference between sensate experiences in general and the experience obtained through experimental investigations.

In introducing the experimental method Galileo is well aware that as sources of human knowledge the senses are obscure and ambiguous. Yet he argues:

> Whenever I conceive of any material or corporeal substance, I am necessarily constrained to conceive of that substance as bounded and as possessing this or that shape, as large or small in relationship to some other body as in this or that place during this or that time, as in motion or at rest, as in contact or not in contact with some other body, as being one, many or few—and by no stretch of imagination can I conceive of any corporeal body apart from these conditions.

> But I do not at all feel myself compelled to conceive of bodies as necessarily conjoined with such further conditions as being red or white, bitter or sweet, having sound or being mute, or possessing a pleasant or unpleasant fragrance. On the contrary, were they not escorted by our physical senses, perhaps neither reason nor understanding would ever, by themselves, arrive at such notions. I think, therefore, that these tastes, odors, colors, etc., so far as their objective existence is concerned, are nothing but mere names for something which resides exclusively in our sensitive body (corpo sensitivo), so that if the perceiving creatures were removed, all of these qualities would be annihilated and abolished from existence. But just because we have given special names to these qualities, different from the names we have given to the primary and real properties, we are tempted into believing that the former as really and truly exist as the latter.[36]

"I am necessarily constrained to conceive of...." This is a strange argument coming from an empiricist! But Galileo did not "conceive of" reality. He defined it.

First he made a distinction between what John Locke later called *primary* and *secondary* qualities. Primary qualities are those aspects of reality that can be measured by comparison with an external standard—a unit of measurement socially agreed upon. All other—secondary—qualities exist only subjectively in our perception. They have no place "out there" in the external world. Reality is in fact *defined* as the totality of primary qualities.

The origin of what has later been denounced as "reductionism," "materialism," and "scientific imperialism" is no doubt to be found right here in the conception of reality as the measurable aspects of existence and the measurable aspects only. David Bohm[8] was right when he referred to measure as "an insight created by man" and warned against the notion "that measure exists prior to man and independently of him" which is precisely the positions which we have called scientific realism. He has also correctly pointed[37] out that "the very word 'measure' has come to denote mainly a process of comparison of something with an external standard" and he continues:

> In a way, techniques of meditation can be looked on as measures (actions ordered by knowledge and reason) which are taken by man to try to reach the immeasurable, i.e., a state of mind in which he ceases to sense a separation between himself and the whole of reality. But clearly, there is a contradiction in such a notion, for the immeasurable is, if anything, just that which cannot be brought within limits determined by man's knowledge and reason.[38]

But Bohm missed the essential point. It is by reducing itself to the measurable aspects of experience that science makes them effable or communicable. The sensous experience of the click of a G M counter is indeed ineffable. But *the number of clicks per unit time* recorded under well defined experimental conditions can be communicated. Although the smell of sulphur cannot be accounted for in any more fundamental terms, its presence or absence in a given test tube can be decided *by comparison* with the smell of elemental sulphur; in other words, by comparison with an external standard—by "measurement."

This is how "objectivity" in science is achieved and this is also all it means. In science *measure* is always used to denote the extent, dimension, capacity etc. of anything or the determination of such quantities, i.e., measurement. If "measure" is understood to mean "a course of action," measures taken to achieve something, it takes on an entirely different meaning.

The superficial similarity between science and mysticism breaks up into a dichotomy.

The scientific language, i.e., the mathematical formula, does not "portray nature, but rather our knowledge of nature" (Heisenberg) whereas the mystical Reality cannot—by nature of its ineffability be expressed. In short: *The scientific language cannot account for Reality and the mystical Reality cannot be accounted for in any language*.

The relation between reality and language needs, however, some further clarification. Meaning in language can be understood in different ways. In the referential theory of language words are supposed to refer to something extra linguistic, something real. Connections between words in the language, and words used to establish such connections, are supposed to correspond to "things" and to connections between "things" in reality. The language "mirrors" the world. Words which do not refer to anything extra linguistic have no real meaning. They tell us nothing. Therefore a proper, precise, and prudent use of the scientific language provides nothing but an image of reality.

It is often taken for granted—not least by the scientists themselves—that this is precisely what science and the scientific language is supposed to do: provide us with a gradually improved, increasingly more comprehensive and basically true picture of the world as it really is. In other words: "the domain of nature becomes a 'thing' devoid of meaning" (Nasr[1]).

The referential theory obviously presupposes scientific realism. It is therefore not applicable to modern (physical) science. When "we assume that concepts correctly mirror the nature of reality, we draw conclusions about ontology from grammar."[39]

This must not be understood to mean that in science we are unable to deal with objects not yet discovered, or more correctly, with experience not yet encountered. It is indeed possible to make predictions in science. In fact much of the convincing power of scientific explanations stems from the "criterion of practice," from the fact that predictions have often proven to be remarkably correct.

The scientific language must be able to provide more than the totality of communicable human experiences and their interrelations. If we subscribe to the theory of use, rather than to the referential theory, we must prove it possible to make meaningful statements about items we have never experienced—and perhaps never will experience—such as Higgs' particles, Wheeler's wormholes or an inflationary universe. These words function in the scientific language because they are thought of in terms which imply the possibility of scientific observation, directly or indirectly.

Suppose somebody asks: "If the planet Neptune never had been discovered would it not nevertheless exist?" It seems strange to answer anything but: Yes!

But, it could be argued, by the same token Brahman, the One, or Einsof could be thought of as existing although none of them have been observed by the scientists (or ever will be).

In this case, however, the answer must be: No!

The point is not that Neptune has been "discovered" and Brahman not. The point is that Neptune was thought of as *discoverable* by scientific means whereas Brahman by its own nature forever dwells beyond scientific inquiry.

It may, however, be argued that Neptune did not exist before the Copernican revolution since there was no place for "invisible" planets in the geocentric system, just as there are no places for phlogiston and instantaneous action at a distance in today's chemistry and physics. Nobody knows what strange objects, whose nature we cannot even imagine, future physicists may claim are right here and now—at least if physicists continue to be of the realistic brand. But Brahman will not be one of these strange objects—this, at least, we can know for sure.

Just as we must not mystify physics we should not physicalize mysticism. They supplement each other, but in a much more profound way than suggested by Zukav, Capra, and others. Presumably this is what Rudyard Kipling—another mystic—meant by his famous words:

> Oh, East is East, and West is West, and never the twain shall meet,
> But there is neither East or West, Border, nor breed nor Birth,
> When two strong men stand face to face, though they come from
> the ends of the earth.

Conclusions

Richard Hubert Jones cites the *Upaniṣads*:

> ...where knowledge is of a dual nature (implying a subject which knows and an object which is known), there, indeed, one hears, sees, smells, tastes and also touches, the self knows everything. Where knowledge, being devoid of effect, cause or action, unspeakable, incomparable, indescribable, what is that? It is impossible to say.[40]

More explicitly St. Teresa of Jesus testifies: "the soul neither sees, hears nor understands, while she is united to God."[41] R.N. Smart, an authority on mysticism, has arrived at the conclusion that the ineffability is simply due to the fact that there is nothing to describe. According to Agehananda Bharati: "there is zero content of a cognitive sort in the experience."[42] But it must be stressed that this "zero content of cognitive sort" should not be understood in a negative sense. Koestler assures as that it is "meaningful though not in verbal terms."[43] Norrman expresses himself somewhat more cautiously:

> Even though there is no theory today that shows that it is possible to identify mystical experiences by a scientific method, there is a basis for developing such a theory in the future, at least as far as the non-content-related properties of the experience are concerned. It is, however, doubtful whether it is of interest to research to establish the non-content-related properties of the mystical experience without finding out what the mystic has actually experienced. At the moment the most interesting aspect of the study of mystical experiences, that is studies of the content of the mystical experiences, appears to be excluded from research.

In *The Logic of Scientific Discovery*, Karl Popper[44] points out that "the empirical basis of objective science has thus nothing 'absolute' about it. Science does not rest upon rock-bottom," and he quoted Hermann Weyl and Reininger:

> What is immediately experienced is subjective and absolute...; the objective world, on the other hand, which natural science seeks to precipitate in pure crystalline form...is relative....this pair of opposites, subjective-absolute and objective-relative seems to me to contain one of the most profound epistemological truths which can be gathered from the study of nature. Whoever wants the

absolute must get subjectivity—ego-centricity—into the bargain, and whoever longs for objectivity cannot avoid the problem of relativism. (Weyl)

Metaphysics as science is impossible...because although the absolute is indeed experienced, and for that reason can be intuitively felt, it yet refuses to be expressed in words. For "Spricht die Seele, so spricht, ach! schon die Seele nicht mehr." (If the soul *speaks* then alas it is no longer the *soul* that speaks.) (Reininger)

But as Sir Thomas Browne once wrote: "The quincunx of heaven runs low and 'tis time to close the five ports of knowledge." For the remaining twelfths we depend on the seven pillars of wisdom, beyond, above but hopefully also within empirical science.[45]

Acknowledgment

I have been much inspired by Christer Norrman's excellent analysis presented in his book *Mystical Experiences and Scientific Method*. This book has also served as a valuable guide to a literature which to a large extent has been unknown to me.

Notes

1. Seyyed Hossein Nasr, *The Encounter of Man and Nature* (George Allen and Unwin Ltd., 1968), 17.
2. *Ibid.*, 21.
3. G.D. Yarnold, *The Spiritual Crisis of the Scientific Age*, 28.
4. E.F. Caldin, *The Power and Limits of Science, A Philosophical Study*, 13.
5. Gary Zukav, (1979), *The Dancing Wu Li Masters* (Fontana Paperbacks, 1982), 331.
6. *Ibid.*
7. Fritjof Capra, (1976), *The Tao of Physics* (Bantam Books, 1977), 294.
8. David Bohm, *Wholeness and the Implicate Order* (Routledge and Kegan Paul, 1980), 23.
9. Zukav, *loc. cit.*, 326–7.
10. Capra, *loc. cit.*, 83.
11. Bohm, (1980), *loc. cit.*, 76.
12. A. Einstein, B. Podolsky, and N. Rosen, *Phys. Rev.* 47 (1935):777.
13. N. Bohr, *Phys. Rev.* 48 (1935): 696.
14. A. Einstein, "Autobiographical Notes," in Paul Schlipp (ed.), *Albert Einstein, Philosopher-Scientist* (New York: Harper and Row, Harper Torchbooks, 1949), 85.
15. A. Aspect, P. Grangier, and G. Roger, *Phys. Rev. Lett.* 49 (1982): 91. A. Aspect, J. Dalibard, and G. Roger, *Phys. Rev.* Lett. 49 (1982): 1804.
16. David Bohm, (1957), *Causality and Chance in Modern Physics* (London: Routledge and Kegan Paul, Harper Torchbook, 1961), 92.
17. Quoted in René Dubos, *The Dreams of Reason* (Columbia University Press, 1961), 102.
18. Zukav, *loc. cit.*, 303–4.
19. Bohm, (1980), *loc. cit.*, 75.
20. T.R. Gerholm, *Danish Yearbook of Philosophy* 14 (1977):103.
21. Christer Norrman, *Mystical Experiences and Scientific Method* (Stockholm: Almqvist and Wiksell, 1986), 43, 47.
22. S. Radhakrishnan, *Eastern Religions and Western Thought* (London, 1969), 116.
23. Plotinus, *The Enneads*, translated by Stephen Mackenna, Fowler ed. revised by B.S. Page. London 5.3.17; 5.3.9. 24.
24. Rudolf Otto, (1976) (1932), *Mysticism East and West. A Comparative Analysis of the Nature of Mysticism* (New York: MacMillan Publishing Co., Inc.), 80.
25. Raymond B. Blakney (ed.), *Meister Eckhart* (New York, Hagerstown, San Francisco, London: Harper and Row Publishers, 1941), 200.
26. Radhakrishnan, (1969), *loc. cit.*, 51.
27. Norrman, (1986), *loc. cit.*, 17.
28. *Ibid.*, 65.
29. *Ibid.*, 69.

30. Cf. R. Ravindra, Chapter 7, this volume. Norrman, (1986), *loc. cit.*, 69 for further references.
31. Paul Henle, *Mysticism and Semantics in Philosophy and Phenomenological Research* 9 (1949):414–22. Also printed in *Philosophy of Religion*, ed. S. Cahn (1970), 274–82.
32. Radhakrishnan, (1969), *loc. cit.*, 67.
33. Martin Buber, (1909), *Ekstatische Konfessionen* (Jena, Eugen Diedrich) 255–274.
34. Arthur Koestler, (1955, 1952) *Arrow in the Blue An Autobiography* (London and Glasgow: Collins Hamish Hamilton Ltd.), 99.
35. Plotinus, *The Enneads, loc. cit.*, 5.3.14.
36. Galilei Galileo, *Il Saggitore*, (1963), translated by A.C. Danto in *Introduction to Contemporary Civilization in the West*, 2nd ed, vol. 3 (New York: Columbia University Press, 1954), 719–24.
37. Bohm, (1980), *loc. cit.*, 22.
38. *Ibid.*, 24.
39. Norrman, (1986), *loc. cit.*, 99.
40. R.H. Jones, "A Philosophical Analysis of Mystical Utterances," in *Philosophy East and West* 29 (1979):255–274.
41. Cf. Norrman, (1986), *loc. cit.*, 80.
42. Agenanda Bharati, *The Light at the Center: Context and Pretext of Modern Mysticism* (Santa Barbara: Ross Erikson, 1976), 48.
43. Cf. Norrman, (1986), *loc. cit.*, 47.
44. Karl R. Popper, *The Logic of Scientific Discovery* (Hutchinson of London, 1959), 111.
45. The Roman unit of measure called *AS* was divided into 12 units called *uncine*. Each multiple had a different name. Quincunx was the Latin expression for five unicae or 5/12. By extension, as the number 12 stands for a complete whole, in the expression "Quincunx of Knowledge" five represents the human senses, our "five ports of empirical knowledge." The "remaining twelfths" represent "the seven pillars of wisdom."

TEN a

COMMENTS On GERHOLM'S PAPER

Ruth Tiffany Barnhouse

The poet W.H. Auden once said that for Europeans Nature was an animal to be tamed while for Americans it was a dragon to be slain. Modern science has certainly been the instrument by which we attempt either to tame or slay Nature. But those who think both approaches are flawed prefer to recognize that we ourselves are inseparable from Nature. Any attempt we make to stand outside and observe it is inevitably contaminated by anthropomorphic projections. To a certain extent the history of science is the history of our recognition of some of those projections, but I believe it is a serious error to suppose that it is either possible or desirable to get rid of them all. The ancient legend of the Tower of Babel casts some light on this difficulty, and it is not insignificant that the result of that human effort to usurp divine objectivity was the confusion of tongues, the proliferation of different languages and vocabularies, making holistic, uncomplicated communication impossible.

Professor Gerholm quotes Bohm to emphasize that measure does not exist prior to or independent of humankind, a specific insight for which I am especially grateful since I have always intuitively felt that the metric system was arrogant, and have much preferred terms like "foot" and others which acknowledge that we are part of the process, not outside of it.

The whole question of "autonomously existing objects" is fraught with difficulty. Do we mean relatively or absolutely autonomous, for instance? And even if there is any such thing, how can we know that our perception of such objects, whether indirect or direct, are not irrevocably conditioned by our own sensory-intellectual apparatus? For instance, [on p. 189] Prof. Gerholm says that Newton's concepts of autonomous existence "make experience possible...we can conceive of space void of all material content but we cannot conceive of matter without having some space to contain it." But is this not the consequence of our experience of our bodies? It is certainly true that we cannot imagine our bodies without intervening space separating us. The same holds true of the fact that "we can conceive of time without material motion, but not the other way around." But since modern biology has demonstrated that each animal body (including our own) is a clock, a clock which measures some aspect of time, how can we be confident that our generalizations, applying our own experience of time and motion to the universe at large are accurate? May they not importantly reflect "what we can conceive?" We heard Sir John Eccles discuss the "creation of the conscious self" which he further defined as the self which knows itself to be unique, not to be confused with some other self. This describes autonomous existence. How can we be sure we are not projecting this experience of ourselves onto the rest of the material universe?

I am not, of course, calling into question any actual observations. I am, however, questioning the categories by which they are interpreted, and also the categories which inform the imagination of those who devise the experiments. For example, [on p. 192] we read that "unless one is willing to accept some mysterious 'spooky' action at a distance, there seems to be no way out but to abandon realism altogether. The spook must be expected not only to act instantaneously, and in some unknown fashion, but it must...also be thought of as endowed with precognition." Further on he tells us that since Einstein and Bohr were unwilling to accept the "spook" there is no validity to the claim that the EPR effect offers a possible explanation for telepathy, etc. Unless I am seriously misunderstanding this passage, the interpretations of Einstein and Bohr are elevated to the status of divine revelation which precludes any other interpretations of the puzzling phenomena. Surely the term "spook" refers to that which is not only not understood, but for which no explanation can be imagined. But it is a pejorative term, one which suggests some aberration of the imagination rather than evidence of a new phenomenon which should be patiently attended until some method of better investigation or understanding presents itself.

Clearly our relation to Nature is fundamental to the entire discussion. This is bound up with the history of consciousness since that is integrated with our way of perceiving reality. In *Saving the Appearances: A Study in Idolatry* Owen Barfield considers this history in detail, beginning with the *participation mystique* described by anthropologists such as Lévy-Brühl. A "representation" or "appearance" is something which is perceived to be there. The particles of physics are that which contemporary science shows to be independently there, but that is not what we perceive. Barfield uses the term "unrepresented" to cover this category. A "collective representation" is that which is consensually validated by others. Thus our familiar world, our joint experience of what is going on in this room now, is a system of collective representations.

Barfield uses the term "figuration" to cover all in the representation which is not sensation. For instance, a person will have a certain sensation on the skin produced, let us say, by a lighted match. They may perceive this in various ways: if awake they will probably decide it is a burn, but if hypnotized to believe that an ice cube rather than a match is producing the sensation they will perceive it differently, and this different perception will alter the physiological response of the body to the stimulus. These variations in the subject's consciousness constitute the "figuration" and are independent of the stimulus/ sensation. Figuration thus is the process by which the mind combines and constructs sensations "into the recognizable and nameable objects we call 'things.'" [Barfield, p. 24] Thus figuration is not a process of thinking about things, but is a way in which variations in our consciousness influence our very perceptual process, and therefore the way in which we arrive at the "representation" or "appearance" which we take to be there. Thus introduction of this intermediate term, "figuration," may be crucial to discussions such as ours here.

Thinking about things Barfield calls "alpha-thinking." This treats representations as external, comparing them with each other. Most scientific and historical thinking, as well as many simpler types, is alpha-thinking. There is a third process which Barfield calls "beta-thinking" which is about the nature of collective representations as such, and about their relation to our own minds. In short, this is thinking about thinking. The distinctions between these three mental operations are theoretically clear, but in practice they affect one another reciprocally.

Barfield calls the participation described by Durkheim and Lévy-Brühl "original participation" and in this there is no alpha-thinking. There is, however, a far different figuration than ours, since the perceiver is symbiotic with the representation. Since thinking is not in terms of cause and effect, there is no consciousness of contradictions such as we have. Barfield considers the gradual changes in consciousness resulting from the rise of alpha-thinking and shows that the last traces of original participation did not disappear from Western consciousness until the scientific revolution.

The essence of that revolution was "a new theory of the nature of theory; namely, that if a hypothesis saves all the appearances, it is identical with truth." [Barfield, p. 51] For Plato, the lowest kind of knowledge was observation since the observed facts were not, as they are today, considered to be truth itself. The highest knowledge was derived from "the contemplation by pure intelligence of the divine ideas." [p. 46] In between came mathematics, and the term "saving the appearances." This meant the use of hypotheses to account for what was observed while retaining the fundamental principles arrived at by contemplating divine ideas. Having more than one hypothesis was not unacceptable, but today it makes many scientists nervous (as in wave vs. particle theories) since we no longer think like that.

Still, Barfield is right to see that it is eventually dehumanizing for us to see nature as a machine. I take this further, believing that our view of Nature is unconsciously anthropomorphic, and that therefore if we see Nature as a machine we are seeing ourselves likewise. Eventually this is suicidal. But a frightened retreat to original participation would not only not help, it would be impossible. Our task is not to get stuck in alpha-thinking, not to confuse facts with truth as we try to work our way through to what Barfield calls *final participation*. This will include a conscious reunion and collaboration with Nature, not the unconscious original symbiosis.

And here is where the question of mystical experience enters. The scientific method deals with parts, not only that, but they are repeatable parts, parts which we, imprisoned in our own finite sensory-intellectual apparatus are able to manipulate. This is, of course, not wrong—we learn much that is noble and useful in this way. What is wrong, however, is to suppose that the sum of these few parts constitutes Reality, and that we have then mastered that. Such an attitude is idolatrous. The Tower of Babel legend alludes to it. But so does the story of the children of Israel who could not wait for Moses to come down from the mountain, who could not stand uncertainty, ambiguity, paradox, who had no patience and insisted that Aaron fashion for them the Golden Calf out of materials which they themselves produced, and which they could discuss with certainty, and to which they need attribute no more mystery than that which could be comfortably tolerated. They need not accept anything truly "spooky."

Mystical experience deals with the whole, not with parts. The mystics have spent at least as long in the practice of strenuous spiritual disciplines before arriving at their experience as have any physicists in the course of acquiring their competence. But the fact that they deal with the Whole, not with parts, means that Professor Gerholm's final hope that all can be elucidated within empirical science—such a hope is entirely vain. He appears to believe that the content of the mystical experience ought to be subject to research, and quotes Norrman's view that would be the most interesting aspect to study. This is wrong, just as Masters & Johnson's "scientific" study of sexual orgasm was wrong, and for exactly the same reason. Neither the mystical nor the sexual experience is reducible to its parts without violating its very nature, and efforts to do so are at least ludicrous and often make serious mischief besides.

Some light can, however, be shed. The studies of modern

depth psychology, particularly the researches of Carl Jung, do offer some indication of what is involved in spiritual disciplines generally, and in the specifics of mystical experience. Jung describes in many contexts and many different vocabularies the reconciliation of opposites, the holding in tension in consciousness of terms which to ordinary ego-awareness seem paradoxical or contradictory. He considers many different manifestations emerging from the unconscious which demonstrate this process. Essential is the willingness to attend, to wait, to listen, to watch, to consider impartially and without prior judgments the images which arise spontaneously. After studying his psychology carefully it is possible to imagine that what the mystical experience consists of is an actual experience of the totality of Reality, not just of a part. This, of course, is why it cannot be verbally communicated in ordinary language. Ordinary language is designed to differentiate, to distinguish, to talk about this, not that, here, not there. Any attempt to list the pairs of opposites whose differences vanish in the Experience is felt to be incomplete, partial, perhaps even a blasphemous attempt at idolatrous reductionism.

It is not wrong for the scientific method to be in some sense reductionistic, provided that it is conscious of its limits. But to say that something is not real, or does not or cannot exist because "there is no place for it in today's chemistry and physics" is wrong. Many of us have direct experience of "instantaneous action at a distance," experience which is not less real because physicists declare it to be impossible. Some of us are no longer willing to be intimidated into keeping quiet about the larger realms of reality.

Nor is it necessary to go to psychology or to Eastern religion to find pointers toward the true nature of the experience. The Judeo-Christian tradition is full of spiritual masters and mistresses, who have expressed themselves in such a variety of ways as to provide guidance to persons of any temperament who are interested in starting on the Path.

ELEVEN

The DISTANCE BETWEEN The LABORATORY And The MONASTERY

SOME REFLECTIONS ON THE ROLE OF VALUES AND EMOTIONS IN SCIENCE

M.W. Padmasiri de Silva

There have been many attempts to compare the logic of scientific investigations with that of the religious quest. In fact, recent attempts have been invariably concerned with the idea that though the methodology of science and religion are different, they seem to converge on the same reality. It has been maintained that the very facts of science makes sense, only if we assume some sort of implicit unifying ground underlying this complex data.

Some of the interesting points of convergence which have emerged in this dialogue may be summarized: rejection of the subject-object duality in the context of knowledge, acceptance of the world and the mind as a great relational network, the limitations of language, grammar, and certain patterns of logic, the integration of apparent polarities, conflicts, and paradoxes to scientific thoughts and a new interdisciplinary spectrum where physics, neurology, biology, and mathematics cross cut into each other's boundary.

However, in this great dialogue between science and religion, an important issue has been glossed over; this is the relationship between types of knowledge and forms of life. It is a central ingredient in the religious quest, that certain styles of living and forms of life are intrinsically related to the generation of certain types of knowledge and the realization of certain insights have a tremendous impact on the orientation towards life.

Wittgenstein used the term "forms of life" to refer to the total context within which language works. It is a complex network of habits, attitudes, skills, and outlook within which language is interlocked. This metaphor may be extended to the strong organic framework within which forms of life and language work in the case of religion.

Affective and *conative* facets of our life are deeply wedded into our *cognitive orientations*, and this applies to the debasing aspects of our knowledge and lives as well as the more refined, valuable and intensive insights. Though a scientist's personal agenda, his devotion, concentration, honesty, etc., can count as important facets of his life and work, yet the practice of science has been embedded in the logical rift between the way of religion and science, which is hard to bridge.

Today, the distinction we make on the one hand between the realm of the academia with the university, the lecture room, the research colloquium, the laboratory, and on the other hand, the temple or the church, the monastic life, meditation and retreats, etc., offers a strong duality which did not exist in very ancient times when the rhythms and tenor of one's life and the search for knowledge and wisdom rested on a more holistic footing.

In this paper, we are especially concerned with the relevance of our *values* and *emotions*, both as the background to the development of cognitive orientations, as well as its consequences.

In exploring this subject, we see a significant area for study which not merely separates religion from science but can account for the one-track limitation in the development of science and some of its social consequences. Perhaps, paradoxically, it is an area which science can investigate: the importance of values and emotions in the growth and refinement of knowledge. It is in this context that this paper will be concerned with *types of knowledge and forms of life*. The search for knowledge when it is deeply grasped is "expressed in the whole area of living."[1]

In a more specific way, this paper is concerned with four issues which seem to throw into relief some important differences between science and religion, or to put it in the form of a more graphic metaphor, the way of the laboratory and the way of the monastery. First, we wish to make an analysis of the "purified view of intellect"; second, the absence of the intentional mode of understanding in scientific investigations; third, certain qualitative shifts in the progress of certain types or levels of knowledge, not completely integrated by science; and finally the modes of communication in scientific and religious discourse.

(1) In general, the scientific enterprise, which is often described as a concern with formal relationships between statements, tends to keep out questions of values and emotions. Even the attack on positivism by such philosophers as Kuhn, Lakatos, Feyerabend, and others has been made within the same framework of conceptions they criticize. The epistemology and the metaphysics of science as such will try to keep questions of moral psychology out. If this viewpoint is to be described as the "purified view of intellect,"[2] such a view attempts to neglect the role of character in the development of the scientific and theoretical intellect.

(2) The object of scientific understanding and the object of an "intentional mode of understanding" are different: "An *intentional* mode of understanding is one that fills the world with meanings implicit in our aims and emotions. Not only is it indispensable to us as rational agents, it may also be irreplaceable by any understanding derived from natural science."[3]

These two points, one referring to a kind of universe, the

other a "form of life" which the scientist does not enter, point towards a third area of importance regarding possible qualitative shifts in the progression towards knowledge.

(3) Western philosophers have made a wide variety of distinctions to differentiate types of knowledge: knowledge by description and acquaintance, knowing that and knowing how, breadth of knowledge and depth of knowledge, and so on. What is important in the religious quest in the context of this paper is the role of the moral agent who not merely develops breadth of understanding, or conventional morality and habits, but through the development of a deeper moral sensitivity seeks a more personal significance in the moral idioms he inherits.[4] It is such a moral sensitivity which can be integrated into what may be called the development of mindfulness. Development of such an experiential mode of understanding cuts across conventional concepts, grammar, semantics, and logic. It is a completely fresh open entry into the reality of the process which goes to condition the nature of human life, the reality of change and transience, the state of disequilibrium and the lack of an essence in events as such. What is discerned is a vast relational network in which the notion of the subject and object dissolves.

While such a reality may be common to the way of science and the way of religion, experiential knowledge in the religious quest is firmly rooted in the moral life. Whether we take the Hindu-Buddhist tradition, or the Chinese and the Japanese Zen tradition, they can respond to the tensions found in the Western philosophical tradition, to a great extent created by the recent discoveries of science, especially in the field of physics. This is because the "eye for paradox" found in these traditions facilitates the easy transition over apparent dualities, keeping up with these dualities (eg. subject-object, body-mind, etc.,) at one level of communication and transcending them at the other level, using conventional dualities at the conceptual level and dissolving them at deeper experiential level. But this is not merely a philosophical or scientific enterprise; it is deeply embedded in the moral culture and the culture of the mind, a complete way of life. When we examine the logic of the religious quest as different from a scientific investigation, what we wish to emphasize is the strong link between the types of knowledge and forms of life.

We have mentioned these three points which very clearly focus attention on the world of values and emotions, as it appears to be a paradoxical preoccupation among scientists who wish to find parallel points of convergence with the religious quest, that they place themselves high on the upper reaches of mysticism, leaving out the world of ethics, values, and the concerns of moral psychology. The burden of this paper will be to throw into relief, this vacuum in value and emotional components in the progress of science and its quest for wisdom. We are not saying that all the ills that fall, in the name of science and technology, on modern society will find a panacea, in the unfolding of the theoretical point emphasized in this paper. It merely focuses on a significant gap, *perhaps a logical gap* between science and religion, not deeply investigated by philosophers seeking points of convergence between science and religion.

(4) Finally, there appears to be an important difference in the kind of format used for presenting scientific findings and religious insights. Philosophers have used both types of format. The scientific abstract, or the professional paper, is a highly structured product of the evolution of scientific and philosophical thought, whereas in religion and in some philosophy, certain dialogues, aphorisms, koans, fragments, diaries, novels, poetry, meditations, and the like will be used. Apart from presenting and recording information, the second type of format is attempting to get the reader to "see things differently." Metaphors, imagery, parables, stories, or exercises aim at a kind of 'transformation' of the audience.

Science and the Purified View of the Intellect

The purified view of the intellect upholds that "intellect, especially the scientific intellect, is or should be purified of desire, emotion, and action." This view which has come down from Aristotle's Nichomachean Ethics has remained as the dominant view in the contemporary English-speaking philosophical world.[5] In general, though, such perspectives remained as the paradigmatic conception of the scientific intellect in the West. Today there is re-thinking on the subject, and more broadbased Eastern conceptions are becoming more attractive.

In neglecting the role of character and the active nature of the intellect, there is a self-imposed limit on the styles of intellectual and scientific activity and the nature of the intellectual life. "People are intellectually honest, intellectually arrogant, intellectually scrupulous, possessed of intellectual care, etc...."[6]

Religion as a way of life will give prime place to those very factors of values and emotions which the purified view of intellect try to eliminate. Also in considering science merely as an articulated body of truths, we overlook the conception of science as an activity, the conception of *doing science*. Intellectual activity is bound to desires and they have ends and goals. Unalienated and whole-hearted participation will make science a way of life rather than merely a body of truths. The point has been well expressed in some contemporary philosophical studies: intellectual activity done for certain goals is a great human good and may form a part of the good human life. A life of such intellectual activity in its fullness will be rooted in intellectual virtues, emotions, desires, and action.

This is the conception of science as a way of life which can offer a parallel to the life of the religious quest. The purified intellect notion has even captured some of the academic discussions in the philosophy of religion; but that is only a facet of our interest in religion and by its nature the religious quest calls for the exercise of a greater variety of human skills, desires, emotions, values, and actions.

Also, in recent discussions of the concept of "creativity" within the dimensions of modern science, scientific activity and more specifically ways of "doing science," interesting references to the role of emotions and values have been made.[7] There are references to both negative emotions and positive emotions in relation to creativity in science. Erich Fromm cites the case of negative emotions which interfere with the grasping of reality, whether it be a thing or person. Something like *experiencing the reality of a person* is a concept which comes within the objects of "intentional mode of understanding." It is something central to the religious quest, but it certainly does not come within the purview of the physical sciences, not even in the biological sciences. It is instead within the social sciences like psychology and within philosophy.

But whether we try to understand *things* or *people*, Fromm says that negative emotions like greed and anger and a wrong cognitive predisposition make us distort the object of understanding and in addition project our own bias. In fact, Fromm draws from the Eastern tradition when he makes these comments and more specifically the roots of greed, hatred, and delusion as discussed in the Buddhist texts. Fromm cites a number of conditions for the development of the *creative attitude*, including the ability to be puzzled, following Poincaré's statement that, "Scientific genius is the capacity to be surprised."[8] The ability to concentrate, which he says is a rare ability in the Western culture, is crucial for creativity.

Fromm says, "We do, if possible, many things at the same time. We eat breakfast, listen to the radio, and read the newspaper, and perhaps at the same time carry on a conversation with our wife and children. We do five things at the same time, and we do nothing."[9] He also cites the importance of the correct sense of 'Identity' for doing science, the ability to accept conflict and polarity (rather than avoid them) and the "willingness to be born every day." As Ravi Ravindra mentions, in Einstein we get the perspective on science as a way of freeing oneself from one's egocentricity. "A noteworthy contemporary example is that of Einstein. For him, certainly an engagement with science was a matter of spiritual vocation, a response to an inner call, a way of freeing oneself from one's egocentricity."[10]

Dealing with the positive emotions and its integration into styles of creativity, Rollo May has observed that in keeping with work done with Rorschach protocols, that "people can observe more accurately precisely when they are emotionally involved."[11] The idea is that a person sees more acutely, sharply, and accurately, when his positive emotions are engaged.

Thus if we make a distinction in using the term "science," between science as body of formulated truths, and styles of doing sciences and science as a way of life, these discussions of creativity are relevant to the notion of doing science. These discussions point towards the limitations of the concept of science upheld by the purified view of the intellect.

Science and the Intentional Mode of Understanding

In the case of the limitations of the purified view of intellect, scientists have made some accommodation by making a distinction between the activity of science and science as a body of truths. But in the case of the intentional mode of understanding, natural science has not and perhaps logically cannot enter the world of meanings and values. Though within the social sciences, there is a current controversy as to whether social understanding deals with social meanings rather than causal regularities,[12] in the case of the natural science, the gap is hard to bridge.

If the religious quest is firmly grounded in ethical values and the ethical way of life, which in turn is intrinsically related to questions of meaning, there appears to be a logical gap between the universe as the object of human intentionality and the universe as the object of scientific understanding (the paradigm grounded in the natural sciences). There are methodological advantages in the interaction between the natural sciences and the social sciences, but at some point logical differences emerge.

It is the same with the study of religion. It is standard to summon scientific method as a guideline for understanding religion. The problem is that the concept science in this context may be loosely used, referring to notions like objectivity, impartiality, belief in causal regularities, etc. But it appears that there is an important difference between summoning natural science paradigms and a social science framework. No religion is complete unless it has a study of the logic of human behavior, its regularities, the rules it follows, and the kinds of meanings enshrined in living (a form of life). Natural science cannot completely touch the full human being. Biological, physiological, neural, physical, and chemical aspects of life do not cover the whole human being. The social, psychological, and the moral aspect are central to the religious quest. Any attempt to generate a dialogue between science and religion has to face this central issue.

Science and Dimensions of Knowledge

In the case of the sciences, it is possible to speak of dimensions of knowledge, in a somewhat 'abstract' manner. For instance, we see some important differences between natural science contexts and social science contexts, and within social sciences, we can make some distinctions of the logically diverse types of knowledge in history, economics, and sociology, or we can look at psychology and distinguish its natural science components and social science components. But in the case of religion, it is a little difficult to talk of dimensions of knowledge in the abstract, as there are different religious traditions. Attempts have been made to find different logical strands over the diverse religious traditions, yet one ought to be aware, in certain contexts, of specific religious traditions. Keeping this note of caution in mind, we introduce a scheme of the different dimensions of knowledge, to talk about types of knowledge across the sciences and religions.

First, there is *theoretical knowledge* which is dependent on using reason to explain an event in terms of a theory or a hypothesis; second, we can speak of *empirical* knowledge which is considered as a kind of objective knowledge gained through sense experience, experiment, etc.; third, there is *existential knowledge* which is a realization through a direct personal encounter with real situations, especially a concept like human suffering. Last, we can refer to a dimension of *experiential knowledge*, which may not be found in the Western scientific tradition but find its paradigm in yoga and meditation.

While the concept of theoretical knowledge is well accepted in the rationalist tradition of philosophy, and empirical knowledge in the empiricist tradition, the existential kind of knowledge has been introduced by existential and phenomenlogical traditions. But experiential knowledge in the true sense is not integrated to the Western scientific tradition; and we can raise the question whether there is a line of separation between science and religion according to our focus on experiential knowledge. If you take the Hindu-Buddhist tradition in religion, all four dimensions of knowledge can be accommodated and integrated within this tradition. In the generation of this experiential knowledge, a crucial role is played by a certain life style and form of living, where the refinement of human values and emotions takes place along with a refinement in the levels of cognitive awareness.

A conference of this sort where scholars in philosophy, religion, and the sciences participate can make an important contribution by emphasizing the possibility of the existence of different conceptual frames of locating man's concern with the nature of the universe and human life. One's own intellectual framework is limited by the semantic, logical, and conceptual tools available within that system. When one comes into contact with another and alternative system, the momentum of the dualities, dichotomies, and dilemmas that is disturbing loses its edge and gets converted into merely a contrasting way of looking at things. In this we find new bases for the mediation of conflicting theories and a new canvas for locating conflicts. It is perhaps due to such cross-cultural and even cross-disciplinary meetings in the past, that scientists in the West have developed an interest in Eastern philosophies and religions.

Though such conceptual adjustments may be made, the conceptual mode is not a substitute for the experiential mode. The religious quest emphasizes that certain types of knowledge are strongly rooted in forms of life, that the affective and the conative aspects are related to one's cognitive orientation. This is one of the general points made in this paper. Second, the question is raised whether there are special barriers between the subject matter of religion and sciences, whether the object of the "intentional mode," of meanings, aims, and emotions can be understood in terms of the natural science paradigms. An awareness of these two issues can always act as a useful reminder of possible barriers, when working out an interesting dialogue between science and religion.

Modes of Communication in Philosophy, Science, and Religion

We have examined the distinction between science as a body of formal truths and science as an activity, and in doing this emphasized the place of values and emotions in the process of scientific exploration, discovery, and creativity. Second, we have mentioned the inability to integrate what may be called the objects of the "intentional mode of understanding" into the scientific universe dominated by a natural science paradigm. Third, we have found some differences between science and religion pertaining to certain levels and types of knowledge. Apart from these three concerns, the process of discovery, the nature of the scientific universe, and the objects of scientific understanding and the development in the progression in knowledge, an interesting subject, somewhat neglected in studies of this sort, is the technique and the format of communication.

An interesting and useful way to explore the subject is to look at philosophy which has been attracted by both the ideal format in scientific communications as well as in religious discourse.

As Arthur Danto has pointed out, philosophy is often a kind of cross breed of science and art[13] where you can discern two types of formats used in philosophical communication. The development of philosophy as a formal academic professional concern has emphasized its sense of community with science with an emphasis on clarity, brevity, and competence. In this context the canonical literary format has been the professional paper. Here philosophers like scientists are building up the edifice of knowledge through a very restricted readership and as a collaborative enterprise.

But there is also another tradition in philosophy concerned not merely with the *imparting of information* but as Danto says with the *transformation of the audience*.[14] In ancient times philosophers were not very much distinguished from sages, saints, and mystics and in certain traditions there were philosophers who were wanderers, ascetics, poets, etc. Within such a tradition, there were certain excesses, but there were the finer refined blends of the philosopher with the sage, saint, the poet, and the artist. The second tradition often used techniques and a format closer to literature than science; and this dimension found in this second and more ancient strand of philosophical thinking can often be shared with the religious traditions. It uses the narrative form more than the argumentative form for communication, dialogues, fragments, aphorisms, paradoxes, commentaries, poetry, parables, stories, etc.

Thus techniques of communication in the Upanishads, the

Bible, Koran, and the Buddhist scriptures do often betray a tendency to use the literary format. If, for instance, one reads the early Buddhist scriptures, it will betray techniques of communication belonging to both types of the philosophical traditions cited above.

The difference lies not merely in these formats and techniques as methods of communication but as methods which try to enter the mind of the *listener*, as well as the *reader*, with the aim of getting them to see things differently, to use a metaphor, a certain kind of "depth," more than merely the "breadth" of information.

It is true that the literary format has entered the arena of scientific writing through science fiction, but that is more in a speculative turn of mind to play with ideas, articulate imaginary possibilities, for popularization etc.

The kind of communication used in a literary form is discussed by Theodore Roszak in his work, *Where the Wasteland Ends*.[15] He refers to Tolstoy's work, *The Death of Ivan Ilyich*, where the dying Ilyich sees a difference between what he learned in his logic books, "All Men are Mortal," and when it strikes him with the resonance of a personal crisis.[16]

Roszak says we are losing our ability to go beyond verbal surfaces and get at the root meaning of words. He makes a distinction between knowing and "knowing": "We are in the position of the Zen master who began as a novice knowing that mountains are only mountains, rivers only rivers, and finished as a sage knowing that mountains are only mountains, rivers only rivers...ah, but finished knowing it *wisely*. How to talk about such things?"[17] Roszak regards the diminishing awareness of such symbolic resonance as a crisis in language.

The linguistic traditions (which in some traditions were orally transmitted in the past) which preserve the handing over of religious ideas have certain logical peculiarities which may be compared with the formal language used in scientific discourse.

Notes

1. David Pole, "Breadth and Depth of Understanding," *Philosophy*, 1990, 119.
2. Michael Stocker, "Intellectual Desire, Emotion, and Action," in Ameli Rorty, ed., *Explaining Emotions* (Berkeley, 1980).
3. Roger Scruton, "Emotion and Practical Knowledge," in Ameli Rorty ed., *Explaining Emotions* (Berkeley, 1980), 533.
4. John Kekes, "Moral Sensitivity," *Philosophy*, v. 59, 1984.
5. Stocker, *Explaining Emotions*.
6. *Ibid.*, 324.
7. Harold H. Anderson, ed., *Creativity and Its Cultivation* (Harper & Row, 1959).
8. *Ibid.*, 44–54.
9. *Ibid.*
10. See R. Ravindra, Chapter 17, this volume.
11. Anderson, *Creativity and Its Cultivation*, 55–68.
12. Alan Ryan, *The Philosophy of the Social Sciences* (London: Macmillan, 1970).
13. Arthur Danto, "Philosophy as/and/of Literature," Presidential Address, *American Philosophical Society Proceedings*, September, 1984.
14. *Ibid.*
15. Theodore Roszak, *Where the Wasteland Ends* (New York: Anchor Books, 1973).
16. *Ibid.*, 349–50.
17. *Ibid.*, 350.

TWELVE

SCIENCE And SIDDHARTHA

CONFLUENCE IN TWO DIFFERING WORLD VIEWS

Alfredo V. Lagmay

Introduction

The problems and aims of classical philosophy, particularly those of the East, have really endured despite developments in science as a different way of defining knowledge and applying it to human problems. The traditional dilemmas posed by pain and suffering and release therefrom, the meaning of life, and the spiritual quest remain in the historical legacy of the great religions, the humanities, and many parts of modern philosophy itself.

We are often reminded that modern philosophy, for having excessively engaged itself in analysis of language and abstract conceptual structures, has lost its basic moorings in what had been regarded as most important in the classical tradition, namely, those questions on the meaning and purpose of life and the cosmos, on appearance and ultimate reality, on good and evil, and on human pain and suffering. This criticism may not altogether be true, that philosophy has lost its moorings. There still is a massive legacy to us that has endured throughout all of history in the great religions, in the arts and literature, in philosophy and the humanities as a whole. And this legacy will continue to be the more important framework within which science will evolve and progress, as it has so done all along.

For there indeed has been a remarkable surge in recent times of wholeness and unity as perspectives in science and technology. The new physics and contemporary cosmology seem to be giving us some renewed feeling for the speculations of the pre-Socratic and Vedic philosophers, though perhaps from somewhat different premises. The environmentalists' concern for the planetary ecology has an almost nostalgic touch of the Oriental view of harmony in man and nature. All over the world there has been a large-scale revival of the ancient philosophical classics such as, to name a few, the teachings of the early Christian fathers, the Tao Teh Ching, the discourses of Siddhartha, the Upanishads, and the Zen classics. A noticeable proportion of the scientific community have referred to these writings in ever-increasing frequency. And the postwar rebirth of existentialism indicates in no unmistakable terms the growing conviction of the primacy of experience and intuition and of the universal human problems of pain, anxiety, and suffering; the problems from which the Royal Society of London, the first and most prestigious academy of science in the world, almost effectively insulated itself when it was founded in the seventeenth century.

And now, with such equal force and pervasiveness as the foregoing observed phenomena, has been the development of studies on serene life cultures—meditative styles of life that have many points of accommodation in psychology and psychiatry, with education and the medical sciences in large measure. It has been said that one of the most significant advances in clinical psychology has been the concept of systematic desensitization to fear, anxiety, anger, and other tension-producing stimuli—a pivotal concept around which a minor revolution in our ideas of psychopathology and psychotherapy has been developing quite rapidly since about three decades ago. An important component of the concept of desensitization is psychophysiological relaxation of the organism, a component that has made the study of serene cultures very important to the scientific world, since the techniques for quieting and relaxing the body-mind had been perfected in the East several thousand years ago. The project of the late Dr. Yoshiharu Akishige and the pioneering work of Dr. Tomio Hirai on the study of Zen meditation are examples of a confluence between the modern scientific idiom and the writings of Patanjali and the discourses of Siddhartha.

More generally, old practices have been brought into the orbit of scientific paradigms, to new levels of understanding by methods and procedures of an essentially modern framework of enquiry. A fair question, therefore, would be: "Is this kind of accommodation necessarily a distortion or a misdirected understanding of the ancient teaching?" The philosophical framework of yoga, Buddhist or Christian meditation may be presumed to be quite different from that of modern psycho-therapy, and there is good reason to believe that this is true.[2] But one could also look at this in another way: that human understanding is really never complete at any stage or point in time. Traditional ways of thinking assume new forms or even new theological paradigms even as the human problems themselves remain constant. Such is the problem of pain and suffering and of early salvation—all very trite statements but as real today as when it was first formulated since no one knows anymore.

Allow me to describe in some detail, at some level appro-priate for most of us educated laymen, what may be considered a spiritual journey in the broadest sense of that phrase, always mindful of something that keeps on making the rounds of my soul: "The question...is not how to escape the mind, or the body, or time, or the world, but rather how to find their right use and place."[3] For in what follows, I seek the right uses of the body and the mind through bodily and mental cultivation.

EEG-Alpha and the Problem of Stress-Related Illness

Medicine has taught us that stress and tension have been implicated in various kinds of bodily and mental disorders, and that the proper remedy, among others, has always been to quiet the individual through rests in its various forms. But it was not until Jacobson[4] came out with his monograph *Progressive Relax-ation* that a full-fledged scientific demonstration of how a wide range of organic and psychological disorders would yield positively to a relaxation technique—a technique which since then has become standard method for quieting physiological arousal and tension of the body. The method Jacobson used was that of relaxing the voluntary muscle system of the body, and, by doing this, he showed that there were profound concomitant changes in pulse rate, blood pressure, and the activity of the parasympathetic nervous system, the state of the vital organs, and a host of others. Unfortunately, Jacobson did not concern himself at that time with the measurement of brain wave potentials or the electroencephalogram, although this technique was already available then through the work of Berger.[5]

It was much later on that workers became interested in the relationship between "quiet physiological states" and the electroencephalogram, particularly on EEG-alpha waves (8–12 Hz) which in many studies had become associated with relaxation. "An abundance of alpha wave activity has classically been considered to represent states of rest (not sleep), relaxation and relief from attention and concentration. Conversely, lack of alpha wave activity and its replacement by beta and waves of faster frequencies (13 Hz and above) has been interpreted as indicating states of alertness, attention, orienting, and anxiety," says Brown.[6] The foregoing terms on faster frequency brain waves are usually associated with tension, stress, physiological arousal, responding to sudden or startling stimuli, and the like. Almost all of the symptomatology of the so-called fight-or-flight (emergency) responses, described by Cannon[7] belong to EEG-beta. When alpha disappears (alpha blocking), as in visual or auditory-orienting responses, or in tension and anxiety, or when the individual is focused on something, as in problem-solving or visual pursuit tracking, beta waves appear on the record. Very early enough, "Berger, Lord Adrian, and later Grey Walter...found that alpha disappeared if the subject engaged in mental activity requiring considerable attention.... By 1935 alpha was known to be importantly related to relief from both visual activity and attention. The situation remains nearly the same today. In the thirty-odd years that have passed, alpha activity has been inspected, counted, dissected, suppressed and distorted in a hundred ways, yet the average brain researcher is unsure whether alpha is associated with mental effort or relief from mental effort," Brown further states.[8]

More recently, however, since some two decades ago, developments in the personal control of muscle relaxation and of the production of EEG-alpha through biofeedback methods, relaxation states have been thrown into greater prominence. The growing literature arising from biofeedback research has shown very clearly and conclusively the significance of stress and anxiety on the one hand and of relaxation and quiet life styles, on the other, in relation to disease and health, respectively. Stroebel and Glueck[9] quote from Shapiro, one of America's leading biofeedback scientists, "...the vast majority of ills and the illness-onset situation itself are clearly not beyond subjective control. These cannot be the private domain of the doctor-scientist but are a matter of the responsibility of each individual.... (Indeed) modern man may require personal demonstration through a structured period of self-learning to incorporate the concept of individual responsibility into his daily life-style in times of both health and illness. This learning may best be accomplished at an early age, with the teaching, for example, of the four R's in the second grade: reading, 'riting, 'rithmetic, and *relaxation*."

Attention Control of Occipital EEG-alpha Activity

Dewan[10] and Nideffer[11] review the subject of focal and non-focal attention in the production of alpha, parts of which are pertinent to this paper.

Berger[12] found in 1930 that alpha waves were blocked when subjects saw patterned visual stimuli. Many investigators thereafter, however, maintained that alpha was produced when there was no visual stimuli. Short and Walter[13] summarize this situation by suggesting that alpha is a non-focal attentive state that would be blocked by attention to either real or imagined visual stimuli. Others have in fact found that, more generally, focal attentive states may be auditory, tactile, or visual and may inhibit alpha waves.[14] It was also found, however, that the relationship between attention to stimuli may not be as invariable as previously supposed. Mundy-Castle,[15] for example, found that there was not exactly a one-to-one correspondence between alpha and attention or visual activity. Furthermore, Dewan[16] found that, in some cases, there could be considerable mental activity and attention, and there would be no alpha blocking. This last finding is important because it is a counter example against the classical position on alpha blocking.

The Oculo-Motor Hypothesis on Alpha Blocking

As early as 1935, Durup and Fessard[17] tried to explain alpha blocking in terms of ocular accommodation (bulging or flattening of the lens of the eye by the ciliary muscles) in order to focus the eyes for greater clarity of vision. Later, Mulholland[18] elaborated on this hypothesis by stating that there is occipital alpha blocking in connection with (1) minimization of the angle between the visual target and the fovea, (2) minimization of target blur, and (3) control of the pupils of the eyes to optimize the level of stimulus input.

The following studies support the hypothesis as developed by Mulholland:

(a) Mulholland[19] found that alpha will be produced by a subject tilting his eyes upward. Alpha could be produced so skillfully that the subject is able to send messages to a computer by the simple expedient of getting dots and dashes of the Morse code electrically translated for long-and short-interval tilts of the eyes upwards.

(b) Fenwick and Walker[20] also found that there is alpha production by a corresponding tilt upward of the eyes, but this was not true for all subjects. However, it was suggested by Dewan that when alpha actually does occur during the eye-tilt upwards, there was a defocus of the eyes and a relaxation of ocular convergence.

(c) Mulholland[21] studied alpha production under three conditions: (1) subject focuses on, and tracks, a moving stimulus; (2) subject blurs the stimulus and continues tracking it; (3) subject blurs the image and refrains from tracking. Alpha production was greatest in the third condition and was least in the first.

(d) In a study by Peper,[22] subjects were unable to prevent blocking of alpha in visual tracking.

In summary, investigations therefore seem to suggest that eye movement, accommodation and convergence are associated with alpha blocking, although this is not always the case. These exceptions will require a separate analysis elsewhere, but we should note it here for our purposes. Likewise, while focusing one's eyes disrupts alpha, and appears to be almost always true in every case, the "almost" part of this statement makes it consistent with the first argument of this paragraph. Indeed, Kamiya[23] found that one of his subjects was able to develop alpha production without tilting the eyes upward, where the entire experiment was ostensibly aimed at the production of alpha by the upward tilt of the eyes. For all these, Mulholland[24] hypothesizes that the relationship between alpha and attention is only a secondary effect of eye movements, which are associated with generalized attentional responses called "orienting reflex." And finally Oswald[25] reported that intense auditory (not visual) alertness could be maintained while producing alpha so long as there was loss of ocular fixation and accommodation.

Non-Laboratory and Quasi-Laboratory Examples of Alpha Production Where the Oculo-Motor Hypothesis May Be Involved

Extensive studies have been made of Zen Buddhist monks in meditation and have found high alpha production in such meditative states.[26] Akishige and his students have demonstrated that high alpha production can be obtained from experienced mediators under conditions of problem-solving, such as those of arithmetic, where there would ordinarily be the expected alpha blocking. The state of alpha quiet however was the result of specialized training stretching usually a number of years. My own question is: "Is there a shorter method suitable for everyday life, as one moves about in work, that can generate perhaps not too high-amplitude alpha but of such strength as to be a significant departure from EEG-beta state?" Zen meditation in all likelihood helps to defocus the oculo-motor apparatus, and one should hope that a direct check on this may be made sometime in the future.

Nideffer[27] cites a personal communication from a certain

Pappas in 1972 which claims that the latter was able to teach speedreading, electrical assembly, pipefitting, taping, and carpet buying to students under alpha state.

More recently, Fritz and Fehmi[28] have developed a method which they claim to produce consistently high alpha by passive attention to "space" (space between the fingers, space several inches around the entire body, space between the two ears, space around the forearms, and so on). He in fact has standardized this method as therapeutic strategy for the relief of anxiety, tension, pain, and a number of psychological disorders. One is reminded, in turn, of the original Jacobson technique of progressive relaxation mentioned earlier, where one pays attention successively to muscle groups of the body (not "space" as in that of Fritz and Fehmi). Harrell and Coles[29] in fact did a laboratory check of this phenomenon and concluded that the sustaining of attention is one of the components of progressive relaxation. I have a strong presumption, held for almost two decades by this time, that when one pays attention to one's body in the aforementioned manner, there is bound to be a defocalization of the body.

Nideffer and Sharpe[30] in fact developed a method for a life-style based on either a narrow focus or a broad focus in the management of one's visual apparatus. A broad-focus visual style has a larger visual field (edge-to-edge), as opposed to a narrow one, where the visual field is narrower and restricted to clear, fovea vision, as in reading, arithmetic problem-solving, and visual pursuit tracking. Nideffer has elevated this kind of attention control training into a therapeutic modality as well as into a life-style that optimizes functioning for both physiological and psychological health.

The foregoing kind of defocusing in all probability has been going on for thousands of years up to the present time in meditative cultures—among the Hindus and Buddhists and similar traditions. Herman Hesse,[31] the novelist, is mentioned in Pennington,[32] as having called our attention to an old game among the gypsies of Europe which, by systematic exercise, develops the broad, defocused type of visual attention. Likewise, Carlos Castañeda[33] of Don Juan, the master of his story, as delineating a procedure as follows: "...walking for long stretches without focusing the eyes on anything directly but slightly crossing the eyes, to keep a peripheral view of everything that presented itself to the eyes. He had insisted, although I had not understood at that time, that if one *kept one's* unfocused eyes at a point just above the horizon (*tilted eyes of Mulholland?*) it was possible to notice, at once, everything in almost 180-degree range in front of one's eyes. He had assured me that exercise was the only way of shutting off the internal dialogue" (*internal dialogue that produces "the tangled knots of thought"*).

In 1976, when I attended a brief workshop seminar with a Zen master named Oshida, I was instructed that the sensation of seeing the visual field should be one of looking as though there was a nearer object that is not there, while the gaze is farther away. Of course, I noticed that there was an automatic defocusing of the eyes and enlarging of the field of vision. According to him this points to the meditative way with eyes open.

There are apparently many ways of defocusing the oculomotor apparatus and thereby getting around to demobilizing the tension-bound state of the body. I recall quite clearly a passage from Krishnamurti, which of his works I no longer remember, of his experience of listening to silence, that is, not to sound but to silence as foreground to everything. Paying attention to silence is a difficult thing at first, but one soon learns to develop a selective attention to it, with any sound emanating from space around you as the background. Silence can either be background or foreground in the perceptual field of attention. Sound ordinarily, in everyday life, is foreground; only when there is absolutely no sound does silence seem prominent and comes to foreground of the perceptual field. This silence can be the foreground all the time as the center of one's attention, and the skill for this is attained with constant practice. The oculomotor apparatus defocuses, the visual field widens, and relaxation ensues. Alpha production goes up and the entire body defocuses.

The advantages of silence as a source for orienting one's attention are obvious:

1. Silence can be foreground or background; others can only be foreground, e.g., paying attention to the rising and falling of the abdomen during breathing, or to a fixation point in space or imagined space, all of which can only be foreground.

2. Silence is continuous and always present, either as foreground or as background.

3. Silence is a non-agitating, "quiet" source which is absolutely compatible with the production of the alpha response.

Those of us who have experienced the alpha state of consciousness will easily see why silence, which enhances this state, could easily be put into the service of basically spiritually-oriented pursuits. The larger dimensions of life itself places a heavy responsibility on all of us to be peaceable, lucid, and kindly, something which the alpha state enhances even if it does not guarantee them necessarily. Whether in sitting meditation, or while actively in motion in the workaday world, one can learn the feel or the sense of deep quiet and tranquility that goes with the alpha state.

Concluding Remarks

I have taken recourse to describing a research area in science which, if regarded separately and without a real-life context to support it, may seem irrelevant to the problem of this conference. But the tremendous interest this type of study has spawned in psychology, medicine, and education may help us to understand why the topic is genuinely related to the alleviation of pain and suffering, and, I am convinced, to the cultivation of mind and body for spiritual ends.

In the EEG-alpha state, it is easier to be free of the tangles and tension of thought, easier to let go of objects, ideas, desires, and obsessions while retaining a lucidity of understanding of situations and meanings. Postures of attack and defense are easily dissipated; and attitudes of greed, anger, hate, and aggression and all the fear and anxiety that go with them are dissolved because profound serenity is the polar opposite of all these. When one is deeply quiet, it is easier to be kindly and generous and forgiving. And true love is silent and also deeply quiet.

This is not to suggest in any way that kind of journey that the sage and the master undergo, from one level of consciousness to the highest stages of transcendental bliss. But I sometimes wonder whether the words of Siddhartha, that watching the breath constantly, continuously, and so gently as one may, as the only way to ultimate salvation, was not really meant for the ordinary man to discover what it means to be free of all those things that we grasp at and cling to and hold on to, while sitting with legs crossed in quiet meditation.

Acknowledgments

This paper is part of a study that was supported by the National Academy of Science and Technology and by the Philippine National Science Society. Their assistance is hereby gratefully acknowledged. Also, the opportunity given me by the Japan Foundation for a brief visit to Sophia University in Tokyo under the sponsorship of Professor Hisashi Hirai afforded some insights into subject matter which would have been unlikely otherwise. I thank all concerned for their help.

Notes

1. Y. Akishige (ed.), *Psychological Studies of Zen*, vols. I & II, Bulletin of the Zen Institute of Komazawa University, No. 1, Tokyo, Japan.
2. Tomio Hirai, "Electroencephalographic study on Zen meditation: EEG changes during concentrated relaxation," *Folia Psychiatrica et Neurologica Japonica* 16, 1960, 76–105.
3. Ravi Ravindra, "Letter to Krishnamurti," in P. Jayakar and S. Patwardham, eds., *Within the Mind: On J. Krishnamurti* (Madras, India: Krishnamurti Foundation, 1982), 118–122..
4. Edmund Jacobson, *Progressive Relaxation* (Chicago: Chicago University Press, 1932).
5. H. Berger, "On the electroencephalogram of man," in Gloom, P. (ed.), *Electroencephalography and Clinical Neurophysiology*, suppl., 28, 1969, 75–93. Originally published in *Journal fur Psychologie und Neurologie* 40, 1930, 160–179.
6. Barbara B. Brown, *New Mind, New Body: Biofeedback, New Directions* (New York: Harper & Row, 1974), 312–313.
7. Walter B. Cannon, *Wisdom of the Body* (New York: Norton, 1932).
8. *Op. cit.*, 313.
9. C.F. Stroebel, and B. Glueck, "Passive meditation; subjective clinical, and electrographic comparison with biofeedback." In *Biofeedback and Self-Control* (Chicago: Aldine Publishers, 1975).
10. E.M. Dewan, "Occipital Alpha Rhythm, Eye Position and Lens

Accommodation," *Nature*, 1967, 214.

11. R.M. Nideffer, "Alpha and the development of human potential." In *Biofeedback and Self-Control* (Chicago: Aldine Publishers, 1972).

12. *Op. cit.*

13. F.L. Short, and W. G. Walter, "The relationship between physiological variables and stereognosis," *Electroencephalography and Clinical Neurophysiology* 6, 29, 1954.

14. I. Salamon, and J. Post, "Alpha blocking and schizophrenia," *Archives of General Psychiatry* 13, 1965, 367–374.

15. A.C. Mundy-Castle, "The electroencephalogram and mental activity," *Electroencephalography and Clinical Neurophysiology*, 1957, 9, 643–655.

16. *Op. cit.*

17. Cited in Dewan, *op. cit.*

18. T. Mulholland, "Feedback encephalography." Reprinted from *Activas nervosa superior* (Prague), 10, 4, 1968. In *Biofeedback and Self-Control* (Aldine-Atherton, 1971).

19. *Ibid.*

20. T. Mulholland, and E. Peper, "Occipital alpha and accommodative vergence, pursuit tracking, and fast eye movements," *Psychophysiology* 8, 1971, 556.

21. *Ibid.*

22. E. Peper, "Feedback Regulation of the Alpha Electroencephalogram Activity through Control of Internal and External Parameters," *Kybernetik* 7, 1970, 107–112.

23. J. Kamiya, "Operant Control of the EEG Alpha Rhythm and Some of its Reported Effects on Consciousness," in C.T. Tart (ed.), *Altered States of Consciousness* (New York: Wiley, 1969).

24. T. Mulholland, 1968, *op. cit.*

25. I. Oswald, "The Human Alpha Rhythm and Visual Alertness," *Electroencephalography and Clinical Neurophysiology* 11, 1959, 601.

26. Akishige, *op. cit.*

27. *Op. cit.*

28. G. Fritz, and L. Fehmi, *The Open Focus Handbook* (N.J.: Biofeedback Computers, Inc., 1982).

29. Harrell and Coles, 1976. [Precise reference not available at the time of printing.]

30. R. M. Nideffer & R. C. Sharpe, *Attention Control Training* (New York: Simon & Schuster, 1978).

31. Herman Hesse, *The Glass Bead Game* (London: Penguin, 1972).

32. G. Pennington, *Little Manual for Players of the Glass Bead Game: The Way of Visual Contemplation* (Wiltshire, England: Element Books, 1983). (First published in 1981 by Irisiana Verlag, Haldenwang, West Germany).

33. Carlos Castañeda, *The Teachings of Don Juan: A Yaqui Way of Knowledge* (New York: Ballantine, 1968).

THIRTEEN

Is RELIGION PSYCHOTHERAPY?

AN INDIAN VIEW

Ravi Ravindra

A related question to the one posed in the title is this: 'Is religion psychology?' In order to make this question a little sharper, let us raise two parallel ones: 'Is religion physiology?' and 'Is religion physiotherapy?'

I have the impression that the answer to any of the above four questions is both 'yes' and 'no.' What I propose to do below is to try to find out how we might understand these questions in the light of the Bhagavad Gītā and the Yoga Sūtras of Patanjali, with occasional help from other sources. These two texts are of paramount importance in Indian religion and psychology, and may be considered representative of the classical Indian view.

Religion as Yoga

We may assume that the Bhagavad Gītā and the Yoga Sūtras have something to do with religion. Their central concern is liberation; this, for our purposes here, describes the point of religion. In order not to become sidetracked by contemporary discussions about the meaning and goal of religion, and whether the word is appropriate or useful to designate what goes on under this label, let me suggest that here we use the Sanskrit word *yoga* for essentially two reasons. The first reason is simply that there is no other Sanskrit word which is more suitable than *yoga* for translating *religion*,[1] and since we cannot avoid bringing in the connotations of whichever word we choose, we might as well choose the one appropriate to the texts we are discussing. Second, and more importantly, the etymologies of *yoga* and *religion* have some close parallels in terms of 'uniting' (or making a bond between) what is human and what is divine, as well as in their explicit associations with 'diligence,' 'attention,' and 'heedfulness.' The importance of yoga in Indian tradition is obvious: a name or an epithet of Śiva is 'yoganāth,' of Viṣṇu 'yogapati,' and of Kṛṣṇa 'yogeśwara,' in each case meaning essentially 'master or lord of yoga.'

One immediate advantage of using *yoga* rather than *religion* is the associated verb form. In the Bhagavad Gītā, for example, the verb form of 'yoga' is used more frequently than the noun form. The word 'religion' does not have a corresponding verb; this leads to expressions like 'having religion.' Similar expressions would sound quite odd in connection with yoga which is closer to a process than to a doctrine. However, any shift of meaning that results from 'religion' to 'yoga,' from being primarily a noun to being equally (or even primarily) a verb is quite warranted, appropriate, and useful. Mythologically, sometimes Yoga is personified as the son of Dharma and Kriyā; Dharma is essentially the order that is the support of the cosmos, and Kriyā, as action and performance, is a *śakti* (energy, power) of Viṣṇu in his Vāmana incarnation. Yoga is 'religion,' 'science,' as well as 'art,' since it is concerned with being (*sat*), knowing (*jñāna*), and doing (*karma*). The aim of yoga, however, both in the Bhagavad Gītā and the Yoga Sūtras, is beyond these three, as well as beyond any opposites they imply. The state of *mokṣa*, i.e., of uncaused freedom, which is Kṛṣṇa's own state (*bhava*), is beyond the dualities of being-non-being, knowledge-ignorance, and activity-inactivity. However, the way to *mokṣa* is yoga, which is religion as path, discipline, and integration.

The Method and Aim of Yoga

The aim of yoga is the transformation of man from his natural form to a perfected form. The *prākṛta* (literally, natural, vulgar, unrefined) state is one in which a person compulsively repeats his actions, in reaction to the forces of *prakṛti* which are active both outside him as well as inside. Through yoga he can become *saṁskṛta* (literally, well made, well put together) and thus no longer be wholly at the mercy of natural forces and inclinations. Corresponding to the root meaning of 'education' is the procedure of yoga; it helps bring out what in fact already is in man but was not perceivable in his unpolished form. The progressive bringing out of *Brahman* in an aspirant is much like the releasing of a figure from an unshaped stone.

The undertaking of yoga concerns the entire man, resulting in the reshaping of mind, body, and emotions. Unlike in a sculpture, the remolding involved in yoga is essentially from inside out, for here the yogi himself is the artist, the stone, and the tools. Lest this analogy should be misunderstood to suggest that yoga leads to rugged individualism, it is worth remarking that the freedom that a yogi aspires to is primarily freedom from oneself. From a strict metaphysical point of view, the yogi *himself* cannot be said to be the artist of his life. The real initiative belongs only to *Brahman* who is lodged in the heart of everyone.

Yoga begins from a recognition of one's situation: one's bondage to nature and the consequent suffering. Since our internal nature is assumed to be made up of the same stuff, and to follow the same principles, as external nature, yoga proceeds by focusing on knowledge of oneself. Self-knowledge may be said to be both the essential method and the essential goal of yoga. Self-knowledge is clearly a relative matter, depending not only on the depth of knowledge but also on what is seen as the self to be known. A progressive change from the identification of oneself as the body (including the heart and the mind) to the identification of oneself as inhabiting the body is the most crucial development in yoga. Ancient and modern Indian languages reflect this perspective in the expressions used to describe someone's death. In contrast to the usual English expression of 'giving up the ghost,' one 'gives up the body.' It is not the body that has the spirit, but the spirit that has the body. The yogi identifies himself less with the body and more with the embodied.

But this identification of oneself with something other than the body-mind and the attendant relative freedom from the body-mind, is possible only through a proper functioning and restructuring of the body and the mind. Here it is useful to use the Sanskrit word *śarīra* in order to steer clear of the modern Western philosophic dilemma called the 'mind-body problem.' Although *śarīra* is usually translated as 'body,' it means the whole psychosomatic complex of the body, mind, and heart. *Śarīra* is both the instrument of transformation as well as the mirror indicating it. The way one sits, walks, feels, and thinks can help one in knowing the relatively more real self. The knowing of this self is then reflected in the way one sits, walks, feels, and thinks.

Śarīra, which is miniaturized or individualized *prakṛti*, is the medium necessary for the completion and manifestation of *svabhāva*, the inner being which is said to be a particle of *Brahman* whose body is the whole manifested cosmos. To view one's *śarīra*, or the world, as a hindrance rather than an opportunity, is akin to regarding the rough stone as an obstruction to the finished figure. *Śarīra* is the substance from which each one of us makes a work of art, according to our ability to respond to the inner urge and initiative. This substance belongs to *prakṛti* and includes our ordinary categories of organic and inorganic processes.[2] She follows strict causal laws, and, although abundantly dynamic in manifestation, is essentially passive before *puruṣa*, the spirit who fecundates her. Each one of us, every existence—movable or immovable—according to the Bhagavad Gītā, comes into being by the union of *prakṛti* and *puruṣa*, or *śarīra* and *ātman*, or the field and the knower of the field. Śiva and Śākti in an intimate embrace symbolize this union resulting in creation. Iconographically, this symbol is further abstracted into Śivalingam (the phallus of Śiva) in intercourse which is viewed from inside the cosmic womb. Each being is the seed placed in the womb of *prakṛti* by Śiva.

Following the Bhagavad Gītā (15.16–17), we can say it in another way. Each man is made up of three beings (*puruṣa*): perishable, imperishable, and the highest *puruṣa*. The first two are said to be basically different from each other. Although the path of yoga aims at a fundamental essential unity of all there is, an intermediate stage is one of recognizing the radical duality between the perishable *puruṣa* and the imperishable *puruṣa*. A yogi sees that part of himself which is independent of his *śarīra*, and thus independent of *prakṛti* according to whose laws his body-mind functions. When he has identified himself with this imperishable *puruṣa* in him, only then can he move towards the yet more basic unity of the highest *puruṣa* wherein all dualities, metaphysical, ethical, or linguistic, are reconciled. In this state, the perfected yogi, the completely integrated man, sees everything in the Self and the Self in everything.[3]

This point is central to the concern of this paper and is worth developing. Man is subject to two major forces or tendencies: one is the downward force of his lower nature, which manifests as desires, inclinations, likes, and dislikes. The other is the upward force of his higher nature which determines his calling. A man's essential being (*svabhāva*) is the lord seated in his heart and making him revolve as if mounted on a machine (B.G. 18.60). Man is advised to follow his *svadharma* which is the law (or demand or vocation) that corresponds to his svabhava. The work done in accordance with this law is *svakarma*. This work must not be abandoned and cannot be abandoned without violating the most essential part of oneself. One is born, incarnated in a specific form at a certain time and place in response to one's previous karma, in order to pursue the dictates of his *svabhāva*. The *svabhāva* of human beings in general corresponds to *brāhmans* (scholars, teachers, seekers), *kśtriyas* (warriors, administrators, rulers), *vaiśyas*, (businessmen, artisans, bourgeoisie), or *śudras* (laborers, serfs, proletariat). Within each of these divisions one can be in the mode of *sattva* (clarity, purity, attentiveness), or of *rajas* (passion, activity, egoism), or of *tamas* (sloth, passivity, heedlessness). Thus the four *svabhāvas* and the three *gunas* constitute twelve types of human beings.

A man is enjoined to persist in his own *svabhāva* and the corresponding *svadharma* and to undertake an upward, qualitative transformation in the *gunas* from *tamas* to *sattva*. *Svabhāva* determines a man's calling, the *guna* predominant in his life indicates the quality of his response. The spiritual principle in man assumes a body for the purpose of perfection. As long as it is unfulfilled, it will continue to incarnate itself, setting aside the body-mind when it becomes unsuitable for its purpose.

Svabhāva, however, is not an end in itself. It is a means by which one can come to share Kṛṣṇa's *bhāva*.[4] If one is in Kṛṣṇa's *bhāva*, one now is truly a microcosm mirroring the macrocosm and one acts as Kṛṣṇa does—in complete freedom, for the sake of sustaining the world order, according to the principle of sacrifice for reciprocal maintenance of cosmic processes (B.G. 3.9–12). The entire course of yoga can be regarded as the transformation in which one's center of gravity and initiative changes its locus from one's lower nature (inclination and desires of *śarīra*) through one's higher nature (demand of *svabhāva*) to Kṛṣṇa nature (or state of *Brahman*).

Yoga as Physio-psychology

Śarīra, the body-mind, is the field, and *ātman* (or *puruṣa*) is the knower of the field, and Kṛṣṇa says that true knowledge consists in knowing both the field and the knower of the field (B.G. 13.2). The knowledge of the field, i.e., of the body-mind and the modes of *prakṛti*, or physics in the broadest sense of the word, is a necessary component of yoga. As yoga proceeds by focusing on the internal manifestation of nature, rather than the external, one may prefer to use the word psychology in this context rather than physics.

We should remember, of course, that in the point of view under consideration psychology and physics are two sides of the same coin, for a strict correspondence exists between the internal and external forces and materials. Furthermore, given the fact that *śarīra* is both 'body' and 'psyche,' one might equally well have replaced psychology by physiology, using these terms in their widest connotations.[5]

As appearance of an unformed stone is different from that of the figure chiselled from *it*, the psychology or physiology of an ordinary, unformed, *prakṛta* man is not the same as that of an educated, *sanskṛta* man. Yoga psychology begins from where one is, but the description and explanation of ordinary man's behavior is only a beginning. The real interest is in the possibility of perfecting man. The concern in yoga is not only the diagnosis of the human condition but also the prescription and effecting of a cure which will make man whole. The healing of the body-mind is an integral part of yoga. Yoga is thus not only physio-psychology but also physio-psychotherapy.

It is perhaps necessary to remark that yoga physio-psycho-therapy aims at a level of being which is quite rare and unusual. The curing of subnormally functioning human beings and helping them live normally is obviously necessary and desirable, but it is not the primary concern of yoga. The healing at issue in yoga is not personal. It is not someone's personal neurosis or defect that yoga wishes to cure; it is the human condition that is of interest. One is heir to one's 'malady' by the mere fact of being human, or, to speak more correctly, by the mere fact of being an existent. No doubt, this condition is expressed in a particular form, and therefore may need particular remedies. Thus at any given moment the yoga prescribed for one person is not necessarily the same as that prescribed for another. Nevertheless, the forces being harnessed in yoga are not exclusive to anyone. The remark of St. Paul, in his *Epistle to the Ephesians* (6:12), that we wrestle not against flesh and blood, but against principalities, powers, rulers of the darkness of this world, and spiritual wickedness in high places, is apt in this connection, in spite of the different idiom.

However, one does not struggle against these large forces single-handedly or only with one's own power. The upward force also is more than personal. Man is between these large forces; he comes into existence owing to their interplay and is constantly subject to them. An image, not uncommon in Indian literature, is of two shores: man's life is the river that connects the two shores; both are needed for a human existence to have a definite form. The *Gītā* speaks of two major tendencies—daivic and asuric, godly and demonic, or upward and downward. Both make demands and create compulsions. Given the thoroughly value-laden, hierarchic system of yoga, we should recognize one demand as 'calling' and the other as 'temptation.' Man is between these two currents; his only choice seems to be to align himself either with the one or with the other, remembering, of course, that 'he that is not with me is against me; and he that gathereth not with me scattereth abroad' (Matt. 12:30).

Yoga thus attempts to reverse the usual, natural order; it is a struggle against *prakṛti*. In the right and proper order, the initiative and movement are from above: the lower parts of man listen to and obey the voice of the higher parts. *Śarīra* should do what *puruṣa* (or *ātman*) demands. Otherwise, from a metaphysical perspective, there will be no point to the present incarnation. The body-mind is animated in order to serve the demands of the inner being. If ill prepared and unable to hear the call or to respond, then *śarīra* has no meaning.[6] From the point of view of the *puruṣa*, this incarnation is wasted, it is an unsuccessful experiment, a mistake. A properly educated man, in response to the inner call of *puruṣa*, does what needs to be done, without undue concern for comfort or discomfort. At the end of the *Gītā* (18.73), when Arjuna says to Kṛṣṇa 'I will do thy word,' it is the informed *śarīra* willingly offering itself as an instrument for the purposes of the highest *puruṣa*.

Within *śarīra* there exists a hierarchy of organs and functions. More or less adherence to the right internal order indicates degrees of preparation of the *śarīra*, the temple, vehicle, and the instrument of the inner principle. The mind (*manas*) can follow the desires of the senses, as is the usual case, or it can be receptive to the initiative of the *buddhi* (higher mind-heart, intelligent will), and direct the senses. Only in the latter case can the call of the *puruṣa* be heard, for *buddhi* alone is capable of this subtle hearing and seeing. If manas and the senses are not guided by *buddhi*, they cannot be useful to *puruṣa*. The first five steps, out of a total of eight, in the *Yoga Sutras*, are intended to bring the senses and the other vital functions, in particular the breath,[7] under a conscious control of the mind. The first two steps aim at a general moral and attitudinal preparation for undertaking yoga. The next three steps concentrate on posture, breath, and inward turning of all the senses. Assuming at this stage a certain quietening of the senses, the last three steps of yoga attempt to bring the mental consciousness (*chitta*)[8] under the subjection of that which is higher.[9]

The various steps of yoga are ordered yet are not sequentially linear in the sense that a completion of one step is required before the next one can be undertaken. Some of the apparent linearity arises from the analytical and linguistic nature of the exposition. Another remark which is useful here is that the earlier steps are preparatory to the later ones, but do not determine them completely. A right physical posture or moral conduct may aid internal development but does not guarantee it; more often, the external behavior reflects the internal development. For example, a person does not necessarily become wise by breathing or thinking in a particular way; he breathes and thinks that way because he is wise.

While moral, physical, and mental cultures are important components of yoga, the point of the effort is beyond the body-mind. The aim of yoga is transcendent. The whole of the physio-psychological work is a preparation of the vehicle to make it fit and suitable for the descent of the spirit. However, none of this work can coerce the spirit. There is no knowledge or method by which we can appropriate the spirit; the only thing we can do is to prepare ourselves so that we may be appropriated by the spirit.[10] Yet the king needs a suitable place for his arrival. It is well recognized in Indian lore that when spiritual experiences occur without a proper preparation of the body and the mind, the tremendous forces involved can shock the organism into severe illness or insanity. There is a legend about sage Bhāgiratha who performed austerities for the descent to the earth of the sacred Ganga, the river which originates in heaven. It was feared that the earth could not bear the shock of her fall. Śiva, the deity of yogis and dancers, caught Ganga on his brow and checked her course with his matted locks, from whence she flowed in seven streams. This is why he is called Gangādhara, upholder of the Ganga. Microcosmically, for the stream of wisdom to descend without destruction, one would need the strength of Śiva riding his bull Nandi, having burnt Kāma, the god of desire, with his third eye, and having withstood the drinking of poison.

The most significant aspect of yoga and the one which distinguishes it from ordinary physio-psychotherapy, is the transcendence of its aim. That which a yogi seeks does not serve his own purposes. In fact, as long as he has his own purposes, he cannot be really open to higher purposes.[11] The whole meaning of religious life can be understood as a progressive freedom from the hindrances that impede one's availability to the purposes of the supra personal intelligence. One of the major hindrances is egoism. The *Yoga Sūtras* (2.6) define egoism (*asmitā*, literally, I-am-this-ness) as the 'identification of the Seer with the limitations of the eye.' The impression that the organs of perception define and prescribe the real perceiver is the root of the delusion that oneself as manifested in one's body-mind is the Seer. This delusion can be dispelled by the clear seeing of *jñāna* (gnosis, wisdom) alone.

Yoga physiology or psychology thus takes its direction and significance from the reality which is beyond the body or the psyche. This renders the physio-psychology of yoga sacred. The cultivation of the body or the mind for their own sake is not yoga.[12] The psychic healing of yoga has its center above the psyche; here the wholeness aspired for is that of holiness.

Normal physical and psychological functioning is necessary but not sufficient; without the movement along the vertical spiritual axis, any adjustment in the psyche constitutes only a horizontal rearrangement of more subtle matter. To confuse these two dimensions is a mistake, to ignore the horizontal dimension is dangerous, and to forget the vertical dimension leads to illusion and bondage.

Notes

1. Dharma will not do for a variety of reasons which are difficult to elaborate here. In the Bhagavad Gītā, dharma is used in many senses, but predominantly as 'order,' 'law,' and 'duty.'

2. The fact that 'mind' and 'body' follow the same laws or the fact that 'organic' and 'inorganic' materials are treated alike does not lead to the sort of reductionism associated with the modern scientific mentality in which the ideal is to describe all of nature ultimately in terms of dead matter reacting to purposeless forces. *Prakṛti*, although following strict causality, is alive and purposeful, and every existence, even a stone, has a psyche and purpose. Creation is from above downward. In contradistinction to modern scientific cosmology, 'mind' precedes 'matter.'

3. This Self is not personal; it is not his nor of someone else. This Self (*Ātman*) is what the Upaniṣads speak of as being identical with *Brahman*. Nor can one think of this as being inside a person and not outside. The *Kaṭha Upaniṣad* (11.1:10) says, 'What is within us is also without. What is without is also within. He who sees differences between what is within and what is without goes everymore from death to death.'

4. Kṛṣṇa identifies himself in the *Gītā* with the supreme *Brahman*, supreme *Ātman*, and supreme *Puruṣa* at various places, and frequently shifts from a personal mode of speaking to an impersonal one. Personal-impersonal, subjective-objective, internal-external and other such dichotomies are too often said to be transcended by sages to be taken rigidly.

5. All these remarks may appear less strange if one keeps in mind older Western connotations of words like 'physics,' 'physiology,' 'psyche.' For Plotinus, for example, a stone has a 'psyche' as a man does. In this connection, see A.H. Armstrong and R. Ravindra: "The Dimensions of the Self: Buddhi in the *Bhagavad Gītā* and Psyché in Plotinus," *Religious Studies*, Vol. 15, 1979, 317–332. This paper is also pertinent to the subsequent discussion particularly as it relates to *buddhi*.

6. Of course, it still has a function as part of nature following laws of cause and effect.

7. The quality of breathing in a person is intimately and directly related with one's inner state, as is apparent from even a superficial observation of oneself. Traditional appreciation of this fact is reflected in words like *pneuma* which in Greek means breath, air, as well as spirit, or *ātman* which in Sanskrit means self or spirit and also means breath like its German cognate *atmen*: to breathe.

8. *Chitta* includes not only reason but also emotions. These emotions, unlike the higher ones proper to *buddhi* such as *bhakti* (love and

devotion) and *śraddha* (faith), arise from *saṁkalpa* which is imagination or desire-well; this in turn is nourished by sensual pleasures and displeasures.

9. Patanjali's yoga ends here for he defines yoga to be the control of the fluctuations of *chitta* (Y.S.1.2). His method is like a frontal attack on consciousness. The yoga of *Bhagavad Gītā* has many more dimensions, which are integrated as several instruments in an orchestra, so that a yogi may conduct a symphony as Kṛṣṇa does on a larger scale. If one does not get stuck in the obvious over-simplification involved, it may be possible to view the *Yoga Sūtras* as appealing initially to the *brāhman svabhāva* in the *rajas* mode, whereas the *Bhagavad Gītā* speaks to a man of any *svabhāva* in either the mode of *rajas* or *sattva*.

10. This point radically distinguishes modern Western science with its external approach and urge to control what it studies, from ancient sciences, Eastern or Western, dedicated to the harmonization and conciliation of the knower and the object of knowledge. In this connection, see Chapter 7 of the present volume, and also R. Ravindra: "Review of Visionary Physics: Blake's Response to Newton by D.D. Ault," *American Journal of Physics*, XLIII, (1975), 1114–16.

11. In this connection, see R. Ravindra, "Self-surrender: the Core of Spiritual Life," *Studies in Religion*, III, (1974), 357–63. See also R. Ravindra, *Whispers from the Other Shore* (Wheaton: Quest Books, 1984), chapters 1 and 6.

12. Examples of this kind are physical and mental gymnastics performed for material rewards or at best for the pleasures of the body or the mind in the sports world and academia. Perhaps the major cause of our contemporary cultural disorientation is the lack of connection between scholarly, artistic, and scientific 'research' and any 'search' for the transcendent. This shortcoming exists not only in practice but even in the prevailing theory of knowledge.

FOURTEEN

SCIENTIFIC KNOWLEDGE And SPIRITUAL UNDERSTANDING

Priscilla Murray

The coming of a spiritual age must be preceded by the appearance of an increasing number of individuals who are no longer satisfied with the normal intellectual, vital, and physical existence of man, but perceive that a greater evolution is the recognized goal of the race. In proportion as they succeed and to the degree to which they carry this evolution, the yet unrealized potentiality which they represent will become an actual possibility of the future.[1]

The Knowledge Which Cannot Be Told

There is a story told in the Chāndogya Upaniṣad[2] about the young Brāhmin, Śvetaketu, who, at the age of twelve, was sent by his father to study the Veda. To be a Brāhmin—a member of the priestly caste—one must be born a Brāhmin, but Śvetaketu's family believed that one could not be a true Brāhmin by birth alone. Śvetaketu left and, having learned the scriptures, returned home when he was twenty-four. He considered himself very knowledgeable and had an extremely high opinion of himself.

His father said to him, "Śvetaketu, you seem very arrogant. I wonder, have you yet asked for that knowledge by which you could hear what cannot be heard, and by which you could know what cannot be known?"

Śvetaketu then realized that even with all his learning he was not yet a true Brāhmin. He sensed for the first time a deeper, richer understanding of what being a Brāhmin might mean; that it would mean not merely adopting the name but being engaged in a study of *Brahman*, the Vastness, connected to that aspect of reality which is eternal and unmanifest.

This story could be retold in a modern context, perhaps about a young woman who after attending university and gaining a great deal of scientific knowledge feels that she knows all there is to know and that she would know more with any advance of science. What could she say if she were asked if she understood the mystery of life and knew the secrets of the universe? Perhaps she would say that he had never been told this knowledge. But can such knowledge ever be told? Can it be known?

How can the knowledge which cannot be told be known and how can the mystery be penetrated?

All of the spiritual traditions have claimed that human beings, as they are, no matter how much they have learned, are incomplete—that they are not whole, not holy. This is expressed in many ways: it is said, for example, that human beings suffer, that they live in sin, in ignorance or in bondage. Those who do not know the mystery of God are often spoken of in the gospels as: "seeing they may see, and not perceive; and hearing they may hear, and not understand."[3] In each of the traditions it is stated that liberation or salvation from this level of existence can be achieved only if a person becomes other than he or she is naturally, by becoming a new person, reborn of the spirit having undergone a *metanoia*, a radical transformation of consciousness.

Except a man be born again, he cannot see the kingdom of God. That which is born of the flesh is flesh and that which is born of the Spirit is spirit.[4]

In order to have new knowledge, a new being is required, for knowledge is a function of being. When there is a change in the being of the knower, there is a corresponding change in the nature of the knowledge which is possible. We see this even in the ordinary process of growth which takes place in a growing child: as the child matures the kind of knowledge accessible to the child changes. But the transformation involved in a spiritual birth is of a much more radical sort. It is not merely a result of learning new facts, of having more general or more inclusive theories, of building larger structures, of seeing smaller entities or even of having better habits. Rather, those who have achieved a new being, which is not natural and which is not given at birth, apprehend the whole of reality differently. They are the saints and sages who have new eyes, new ears and who can see and hear what we cannot ordinarily see and hear. Although such a transformation is rare, it is possible for humankind by way of a spiritual path.

The Reasoning Mind

The characteristic which distinguishes human beings from animals is the possession of a certain quality of mind and the possibility of a corresponding quality of knowledge. This level of mind, which may be called 'the reasoning mind,' is not only intellectual, but at its best, allows human beings to function as intelligent, sensitive and perceptive beings capable of producing change in the world. It refers to a certain quality of thought, feeling, perception and technical ability through which an understanding of the world and our relationship with it may be reached and by which what we understand is revealed.

Science, art, and philosophy represent several ways of reaching such an understanding, although what is sought may be named in a variety of ways such as reality, beauty, truth, or power. In each of these fields—science, art, and philosophy— the use of a different aspect of the mind is emphasized, although not to the exclusion of the others, and each relies on a distinctive methodological approach. The statements and the expressions from these disciplines are the knowledge which we as humankind have.

It is certainly not the case that all humans are equal. Not everyone has the same capacity of mind: some are more intelligent, others more sensitive or perceptive, while others may be more able to produce results. Talent, experience, and training of the mind are all required in order to reach and to express the highest possible quality of scientific, artistic, or philosophic understanding. Einstein's theory of relativity, the Taj Mahal, Bach's fugues, and Kant's *Critique of Pure Reason* are all products of this mind. But it is also the same reasoning mind which permits even a very rudimentary inquiry about the world, or a primitive expression of a feeling, or allows any question of value to be raised. So although the quality of this mind can vary enormously in different people, or in the same person at different times, animals below the level of humanity can never be scientists, artists, or philosophers in any sense.

This capacity of mind is also responsible for results representing a great range of moral standards, from the good of humanitarian efforts in the world to the evil of the Holocaust. The concerns of the reasoning mind vary greatly in size and scale, from a study of the universe to an investigation of subatomic particles, and from the development and use of the nuclear bomb to the concern about the right color of shirt to wear.

Although it is a very complex issue, this whole level of mind can be characterized by the ability to separate whatever is known from the process of knowing, and thus to regard what is known as an object.[5] This is so whether what is seen is external, like a stone, or a diagram, or an object which is inferred such as an electron, or whether it is internal, such as thoughts, feelings, and sensations, or whether what is known is the observer himself. Self-consciousness, in the sense one can be aware of oneself as an object and of the things which go on in oneself, together with conceptualization, the naming of objects, memory, judgment, and reflection are all made possible by the functioning of the reasoning mind. It is because we have this level of mind that we have the particular knowledge of the world which we have.

We do not always behave with the kind of objectivity which enables us to separate ourselves from the objects of our perception and thought. There are occasions, more or less often for each of us, when we are lost in the situation, when we do not see what is going on and therefore react in either an instinctive or a habitual way. This sort of response is often spoken of in the vernacular as acting absent-mindedly or blindly, although both mind and sight are present in the physical sense. The sight which is lacking in such an instance, when we operate with less than full human potential, is the sight made possible with the reasoning mind. I would suggest, although I do not wish to defend this position here, that this more mechanical way of being is the usual state. It is difficult to act effectively, or to take thought, or to have sensitivity, or to be perceptive, and when all of these function simultaneously it is indeed a cause for celebration. The reasoning mind allows a wonderful and valuable relationship with the world which has infinite possibilities and which needs to be and can be nurtured and developed.

Scientific Knowledge

In the whole wide and wonderful kingdom of the reasoning mind, science has become the queen. She has become so because of the power that can be realized with the application of the results of scientific knowledge. The prediction and control of phenomena which science allows can be used to satisfy, as far as possible, the fundamental human wish to obtain what we need or desire and to avoid what we dislike or fear. With every advancement of science a greater likelihood of satisfaction is anticipated, a greater power is expected. Science has already given us immense power. Through the amazing achievement of scientific knowledge men have walked on the moon, smallpox has been eliminated, people have been revived from near death, and weapons are available which could destroy the nation of any of those whom we fear. What could be more seductive?

The possibility of prediction and control is guaranteed by the very process by which scientific knowledge is produced. Among other requirements, a statement of scientific law is accepted as true only to the extent that, based on the observation of previous events, its application can be used to successfully predict what will happen in a controlled situation. Thus, if the relevant natural laws are known, then insofar as the necessary conditions can be produced or avoided, there is a corresponding control of the results. Science is concerned with the laws correlating successive events—with understanding the regularities in natural processes; and the secret of the power of science consists in the fact that a knowledge of these laws can be used to effect changes in the world which will be useful for our purposes. What our purposes are or what they might be is another question.

The public nature of scientific knowledge has always been regarded as an important characteristic of its objectivity. In order to eliminate the influence of what is merely personal, all scientific observations are required to be publicly verifiable; that is, given the same experimental conditions, they must be repeatable by another who is equally competent. The quality of the person observing is not relevant. In fact, a mechanical or electronic instrument which can take the appropriate measurements is likely to be more reliable than a human, since it does not have unpredictable personal idiosyncrasies. What is to be observed must also be quantifiable in order to remove the need for any subjective judgment. Any scientific theory or hypothesis must also satisfy the requirement for publicity. A theory or hypothesis must be capable of being formulated so that it could be understood and verified by others of equal competence and training, and it must be consistent with and related to the whole body of accepted scientific knowledge; otherwise, it cannot be considered reasonable.[6]

In science what can be said to be true and, therefore, what can be known is limited to facts which are empirically observable, to statements of laws which can be used to predict events, and to theories which can explain coherently a large number of facts and laws. No revelation or insight will be accepted as true or as knowledge unless it satisfies all the conditions of verifiability established within the scientific process. Thus for science, there can be no knowledge except scientific knowledge. This seems a terrible conclusion, but of course it must be so. It does not follow from this that scientists can have no knowledge except scientific knowledge. Only those scientists who acknowledge a larger truth than scientific truth, whether such a possibility is or could be articulated, can have other knowledge. Similarly only those who acknowledge a larger truth than is possible for the reasoning mind can have more knowledge, such as a knowledge which is not of something separate from the knower, but which is a knowledge of the being of the knower. Only when Śvetaketu suddenly realized this possibility as his father questioned him was he able to receive a teaching of another order of knowledge.

Science, as well as demanding objective criteria for the gathering of data and the testing of claims, is objective because it studies entities, which are separate from the knower—large and small, internal and external, visible and invisible. It is concerned with the properties of matter and energy and with events which involve the movement or the change of matter. Physics is the most fundamental of the sciences because the objects of study are the basic components of matter and energy and the laws which govern the relationship between them. Since everything which can be investigated is made up of matter and energy of some kind, the truths of physics are considered to be the most general and the most universally applicable.

Yet some of the objects which are formed of matter and which have energy are also alive. The science which studies these objects is biology. The basic unit of living entities is the cell, although cells are made up of matter and energy. Some things have the property of life, others do not. Those things which are alive can be studied as if they were dead matter. In fact it is more correct to say that they can be seen to be merely a complex way. It is assumed matter, organized, to be sure, in that from this complexity the characteristic properties and variety of life arise, yet an increase in complexity is a quantitive change and may not result in a qualitative change. So although biological substances and processes are regarded as more complicated than simpler physical materials and events, there is a subtle implication that since physics investigates not merely that which is common to everything but is engaged in the study of the basic components of which everything is ultimately made, it knows or might come to know about everything, and thus biology is really a branch of physics.

If science does not acknowledge that the presence of life

indicates the existence of a radically different category of systems, rather than being another property of the same matter and energy which also constitutes non-living entities, then it remains basically reductionist and must always conclude that there is nothing else to know about except physical matter and energy and the laws which govern their behavior.

Just as living beings often are regarded as if they are the same as non-living systems but with different properties, those higher level beings which have an animal nature or those who have a reasoning mind are often considered to be merely physical systems possessing certain properties which arise from the increasingly complex organization of that matter and energy. Although the assumptions from which this attitude springs are not necessary for a scientific inquiry, the materialistic perspective has become the predominant view of modern science and has come to seem to be the only possible one which a reasonable scientist could hold.

Scientific methods of investigation and of theoretical explanation can be and are applied to those things which exist at the level of animal life and at the level of the human mind. The resulting branches of science—zoology, medicine, psychology, and sociology—have different domains, yet with an assumption of scientific materialism, they can only be branches of physics in the same way that biology is.

From another perspective, which also regards the emergence of life as completely unaccountable and anomalous yet understands that those things which are alive or which are dead, having been alive, comprise another kind of substance than matter which is not and has never been alive, physics could be regarded as a science of non-living systems of matter and energy, or of the matter and energy of living systems, but not of the life of these systems. From such a perspective it is clear that physics cannot study all there is.

Similarly if the levels of life with animal nature and with a reasoning mind are understood to represent different forms of existence from the levels of the simplest classes of life or of matter, then it is clear that a knowledge of the physical substances and the laws of their interactions is a very partial knowledge. All spiritual traditions have considered that the physical sciences are only concerned with a very small part of the world to be studied and learned about and moreover that the knowledge about the world which is reached through the scientific undertaking can be said to be true only within a very limited context.

Objective Knowledge

Modern scientific knowledge is essentially objective knowledge, in both the sense that it is intersubjective and that it is about objects which are understood to be separate from the knowing subject. It is therefore a knowledge *par excellence* of the reasoning mind. Because of the great success of the scientific method it has sometimes been assumed that the particular way of seeing objectively which has been developed and codified within the sciences is the only way of reaching objective knowledge, but not all objective knowledge is scientific knowledge.

Although scientific knowledge is impersonal knowledge because of the need which has been perceived to eliminate the subjective element of observation and judgment in gathering data or in verifying hypotheses, every man, every woman, and every scientist has more knowledge than scientific knowledge, but which is not verifiable in the same impersonal way that scientific knowledge is. That which is sensitive or perceptive or thoughtful within us may also have knowledge which is entirely reasonable, produced by the reasoning mind about the world which is its object. This knowledge may be expressed in many ways other than by statements of empirical fact and theoretical explanations about them. Knowledge may be manifested, for example, through artistic expression of all sorts, through philosophical reflection and in relationship, both between individuals and within the larger societal structure.

Value judgments, philosophical theory and aesthetic considerations may be merely personal, but they may also be supra-personal; that is, they may express not only selfish concerns and interests but they may represent and call for the highest standards of behavior, thought, feeling, and perception. At their best, they seek what is good, possible, and beautiful, whereas science seeks what is true. Philosophy and art are objective both in the sense that they seek to understand and know about the world and our situation in it and in the sense that they have standards which are not merely personal.

Einstein wrote[7] of the role of science in ascertaining what is, in determining how facts are related and conditioned by each other, yet he saw clearly that science could not determine what the goals of human aspiration should be. He realized that value judgments and ethical concerns remain outside the domain of science but that they are always necessary. The feeling he had which arose from his deep conviction of the rationality of the universe and the awareness he had of the marvelous order, revealed both in nature and in the world of thought, he called "a cosmic religious feeling."[8] It was this sense of wonder which he felt inspired men and woman in their work. Such an appreciation of the world constitutes more of an artistic relationship with it than a scientific one. It is not therefore an invalid one, but a different one.

Many other great physicists, such as, Heisenberg, Planck, Eddington, and Schroedinger, have also understood that the statements which can be made by modern science are valid only within a limited framework.[9] Those scientists who have worked at the frontiers of science are the ones who can best see the limitations of science, both because they have direct experience of its boundaries and because, in general, they have reached such a position due to an excellent quality of mind.

While science has limited itself to a study of what is material—of the fundamental particles of matter—philosophy and art do not have the same limitation, although they have others. They are generally not materialistic in the way that science is, although they may be. Or it may be claimed that they are vitalistic, idealistic, or personal, terms which are frequently used in a derogatory manner by those who make the assumption of materialism.

Science, philosophy, and art are all produced by that capacity of mind which is able to regard what is seen as object; yet they are different enterprises with different approaches even to the same thing. If the object of inquiry were a particular man, a scientist, an artist, and a philosopher would treat him very differently. The scientist would subject this person to experiment, take measurements, and gather data from which to draw conclusions based on theory and hypothesis; the artist would try to see his essential nature clearly and express it; and the philosopher would wonder how this person could be known and what could be said truly about his position in the world. A psychologist, for instance, could engage with this person scientifically, artistically, or philosophically, or perhaps in a way which combined these perspectives.

Whereas science is engaged with a discovery of natural laws, art is concerned with an appreciation of the forms perceived in the world, and philosophy is interested in the evaluation of standards and methods, in ethical and moral considerations, and in a reflection upon the possibility and limits of the situation. There is far more objective knowledge possible for humans, who possess reason, than scientific knowledge alone.

The knowledge of the world available to human beings has infinite variety, unlimited possibilities for discovery, and a continued need for improvement of standards and techniques. Within the scope of this knowledge there will never be an end to what can be gained. We might well be satisfied to stay within this realm, striving for more and more knowledge and more and more power, unless we are faced with some questions which cannot be answered from within this place, no matter how extensive our knowledge. These are the questions which have always been called ultimate questions, like 'Why is it so?,' 'What purpose might we serve?,' 'What is death?' or like the one which Śvetaketu was asked by his father: 'Can you hear what cannot be heard?'

Or, having heard of or having had the experience of being different, of knowing differently, in such a way that what is known is not a matter of question and answer, of argument and proof, we can no longer be completely satisfied with this way of knowing, this way of being.

Spiritual Knowledge

There are two kinds of spiritual knowledge, and it is important to be clear about the distinction between them. One kind of spiritual knowledge is a knowledge about the spirit, as object, which can be gained by the reasoning mind. The object of study, of inquiry, of attention in this case is what may be called spirit, that quality of aspiration which has a more subtle quality than even an intelligent, sensitive, and perceptive mind and which is said by the sages of all the traditions to inform all levels of existence and materiality and to be the origin or the root of all there is. Before any study of the spirit can be undertaken there must first of all be an acknowledgment that such a quality exists and an ability to recognize it.

The objective knowledge about the spirit may be a scientific knowledge. If a modern scientist were to admit that some things, some people, could be classified as possessing the property of being spiritual and then proceeded to investigate them he or she would examine the properties of these subjects under certain conditions, perhaps by measuring the brain-wave activity or the changes in body-temperature. The subject's statements about childhood experiences or reactions to various stimuli could be recorded. Reason could then be brought to bear to examine the data in order to explain it and to develop theories which could be used to predict future results.

The scientist, as scientist, is interested in discovering the natural laws that govern the changes which take place, interested in an explanation and the consequent possibility of the prediction and control of events; thus what is learned will be useful in producing certain results and avoiding others, such as the prolonging of life or the prevention of illness due to stress—nothing else will count as knowledge. The concerns and methods of science determine what can be known. Science consists of no other knowledge except scientific knowledge, although it may be specifically about those things which are said to be 'spiritual,' or to have the property of possessing spirit.

But an objective knowledge about that which exists at the level of the spirit may also be artistic or philosophical. An artist may appreciate the quality of spirit and attempt to express this appreciation in some form of visual, aural, or verbal statement with more or less sensitivity and with more or less technical ability.

A philosophical knowledge about the level of the spirit may be gained by a study of the words and works of recognized spiritual masters or students of many traditions, who have lived through the spirit. Moral injunctions, rules of behavior, and ethical systems may be derived from this and then elaborated, interpreted, or followed. The cosmological theories implicit in the statements of the wise ones of the traditions may be discussed, analyzed, and clarified; the truth-claims and statements of purpose which they have made may be argued about or explained by reference to an accepted body of knowledge. Norms of social relationships, systems of justice, and theological theories, all of which form a part of the philosophical basis of the society, are often based upon an expression of the understandings of those who have a deeper insight into the nature of things.

The attempt to recognize and to understand something of the level of the spirit requires a mind which can be sensitive and attentive to the statements and accomplishments of those who have experienced reality differently—who have had spiritual knowledge of another kind. This other kind of spiritual knowledge is rare. It requires a transformation of being—becoming radically different in mind and body, being reborn of the spirit.

From the level of our ordinary understanding it is impossible to comprehend this different way of being or to know what those who have this extraordinary sight know, but because we are human, with the possibility of experiencing all levels of being, it is likely we have had some moments when we have been aware of ourselves, others, and the situation more directly. Yet perhaps the kind of knowledge the saints, sages, and seers have can most easily be understood by analogy. Their knowledge is related to that of ordinary humanity in a way similar to the way that human knowledge is related to that of animal creatures. Those who have this kind of spiritual knowledge know differently because they are different—they participate in another order of existence.

The process required to forge a new being is a spiritual path which gradually allows or causes a detachment from the way of being which sees everything as an object. This is not a simple accomplishment; it may be gained only at the cost of great suffering and sacrifice of oneself. It is said again and again, in the scriptures of every great religion, that one must die to the self, become selfless or empty of the self in order to make room for a new self. It is sometimes also said that one must empty the mind or become mindless. This is not in order to become brute-like and less than human, but in order to have room for more than this ordinary mind, in order to be able to see from a higher level of consciousness.

Those who have achieved a new being have a different kind of relationship with the world than is ordinarily the case. The characteristic of greater consciousness which is common to them is marked by a degree of understanding of and compassion for the self, others, and everything which exists which is only possible with a more direct awareness of reality rather than from a discursive knowledge about it. If a person in touch with a more developed spirituality were to meet the same man who had earlier been studied by the scientist, the artist, and the philosopher, such a seer would know his whole history and how it would be to be that man. Those people who have met a sage often report that they feel they have been completely seen with great love and without judgment. In sensing this they recognize the presence of a higher level of consciousness. In the gospels, Nathanial is amazed at Christ's insight. "Whence knowest thou me?" and then acknowledges "Rabbi, thou art the Son of God."[10] The Samaritan woman reports on her meeting with Jesus, "Come see a man who told me all that ever I did. Is not this the Christ?"[11]

These wise ones do not only know about higher objects, but they realize being in the world. It is based upon a different way of seeing rather than on an increasing amount of information. Yet with this greater sight there is a corresponding increase in responsibility; those who are able to see the situation with clarity are required to act from this knowledge.

When someone undergoes such a radical transformation of consciousness so that life can be lived from the higher level of the spirit, that one will be a new person and will have new knowledge. With such a transformation Śvetaketu would be able to hear what cannot be heard and to know what cannot be known. With such a transformation the world becomes different, and he becomes one to whom it can be said, "Blessed are your eyes for they see, and your ears for they hear."[12]

Acknowledgment

Over the years Ravi Ravindra and I have had many discussions about the possibility of a greater spiritual understanding and about the nature of the knowledge which we have. My thinking has been greatly influenced by his fresh and inclusive approach.

Notes

1. Aurobindo Ghose, *The Human Cycle in Social and Political Thought*, Sri Aurobindo Birth Centenary Library, Vol. 15, Sri Aurobindo Ashram Press, Pondicherry India, 1970.
2. *Chāndogya Upaniṣad* VI.1.i,ii,iii.
3. Mark 4:12. The quotations from the Bible are taken from the King James Version.
4. John 3:3,6.
5. There is a great deal of discussion about the way the knower and the known are related and how they affect each other. This way of speaking about a separation does not imply that there is no interaction between them.
6. For a useful examination of some of the assumptions of science, see "Experience and Experiment," Chapter 7, this volume.
7. A. Einstein, "Science and Religion," in *Ideas and Opinions* (New York: Bonanza Books, 1954), 45.
8. A. Einstein, "Religion and Science," in *Ideas and Opinions*, 38.
9. Ken Wilber, *Quantum Questions* (Boston: Shambhala, 1984). A selection of writings of some of the great modern physicists on the role and the limitations of the scientific enterprise.
10. John 1:48–49.
11. John 4:29.
12. Matthew 13:16.

FIFTEEN

YOGA And KNOWLEDGE

Ravi Ravindra

The Aim of Yoga

It should be stressed right at the outset that the point of view informing Yoga theory and practice originates from above, that is to say, from the vision of the highest possible state of consciousness. It is not something forged or devised, or even understood by the human mind, however intelligent such a mind may be. Yoga is a supra-human (*apaurusheya*) revelation, from the realm of the gods; mythologically, it is said that the great God Shiva Himself taught Yoga to his beloved Parvati for the sake of mankind. It is not validated or refuted by human reasoning; on the contrary, the relative sanity or health of a mind is measured by the extent to which it accords with what the accomplished sages transformed by the practice of Yoga say. It is a vision from the *third eye*, relative to whose reality the two usual eyes see only shadows.

However, it is important to emphasize that no mere *faith*, certainly nothing opposed to *knowledge*, is needed in Yoga; what is in fact required is the utmost exertion of the whole of the human being—mind, heart, and body—for the practice which would lead to a total transformation of being, a change not less than in a species mutation. Thus, Yoga not only brings the vision from the third eye of Shiva and of the sages for us to receive, but aims at helping us develop and open the third eye

267

in ourselves so that in reality we may be of like spiritual vision with Shiva and the sages. This is conveyed by the etymology of the word *yoga*: it is derived from the root *yuj*, meaning to yoke, unite, harness. When the human body-mind is harnessed to the Spirit (*Purusha, Ātman, Brahman*), which is as much within a human being as outside, he is in yoga.

Yoga is as much *religion*, as *science*, as well as *art* since it is concerned with being (*sat*), knowing (*jñāna*), and doing (*karma*). The aim of Yoga, however, is beyond these three, as well as beyond any opposites that they imply.[1] Yoga aims at *moksha*, which is unconditioned and uncaused freedom; by its very nature this state of freedom is beyond the dualities of being-nonbeing, knowledge-ignorance, and activity-passivity. The way to *moksha* is Yoga, which serves as the path, a discipline, and integration.

The aim of Yoga requires the transformation of a human being from his natural and actual form to his perfect and real form. The *prākrita* (literally, natural, vulgar, unrefined) state is one in which a person compulsively acts in reaction to the forces of *prakriti* (nature, causality, materiality) which are active both outside him as well inside. Thus the common man is a slave of the mechanical forces of nature; all his actions are determined by the *law of karma*, the law of action and reaction. Through Yoga he can become *sanskrita* (literally well-formed, cultured, refined), and thus no longer be wholly at the mercy of natural forces and inclinations. The procedure of Yoga corresponds to the root meaning of the word *education*: it helps draw out what in fact already is in man but was not perceivable in his unpolished form. The progressive bringing out of The Real Person within (*Purusha*) in an aspirant is much like the releasing of a figure from an unshaped stone.

The undertaking of Yoga concerns the entire man, resulting in the reshaping of mind, body, and emotions; in short in a *new birth*. Unlike sculpture, the remolding involved in Yoga is essentially from the inside out, for the yogi himself is the artist, the stone, and the tools. Lest this analogy be misunderstood to suggest that Yoga leads to a rugged individualism in which a man is the maker of his own destiny and there is nothing above him, it should be remarked that the freedom that a yogi aspires to is less a freedom *for* himself, and more a freedom *from* himself. From a strict metaphysical point of view, the yogi *himself* cannot be said to be the artist of his life; the real initiative belongs only to *Brahman* who is lodged in the heart of everyone. A person does not create the state of freedom; if he is properly prepared, and does not insist on possessing and controlling everything, he can let surface, and be possessed by, what is deep within himself.

The Body and the Embodied

Yoga begins from a recognition of the human situation: human bondage to nature and the consequent suffering. Since our internal nature is assumed to be made up of the same stuff and to follow the same principles as external nature, Yoga proceeds by focusing on knowledge of oneself. Self-knowledge may be said to be both the essential method and the essential goal of Yoga. Self-knowledge is clearly a relative matter, depending not only on the depth and clarity of insight, but also on what is seen as the *self* to be known. A progressive change from the identification of oneself as the body (including the heart and the mind) to the identification of oneself as inhabiting the body is the most crucial development in Yoga. Ancient and modern Indian languages reflect this perspective in the expressions used to describe a person's death: in contrast to the usual English expression of *giving up the ghost*, one *gives up the body*. It is not the body that has the Spirit, but the Spirit that has the body. The yogi identifies himself less with the *body* and more with the *embodied*.

But this identification of the person in oneself with something other than the body-mind and the attendant freedom from the body-mind is possible only through a proper functioning and restructuring of the body and the mind. Here it is useful to retain the Sanskrit word *sharīra* in order to steer clear of the modern Western philosophic dilemma called the 'mind-body' problem. Although *sharīra* is usually translated as *body*, it means the whole psychosomatic complex of the body, mind, and heart.[2] *Sharīra* is both the instrument of transformation as well as the mirror indicating it. The way a person sits, walks, feels, and thinks, can help him in knowing the relatively "realer" self;

the knowing of this self is then reflected in the way he sits, walks, feels, and thinks.

Sharīra, which is miniaturized or individualized *prakriti*, is the medium necessary for the completion and manifestation of the inner spiritual being, which itself can be understood as individualized *Brahman* (literally, The Vastness) whose *body* is the whole of the cosmos, subtle as well as gross. There is a complete correspondence between the microcosmos which is a human being, and the macrocosmos; the more developed a person is, the more he can also correspond to the deeper and more subtle aspects of the cosmos; only a fully developed human being (*Mahāpurusha*) mirrors completely the entire creation. To view the *sharīra*, or the world, as a hindrance rather than an opportunity is akin to regarding the rough stone as an obstruction to the finished figure. *Sharīra* is the substance from which each one of us makes a work of art, according to our ability to respond to the inner urge and initiative.

This substance belongs to *prakriti* and includes what are ordinarily called psychic, organic, and inorganic processes. The view that *mind* and *body* follow the same laws, or the fact that the *psychic, organic*, and *inorganic* substances are treated alike, does not lead to the sort of reductionism associated with the modern scientific mentality in which the ideal is to describe all of nature ultimately in terms of dead matter in motion reacting to purposeless forces. *Prakriti*, although following strict causality, is alive and purposeful, and every existence, even a stone, has a psyche and purpose. Creation is from above downward; in contradistinction to modern scientific cosmology, *mind* precedes *matter*.

Seeing through the Organs of Perception

Although there are many kinds of yogas, such as *karma yoga* (integration through action), *bhakti yoga* (union through love), *jñāna yoga* (yoking through knowledge), and others, the Indian tradition has in general maintained that there is only one central Yoga, with one central aim of harnessing the entire body-mind to the purposes of the Spirit. Different yogas arise owing to the varying emphasis on the methods and procedures adopted by different teachers and schools. The most authoritative text of Yoga is regarded to be the *Yoga Sūtra*—aphorisms of Yoga—compiled by Patanjali sometime between the 2nd century B.C.E. and the 4th century C.E. from the material already long familiar to the gurus (teachers) of Indian spirituality. It is clearly stated by Patanjali that clear seeing and knowing are functions of *Purusha* (The Person) and not of the mind. The mind is confined to the modes of judging, comparing, discursion, association, imagination, dreaming, memory through which it clings to the past and future dimensions of time. The mind with these functions and qualities is limited in scope and cannot know the objective truth about anything. The mind is not the true knower: it can calculate, make predictions in time, infer implications, quote authority, make hypotheses or speculate about the nature of reality, but it cannot see the objects directly, from the inside, as they really are in themselves.

In order to allow the direct seeing to take place, the mind which by its very nature attempts to mediate between the object and the subject has to be quietened. When the mind is totally silent and totally alert, both the real subject (*Purusha*) and the real object (*prakriti*) are simultaneously present to it: the seer is there; what is to be seen is there; and the seeing takes place without distortion. Then there is no comparing or judging, no misunderstanding, no fantasizing about things displaced in space and time, no dozing off in heedlessness nor any clinging to past knowledge or experience; in short, there are no distortions introduced by the organs of perception, namely the mind, the feelings, and the senses. There is simply the *seeing* in the present, the living moment in the eternal now. That is the state of perfect and free attention, *kaivalya*, which is the aloneness of seeing, and not of the seer separated from the seen, as it is often misunderstood by the students of Yoga. In this state, the Seer sees *through* the organs of perception rather than *with* them.

It is of utmost importance from the point of view of Yoga to distinguish clearly between the mind (*chitta*) and the real Seer (*Purusha*). *Chitta* pretends to know, but it is of the nature of the known and the seen, that is, an *object* rather than the pure *subject*. However, it can be an *instrument* of knowledge. This misidentification of the seer and the seen, of the person with his organs of perception, is the fundamental error from which all other problems and sufferings arise (*Yoga Sūtra* 2:3–17). It is from this fundamental ignorance that *asmitā* (I-am-this-ness, egoism) arises, creating a limitation by particularization. *Purusha* says 'I AM'; *asmitā* says 'I am this' or 'I am that.' From this egoism and self-importance comes the strong desire to perpetuate the specialization of oneself and the resulting separation from all else. The sort of 'knowledge' which is based on this basic misidentification is always colored with pride, a tendency to control and fear.

The means for freedom from the fundamental ignorance, leading to all sorrow, is an unceasing vision of discernment (*viveka khyāti*); such vision alone can permit transcendental insight (*prajñā*) to arise. Nothing can force the appearance of this insight; all one can do is to prepare the ground for it; it is the very purpose of *prakriti* to lead to such insight, as that of a seed is to produce fruit; what an aspirant needs to do in preparing the garden is to remove the weeds which choke the full development of the plant. The ground to be prepared is the entire psychosomatic organism, for it is through that and in that whole organism that *Purusha* sees and *prajñā* arises, not the mind alone, nor the emotions nor the physical body by itself. One with dulled senses has as little possibility of coming to *prajñā* as the one with a stupid mind or hardened feelings. Agitation in any part of the entire organism causes fluctuations in attention and muddies the seeing. This is the reason why in Yoga there is so much emphasis on the preparation of the body for coming to true knowledge. It is by a reversal of the usual tendencies of the organism that its agitations can be quietened, and the mind can know its right and proper place with respect to *Purusha*: that of the *known* rather than the *knower* (*Yoga Sūtra* 2:10; 4:18–20).[3]

Samyama Attention as the Instrument of Knowledge

In classical Yoga, there are eight limbs: the first five are basically concerned with a purification and preparation of the body, emotions, and breathing and acquiring the right attitude; the last three limbs are called inner limbs compared with the first five which are relatively outer. The three are *dhāranā, dhyāna,* and *samādhi, Dhārāna* is concentration in which the consciousness is bound to a single spot. *Dhyāna* from which is derived the Japanese *Zen* through the Chinese *ch'an,* is contemplation or meditative absorption in which there is an uninterrupted flow of attention from the observer to the observed. In these the observer acts as the center of consciousness which sees. When that center is removed, that is to say when the observing is done by *Purusha,* through the mind emptied of itself, that state is called *samādhi*—a state of silence, settled intelligence, and emptied mind, in which the mind becomes the object to which it attends, and reflects it truly, as it is.

The insight obtained in the state of *samādhi* is truth-bearing (*ritāmbharā*): the scope and nature of this knowledge is different from the knowledge gained otherwise, by the mind or the senses. Unlike the latter, the insight of *prajñā* reveals the unique particularity, rather than an abstract generality, of an object. Unlike the mental knowledge, in which there is an opposition between the object and the subjectivity of the mind, an opposition that inevitably leads to sorrow, the insight of *prajñā,* born of sustained vision of discernment, is said to be the *deliverer.* This insight can pertain to any object, large or small, far or near; and any time, past, present, or future, for it is without time-sequence, present everywhere at once, like light in physics.

The three inner limbs of Yoga, namely, *dhāranā, dhyāna,* and *samādhi,* together constitute what is called *samyama* (discipline, constraint, gathering). It is the application of *samyama* to any object which leads to the direct perception of it, because in that state the mind is like a transparent jewel which takes on the true color of the object with which it fuses (*Yoga Sūtra* 1:41). The special attention which prevails in the state of *samyama* can be brought to bear on any aspect of *prakriti* which encompasses all that can be an object of perception, however subtle.

The Natural Science of Yoga

The basic research method of the science of nature according to Yoga is to bring a completely quiet mind and to wait without agitation or projection, letting the object reveal itself in its own true nature, by coloring the transparent mind with its own color. This science is further extended by the principle of analogy and isomorphism between the macrocosmos and the microcosmos which is the human organism, so that *self-knowledge is at the same time a knowledge of the cosmos*. An example of this isomorphism is to be found in the *Yoga Darshana Upanishad* (4:48–53) where the external *tīrtha* (sacred ford, place of pilgrimage, holy water) is considered inferior to the *tīrtha* in the body, and external mountains and other places are identified with the various parts of the organism: "The Mount Meru is in the head and Kedara in your brow; between your eyebrows, near your nose, know dear disciple, that Varanasi stands; in your heart is the confluence of the Ganga and the Yamuna..."

A large number of aphorisms in the *Yoga Sūtra* (3:16–53) describe the knowledge and the powers gained by attending to various objects in the state of *samyama*. For example, we are told that, through *samyama* on the sun, one gains insight into the solar system, and, by *samyama* on the moon, knowledge of the arrangement of the stars (*Yoga Sūtra* 3:26–27). Similarly, many occult and extraordinary powers (*siddhis*) accrue to the yogi by bringing the state of *samyama* to bear upon various aspects of oneself: for example, by *samyama* on the relation between the ear and space, one acquires the divine ear by which one can hear at a distance or hear extremely subtle and usually inaudible sounds. Many other powers are mentioned by Patanjali; however, none of them are his main concern. There is no suggestion that there is anything wrong with these powers; no more is there a suggestion that there is something wrong with the mind. The point is more that the mind, as it is, is an inadequate instrument for gaining true knowledge; similarly, these powers, however vast and fascinating, are inadequate as the goal of true knowledge.

It is wrong to suggest that Yoga is not interested in the knowledge of nature and is occupied only with self-knowledge. From the perspective of Yoga, this is an erroneous distinction to start with, simply because any self, however subtle, that can be known is a part of nature and is not distinct from it in substance or laws or principles. And the deepest self, to which alone belongs true seeing and knowing, cannot be known; but it can be identified with. One can become that self (*Ātman*,

Purusha) and know with it, from its level, with its clarity. In no way is *prākriti* considered unreal or merely a mental projection; she is very real, and though she can overwhelm the mind with her dynamism and charms and veil the truth from it, yet in her proper place and function she exists in order to serve the real person (*Purusha*).

However, it is certainly true that the procedures, methods, attitudes, and perceptions involved in Yoga are radically different from those in modern science, as are the aims of the two types of knowledge.[4] In a summary way, one can say that in contradistinction to modern science the knowledge in Yoga is a third eye knowledge, transformational in character, without violence to the object of its investigation; it is a knowledge by participation, rather than by standing apart or against the object and is ultimately for the sake of true seeing and the corresponding freedom.[5]

Yoga, Prāṇa, and Qi

Proper breathing plays an extremely important function in Yoga. The quality of breathing in a person is intimately and directly related with his inner state, as is apparent from even a superficial observation of oneself. Traditional appreciation of this fact is reflected in all ancient, particularly scriptural, languages, in which the words for spirit, breath, and air are either the same or very close to each other. This is, for example, true in Sanskrit, Pali, Chinese, Hebrew, Arabic, and Greek. One of the eight limbs of classical Yoga is *prāṇāyāma*, which involves a training in right breathing. *Prāṇa*, which is translated as *breath*, is in fact the whole subtle energy of life, connecting mind with consciousness. *Prāṇa* is said to be present everywhere at all times. In Indian thought, *Prāṇa* is equated with *Purusha* and *Ātman* and with the cosmic essence and with *Brahman*. It is the vital energy making anything alive, the quality of being corresponding to the quality of *Prāṇa*.

Even at the most ordinary level of physical culture, tremendous feats of strength are accomplished by people who are able to control their breath. However, it is important to emphasize that to the extent *Prāṇa* comes closer and closer to the Spirit (*Purusha, Pneuma*), it cannot be manipulated or controlled from below, by the mind or the body. What one can do and needs to do is to allow the mind and the body to be pervaded by the subtle *Prāña*, which by itself will bring about an alchemical transformation of the organism making it more and more sensitive. Thus, in the final analysis, it is less a matter of controlling *Prāña* and more a matter of being controlled by *Prāña*. Therein lies the chief difficulty of making a scientific study of *Prāña*: what can be studied by the mind in the modern scientific mode is only that which can in some senses be manipulated and controlled by the mind and is thus below the level of the mind.[6] In the presence of something higher than itself, the mind needs to learn how to be quiet and listen.

Another remark needs to be made about the various practices of Yoga: what is below cannot coerce what is above. One cannot force higher consciousness or Spirit by any manipulation of the body or the breath. A right physical posture or moral conduct may aid internal development but does not determine it or guarantee it; more often the external behavior reflects the internal development. For example, a person does not necessarily become wise by breathing or thinking in a particular way; he breathes and thinks in that way because he is wise.

From what I can gather and understand about the notion of *Qi* in the Chinese, Korean, and Japanese traditions, it strikes me as very close to that of *Prāña* in Indian thought, with a similar range of breadth and subtlety, as well as similar difficulty of explication in the usual scientific terms. However, I may be entirely mistaken, and we may be dealing with quite different notions which only partially overlap.

Notes

1. In this connection, see R. Ravindra, "Is Religion Psychotherapy?—An Indian View," *Religious Studies* 14, 1978, 389–397. [Chapter 13, this volume.]
2. *Sharīra* here has the same import as *flesh* in the *Gospel According to St. John*, for example in John 1:14 where it is said that "The Word became flesh and dwelt in us." In this connection, see R. Ravindra, *The Yoga of the Christ in the Gospel According to St. John* (Shaftesbury, England: Element Books, 1990). The important point, both in the Indian context and in John is that the spiritual element, called *Purusha, Ātman,* or *Logos (Word)* is above the whole of the psychosomatic complex of a human being, and is not to be identified with *mind*.
3. In this connection, see. R. Ravindra, "Yoga: the Royal Path to Freedom," in *Hindu Spirituality: Vedas Through Vedanta*, ed. K. Sivaraman, Vol. 6 of *World Sprirtuality: An Encyclopedic History of the Religious Quest* (New York: Crossroad Publ., 1989) pp. 177–191.
4. In this connection, see R. Ravindra, "Perception in Physics and Yoga," *Re-Vision: Jour. Knowledge and Consciousness,* 3, 1980, 36–42. [Chapter 16, this volume.]
5. The reader's attention is drawn to R. Ravindra, *Whispers from the Other Shore* (Wheaton, Illinois: Quest Books, 1984), especially Chapters 1, 2, and 6.
6. In this connection, see R. Ravindra, "Experience and Experiment: a Critique of Scientific Knowing," *Dalhousie Review,* 55, 1975–76, 655–674. [Chapter 7, this volume.]

SIXTEEN

PERCEPTION In YOGA And PHYSICS

Ravi Ravindra

Knowing and Being in Physics and Yoga

One can say quite straightforwardly, and without any ambiguity, that both yoga and physics are interested in objective knowledge. (By physics I really mean science in general, physics in a more comprehensive sense.) On the other hand, I think it is rather a straightforward fact that the two 'knowledges' are different from each other. Many of the differences between them are centered around the nature of perceptions in the two disciplines. The primary reason for pointing out some of these differences is to avoid settling for an easy integration, a superficial reconciliation, for nothing is more soporific than to imagine there is peace when there is no peace. What will stop us from seeking further is an illusion that we have already found what we need.

In spite of our wish for a reconciliation between science and mysticism, we are very far from even having clear questions to raise in this context. We wish these disciplines to be reconciled because they appear to us to be, after all, significant manifestations of the human psyche, both very profound. We wish to imagine that somehow in modern times we have got hold of this reconciliation. Of course, we tend not to be very clear as to whether we are thinking of the scientific revolution of 1905 when Einstein put forth his theories, or of quantum mechanics in the 1920s, or of holography in the 1960s; it depends on whom one is talking to.

Every age in science has always thought, as we do today, that now we have the right scientific answers; now we know; now we are talking about precisely the same thing as the great mystics or the wise men of the past ages—if that seems to be an acceptable style.[1] If their answers don't appeal to us, then we say that now we really have the answers and the earlier people all missed out. Every age somehow believes that the present scientific theories have really got the answers or will soon have them. Still, we remain inwardly fragmented and in sorrow.

Let me make a simple observation. The sages of the Vedas and the Upanishads or the biblical prophets were saying whatever they were saying not just yesterday; they have been saying this sort of thing for thousands of years, and we find that there is much in common among them, across the races, across the ages, across space. Then, suddenly, we come on the scene with our scientific pronouncements which are likely to change in ten years or a hundred years or one thousand years. Almost certainly they will change in another three or four thousand years, which is the length of time over which we have had these sages and the prophets saying things which have not changed. So, one wonders about this easy equation of something which is very transient with something which we ourselves say has not changed and will not change because it is eternal and timeless. Six thousand years from now the sages of the Vedas and other mystical sages will still say the same things, whereas we can be completely certain that the physicists will say different things. Unless we imagine that in our steadily progressive science, we scientists are saying today the same things as the Buddha or Laotze, and therefore that in the next hundred years we will be able to say wiser things, then we must see what the differences are in what the scientists and the mystics say and seek.

It is obvious that observations and perceptions play a very great role in scientific knowledge. In fact, if anything, one might say that this was one of the great hallmarks of the scientific revolution of the sixteenth and seventeenth centuries—the insistence on the part of the new natural philosophers that observations were relevant to coming to truth, that one could not just sit down, think, and come to truth. The same is, of course, true in yoga. The whole point of yoga is to come to certain sorts of perceptions. Thus it is clear that the problem of perception is really a central one.

Before proceeding further, it is useful to be clear about what I mean by *yoga* here. Let me tell you a little story so that we can come to an understanding of what yoga means. It is a story from the Chandogya Upanishad. There was a famous sage who had a very bright son, Shvetaketu. When the boy came of age, his father said to him, "Look son, in our family we have been brahmins not only in name but also as real seekers of Brahman. (This is a little different from Brahma; Brahman means the vastness, the greatness.) We have been ardent seekers of this vastness, this is why we are called brahmins. Therefore you must go and seek the knowledge of Brahman."

So this bright young man goes out seeking the knowledge of Brahman and he studies, as is said, for twelve years. Then he returns, having mastered all the sciences, very learned, very arrogant, very self-assured, and he comes and tells his father about his learning. The father listens to him and asks him questions and determines that indeed his son is very learned. Then the father says, "Shvetaketu, now you are so learned and so wise and so arrogant. Did you learn that teaching by which the unhearable becomes heard? And by which the unseen becomes seen?" One can guess the answer Shvetaketu gave; he had not heard of such a teaching, he had not been taught this; otherwise he would not be so arrogant. Then he asks for instruction from his father who has knowledge of altogether another order of reality.

For our purposes here, what I mean by yoga is that teaching by which the unhearable becomes heard and the unseen becomes seen. I do not mean any specific path by this, but any spiritual path by which an internal integration takes place such that one becomes available to an altogether different, more subtle and more comprehensive order of reality. Literally, etymologically, the word yoga means integration. A yogi is one who is integrated.

Experiment and Experience

So any path by which human beings can be made whole and integrated is yoga. It is important for us to be clear about the distinction between whatever we have come to call *religion* and a *spiritual path*. I think these two can happily exist apart from each other; in general they seem to exist apart from each other. It may even be the case, at least this is my own personal impression, that most of what we call religion is actually an obstruction in the spiritual path. I wish here merely to draw a distinction between these two and speak only about the path, the way of yoga.

Perception is very important in both physics and yoga. They are both looking for objective knowledge, and they are both interested in empirical verification. They are experimental or experiential and empirical. But let me again draw a distinction. The distinction is between two words, *experiment* and *experience*. I wish to stress that the modern natural sciences are thoroughly experimental in character, but they are in fact almost determinedly contra-experiential. The fact is that these two words are often used as if they meant the same thing.[2]

Experiment comes from the Latin word *experimentum* and experience from the Latin word *experientia*. They are both derived from *experiens*, the present participle of *experiri*, which is made up of two parts, *ex* and *periri*. The second word is connected with the same root from which the word peril comes in English. Ex means 'thoroughly' in this connection. So, to try something thoroughly, to put oneself in peril, to risk one's self, to undergo—these are the root meanings of the word experiens. Experiment is also derived from this word; but for nearly three hundred years the words experiment and experience have been used in very different contexts. Experiment is no longer used as a transitive verb; it is used only intransitively, unlike experience.

For example, I can experience a flower but I cannot say I can experiment a flower. I have to say I can experiment on a flower, with a flower. One might think that this is just linguistic finesse and it doesn't really matter, but what is important is to draw attention to the fact that the word experiment, and the underlying attitude involved, already sets things apart from oneself.

One experiments on something; one can experiment on human beings, with LSD, on rats, on flowers, or whatever. What one experiences is something different. And what a scientist does in his laboratory is experiment with things, he makes measurements based on those experiments; it is wholly erroneous to say that he experiences those things.

Personal Equation

No doubt, if one is thinking of simpler observations, sometimes experimenting and experiencing may coalesce, come closer to each other. But this is so when one thinks of really simple observations, and would exclude practically all observations now made in science, especially in physics. What I am trying to get at is the question of the involvement of the person in perceptions in science. It is obviously rather a complicated question; I can go into only some parts here.

What is significant to point out is that as scientists we must try, as assiduously and carefully as we can, to avoid what we call the *personal equation*. This question has nothing to do with this whole business of whether quantum mechanics has reintroduced the observer into the picture; that is quite irrelevant here. What I am trying to say here is that whether I am feeling angry or happy, whether I love my wife this morning or I don't, whether I am short or tall, or any of these considerations, whether I am a Buddhist or a Hindu or a Christian, whatever one means by any of these, one must try to eliminate all such considerations from the experimental observations.

To be sure, historians of science have often pointed out that it is not always easy to be free of these considerations. When one actually looks at some previous scientific work, one can sometimes see that because so and so was a German, he was thinking along such lines, and because someone else was English, he thought along different lines. There are national styles of doing science, and there are specific decades and centuries during which specific problems were considered more important in England than in France, etc. A scientist's cultural and personal conditioning naturally affects the style and the direction of his inquiry. Nevertheless, one must try to eliminate from science what we call the personal equation.

We should follow this a little further because it is an important matter. Often it is said that this effort to eliminate the personal is what makes science international; this is what makes science intersubjective because we are not caught up in our subjective emotions. Underlying this is a wish for objectivity and also a very correct perception that most of our emotional life, ordinary emotional life, is contradictory. It is based on "I like this" or "I don't like that"; or it is based on fear or pleasure. It is a good idea for the sake of objectivity not to fall for these subjective ramblings of the heart or the mind. There is a right perception underneath all of this, and the attempt in science has been, more particularly since the great scientific revolution of the sixteenth and seventeenth centuries, to be freed of these personal wishes and concerns in the process of making scientific observations and forming hypotheses.

On the other hand, what science has done is to throw the baby out with the bath water. It is a unanimous understanding in all spiritual disciplines (and this is the way I am using the word yoga here, namely, a spiritual discipline, as long as it is a discipline rather than merely a set of beliefs), that the feelings themselves are an agency of knowledge, instruments for the highest knowledge. What is required is a cleansing or a deepening of these feelings, making these feelings so honed that one can come to objective knowledge through feeling. One of Goethe's very perceptive remarks was that mysticism is a dialectic of feeling. By contrast, one could say that science is a dialectic of reason. Even observations and experiments in science are primarily generated by reason and are in the service of reason.

There is no doubt that both in yoga and physics there is an interplay between theory and observations, or, if you like, between conceptions and perceptions. But they enter these disciplines differently. In physics, experimental data, observations, and perceptions are all in the service of theory. They are either testing theories or generating larger theories. What we ultimately end up calling scientific knowledge is an ensemble of theories. Whereas, completely by contrast, the point of theory in yoga or any spiritual discipline is that it is in the service of perception. And it ultimately doesn't matter very much what theory one has. Theory is a device, a trick to quiet the mind or engage the mind or enlarge the mind. Of course, theory is required in yoga as well. As everyone knows, along every path one has to study a lot of metaphysical theory.

However, if a spiritual discipline remains within that, or remains in the service of enhancing further theories, it is the surest test that there is merely empty theological talk. Such speculative talk is pervasive enough for us to know that one can be easily caught up in this; all sorts of theology schools and philosophy departments are dedicated to this. We should remember that the usual religious person or an ordinary yogi or a common man aspiring to be a mystic is as far from the Christ or the Buddha as an ordinary scientist is from Newton or Einstein. We might as well keep our attention on great men so that we can understand the deep differences among them by looking at the best practitioners of their respective crafts. So what is at issue here? I don't think that ultimately the point about the Buddha or the Christ is that they have a metaphysics, a theory. But the point about Newton and Einstein is that they have a theory. That is their importance. So perceptions and conceptions play roles in physics different from the role played in yoga.

Now I wish to look at the other point mentioned earlier, the business of trying as carefully as possible to eliminate the personal equation. Underlying this is the great motivation for objectivity. Elimination of oneself or one's emotions from scientific observation has far-reaching consequences. The point is that, strictly speaking, the nature of the scientist should not affect the observations he makes. Let me give an example: The only thing that is relevant to physical optics is that which would be available even to a blind man.[3] We need to ponder over this for a moment. In physics, when we come to constructing theories or devising experiments in optics, they should be available even to a blind man. What it also means is that the state or the nature of the scientist is irrelevant to his observations.

For example, whether it is the Buddha looking at a bunch of electrons or whether it is an ordinary person looking at them, even though they may see different things, we must select only that part of their perceptions which is common to both of them.

I think this is a way of impoverishing our perceptions. Since the state of consciousness or the state of being of the scientist is irrelevant to his observations, the net result is that all scientific observations in reverse are irrelevant to the state of consciousness of the scientist. Nothing in science would help raise anybody's level of being, at least nothing in science as we know it now, as we practice it now.

It is actually built right into the metaphysics of modern science that the state of being of the scientist is irrelevant to the science he produces. Whether he is a good man or a bad man, whether he is fearful, hateful, or kind, is beside the point in determining his qualities as a scientist. (One should keep in mind that a majority of all scientists and technologists in the world actually work for the military in one form or another.) It is built right into our procedures and assumptions that the state of a person's consciousness or the level of his moral preparation is irrelevant to the quality of science he does. Now I am simply pointing to the obverse of this idea; whatever we know in science or via science is going to be impotent in changing our level of being.

What is partly involved here is a very old philosophical debate which necessitated this kind of limitation on oneself. This is a debate which took on particular importance in the sixteenth and seventeenth centuries in Europe, namely the distinction between primary and secondary qualities. Since one wants to get on with the business of gathering knowledge, one cannot take everything into account; one has to impose a certain limitation. Now the question arises: Which qualities or which properties of matter do we think are fundamental to reality and which are somewhat, relatively speaking, superficial?

Or in what basic terms should we attempt to explain the whole of nature? During the sixteenth–seventeenth centuries, very definite decisions were made about this, sometimes self-consciously, sometimes not so self-consciously; namely, that those properties which can be mathematically and quantitatively determined—such as mass, size, and proportion—should be considered primary. Later on, charge was also added to this list. But aspects of color, taste, smell, and touch should not be considered primary; these are subjective, secondary qualities.

Let me give a specific example. Physicists can talk at length about their methods; there may be uncertainties, but within those limits there are procedures and ways to determine what is the mass of an electron, and what is the charge of an electron. But if we were to ask what is the color of an electron, that sounds a little ludicrous, although some physicists do have fun with this kind of thing. Then we ask, what is the taste of an electron? That is a little subjective already, because what constitutes primary reality is mass and charge.

The interesting thing about these is that neither can be sensed directly by anybody; they are very abstract concepts. Then if one were to ask, "Well, what is the purpose of this electron?" then one is out of the scientific arena altogether. There are only certain properties of matter which are considered, somewhat *a priori*, fundamental. When we come to aspects like color, we can explain these in terms of other entities, in terms of vibrations of matter, vibrations of electric field, etc., ultimately related with mass and charge. Obviously, some lucky guesses were made in the sixteenth–seventeenth centuries; so much of physics has been based on these with such remarkable success. It is worthwhile pointing out that this distinction between primary and secondary qualities which made color essentially subjective and not a fundamental constituent of reality used to bother Goethe very much; this was an important point in his profound (but completely ignored) critique of Newton.

Perceptions in Yoga and Science

Coming back to perceptions again, what we are trying to do both in science and in yoga is to proceed from the assumption that reality as revealed by our ordinary senses is not quite what it in fact is; it is not the real reality. With unaided or unrefined senses one does not quite see the truth behind the appearances. On both sides this will be agreed upon. The direction from there for a physicist would be to enhance one's organs of perception through the development of scientific instruments. This enhancing of organs of perceptions is largely quantitative. I look at an object with whatever sorts of eyes I have; now with a microscope I can see smaller objects, or with a telescope, far-away objects, but I still look at them in exactly the same way; my valuation of them does not change. That is what I mean by quantitative extension here.

On the other hand, the direction in yoga would be much as expressed by William Blake, who was as great a visionary as any, namely, trying to cleanse one's organs of perception. That cleansing is qualitative, and perception of the same reality before and after cleansing has different quality and significance. This is why every spiritual discipline subjects the student to a great deal of personal suffering, because in a spiritual discipline the sculptor, the chisel, and the stone are all oneself. One is trying to sculpt something out of the given stone and with means which are really in oneself. (Of course, teachers can help, etc.; here I am not outlining the whole procedure.)

What is involved here is a cleansing of the organs of perception internally, and whenever one becomes aware of the muddiness of one's perceptions, then ensues something like the Dark Night of the Soul, causing much suffering to the person experiencing it. What is at issue here is not the elimination of feelings because they are unreliable, but the recognition that uneducated feelings are unreliable, preliminary to undertaking a discipline of training of feelings so that one can come to reliable feelings, more objective feelings.

What is happening is a complete reversal of direction. In physics we externalize our perceptions, even those things which are inside us we project outside, and in a way one can completely abstract even ordinary organs of perception and put them, as it were, in a sensor, in a computer. If we look at an actual scientific experiment, it is possible for us, given enough research grants, to set up a mechanism so that the scientists can go home to lunch, and the data will be there when they come back.

This is a very important point, particularly for people working in parapsychology or paraphysics because this is where the difficulty actually comes in. It seems that the parapsychological data are not available to a computer or a robot making measurements, and that it requires another sympathetic consciousness. In the usual scientific experiments, in general, the actual presence or participation of the human scientists is not necessary for the collection of data. Of course, a scientist is necessary in setting up the whole thing, in interpreting the data, etc.; so I am not proposing an elimination of the scientist from science. What I am saying is that the actual scientific perceptions—precisely where there is a direct contact with reality, whether one is measuring the scattering of electrons, studying the heartbeat of a fetus in the uterus, or investigating the reactions of rats towards certain kinds of controlled stimuli—do not need real, alive human beings. Perceiving can be done without the presence of the scientists as far as the collection of data is concerned. That is to say, perceptions can be completely externalized and one's organs of perception can be taken outside and quantitatively extended. This is not the case in yoga where, if anything, it is a complete and total internalization that is taking place. In both cases, however, the assertion is that our ordinary organs of perception, as they are, are not quite adequate for perceiving reality.

In yoga, an assumption is that as one is, so one sees. This is not at all true in science. Because only those perceptions must be admitted, or are allowed to be admitted, in which it is irrelevant what kind of a person one is. What is at issue here is the great sundering or separation between knowing and being; that the level of being of a person, or the state of consciousness of a person, is irrelevant to the sort of knowledge one produces. What is really underneath it is another point: What is the point or what is the purpose of the knowledge involved in these two cases? Why are we so excited about scientific knowledge? Supposing we knew all about Mars, what would that change? There is a remark of Albert Camus which really used to bother me when I was a young scientist. He said, in his Myth of *Sisyphus*, that whether the moon goes around the earth or the earth goes around the moon is quite irrelevant in life. I used to think what a strange kind of philosopher is this. But really, when you ponder over it, why are we so interested in scientific knowledge?

Knowing and Being

It is hard to answer this question readily. If one sees the uses to which scientific knowledge is actually put, in general, there seems to be a very strong wish for control and manipulation of whatever one studies. Of course, one recognizes that there are many things one studies which may not be subject to control, not easily. They may be too far; most things in astronomy are like this. Still the methods and procedures that have been developed are based on the wish for control. And it was classically so expressed by Francis Bacon, the patron saint of the Royal Society, that man should study nature in order to control her and utilize her for the betterment of the estate of man.

Now, this is hardly the point of view taken in yoga. I raise this point here to draw attention to a recent, in the last 15–20 years, emphasis in some circles on the study of consciousness. The important point is that as long as we approach the study of consciousness with our present scientific attitude, what we are always going to ask is how can we control it, how can we use it?

When this attitude comes into psychology, particularly in the transition zone between the psyche and the spirit, it always leads to what classically used to be called demonic tendencies.[4] If we proceed with the present scientific attitude to the study of the spirit, what we are going to be concerned with, even if we don't actually formulate it as such, is how can we appropriate the spirit for our purposes for our uses? So we ask, how can we use meditation to get ahead in business, to be better lovers, or to be more successful? In the matters of the spirit, the yoga attitude would be not how I could appropriate the spirit for my use but how could I be appropriated by the spirit for its use? There is a fundamentally different attitude to the purpose of knowledge, and to the value of knowledge; different kinds of perceptions and the means of perception are connected with it.

We might now take another step forward. One could say that in yoga the point of knowledge really is the ending of knowledge. This is how the word vedanta literally translates, meaning the end of knowledge. When one comes to the understanding or the realization of an essential unknowability of this Vastness (Brahman) of which one is a part, then one can become quiet in mind and heart and come to participate in this Vastness. In that sense, he who knows the Brahman becomes Brahman. One cannot know it, as it were, from apart. What one is saying here is that the central problem is of being, not of knowing. In yoga, knowledge or knowing is in the service of being, and ultimately it is like a self-destructive art. If it serves a certain function, then that knowledge is transcended, it is gone beyond. In the classical metaphor, knowledge is like a ladder one uses to go up; once one is up, it is somewhat stupid to be carrying the ladder. Science has a fundamentally different metaphysics underneath it, and it is a part of that metaphysics that being is not at all relevant to knowledge.

In the sense that ultimately the point of yoga is to end knowledge, one could say that the point of yoga is also to end individuality, to end the observer, the perceiver. As is said, it is only when one can leave one's self behind that one can follow Christ. This is what this little self is made up of, all this knowing: the past, present, and future; fears and pleasures; likes and dislikes. When one speaks of the path of yoga as chiseling a stone to help something else emerge, to help the sculpture emerge, it is precisely the chiseling away of the unnecessary parts that one has in mind.

This is how the right order emerges, as does the end of knowledge, the end of individuality, the end of separation, and the end of time. According to Patanjali, the celebrated author of the famous *Yoga Sutras*, the greatest illusion is what he called *asmita*. It is difficult to render this into English, but it is something like I-am-this-ness, the egoity. He went on to define this (and one can recognize a very similar remark made by William Blake) as the misperception that the Seer is limited by the organs of sight. Thus, the point of yoga really is to go beneath, behind, beyond—as the Upanishads say, he who does not see that what is inside is also outside is verily deluded—these ordinary organs of perception. Since to assume that the Seer is constrained by the apparatus of seeing is a fundamental error, a yogi purifies and integrates his perceptions so that he sees not as much with the eyes as through the eyes.

Let me end the discussion of this particular point by quoting part of a dialogue from a famous mystic, Jacob Boehme. A disciple says, "Oh, how may I arrive at the unity of will, and how come into the unity of vision?" And the master replies,

> Mark now what I say; the Right Eye looks in you into eternity. The Left Eye looks backward into nature, and the things of time, it

will be impossible for you ever to arrive at the unity you wish for. Remember this; and be on your guard. Give not your mind leave to enter in, nor fill itself with, that which is without you; neither look backward upon yourself....Let not your Left Eye deceive you by making continually one representation after another, and stirring up thereby an earnest longing in the self-propriety; but let your Right Eye command back this left...and only bringing the Eye of Time into Eye of Eternity...and descending through the Light of God into the Light of Nature...will you arrive at the Unity of Vision of Uniformity of Will.

These days all sorts of what used to be esoteric knowledge is readily available for $5 in any bookstore, and this knowledge, within this culture as well as from other cultures far away in space and time, is easily and promiscuously accessible. This is partly because of our scientific mentality which gives no importance to the distinctions between levels of being and between levels of knowledge. In such circumstances, where are our guardians? What are our safeguards? There is a traditional notion, not only in India but in every classical tradition of which I am aware, that truth is something for which one has to be prepared in order to understand it. But not only that; one has to be prepared to withstand it as well, because truth can be devastating. How are we preparing ourselves for all this profound esoteric knowledge so that we not only understand it but also withstand it? What preparation do our intellectual or political leaders have so that they don't misuse this knowledge? How is this esoteric knowledge going to transform our being if we regard it just as we regard scientific knowledge?

To imagine that our science of today is equivalent to ancient esoteric knowledge, presumably because of some superficial similarities in some expressions, is an indication of complete ignorance of the methods and aims of ancient spiritual traditions. Implicit in these sentimental assertions of similarity and equivalence of modern science and esoteric knowledge is a naive and arrogant assumption that tomorrow—next decade, next century, or surely by the next millennium—our science will far surpass the ancient mystics, sages, and prophets. From a spiritual and traditional point of view, such assertions are not merely innocent, but dangerous and soporific; they are ways of nullifying the impact of esoteric knowledge in bringing man into a state of wakefulness—to his proper place in the cosmos, to his responsibility in the maintenance of right inner and outer order, and to his real possibilities.

It is easy for us, individually and culturally, to be lulled back to sleep, away from a disquieting moment of waking up and seeing, into a dream in which we plan conquest of inner space and of consciousness and imagine ourselves at the same level of understanding as the greatest of past sages while remaining content with superficial appearances.

By our refusal to be woken up by esoteric knowledge, and by our wish to master it for our own egoistic purposes, we do not allow this knowledge to work in us to transform our being, to bring us to the end of knowledge that gives us acquisition and control, to help us be freed of ourselves and to bring us to a stillness in which we are aware of our essential unknowing and are not paralyzed by it into inaction nor frightened into the lap of deceptive security of explanations. Above all, we need right discrimination in order to see our situation clearly, and enough strength to bear the ravages of transformation.

Let me end with a little story which is relevant to this. There was a great sage in India called Bhagirtha. He made great efforts and undertook spiritual austerities; he was blessed with a boon by higher forces. Because he saw human beings parched for the life-giving waters of real knowledge, he asked the gods to let the river Ganga that usually flows in heaven descend to the earth. The boon was granted; but it was feared that since the river Ganga, which we might take here as esoteric knowledge, is used to flowing only in heaven, if it were to descend to the earth, the planet—ourselves as an ordinary body-mind— not being prepared to receive the shock of Ganga's descent, would be shattered. Shiva, the lord of the yogis, agreed to take the impact of the descent of the river on his head. From there, it comes down to the earth in seven life-giving streams. Of all the gods, Shiva is the guardian deity of transformation. He alone is able to overcome the sleep of illusion and subdue the force of desire with the fire of discriminative vision of his third eye. Who among us will act as Shiva in the present moment of deep crisis and radical opportunity?

Notes

1. It is not generally well known that Newton, whose mechanics are now considered heartless *bête noir* by all those who think that contemporary physics is mystically inclined, self-consciously attempted to model himself after the Chaldean mystic-scientists. He was convinced that he was not saying anything new which was not known to the wisemen of the ancient world. He said that even his inverse square law of gravitational attraction was known to Pythagoras and Moses, among others, and that he was merely espressing it in a form more understandable in his times.
2. For details, see R. Ravindra, Chapters 7 and 8, this volume.
3. This was especially emphasized by the positivist philosophers of the Vienna Circle.
4. For some distinction between the psyche and the spirit, see R. Ravindra, Chapter 13, this volume.

SEVENTEEN

SCIENCE And The MYSTERY Of SILENCE

Ravi Ravindra

"When I consider thy heavens, the work of thy fingers, the moon and the stars, which thou hast ordained; What is man, that thou art mindful of him?" – *Psalms* 8:3

Throughout human history, in every age and culture, whenever human beings have been struck by the grandeur of the cosmos and its workings, they have wondered what place they have in it. What meaning could our life, with all its limitations and smallness, have in the midst of very large forces operating in the universe? Is our earth significant when galaxies are continuously emerging and dissolving? Is "three score and ten years" of our existence, or a "hundred years" as the Vedas say, meaningful in the billions of years of cosmic expansion and contraction? What purpose does our life have when each year, on the average, one hundred million of us die? We die and are replaced by others, like you and me—with our ambitions, fears, and hopes. Why? For what?

Every human being sometimes wonders about the universe he lives in: its vastness, the variety of manifestations in it, with its endless transformations of substances and energies, and the intricate laws by which all this is regulated. That the universe exists is a wonder! And that it works and continues to exist is even a greater wonder. Each one of us is thus some sort of a scientist. We may not undertake investigations of the cosmos, and the forces and laws governing it, rigorously or in any systematic manner, but we could hardly be uninterested in the place where we have our being, where the Spirit manifests itself, where all the aesthetic possibilities are realized, where precise intellectual formulations find their concrete expression.

And, not to wonder about one's own existence—its meaning, function, and purpose? Is that possible? Unless one is determinedly partial and fragmented, one could hardly be oblivious either to the mystery of one's own existence, or to the mystery of the cosmos. Both mysteries exist, perhaps parts of one larger mystery. In the vastness of the universe, I am a small particle, a mere nothing! But, equally truly, I am the center of the cosmos, of my cosmos! What is myself?

How am I related with all there is? What perception is needed for me to hold the truth of my nothingness and my centrality in proper perspective?

These and such questions are not new; they are as old as mankind. In different forms and languages—myths, ideas, colors, musical notes, sculpture—these questions have engaged human beings everywhere.

When we are driven by other necessities of survival, or assertions of our ambitious egos, we may forget these questions for short or long periods. But something in us is always deeply unsatisfied unless we keep returning to some form of inquiry about our own nature and our relationship with others and the cosmos. Who am I? Why am I here?

It is hard to imagine an intelligent human being who is not interested simultaneously in the entire psycho-somatic complex of the cosmos and the animating spirit behind it. Whether one considers this at the scale of an individual body-mind and soul, or at the scale of the whole universe and the Cosmic Spirit, neither the perceived nor the perceiver can be ignored.

In the language of the *Bhagavad Gita* (13.2), "knowledge of the field and of the knower of the field is true knowledge." In Sanskrit, other words which are often used to describe the two realms are *prakriti* and *purusha. Prakriti* is nature in all its various aspects and levels of subtlety, including also the subtle psychic and parapsychic phenomena; it is the total domain of materiality and laws, everything that can become an object of study or thought or perception.

Purusha, on the other hand, is the perceiver, the self, and the spirit. Just as there is an underlying unity behind all natural entities and processes, all having arisen from common subtle matter obeying the same laws, there is an underlying unity behind all the knowing selves or consciousness. Individual consciousness is differentiated from a larger common consciousness through different mind-bodies, the material instruments of perception and action. This is one of the resounding affirmations of the Upanishads, namely that *atman* is *Brahman*. This is one of what are called "great utterances" (*mahavakya*) in the Indian tradition: individual consciousness is identical with the consciousness of the All, in essence. Or, as Krishna (the highest Purusha) says to Arjuna (who symbolizes an awakening individual consciousness), "know me as the Knower of the Field in all fields" (*Bhagavad Gita* 13:2).

Anyone who wishes to know Krishna must learn to know his own innermost self, for Krishna is not any particular being, born at this or that place, of this or that form or shape or color, but the innermost and the highest Purusha who is seated in the heart of everyone, the essential self of all selves.[1] He is represented in dark colors precisely because he is mysterious and unknown. He is often painted blue because he is vast as the sky or the ocean, as is our own self, which as said earlier, is declared by the Upanishads to be the same as Brahman (literally, Vastness).

However paradoxical it may appear on the surface, to come to one's own innermost self, most of us need guidance and instruction. The various spiritual paths and disciplines, often quite varied in their emphases and methods owing to different periods and places of their development and different types of psyches to which they are addressed, aim at precisely this: to prepare a seeker to come to and to stay in front of the naked truth in the deepest level of his being, without fear and anxiety which lead one to take the crutches of some doctrine or belief.

Here is a remark of the Zen master, D.T. Suzuki: "Meditation opens the mind of man to the greatest mystery that takes place daily and hourly; it widens the heart so that it may feel the eternity of time and infinity of space in every throb; it gives us a life within the world as if we were moving about in paradise; and all these spiritual deeds take place without any refuge into a doctrine, but by the simple and direct holding fast to the truth which dwells in innermost being."2

As long as a person is interested both in the Spirit and its dwelling place, *Brahman* and *Brahmanda*, one's inner self and the cosmos, *purusha* and *prakriti*, the knower of the field and the field, realm of purpose and that of action, one cannot but be interested both in the spiritual traditions and science. Although, as the *Bhagavad Gita* (13.26) says, all existences, moving or unmoving, arise from the union of the field and the knower of the field, human beings are particularly endowed with the possibility of the self-awareness of their real nature. This self-awareness itself has many levels and is something that needs to be cultivated and deepened and should not be confused with any supposed characteristic of homo sapiens which at some stage in history become a part of man and which he now automatically has from birth. Also, one must not fall into the easy temptation of thinking that since there is some sort of unity of spirit and body in all the creatures, nothing needs to be understood further. To refer to the *Bhagavad Gita* (13.34) again, real discernment of the differences between the field and the knower of the field is essential for coming to the supreme goal of liberation.

It is also good to remind ourselves that any real reconciliation of the demands of the spirit and those of the body is not a matter of general mental abstractions such as "science" and "religion." It is only in a unique particular in an individual's soul that any such reconciliation has any meaning. It is only in the concrete existential situation in which I simultaneously experience and intentionally embrace the different forces of the two realms of spirit and body or religion and science that I have a possibility of wholeness. Otherwise, one remains fragmented, thinking about or wishing for wholeness.

However, there are occasions when we reflect, from the outside as it were, about science and religion as cultural and social endeavors, and consider their procedures and presuppositions, their similarities and differences. The first thing a person notices both about the spiritual traditions and about science is their internal diversity. Not all traditions are alike, any more than all the sciences at different periods or in different cultures are exactly alike. After all, the keepers of the Jewish tradition differed enough from the Christian understanding to crucify Jesus Christ! And the orthodox Brahmins for centuries struggled against the Buddha and the Buddhists. In every tradition there have been many heretics; and many of these were far more passionate and divinely inspired about Truth or God than the orthodox. There is an inevitable hardening of any tradition with the passage of time, although, clearly, a tradition can be periodically renewed from within by those who are willing to seek beyond the dogmas and comforts of religions and are able to recapture the original vibration of the impulse, often in a new form for a new age.

Ultimately a true son of God brings no new teaching. His teaching is original but not novel, for wisdom that is eternal is not of time. It is the ancient way that he uncovers and reveals afresh for a new generation. "I have seen," the Buddha says, "the ancient way, the old road that was taken by the formerly All-Awakened, and that is the path I follow" (*Samyutta Nikaya* 2; 106). Yajnavalkya, in the oldest upanishad, quotes verses which were already old by his time, and which mention "the narrow path which stretches far away," by which "the wise are set free and ascend" (*Brihadaranyak Up.* 44:8). And nobody arrogates the honor of being a high priest to himself: he is called by God, as was Christ in the succession of Melchizedek (*Hebrews* 5:1–10).

Nevertheless, all teachings and great revelations degenerate; they get defiled by men like us—self-seeking and self-important. We move from inquiry to dogma, from exploration to explanation, and from spiritual paths to religions. In the process, we are once again trapped in beliefs and doubts, fears and desires. From seeking ways for freedom and love, we get taken by the means for possession and control. In the ancient simile of the many fingers pointing to the moon, rather than a transformation of our being so that we may come to the oneness of the moon of the spirit, we get continually occupied with the exclusivist fingers of religions and sects.

Science too is not the same everywhere and at all times. The Chinese sciences and the European sciences are different from each other in their fundamental attitudes toward nature. Within Europe, there are profound differences in the procedures and assumptions of post-sixteenth-century modern science and the earlier sciences. I have elsewhere tried to point out some of the presuppositions of modern science, which are persistent and continuous with the contemporary sciences in spite of some major revolutions within modern science in the twentieth century.[3]

Here, let me mention only three of these assumptions. The first one is that in modern science, in complete contrast to all traditional sciences, creation is assumed to be from below upward. Matter somehow came into existence, then, chronologically later and ontologically dependent on matter, arose intelligence and, later still, if it is admitted at all, somehow came the spirit. In that sense alone (and not in the sense of being interested only in the lower things of life) are scientists professionally all materialists; that is to say, they regard matter as prior to and the basis of everything else. For them, it is the body which has the spirit, whereas in the traditional cosmologies, it is the spirit, which for its own purpose and according to natural (not supernatural but "subtlenatural") laws, takes on a body. For example, in all the Indian languages, one would traditionally say that a person who has died "has given up the body." Presumably now he has gone into another form of existence and he may, if necessary according to the laws of *prakriti*, be reincarnated in another body. In a summary form, one might say that for the traditional cosmologies, matter is coarsened spirit, whereas for modern scientific cosmology, spirit is organized matter.[4]

Another extremely consequential aspect of the modern scientific procedures is that whatever is investigated is in principle capable of being subjected to control and manipulation by the scientists-technologists. The subject matter under investigation may be an elementary particle, or another culture, or the human mind, or extra-sensory perception; the general scientific attitude is of manipulation and control. What does this insistence on control and manipulation amount to in knowing something? Does it not guarantee that we cannot know, by these methods, anything more subtle or more intelligent than ourselves, anything that is higher than we are, if such a being or force is not susceptible to our control? If scientists speak of lacking evidence of anything higher than man, that is to be expected, for their procedures specifically preclude the possibility of such evidence.

The third aspect that needs to be mentioned here is the fact that, according to the metaphysics of modern science, the state of being of a scientist is irrelevant to the type of science he produces.[5] A related aspect is that in much of contemporary science, given enough research grants, a scientist can so set-up his experiments that the actual collection of data, precisely the place where he actually observes something about nature, can be done by a computer. This is true in experimental psychology as in physics. The state or the nature of the scientist is irrelevant to his observations, or more precisely, only those observations will be admitted into science to which his state is irrelevant. Whether it is the Buddha or an automaton collecting scientific data, only the aspects of their perceptions which are common to both will be accepted. In this impoverishment of our perceptions, the reverse principle naturally operates. Nothing in science can in principle change anybody's level of being; at least nothing in science as we know it now, as we practice it now. This change of a person's level of being, on the other hand, is the sole *raison d'être* of spiritual paths.

To point to these differences in some of the fundamental concerns and assumptions of the modern (and contemporary) sciences and the concerns of the spiritual traditions is not to say that an individual scientist cannot approach his work in the spirit and attitude of a spiritual discipline. Science, like all other activities, has the possibility of being a spiritual way, a ladder connecting different levels of being, for its practitioners. A noteworthy contemporary example is that of Einstein.[6] For him, certainly, an engagement with science was a matter of a spiritual vocation, a response to an inner call, a way of freeing oneself from one's egocentricity. But this attitude is as possible today as it was a hundred years ago, or three hundred years ago; and it is as little practiced now as it was then.

An integration of our intellectual and spiritual tendencies, or of science and religion as Einstein understood them—without meaning thereby anything denominational or institutional—is essential for the healing of ourselves and of the whole culture. It is important to stress, however, that the primary reconciliation that is needed is a harmonization of the various aspirations in the same person. The locus of reconciliation is within the soul of a single human being. The more an individual is integrated in his various faculties the wiser he is likely to be, in whatever specialty his own particular calling and capacities engage him. What makes any career a spiritual path is the breadth of view with which one understands its purpose and the motives for which one pursues it. So long as an occupation is primarily motivated by ambition for self-advancement and self-aggrandizement, or by fear and insecurity, or by gratification of personal pleasure and inclinations, it cannot become a spiritual path. Freedom from oneself is a necessary prerequisite for apprehending reality as it is rather than as we wish it to be. Freedom from one's personal subjectivity, however, is not obtained by appealing to a collective subjectivity which remains an extension of oneself in a horizontal plane. Real objectivity seems to include an altogether different dimension. When Christ says, "He who would follow me must leave self behind," he is calling for movement along a vertical axis of being. In this connection it is worth recalling a remark of Einstein as well: "The value of a human being is determined primarily by the measure and the sense in which he has attained liberation from the self."[7]

When science does serve as a spiritual path, then there are moments when one is bathed in the wonder of it all. One stays in front of the mystery in amazement. It is a mystery that broadens and deepens with contemplation. It is not a who-done-it type of mystery which will sooner or later be resolved by a new theory or a fresh clue or an innovative experiment. It cannot be resolved; it can be loved and deepened. One comes to the mystery of oneself and the mystery of it all. One knows somewhere that one must ask questions, one must do science, just as some others must write poetry or make music. All this is man, and precisely why the Old One, as Einstein occasionally called God, must be mindful of him as of everything else. It seems we must theorize to go beyond theory, we must intellectualize to come to a stillness of the mind, and we must make music to come to the silence.

Notes

1. This is a point worth emphasizing; otherwise Krishna can become a sectarian god in competition with others, as Jesus Christ has become in Christianity. Here we have in Christ a true messenger of the highest God, who like the Upanishadic sages says that he is one with the Father (*atman* is *Brahman*) and in order to follow whom, we have to leave our ordinary selves aside and delve deeper into our forgotten Ground. But Christians generally put an ordinary self on him with particularities of name, form, and place, and turn him into a sectarian miracle worker in whom they then believe with all the exclusivism and emotional vehemence of a frightened man, substituting believing for seeing and the crutch of dogma for the sword of gnosis.

2. Quoted on page 312 of *The American Theosophist*, vol. 68, no. 10, 1980.

3. See R. Ravindra, Chapter 7, this volume.

4. It is worth remarking that in neither case is it easy, if possible, to give a clear, rational explanation of how one level of existence arises from another. A very intriguing and engaging contemporary attempt is made by G. Gurdjieff as reported by his pupil, P.D. Ouspensky, *In Search of the Miraculous* (New York: Harcourt, Brace & World, Inc., 1949).

5. In this connection, see R. Ravindra, "Modern Science and the Spiritual Paths," *The American Theosophist*, vol. 68, 1980, 340–8.

6. See R. Ravindra, Chapter 24, this volume.

7. Albert Einstein, *Ideas and Opinions* (New York: Crown Publishers, Inc., 1954), 12. (Italics are in the original.)

EIGHTEEN

In The BEGINNING Is The DANCE Of LOVE

Ravi Ravindra

It is a reflection of our collective world-view, perhaps since the publication of Newton's *Principia* in 1687, that we regard questions concerning the origin, development, measure, and meaning of the cosmos as pertaining almost exclusively to the domain of science, and in particular to that of physics. In other words, for us moderns, cosmology is a branch of physics, a subject that since the sixteenth century has concerned itself with understanding the cosmos ultimately in terms of dead matter in motion in reaction to external and purposeless forces.

As is well known, natural theology has a long history. At the beginning of modern science, Kepler regarded himself as a priest of God in the temple of Nature. And for Newton, all his scientific work was a gloria in praise of God. Since his time scientists have felt increasingly uneasy about mentioning God, at least in their scientific publications. A long and hard struggle was necessary to establish natural science as an independent mode of inquiry, free of the tyranny of theology and the church, which had been coupled with temporal power. Now, especially since the making of the atomic bomb in 1945, it is science that is associated with power; and a similar struggle may be necessary to rescue genuine spiritual inquiry from the tyranny of scientific rationality.

Contemplation of the heavens has always played a significant role in bringing human beings to wonder about the meaning and purpose of the cosmos and of their own existence. The heavens have always seemed to be the abode of the sacred, inspiring reflection and awe. However, a subtle shift has taken place in our attitudes, owing to the rise and development of modern science. Let us take a familiar example from *Psalms* 8. The psalmist asks: "When I consider thy heavens, the work of thy fingers, the moon and the stars, which thou hast ordained; What is man, that thou art mindful of him?" We too have contemplated the heavens and other things in the light of the latest scientific knowledge, but our attitudes, and our questions, are different. If I may be permitted a modern rendering of the psalm, the scientist is more likely to ask: "When I consider the heavens, the work of our equations, the blackholes and the white dwarfs, which we have ordained; What is God, that we are mindful of him?"

Ideas and activities flourish in the context of a world-view, although world-views themselves are permeable and elastic, and change. It is science that is the major component and the strongest constituent of the present paradigm, and it is in the assurance of a shared scientific rationality that all our intellectual discussions now take place.

I do not have any new data to bring for consideration to the symposium on "Origin and Evolution of the Universe: Evidence for Design?" And I do not really believe that what we need, collectively or individually, is additional data to come to a proper sense of a design or its absence in the cosmos, and of our relationship with it. What I propose to do is to raise some questions and make some comments about and around the theme of the symposium and of this volume, organizing my discussion under the subheadings conveniently provided by the key words and associated ideas of the title: *origin, evolution, universe, evidence,* and *design.* These terms conform to a particular kind of rationality and circumscribe our deliberations here.

Origin

The question of the origin of the universe is intimately connected with the understanding of time. It is practically impossible for the Western mind, particularly since Augustine in the fourth–fifth century, not to think of time linearly. The notion of linear time has entered deeply into the structure of scientific thinking. Even when we think of non-linear time, as we sometimes do in contemporary physics, we look at the non-classical properties of time: what its conjugate variables are, how it works in other dimensions and spaces, etc. But what is important to emphasize is that in physics we are always dealing with some dimension of time, and never the sort of situation when "time shall be no longer" as is said in *Revelation* 10:6. Of course, when we extrapolate along the dimension of time, we might run into a singularity, as we do for example in equations dealing with gravitational collapse or the cosmological solutions leading to the "big bang" theory of the origin of the universe. There our notions of time go awry, and we need some very ingenious methods to get around these difficulties.

The thing to note, however, is that from the point of view of the physical cosmologists, the questions concerning the beginning of the universe have entirely to do with smaller and smaller amounts of time from the initial event when all this began. However many theoretical or practical difficulties we might encounter, what in fact we are trying to do is to follow the time coordinate back to zero. We have theories now dealing with the state of the universe at time spans of the order of 10^{-23} seconds after the absolute zero of time. There are theoretical reasons for believing that this may be the closest we can get to the absolute beginning along the time coordinate. What that in fact means is that according to our present notions of time it makes no sense to talk about time any closer to that beginning and certainly not prior to it.

What I should like to suggest, however, is that the sort of beginning that the physical cosmologists search for is not the beginning spoken of in the mystical or the mythical literature. When it is said, for example, in the opening lines of *Genesis*, "In the beginning God created the heaven and the earth," we are tempted to think that according to the Bible the heaven and the earth were the first manifestations. To do so, however, is a mistake, as we see from the immediately following verses. The heavens were not created until the second day and the earth not until the third; and the heavens, also called the firmament, were created in order to divide the waters above from the waters below. These waters, one should notice, existed before the existence of the heavens and the earth, which, on the other hand, were said to be created in the beginning. Perhaps we are presented with two different kinds of heavens and two different kinds of earth. I shall not engage in biblical exegesis here; all I wish to suggest is that we have here a notion of a beginning that is different from the scientific notion.

Of course we may here be encountering difficulties with language that are endemic to all religious literature, often also to poetry, as well as to almost any situation of intimacy. But there is no reason for us to imagine that the scriptures are meant to be at our service and that they must be clear to us while we remain as we are. I imagine that, at the least, scriptures summon us to realities that we do not ordinarily perceive. There is universal agreement among all spiritual traditions that for us to perceive these hidden realities something in us needs to change. We cannot remain as we are and come to the Mystery. That change is called by many names: a change in the level of being, a change in consciousness, a deepening of faith, a new birth, the opening of the third eye, the eye of true gnosis, and so on. One of the fundamental changes that is said to occur when the doors of perception are cleansed concerns time: not only does one's sense of duration change but, more important, what alters radically is one's relationship with the passage of time.

Statements like "In the beginning was the Word," in spite of their appearances, are not statements concerning ordinary time, the sort of time on a coordinate axis whose point of origin is the beginning. These statements carry weight and significance precisely because they were uttered and received in heightened states of awareness. It is true that scriptures can be and have been misused to cover up intellectual laziness, to foster fear, hatred, bigotry, and the like. Such misuse can make a spiritual document or symbol fearful and even hateful to people of goodwill. Nevertheless, whenever these writings and symbols speak to anyone spiritually, it is because they carry a higher level of energy and not primarily, or even at all, because of any logical clarity or agreement with our scientific notions of space and time.

This other kind of time, that of myth and mystical writing, is certainly not contradictory to our ordinary time. Nor is it, however, merely an extension of it—in either direction of the time coordinate, to the beginning or to the end. Just as the scriptural *beginning* is not the zero of the time coordinate, mystical *eternity* is not an infinite extension of time. Thus what is everlasting is not necessarily eternal. It appears that spiritual time is in a way orthogonal to scientific time, in the sense that the mathematicians use the notion of orthogonality, which is to say that it lies in a dimension wholly independent of the domain of time, although it is able to intersect with time at any moment. Thus, even if we were to consider time multi-dimensionally, or even non-sequentially, or any other way, no manipulations of time or in time could lead to the dimension of eternity that is orthogonal to it, and in which mythic beginnings and endings are spoken.

Evolution

As long as there is time there is change. That is how we understand and measure time; that is how we know that time exists and that it passes. It is only in this minimal physical sense, of state A changing into state B, that we speak about the evolution of the universe in physical cosmology. But there is an ordinary use of the word "evolution" that has a certain emotional connotation of which we need to be careful; otherwise we only introduce a philosophical problem where we do not intend to. Ordinarily, one thinks of evolution as containing within it an idea of change in a desirable direction, so that the end product is at a level higher than the antecedents.

Now, it is very difficult to say in what sense one understands "level." There are, however, also connected notions like development, growth, progress, and the like. Something or someone who is at a higher level may have more being, more consciousness, more wisdom, or the potentiality to perform more complicated tasks than one at a lower level. What is important is that the idea of hierarchy is built right into the notion of levels and of evolution, and that furthermore we specify from our point of view which is higher or lower, or whether a process is degenerative, progressive, or static. What cosmologists really talk about is physical change, without attaching any notion of hierarchy of being. But once the universe unfolds what is seen may be judged from a particular point of view. As in the *Genesis* account of creation, at the end of each day and each new manifestation, God looked at it and pronounced it to be good. Our cosmologists consider what they think happened and pronounce the change to be evolution. All that our physical laws describe is change in time. There is nowhere any place in them for intention, purpose, or evolution as long as it contains the emotionally laden sense of progress in it.

It is worth paying a little more attention to this point. In the history of natural philosophy, ideas relating to change and the laws governing the dynamics of nature have been intimately connected with the notions of causality, and for obvious reasons. Three distinct notions of causality can be distinguished for our purposes here: metaphysical, physical, and biological.

The metaphysical notion of causality, which prevailed until the sixteenth century, assumes that the cause is greater than the effect. Thus, in theology, the creator is naturally greater than the creation, at a higher level of being, intelligence, and power. This principle was applied also in natural philosophy and was, from the point of view of the subsequent developments in science, a stumbling block to a proper understanding of nature.

During the sixteenth century, a new understanding of physical causality emerged, according to which the cause and the effect were at the same level. This was a time in history when, in my view, there was a general leveling off in every field of human culture and society. Now in natural philosophy one did not speak of a cause being higher than, or in some senses containing, the effect. Instead, one spoke of change, change of one state of matter into another, without raising or lowering its level of being or intelligence or desirability. It was a subtle shift from the domain of intentions, will, reasons, and purposes, and the forces and laws (or, in another language, angels and powers) required to carry out these intentions in nature, to a field of forces and laws operating in nature without any purpose. (The philosophical and theological controversy between Leibniz and Newton was connected with this shift in the understanding of causality and the consequent sundering of the realm of facts from the realm of intentions, or of nature from spirit.)

In the nineteenth century a biological notion of causality emerged, according to which the cause is lower than the effect. That which is inferior, ontologically or in intelligence or in the subtlety of cellular organization, gives rise to what is superior. Thus amoebae would give rise, in time, to Einstein. Since what follows is more desirable than the antecedent, from the human point of view, this notion of causality is rightly called evolution. This principle is the inverse of the metaphysical and the theological notion of causality: rather than proceeding from above, creation, including human beings, now proceeds from below. In its wake this idea naturally brings an immense amount of anxiety and unease, especially to those who are comforted by a belief in some ultimate cause, or God, who is personally concerned about their welfare.

Returning now to scientific cosmology, it was only sixty years ago that the idea of the entire universe itself being dynamic was formulated precisely. One of the solutions to the field equations of General Relativity demanded that the universe as a whole be dynamic; otherwise the solution was unstable. This notion of the dynamism of the cosmos seems to have been such a revolutionary idea in the Judeo-Christian world that even a radical thinker like Einstein balked at it. He tinkered with his equations and introduced another factor into them called the cosmical constant, which was helpful in obtaining a stationary solution to the field equations. Soon after, it was discovered that even with this new, somewhat arbitrarily introduced, constant, dynamic solutions of the equations still resulted.

Also, within a few years, Hubble discovered from observational data that the galaxies were receding from each other at the speed of light and that the universe was therefore expanding. This was the most significant observational confirmation of Einstein's theory of General Relativity, and Einstein himself later remarked that the introduction of the cosmical constant in his field equations was "the greatest blunder of [his] life." The point of these remarks here is that the fundamental equations on which modern physical cosmology is based have nothing to do with evolution, except in the minimal physical sense of change. Modern cosmology is just like the rest of physics as far as the notion of causality is concerned: it describes the change in matter-energy from one state to another. Naturally, from our point of view, the emergence of the stars, galaxies, the solar system, and ultimately of ourselves is more desirable than their non-emergence, and so we feel justified in describing this change as evolution.

What we need to be aware of is that in this process we are combining two different notions of causality described earlier. One of these we actually need for our knowledge; the other is an emotional overlay for the obvious reason that we humans are at the end of the corresponding change. So we get saddled with a philosophical problem because of our sentimentality about human beings while nevertheless insisting on a limited physico-biological view of man. We do not need so limited a view of cosmology that the deepest, spiritual part of ourselves, cannot be taken into account. In physical cosmology, which is a perfectly legitimate and wonderful study in its domain, it is change in the physical form of matter-energy that is our concern; we do not speak, indeed we cannot speak within the assumptions and procedures that govern the subject, of spiritual evolution. Of course, human beings have always had a need and a sense of the sacred; this alone gives meaning and purpose both to ourselves and to the cosmos. Fundamentally bereft of the sacred we are riddled with personal anxiety and adrift in the meaningless vastness of space-time. Physical theories concerning the static or the dynamic nature of the universe are not, nor do they pretend to be, about the dimension of significance or purpose.

Universe

What do we mean by universe? Presumably, all there is. Does a cat or a bee have the same universe as a man? Does a tone-deaf or a color-blind person have the same universe as the one who is musically gifted or is a painter? Does a person who is blind to symbols or to spirit, or who is insensitive to wonder, beauty, or spiritual presence have the same universe as a scientist or a poet or a mystic?

What there is is a function of who sees. This axiom is not meant to support the philosophical position that claims that a thing does not exist unless there is someone to see it. My concern is our knowledge: what we know, actually and potentially, about the universe depends on the procedures, methods, and interests that we bring to our observation of it. If we do not know how to find angels and we are not interested in them, we will say that the angels do not exist. And it is true that they are not a part of our scientific universe. Nor are "the clouds which brood," which were a part of Wordsworth's universe, nor are the dancing colors inhabiting Blake's universe, nor are the cherubim and the seraphim singing "Holy, holy, holy" who were a part of Bach's universe. The physical cosmologist's universe, vast and marvelous as it is, is not all there is. As Shakespeare would have put it, "There are more things in heaven and earth than are dreamt of in your philosophy."

Even when allowance has been made for error and illusion, which can, of course, as much blight the cosmologist as the poet, the musician, or the mystic, it is difficult simply to dismiss these other fields. Hardly anyone of sound judgment and goodwill dismisses the arts out of hand. But it is astonishing how so many people find it much easier to dismiss the mystic and the theologian. There are understandable historical reasons for this, but what concerns us here is that in intellectual circles none of these fields are now considered as relevant to deliberations concerning the cosmos. Witness, for example, the contents of this volume. The universes inhabited by what is regarded as the most precious by the artist, or the musician, or the mystic are somehow relegated by us to a murky and imaginary realm, not entirely real. And certainly not as real as the multiple universes or the shadow universe or the anti-universe or the other weird universes that make up the speculations of physical cosmologists.

The important point is that it is our assumption now that whatever else the musicians, artists, or mystics might be doing, they are certainly not producing knowledge. Knowledge is produced exclusively by scientists, we would say, and by nobody else. And contemporary philosophers, with all their love for wisdom, in general agree. We might not now say, with the positivists, that "non-science is nonsense," but we would surely, say that non-science cannot lead to knowledge and truth.

In connection with what we include in the universe, mention needs to be made of a traditional idea of levels of materiality. As is well known, medieval philosophers in general held that the matter on different planets was different, as were the laws in operation there. It was a considerable advance in astronomy to establish that fundamentally the same sort of matter prevailed throughout the universe, subject to the same laws everywhere. However, when we move from medieval natural philosophy, whether expressed in alchemy, astrology, mathematics, or cosmology, to the modern sciences, our general reaction to the backward-looking nature of the past and our excitement over new discoveries blind most of us to the predominantly symbolic and analogical nature of medieval thought. We would do well to remind ourselves of the ancient analogy between each human being and the universe, between the cosmos and the microcosmos that inwardly mirror one another's essential principles.

We might then realize that the various planets, the different materials on them, and the different laws operating there were all symbols of different levels of interiority within a human being, and that the quality of matter-energy at different levels of the mind is different from the matter-energy of the body and subject to different laws. Sometimes this idea was explicitly shown in various diagrams, but the prevalence of symbolic and analogical ways of thinking meant that it was often just assumed, much as we today assume that everyone in all reasonable gatherings naturally accepts the mode of scientific rationality. It is plain and obvious, as Blake succinctly put it, "Reason and Newton are quite two things." What goes on in our minds and our feelings, and not only what takes place in our bodies, also contributes to all there is.

By bringing in mental and psychic functions, I do not wish to suggest that these are in principle outside the domain of scientific knowledge. I am not proposing anything supernatural, as opposed to natural, that is excluded from the investigations of natural philosophy. There is nothing supernatural about most of what gets labeled extrasensory perception, or miraculous. These, to be sure, are at present extra-science perceptions, but there is nothing inherently beyond nature or beyond science in them. It may well be that a radically altered science will be required to understand what is now extrasensory perception, just as a radically altered science was required to understand lightning in the sky or the light of the sun, which might have seemed quite supernatural from the perspective of fourteenth-century scientists. It is important to distinguish, as St. Augustine did, between what we claim really is nature and what we know of nature. The limits of our knowledge are not necessarily the limits of nature.

But it is still more important to realize that even with a radically altered science that could take account of extrasensory perceptions and other miraculous happenings, we cannot come to the end of all there is. All there is far exceeds the realm of nature, the domain of causality and materiality, however subtle our descriptions. To say that we do not yet know certain levels of nature is not to say that nature is all that there is to know or that can be. In fact, practically without exception, all great spiritual teachers, such as the Buddha, the Christ, Patanjali, Krishna, and Moses, have warned against an excessive fascination with miraculous phenomena and occult powers, which are said to be diversions from the true spiritual paths.

Two related, although somewhat parenthetical, remarks may be made here. One of them concerns an important distinction, made in the scientific revolution starting in the sixteenth century, between the primary and the secondary qualities of matter. This distinction played a crucial role in the development of the physical sciences and also in the subsequent impoverishment of nature. The primary qualities were extension, mass, and velocity; to this list was added charge in the nineteenth century and spin, strangeness, charm, and others in the twentieth. The secondary qualities consisted of taste, color, smell, and the like; they were not considered objectively to be a part of nature, but were subjective and rather unreliable.

Considered even more subjective and unreliable were tertiary qualities, feelings of beauty, purpose, or significance.

The secondary and tertiary qualities were gradually eliminated not only as instruments of inquiry into nature but also as fundamental constituents of nature. They could not, properly speaking, be studied as themselves constituting reality, but as something which needed to be explained and understood in terms of the primary qualities. Thus a deep-seated reductionism is built into the fundamental presuppositions of scientific inquiry. A division into *res extensa* and *res cogitans* carried within it a certain instability attached to the realm of the mind. From a scientific point of view, as we see clearly in behavioral psychology, all psychic functions must be reducible to external motions.

On the other hand, we have the philosophical problem of mind-body dualism. In some theological circles it is really understood as soul-body dualism, in which the soul is supernatural, removed from the realm of nature and scientific investigation altogether, and placed in the realm of faith away from knowledge. Any real knowledge of the psyche or the soul thus gets rather short shrift: the scientists deny the existence of anything in it which they cannot study by physical means, and the theologians deny the possibility of any knowledge of it. But in neither case can spiritual qualities have any independent existence in the cosmos that we can study.

The other related remark derives from a comparative study of the history of ideas in the Western world and in India. In Greek philosophy, and in the early Christian writers, as well as in the Indian tradition, there was a tripartite division of a human being into spirit, soul, and body, or, to use the terminology of St. Paul, *pneuma, psyche,* and *soma*.[1] Gradually this threefold division shrank into a two-fold division: spirit and nature, or mind and matter, or soul and body. The *coup de grâce* was dealt by Descartes, who explicitly identifies spirit with soul and both with the mind.[2] In the Western world, since the time of Descartes, soul is in general regarded more or less completely as spiritual rather than natural. A partial reduction of the threefold division into a two-fold one took place in India as well. However, there, in general, the psyche has been considered in the realm of nature, and therefore subject to the laws of nature and amenable to scientific inquiry. Thus thoughts and feelings, and psychic phenomena, including those considered paranormal, are in the realm of *prakriti*, nature, that is to say, in the domain of materiality and causality. According to Indian thought, the so-called miracles, for example those mentioned in the Bible, are not supernatural or spiritual, even though they are unusual and extraordinary. Spirit is still beyond.

Evidence

We have already spoken about the somewhat obvious fact that our knowledge depends on the procedures, methods, and interests that we bring to knowing the cosmos. Neils Bohr was quite right in saying: "It is wrong to think that the task of physics is to find out how nature is. Physics concerns what we can say about nature."[3] Of course, even what we can say about nature depends on the mode of discourse a community of scientists accepts as the appropriate mode. In that universe of discourse only certain kinds of data are acceptable as evidence, and certain other data are not acceptable. For example, the angels, so very real to Blake, are not acceptable scientific data, nor are Bach's fugues. In fact, no interior experience is a part of scientific data.

Although one may speak in general of the scientific experience, it is necessary to distinguish between *experience* and *experiment*.[4] What we utilize in the sciences, and more particularly in the physical sciences on which our cosmology is based, are experiments and certainly not experiences. The words experiment and experience are derived from the Latin words *experimentum* and *experientia*, which in turn are both derived from *experiens*, the present participle of *experiri*, which means to try thoroughly, to risk, to go through; the clear implication is that this involves some personal participation and risk. We still use experience in this sense, but experiment has not been used in this sense for nearly three hundred years. *Experiment* is used these days as an intransitive verb, and no longer transitively as *experience* is. We can experience a flower, but we can only experiment with or on it. The scientific evidence about something is not gathered by experiencing it but by experimenting upon it.

The knowledge thus produced is not a knowing-by-participation, but a knowing-by-distancing. It is not an I-thou knowing but an I-it one. Thus we see that scientific knowledge is indeed objective; but it is not objective in the mystical sense in which the observing self is so completely emptied or naughted that the object reveals itself as it is, the thing in itself, in all its numinosity and particularity. Sages in all cultures have said that it is only in this state of consciousness, devoid of the self, that an object is known both in its oneness with all there is and in its distinct uniqueness. An entity—be it a tree, or a person, or a culture, or the whole cosmos—is then understood both in its interiority and its externality, including its generality and specificity. Scientific objectivity comes from another route, even etymologically, when we throw ourselves over and against something, as is understood in our word *objection*. One mode is that of love, the other of combat.

Mystics, as everyone knows, are constantly speaking about love. We are told that God is love, as in the New Testament, or that love is what supports the whole cosmos, as in Dante's *Divine Comedy*, or, as in the *Rig Veda*, that love was the first creation and absolutely everything else came from it. But by our scientific methods we wish to conquer nature as if she were an adversary. In fact, scientists almost never refer to nature as *she*; she is always called *it*.

Naturally, what is dead or was never alive can hardly have intentions, purposes, reasons, or feelings. In short, it can have no interiority. Evidence that involves this sense of interiority, that is based on an I-thou relationship, is out of the scientific arena altogether.

What is at issue here is a different sort of knowing. The important thing is not to see different things, but to see differently; not changed or expanded contents of the same consciousness, but a different quality of consciousness. Just as one can be in an I-thou relationship even with a cat or a tree, as Martin Buber used to say, one can also bring the I-it attitude to human beings, or even to God, if we seek only to use them as objects. Such, for example, was the attitude of Newton, perhaps the greatest of all scientists; as one of his biographers, Frank Manuel, has remarked, "For Newton, persons were usually objects, not subjects." The suggestion is not that scientists have any monopoly on the I-it attitude or that they are, as a class, devoid of the I-thou intercourse, but that in science, as distinct from some other possible activities of scientists, the I-thou attitude and any observations based on the inclusion of interiority of the object are automatically excluded from the body of scientific evidence.

In the last four centuries, there has been a virtual explosion in the number of scientific instruments that have extended our ability to observe the very small and the very far away and to measure extremely small amounts of time. In this immense quantitative expansion of the field of our observation, it cannot be said that we now see the cosmos with different eyes. There has been an extension of our eyes but not their cleansing, as Blake or Goethe would have understood it. There is nothing in the nature of science itself which might make one invoke, with St. Francis, "Brother Sun; Sister Moon."

Any one of us can, of course, be deeply moved by a sense of our oneness with the cosmos, scientists as well as non-scientists. Furthermore, one can be struck by the wonder, the mystery, and the design of the cosmos as much today as in the days of Newton or Archimedes or Pythagoras, although unfortunately most of us are all too rarely struck in this way. These feelings and perceptions lie in dimensions different from the ones in which our scientific observations are extended. No amount of quantitative expansion of data and theories can lead to the dimension of significance, any more than an endless extension of time can lead to eternity.

Design

It is hard to imagine a scientist who does not see order in the universe, a harmony of the various forces that permit the continued existence of the world, and a pattern involving regularity of phenomena and a generality of laws. The more we know about the universe, the more elegantly and wonderfully well ordered it appears. Most scientists share with Einstein a "deep conviction of the rationality of the universe," and his feeling that no genuine scientist could really work without a profound "faith in the possibility that the regulations valid for the world of existence are rational, that is comprehensible to reason." Einstein himself called this a "cosmic religious feeling," which he regarded as the "strongest and noblest motive for scientific research." Even though other scientists may be shy or embarrassed by the word religious, they are by no means strangers to the feeling that Einstein is describing.

What puts scientists on guard is not the idea or the feeling of design in the universe, but a suspicion that lurking behind the slightest concession in using the word is a theologian who will jump with glee and immediately saddle them with the notion of a Designer and all that goes with it. It is not the design that the scientists are uneasy about, but the designs that they smell hiding behind the slightest admission of it! It is no use telling them that the theologians have been on the defensive now for nearly three hundred years and are so eager to gain any approval from their scientific colleagues that they get a little over enthusiastic if they sniff any possibility of truce. All of science is a celebration of pattern, regularity, lawfulness, harmony, order, beauty; in other words, all the marks of design. What it does not have much to do with is the Designer, who is over and above the design, occasionally interfering in the universe in contravention of natural laws. Already in the seventeenth century, Leibniz was able to remind Newton that his God was like a retired engineer: having created perfect laws and having set the universe initially in motion, He was no longer needed, and could be on a permanent sabbatical. The very perfection of scientific laws and their comprehensibility make the continued presence of this sort of God less necessary.

To have to infer the Designer from the design is largely a particular type of theological and linguistic habit. It is based on a notion of design that is more technological in character than scientific or artistic. In art there is always present a definite element of play, improvisation, and surprise. No creative work is like painting by numbers; the artist does not know beforehand what the finished product will be like. And any scientist who already knows what he is going to find at the end of his work does not need a research grant, for he hardly needs to carry out the research.

I am not discounting the intuitive conviction that a scientist can have about a particular idea or a method, so that he knows prior to engaging in a detailed calculation or an experiment what the outcome must be. But every good scientist, even an Einstein or a Newton, has many intuitive convictions that just do not lead anywhere. In the actual working out of the ideas, and their encounter with what is, is the real delight, excitement, and even terror of creativity. Without them, scientific and artistic activity would be very dull.

And any God who might create the universe without delight, without playfulness, without wonder, and without freedom and fresh possibilities would be a very dull God indeed. He would be a God of grim specialists, but not of the dilettantes, those who delight in what they do and study. Such a God could be a good technician carrying out a technical design, or a good bureaucrat keeping everyone in his place, or a thorough accountant keeping track of everyone's actions for later dispensation of necessary judgments; he might even make a good president of a large corporation like a modern university. But he certainly would not make a good scientist, artist, or mystic. Such a God could not be the God of love or of wisdom, and it would be very difficult to take delight in Him.

Etymologically, *design* is also related to *sign from*. Sign from whom? Historically, in Christian theology, with rare exceptions, the signs are always from a personal God. However, there are profound and fundamental incompatibilities between scientific knowledge and the idea of a personal God, in spite of the fact that many very great scientists, for example Newton, were deeply committed to a personal God. Here is a brief excerpt from a manuscript of Newton, now in the Jewish National and University Library (Yehuda MS. 15.3, fol. 46r):

> We must believe that there is one God or supreme Monarch that we may fear and obey him and keep his laws and give him honor and glory. We must believe that he is the father of whom are all things, and that he loves his people as his children that they may mutually love him and obey him as their father. We must believe that he is Lord of all things with an irresistible and boundless power and dominion that we may not hope to escape if we rebel and set up other Gods or transgress the laws of his monarchy, and that we may

expect great rewards if we do his will...To us there is but one God the father of whom are all things and we in him and one Lord Jesus Christ by whom are all things and we by him: that is, but one God and one Lord in our worship.

However, since Newton's time, and at least partly owing to the very science he took a major hand in creating, scientists are much less comfortable about accepting such a faith in a personal God, and certainly in expressing it. There is a feeling of a fundamental incompatibility between science and such a faith. Most scientists these days are likely to agree with Einstein in his description of what he called his religious feeling as:

> one of rapturous amazement at the harmony of natural law, which reveals an intelligence of such superiority that, compared with it, all the systematic thinking and acting of human beings is an utterly insignificant reflection....The most beautiful thing we can experience is the mysterious. It is the source of all true art and science....To know that what is impenetrable to us really exists, manifesting itself as the highest wisdom and the most radiant beauty which our dull faculties can comprehend only in their most primitive forms—this knowledge, this feeling, is at the center of true religiousness. In this sense, and in this sense only, I belong in the ranks of devoutly religious men. (*Ideas and Opinions*, 1954)

Many people who knew Einstein personally insisted that he was the most religious person they had ever met. But he was not religious in any church or denominational manner. As he said, many times and in many ways, "My religion consists of a humble admiration of the illimitable superior spirit who reveals himself in the slight details we are able to perceive with our frail and feeble minds. That deeply emotional conviction of the presence of a superior reasoning power which is revealed in the incomprehensible universe forms my idea of God."

Here we see a very good illustration of the fact that being struck by the beauty, harmony, order, and design in the universe does not necessarily mean accepting a personal or a sectarian God. It is worth quoting Einstein at some length on this point, from a remarkable address at a symposium in 1941:

> The main source of the present-day conflicts between the spheres of religion and of science lies in this concept of a personal God. It is

the aim of science to establish general rules which determine the reciprocal connection of objects and events in time and space. For these rules, or laws of nature, absolutely general validity is required—not proven. It is mainly a program, and the faith in the possibility of its accomplishment in principle is only founded on partial successes....The more a man is imbued with the ordered regularity of all events the firmer becomes his conviction that there is no room left by the side of this ordered regularity for causes of a different nature....To be sure, the doctrine of a personal God interfering with natural events could never be refuted, in the real sense by science, for this doctrine can always take refuge in those domains in which scientific knowledge has not yet been able to set foot.

But I am persuaded that such behavior on the part of the representatives of religion would not only be unworthy but also fatal. For a doctrine which is able to maintain itself not in clear light but only in the dark, will of necessity lose its effect on mankind, with incalculable harm to human progress. In their struggle for the ethical good, teachers of religion must have the stature to give up the doctrine of a personal God, that is give up that source of fear and hope which in the past placed such vast power in the hands of priests. In their labors they will have to avail themselves of those forces which are capable of cultivating the Good, the True and the Beautiful in humanity itself. This is, to be sure, a more difficult but an incomparably more worthy task. ("Science and Religion," in Einstein's *Out of My Later Years*, 1950)

In my judgment, which in this regard is different from Einstein's, the major cause of the incompatibility between science and theology or church religion, which should certainly not be confused with spirituality, is not so much the concept of personal God per se, as the restricted view of knowledge that prevails in scientific circles, as remarked earlier, and the limited notion of the Spirit or Divinity that the theologians have. To have understood rightly that Divinity is at least at the level of the human person does not mean that it is only personal. The personalist aspects of Being, such as intelligence, intention, will, purpose, and love, which are all marks of interiority, do not have to lead to a concept of a personal God made in the external image of man, with definite form and being separated from others. Uniqueness of any level of being, seen separated from the oneness of all Being, leads to a limitation of vision, to partiality, and to exclusivism.

As the scriptures tell us, man is made in the image of God, which I take to mean that man is potentially able, in the deepest part of himself, to be one with the Divine. This is what the sages have always said, everywhere, whether the expression is *aham brahmāsmi* or "My Father and I are one." However, if we forget the summons for an inward expansion to God, we are bound to reduce God in an outward contraction to man.

Concluding Remarks

I have argued that there is more to the universe and to knowledge, and the corresponding evidence, than is encountered in physical cosmology; that there are dimensions of the existence and development of being other than in time; and that one can be very spiritual with a personal God or without one. These are practically truisms. In any case, my observations have nothing to do with being Eastern or Western. Of course, one is conditioned by one's cultural background. However, the more deeply one delves into oneself, the more one discovers one's common humanity with others, and one's commonality with all there is, without thereby losing one's uniqueness. In this necessary realization of our oneness as well as uniqueness, we may, each one of us, have to travel paths we do not ordinarily travel, in lands we do not usually inhabit, and experience modes of being not habitually ours.

Different modalities and levels of being, and the corresponding levels of thought and feeling, exist in every human being and even more so in every culture. Some contingent, historical factors can overwhelm or underscore a particular modality at any given time. The tremendous impact of science and technology in the West in the last two centuries has made some modes of being now appear to be non-Western. Yet we are now in a particularly exciting situation of a global neighborhood demanding a larger vision of ourselves. A special kind of insensitivity is now required for us to remain culturally parochial, refusing to become heirs of the great wisdom of mankind: as much of Plato as of the Buddha, of Einstein as well as Patanjali, of Spinoza no less than that of Confucius.

A major conceptual revolution was created in the Western world when the works of Aristotle were discovered by the Latin

West through the Arabic philosophers in the eleventh and twelfth centuries. The revolution went on for several centuries, leaving no area of thought and culture untouched. It appeared for a time that the major synthesis brought about by Thomas Aquinas between Aristotle and Christian thought was a culmination of this revolution. But no: it rolled on until and including the major scientific revolution of the sixteenth and seventeenth centuries that was finally brought to a close by Newton. Since the end of the nineteenth century, we have been in the middle of another very major encounter of different cultures and different streams of thought, of the West with the East. There is, moreover, an important aspect of the contemporary situation, since the Second World War: for the first time in history major cultures are juxtaposed as neighbors without being in the position of either the victor or the vanquished. Who knows where the resulting cultural revolution will end?

One thing, however, is certain: a consequence of this revolution is bound to be a recognition, in addition to the experimental science of nature that has been a particular achievement of the modern West, of an experiential science of the Spirit freed from all sectarian theology. This science of the Spirit is not the same thing as an extension of our present science to include occult phenomena and extrasensory perceptions. Also, one should not let oneself be seduced by superficial parallels between certain expressions and paradoxes of contemporary science and ancient Oriental thought. It is true that here and there are beginning to appear, in the long column of Western appellations in the honor rolls of science, names like Chandrasekhara Venkata Raman, Tsung Dao Lee, Hideki Yukawa, Abdus Salam, and Chen Ning Yang. In his day Kepler was convinced that the Sun was the Father, the circumference of the solar system the Son, and the intervening space the Holy Ghost. A latter-day scientist, brought up on different symbols and metaphors, might see in the patterns appearing in the cloud chamber the dance of Shiva, or be moved to find in the complementarily appearing in the quantum phenomena *yin* and *yang* encircled together, or discover the resolution of the various paradoxes of contemporary physics in the ineffable Tao. These parallels or interpretations are as true or false now

325

as they were then. They add nothing, either to true science or to true spirituality.

There is a deep-seated need in human beings to seek an integration of all their faculties, and a unity of their knowledge and feeling. We are fragmented and thirst for wholeness. This thirst, however, cannot be quenched by mere mental conclusions and arguments about the parallels between physics and Buddhism or about the existence and nature of the design in the cosmos. What we need is a radically transformed attitude—in the deepest sense, including the posture of the body, as is happily conveyed by the corresponding French word—which would permit us to receive true wisdom and intelligence from above ourselves, and to use our science and technology with compassion and love.

Without this attitude we cannot reconcile Blake and Newton, and their future heirs. And the lament will continue:

> O Divine Spirit sustain me on thy wings!
> That I may awake Albion from his long and cold repose.
> For Bacon and Newton sheathed in dismal steel, their terrors hang
> Like iron scourges over Albion, Reasonings like vast Serpents
> Infold around my limbs, bruising my minute articulations...
> In heavy wreathes folds over every Nation; cruel Works
> Of many Wheels I view, wheel without wheel, with cogs tyrannic
> Moving by compulsion each other: not as those in Eden: which,
> Wheel within Wheel, in freedom revolve in harmony and peace.
> (William Blake, *Jerusalem* 15:9–20)

The tension between the two major contributing streams to the Western mentality, the Greek and the Hebraic, with their respective emphases on the cosmological and the theological perspectives, is very old. Whitehead once remarked that this tension may have been the main source of the creative dynamism of the Western culture for centuries. However, now there is almost a complete separation between these two perspectives. As I said earlier, scientists are deeply committed to the cosmological perspective to the exclusion of the person. On the other hand, neither theology nor philosophy has been an experiential science for many a century. If we were to take the corresponding experience seriously, as with great mystics and spiritual masters, one thing would become immediately clear: there is not much meaning to consciousness or intelligence, and thus to God, without the accompanying attributes of action, love, and delight. These are not so much attributes of the Spirit, added from the outside and without which the Spirit could exist, as they are the means by which we recognize the presence of the Spirit or Consciousness or Intelligence.

Thus God is not only omniscient, but also omnipotent, omni-amorosus and omnidilettante! This is precisely what makes the Spirit omnidelectabilis so that human beings are constantly drawn to Her and in love with Her. Occasionally, they write poems of ecstasy for the Spirit, as did Alexander Skryabin, a Russian composer and poet of the early twentieth century:

> The Spirit playing,
> The Spirit longing,
> The Spirit with fancy creating all,
> Surrenders himself to the bliss of love...
> Amid the flowers of His creation, He lingers in a kiss...
> Blinded by their beauty He rushes, He frolics, He dances,
> He whirls...
> He is all rapture, all bliss in this play
> Free, divine, in this love struggle
> In the marvelous grandeur of sheer aimlessness,
> And in the union of counter-aspirations
> In consciousness alone, in love alone,
> The Spirit learns the nature of His divine being....
> *(Poem of Ecstasy)*

Thus the design, the intelligence in it, behind it, and above it, turns into a dance. Some dancers come and go, join the dance, or stop to watch it; but the dance goes on eternally, in the beginning as now, in love and delight. In moments of wholeness, of deep feeling and clarity of awareness, each dancer is unique in himself and one with the cosmos, and he knows that In the Beginning Is the Dance of Love.

Notes

1. In this connection, see A.H. Armstrong and R. Ravindra, "The Dimensions of the Self: *Buddhi* in the *Bhagavad Gita* and Psyché in Plotinus," *Religious Studies* 15 (1979): 327–342.
2. We see a good example of this identification in French: the last words of Jesus Christ before his crucifixion, in the Gospel according to St. *Luke* 23:46, are translated into French as "Père, je remets mon esprit entre tes mains." The word *esprit* now means what is conveyed in English by both *spirit* and *mind*. It was pointed out to me by the French physicist Jean Charon that Descartes in *Meditations VI* seems to make some room for an entity higher than both the body and the soul. Perhaps; but the Cartesians?
3. Quoted in Ruth Moore, *Neils Bohr* (New York: Knopf, 1966), 406.
4. In this connection see R. Ravindra, Chapter 7, this volume.

NINETEEN

To The DANCER BELONGS The UNIVERSE

FREEDOM AND BONDAGE OF NATURAL LAW

Ravi Ravindra

The Challenge of Being Human

There are five billion of us on the surface of this planet. Five billion human beings, like you and me, each one with aspirations and regrets, fears and ambitions, memories and hopes. We all have our occasional grand philosophical moments—in the midst of much longer periods of uncertainty, hesitation, and habitual repetition. And each one of us occupies a place in a gargantuan funeral march, each day moving closer to the exit by steady steps. Between now and a year from now, a hundred million of us will die: a hundred million sparks of consciousness will be extinguished, some barely sparking, some ablaze in glory, but each one coming to a definite and discernible end.

However, life and consciousness will continue to assert themselves, and a hundred million or more centers of awareness, with fresh memories and new hopes, will be born. This cycle of life, which includes both the being born and the dying, has continued for hundreds of thousands of years, creating an astounding variety of human beings, each one completely unique and yet each one quite replaceable in the mammoth Dance of Life. Dancers come and go, but the dance continues. Each new beat of the drum presents to time new faces to see, as the old ones disappear from view. No wonder that in the myths of so many ancient cultures the Earth is spoken of as the Great Goddess with an extremely fecund womb and a very destructive jaw, producing and devouring at the same time.

What meaning has this Great Dance of Life? Perhaps that is too large a question to raise now. So, let us ask, what place do we human beings have in this Dance? First of all, collectively, as mankind: what role have we in the cosmic economy? As is well known, our colleagues in Biology, especially in Marine Biology, have very clear ideas about the role and function of almost every animal in a large scale ecological chain. They can tell us, for example, how kelp is needed for the lobsters to grow, how the sea urchins are also necessary in this chain except when they become too abundant, and so on. Every creature has its place and function so that the whole eco-system can flourish. So we may rightly wonder: What function has mankind? What do we contribute towards the smooth and harmonious working of the system of the earth? We depend on the Earth; but does the Earth need us? Does the Sun? This is not a new question; as long as mankind has existed, the awareness of the vastness of the universe has made human beings aware of their small-ness and has raised questions about their place. Perhaps the example most familiar to this audience is that of *Psalm* 8:

> When I consider thy heavens, the work of thy fingers, The moon and the stars, which thou hast ordained; What is man, that thou art mindful of him?

Our contemporary idiom may be a little different, as is our knowledge about the solar system and the far from central place the Earth occupies. We know that we live on a quite mediocre planet moving around a peripheral and third-rate star in an average galaxy. But we also wonder about our place in this largeness. There are immensely vast stretches of time and of space, and mankind exists like an excrescence confined to a few meters depth on the skin of the Earth. What is mankind in the midst of this immensity? No one can fail to appreciate the vastness, intricacy, and delicacy of the whole structure of the universe. The physical and chemical characteristics not only of the environment on the Earth but also on the largest cosmological scale seem to be so artfully and finely tuned, with mankind precariously balanced in a state of extreme fragility, that one cannot but endorse the cosmic feeling of awe which Einstein described as one of "rapturous amazement at the harmony of natural law, which reveals an intelligence of such superiority that, compared with it, all the systematic thinking and acting of human beings is an utterly insignificant reflection."[1]

It is a consequence of this amazing harmony of natural law that mankind is here, that a hundred million of us die every year and a hundred million or more are born. We are not here contrary to law. We may not know the precise mechanism by which we came to be, and we may not know the function we have in the vast universe. There may be enough uncertainty about all this that some of us may declare ourselves to be here by random chance, just as some thinkers have been driven to conclude that the universe is chaotic and absurd because they could not make sense of the events around them. Making an exception for such desperation, it is hard to imagine a scientist who does not see order in the universe, and a harmony of the various forces which permit a continued existence and a constant unfolding of the world, and a pattern involving regularity of phenomena and generality of the laws. The more we know about the universe, the more elegantly and wonderfully well-ordered it appears. Most scientists share with Einstein his "deep conviction of the rationality of the universe," and his feeling that no genuine scientist could really work without a profound "faith in the possibility that the regulations valid for the world of existence are rational, that is comprehensible to reason."

Einstein himself called this a "cosmic religious feeling" which he regarded as the "strongest and noblest motive for scientific research." Even though other scientists may be shy of the label *religious*, they are by no means strangers to the feeling described by Einstein. What is essentially at issue is the fundamental lawfulness of nature. This is not something that can be proved by scientific research; this is a philosophical and psychological prerequisite for such research. Of course, at any stage of development of scientific thought, the precise range and applicability of a given set of natural laws may undergo a radical revolution, as happened for example in the establishment of quantum mechanics where the laws turned out to be statistical, applying to ensembles of particles rather than to individual particles. But we do not abandon the idea that there are laws of nature. That idea is needed for us to think coherently about nature and to communicate our thoughts to each other.

Returning to our initial question about the place of we human beings in the lawful Dance of Nature, but now individually: What is my place? Why am I here? What am I? Maybe mankind on the large has some function to play in the ecology of the earth, but what about me personally? Am I completely replaceable in an ensemble of human beings as far as the vast cosmos is concerned? What meaning is there to my individual existence? What significance to my personal hopes and aspirations? What was said several thousand years ago by a poet in the *Rig Veda* (I, 164, 37) can be said by any one of us: "What thing I am I do not know. I wander alone, burdened by my mind." This burden of the mind, this wandering alone in inquiry, this passion for knowing what one is and how one is related to the cosmos is peculiarly human. Inhabiting a dying animal as we all do, each one of us is nevertheless condemned to question and search for self-awareness.

Concern with these sorts of eternal questions is what gives great spiritual documents of humanity their abiding quality. But they have more than questions: they point to another level of consciousness, another mode of existence, towards which we could aspire, and where questions about our individual and collective significance can come to rest and find some resolution. The above hymn of the *Rig Veda* continues: "When the Firstborn of Truth has come to me I receive a share in that selfsame Word." How do I prepare to receive the Firstborn of Truth which elsewhere in the *Rig Veda* is said to be Love? How do I dwell and participate in the Word which is from the Beginning? Some of you will recognize echoes from the Gospel

According to St. John. Using a metaphor from that gospel one may ask: Lambs of nature as we are in any case, how can we also become lambs of God?

Transformation as a Human Imperative

In asking this question we are asking about the possibility of transformation from one level of being to another. It is as though we are unfinished creatures as we are; and the world is incomplete and unfinished along with us. However well balanced and ecologically sound the universe may be without our human interference, we seem driven by our deepest internal necessity, possibly in fulfillment of a requirement of the cosmos, not only to understand the cosmos but also to transform it. We cannot be human unless we intervene in the natural order—both inside us as well as outside. Man is a creature who must intervene; he cannot leave himself or the cosmos the way he finds them.

By *transformation* I do not mean *change*—all the changes brought about by human intervention do not necessarily lead to transformation either of man or of the cosmos. Everything in the universe is constantly undergoing change; that is how we measure time. Change is a truth and law of nature; it is natural. Transformation on the other hand is intentional change; it is not natural. All works of art are examples of transformation. To bring into existence a sculpture from the material of a stone needs the intentional intervention of a human being. We are constantly called to make ourselves, the earth and the whole universe into works of art.

In the transformation of a human being, in what the alchemists called the Great Work, great art is needed. To live and die as a lamb of nature is natural. But to live and die as a lamb of God is not natural; it requires a teaching, a spiritual path, effort and grace. The transformation from one kind of lamb to another requires intentional change; it is brought about by art and the corresponding skill and hard work. In the Sanskrit language, an ordinary person, as he is born and lives, is called *prākrita*, which means natural, vulgar, common, unrefined. But, if he is able to intervene in his internal cosmos, and is properly educated, he can be transformed into a *sanskrita* person: well made, refined. Such a person is not wholly controlled by his natural inclinations; he is not completely determined or bound by natural law.

Every man is an artist of his life: starting from the raw material of his own self, he sculpts something from it which corresponds to his aspirations, his understanding, the level of his engagement, his skill and sensitivity. What he makes of himself does not depend only on his own abilities and work, but also on the various forces assisting or hindering him. But he must engage in the work of transformation; this is an imperative of his human existence. Even our most superficial good manners indicate a wish for right internal and external order; and the most dedicated social climber among us nevertheless expresses a wish for larger and freer being.

Two Natures of Man

We need to be careful and to avoid the pitfalls that we can anticipate. The first difficulty lies in the use of the words nature and natural. In saying that transformation is not *natural*, I do not mean to suggest that it is *artificial* in the pejorative sense of that word. I more mean to say that it requires art and work and will not be done automatically by itself. Another way of saying this is that human beings have a *purpose* to their existence; they are needed in the cosmos. A human being fulfills this purpose when he engages in the work of inner and outer transformation.

We may distinguish *purpose* from *function* in the same way as *transformation* from *change*, namely by the necessity of intentional intervention. Whatever our function in the scheme of nature—it may simply be to produce a certain amount of carbon dioxide for the trees, to add to the humus in the soil or to produce food for the worms—it will in any case be performed automatically in response to natural forces, as are the functions of kelp and lobsters. As we are born, breathe, procreate, and die, we fulfill our natural function whatever it may be. The hundred million who die this year fulfill this natural function. But, the fulfillment of our purpose needs an active participation on our part, a certain degree of choice and intention. This is what gives meaning and significance to our lives. Our function could be fulfilled collectively and interchangeably by one person for another; but the accomplishment of our purpose requires a unique engagement by each one of us. A person may not know what his purpose in life is; if he senses what it is, he could still fail in the fulfillment of his purpose; and he could even refuse to engage with it at all.

Perhaps not quite. It does seem that some human beings, and the most sensitive and creative among us belong to this group, are unable to refuse to engage with the whole complex of purpose, meaning, significance and transformation. They are condemned to it, and cannot deny it without denying their own humanity. They have an internal daimon, as Socrates had, which drives them, or they are compelled by the Muse, or they are hounded by God, as was the case with practically all the prophets in the traditions of Judaism, Christianity, and Islam. At least in their cases it seems more accurate to say that it is a part of their nature which compels them to struggle against other parts of themselves to do what they must, in response to what they recognize as their higher urges. In fact, it is common place in many ancient traditions to speak in terms of two natures of man, often labeled *higher nature* and *lower nature*, frequently in conflict with each other, one concerned with purpose and the other occupied with function, possibly symbolized by the vertical and the horizontal dimensions of the cross.

In order to make the distinction between the two natures clearer, we should recall that sometimes their tendencies are called *natural* and *supra-natural*, and more often as *natural* and *spiritual*.

All these labels have their difficulties, especially when they are considered without reference to any experiential data, as is generally the case in philosophy and theology. What we need is a super-science, a science of the higher nature or of the spirit, a science dealing with the whole arena of purposes and significance and the transformation of being and the laws pertaining to them, one in which actual experience has an important place in validating or refuting the theories, statements, and claims. This super-science would deal with human beings not only as they ordinarily are but as they could be.[2]

In spite of the difficulties associated with the label *higher nature* for the spiritual aspect of a human being, there is one great advantage. We are used to the idea that there are laws in nature, that there is causality, that there is a possibility of inquiry and investigation. To be sure, this inquiry needs to take into account higher-order laws, it needs to make room for human intention and purpose; nevertheless, it is an empirical inquiry and not something accepted without experiential investigation and reference to objective experience.

It should be remarked here that by "objective" is not meant anything exclusively or even necessarily *external*. That is why this super-science has to be fundamentally different in its assumptions, procedures, and goals from other natural sciences which have attempted to model themselves after physics for the last three centuries. No interior experience is at present a part of scientific data, especially of physics, a subject which since the sixteenth century has concerned itself with understanding the cosmos in terms of dead matter in motion in reaction to external and purposeless forces. Although one may speak in general of the scientific experience, it is necessary to distinguish between experience and experiment.[3] What we utilize in the sciences, and more particularly in the physical sciences on which are based all other natural sciences, are experiments and certainly not experiences.

The words *experiment* and *experience* are derived from the Latin words *experimentum* and *experientia* which in turn are both derived from *experiens*, the present participle of *experiri* which means to try thoroughly, to risk, to go through. The clear implication is that this involves some personal participation and risk. We still use *experience* in this sense, but *experiment* has not been used in this sense for nearly three hundred years. Experiment is used these days as an intransitive verb, and no longer transitively as experience is. We can experience a flower, but we can only experiment with or on it. The scientific evidence about an object is not gathered by experiencing it but by experimenting upon it. The knowledge thus produced is not a knowing by participation, but a knowing by distancing.

The objectivity of the natural sciences can relate only to those aspects which can be externalized. All aspects of interiority, such as intentions, purposes, and significance—all the aspects which easily come to mind when one speaks about the higher nature of man—are left out. The usual scientific knowledge is objective in many senses, but it is not objective in the mystical spiritual sense in which the observing self is so completely emptied or naughted that the object reveals itself as it is, the thing in itself, in all its numinosity and particularity. As sages in all cultures have said, in this no-self state of consciousness alone an object is known both in its oneness with all there is and in its uniqueness. Any entity—be it a tree, or a person or a culture or God—is then understood both in its essential interiority and its wholeness, including generality and specificity. Such is the state of insight described as truth-bearing (*ritāmbharā*) in Patanjali's *Yoga Sutras*, the classical text of Yoga. In another cultural metaphor, he who can be so completely emptied of himself that he could say that "I am not myself the source of the words I speak: it is the Father who dwells in me doing His own work" (*John*. 14:10), can speak authoritatively both of the uniqueness of the Father as well as of oneness with Him. For him there is no contradiction between these two statements which are both objectively true, namely, "The Father and I are one" (*John*. 10:30) and "The Father is greater than I" (*John*. 14:28).[4]

The fact of two natures of man is a matter of experience and cannot be denied. Too bad for any system of thought that does not make room for both of these. We ought not deny one or the other, nor assume that they are the same or that one is reducible to the other. The two natures are born of different parentage: every man is born of human parentage, but it is possible, according to all spiritual traditions even though their precise metaphors and nuances are quite different from each other[5] for a person to be born again of divine parentage, "begotten not by blood, nor by carnal desire, nor by man's willing, but by God" (*John*. 1:13). This birth of an inner being is a virgin birth because it is a spiritual birth without any carnal intercourse.

No literal, sex-related, impregnation of Mary by the Holy Spirit can possibly be intended by the Gospel writer. The masculine association with the *Holy Spirit* in English is derived from the corresponding Latin word, *Spiritus Sanctus*. This in its turn is the translation of the Greek word *Pneuma* which is neuter. Although the gospels are written in Greek, in the circles of Jesus and his disciples the language of ordinary usage was Aramaic, whereas Hebrew was used for sacred purposes. The two words from Hebrew which are both translated into Greek as *Pneuma* are *rhuh* and *shekinah*. However, both of these words in Hebrew are feminine.

Whether we speak in terms of two natures of man or two beings in him, spiritual and physical, where the physical includes the mental and the emotional, we cannot escape the fact that these two beings follow different laws, the law of spirit and the law of flesh. There are teachings, for example in Tibetan Buddhism, in which inner birth is spoken of in terms of several subtler bodies arising from the gross body by alchemical transformation of substances. St. Paul also has fragments of this doctrine. The point to be emphasized here is that just as there are levels of physical and mental development within the lower nature, similarly there are levels of development in the spiritual nature; and different laws, permitting different degrees of freedom, apply to different levels.

Spirit, Soul, and Body

There is a saying (hadith) related to the Prophet of Islam. Upon returning from a battle, Prophet Mohammed said to his disciples, "We have returned from the little holy war to the great holy war." When the disciples pressed him for clarification, he said, "The little holy war is a war against the infidels, but the great holy war is the war against one's own soul."

In the Christian world in the modern times, *soul* is considered to be so wholly good and spiritual that the idea of waging a war against it is likely to sound like siding with the devil. It is therefore useful to make a brief historical remark concerning this. In many ancient traditions, and certainly in early Christianity, Greek philosophy and Indian thought, a developed or mature human being was regarded to have three distinct parts: Spirit, soul, and body, or to use the New Testament terminology, and especially of St. Paul, *Pneuma, psyche,* and *soma*.[6] In this division, *Pneuma* (Spirit) is supra-personal, manifesting itself in or through a person or in other ways, whereas *psyche* (soul) belongs to the person. Thus it makes sense to speak of 'my soul' but not of 'My Spirit.' On the other hand, one can speak of 'the Spirit' or of the 'spirit in me.'[7]

Gradually over the centuries this three-fold division shrank into a two-fold one: spirit and nature, or mind and matter, or soul and body, or higher nature and lower nature. In Western thought, the *coup de grâce* was dealt by Descartes who explicitly identified spirit with soul and both with the mind. Since his time, in the Western world, soul is in general regarded more or less as completely spiritual, as contrasted with natural. In India also a partial shrinkage of the three-fold division into a two-fold one took place. However, there, in general, psyche has been considered to lie in the realm of matter, and therefore subject to the laws of material nature and amenable to natural scientific inquiry. The psychic functions, such as thoughts and feelings, and the psychic phenomena, including the so-called paranormal ones, are in the realm of *prákriti* (nature), that is to say, they are in the domain of materiality and causality. According to the Indian thought, the so-called miracles, for examples those mentioned in the Bible, are not supernatural or spiritual, even though they are unusual and extraordinary. In this connection, it is good to remind ourselves of an obvious truism that what we know about nature is not all there is to nature.

Returning to the saying of the Prophet Mohammed, the war against the soul, in the context in which it is spoken, is a war against one's own lower nature. Similarly, Jesus Christ says several times, in Luke 14:26 for example, that he who does not hate his psyche—which is to say his soul or self—cannot be a disciple of his. Soul there, as in the Indian thought, belongs to the lower realm. However, it is within this lower realm (also spoken of as the realm of the *world* or of the *flesh*, as in the Gospel According to St. John) lie the possibilities of a new life, a birth into the higher world of the Spirit. In a three-fold division of a human being, which is philosophically clearer and more satisfying than the two-fold one, the struggle between the spiritual and carnal natures of man is waged in the psyche of man. In the play of forces in his own soul, a human being can side completely with one or the other side, becoming wholly an animal or an angel, or he can keep both of them in their proper balance and be truly human. A properly ordered person does not deny the body-mind, but he is not driven by it. For him the body-mind is like a horse for the Spirit to ride, and needing to be disciplined as well as befriended but certainly not to be brutalized. To use a classical analogy: the Spirit has the vision, but is lame; the body-mind is blind but it can carry and move. Together they can constitute an integrated and whole person— with both the vision to see what needs to be done and the ability to carry out the corresponding action.

Different Laws for Different Levels

At the level at which most of us live, practically all our behavior and everything else about us is completely determined by ordinary laws. The more developed a person is spiritually, which requires an intentional intervention on his part and which is by no means automatically accomplished in nature, the more he develops those aspects of being which are free of the lower laws and subject to the higher laws. Whether we follow the essentialist metaphor, as used in most religions, and say that a person can discover his deepest spiritual Self or God which is already in him, or whether we follow the existentialist metaphor so that a person has to create this spiritual part, the important point is that some purposeful action, an intentional undertaking, is required from man. Speaking in a religious mode, even as we see that without God it cannot be done, we also see that without man it will not be done.

However, not everything in a developed human being becomes free of the usual laws of birth, change, and decay. His physical body still obeys the laws of its own level; but he discovers or creates and progressively lives from a more subtle part of himself which itself is relatively freer of the laws to which the body is subject. Only at the highest possible inner development of a person could one say that the most spiritual part of himself—God, the Absolute, Brahman—is beyond all laws, and is therefore completely and absolutely free. But this is like a theoretical limit, where our mental concepts break down, as in dividing a number by zero, and we need to be extremely careful about extrapolating from that sort of a limit to anything practical. Whereas it may be true to say in some cases, for example for Jesus Christ when he is one with God, that for them the law is ended, still that does not mean that there are no laws in the realm of the spirit. The spiritual and the natural realms may be distinguished by different sorts of laws, but they are not separated by an abundant lawfulness in the one realm and its absence in the other. There may in fact be more of a continuity in practice between these realms than is allowed by theoretical theology which has brought in its wake disastrous consequences wherever it has prevailed. On the one hand, it has cut off the spirit from the bodily center of man in the natural rhythms of life, and on the other, it has fostered an opposition between natural science and spiritual life. Above all, it is spiritual life that has suffered by losing touch both with the body and with the intellectual principles of empirical inquiry.

The fact that so far while speaking about the two natures, spiritual and carnal, our attention has been confined to human beings should not blind us to the possibility that even in the cosmos these two realms with different laws exist, containing many gradations within them, and that the whole creation participates both in materiality and spirituality. All creatures and constellations, however brutish and solidly material they may be, have the possibility of consciousness, even if only at a rudimentary level.

Also, there was a well-nigh universal idea throughout the ancient and medieval world that a developed human being is a microcosmos mirroring inwardly in essential principles the large cosmos, and vice versa. The presence and action of subtle spiritual energies and beings, variously labeled *angels, devas, gods, fairies, spirits,* and the like are globally attested. The fact that we cannot detect these with our ordinary scientific concepts and instruments does not mean that they do not exist.

What we know—actually and potentially—about the universe depends on the procedures, methods, and interests that we bring in looking at the universe. If we do not know how to find angels and we are not interested in them, will we be right in concluding that they do not exist?

It is true that angels are not a part of our usual scientific universe. Nor are "the clouds which brood," which were a part of Wordsworth's universe, nor are the dancing colors, inhabiting Blake's universe, nor are the cherubim and seraphim singing "Holy, holy, holy," who were a part of Bach's cosmos. The physical cosmologist's universe, vast and marvelous as it is, is not all there is. Spiritual realities cannot be seen with ordinary eyes or their extensions at the same level; a new being and a transformed vision are needed for their apprehension. As Plotinus said (*Enneads* I.6.9), "to any vision must be brought an eye adapted to what is to be seen, and having some likeness to it. Never did eye see the sun unless it had first become sun-like, and never can the soul have vision of the First Beauty unless itself be beautiful."

In a science of higher nature a mind with steady attention and a heart cleansed of egoistic cravings may be the greatest scientific instruments. What can be perceived by a person with a disciplined body, steady mind, and clear heart, in other words, a *third-eye universe*, is quite different from what can be seen by the two ordinary eyes and their quantitative extensions. We do not need more and more things to see with the same eyes; what will really affect us is to see, even the same things, with different eyes.

New Physics and Human Freedom

There is something particularly sad about the eagerness with which many so-called religious people have latched on to one or another discoveries or theories of modern physics to justify their faith or to find some room for their religious positions. Before the sixteenth century in Europe, every activity had to be justified in the light of Christian theology, just as for decades in the twentieth century in the U.S.S.R. everything had to be justified in the terms of dialectical materialism. In the Western world for a couple of centuries now, and increasingly in the rest of the world as well, the true intellectual orthodoxy is that of science. If you want to sell anything or promote anything, it is better to have science prove its value—whether it is a particular kind of toothpaste or transcendental meditation. Every guru feels a little securer if he can have a scientist, especially a physicist with a Nobel Prize, sitting next to him on the dais! Now even God has to be scientifically acceptable. Last year in a paper to the Royal Society of Canada I suggested that our modern attitude is better reflected in the following rendering of the verse from the *Psalm* quoted earlier:[8]

> When I consider the heavens, the work of our equations, the blackholes and the white dwarfs, which we have ordained; what is God, that we are mindful of him?

I wonder what we expect science to do for us? What do we hope from it? Wisdom? Freedom? Salvation? Can any discoveries or creations of science bring about a transformation of our own inner being where alone true freedom and bondage lie? Can any theory or external authority do this for us? For that matter, even in the realm of the scriptures, whose total concern is with salvation or enlightenment, what sort of knowledge of them will do? Are the theologians who have studied all the influences which have shaped the scriptures saved? Are the physicists who can solve the latest conundrums in magnetogeometrodynamics enlightened? What is it that we need? It surely must reflect a peculiar kind of psychological uncertainty to require a bolstering by the up-to-date findings of quantum mechanics, or to be assured of free will by them. Did the Buddha have to wait for the proof of Bell's theorem? Or of the theory of relativity or of holography? Is next year's Nobel Prize winner in physics more unified or whole than Kepler, or than Pythagoras? Is he freer?

If we are totally out of touch with our own center, we can have no inner orientation; then the sense of ourselves needs to be supported by the changing theories in science, or in theology. This kind of external prop can substitute for the discipline of an actual inner search and block a real centering of oneself. The more we rely on mental constructs rather than a direct seeing of ourselves, the farther we get from our own inner essential core, or from the *hara* where Zen satori takes place, or from the belly from where the rivers of living water flow according to Jesus Christ (Jn. 7:38). Einstein was right when he said, "The present fashion of applying the axioms of physical science to human life is not only entirely a mistake but has also something reprehensible in it."[9]

Schroedinger was even clearer: "Physics has nothing to do

with religion. Physics takes its start from everyday experience, which it continues by more subtle means. It remains akin to it, does not transcend it generically, it cannot enter into another realm."[10] He characterizes such attempts as "sinister." "The territory from which previous scientific attainment is invited to retire is with admirable dexterity claimed as a playground of some religious ideology that cannot really use it profitably, because its [religion's] true domain is far beyond anything in reach of scientific explanation."[11]

Also, we should not let ourselves be seduced by superficial parallels between certain expressions and paradoxes of contemporary science and ancient Oriental thought. They are entirely different from each other in their procedures, intentions, goals, and consequences simply because they deal with two different kinds of nature.[12] Furthermore, these parallels are, in general, pressed by people who although themselves derive from the Judeo-Christian traditions, yet have very little sympathy with the principles and idioms of the Western spirituality which they regard to be fundamentally different from the Oriental one. However, it is true that here and there are beginning to appear in the long column of Western appellations in the honor rolls of science names like Chandrasekhara Venkata Raman, Tsung Dao Lee, Hideki Yukawa, Abdus Salam, and Chen Ning Yang. In his day Kepler was convinced that the Sun was the Father, the circumference of the solar system the Son, and the intervening space the Holy Ghost. A latter day scientist, brought up on different symbols and metaphors, might see in the patterns appearing in the cloud chamber the dance of Shiva, or be moved to find the complementarity appearing in the quantum phenomena pointing to *yin* and *yang* encircled together, or discover the resolution of the various paradoxes of contemporary physics in the ineffable Tao.

These parallels or interpretations are as true or false now as they were then for Kepler. They add nothing, either to true science or to true spirituality. Any true science of the Spirit, which is not merely an extension of the present scientific procedures and assumptions to include occult phenomena and extrasensory perceptions, must rely upon the perceptions and understanding of transformed human beings so that the levels of reality which are generically and qualitatively different from the ones now studied by the natural sciences can be apprehended. Such sacred sciences have existed for centuries, as Yoga, Zen, alchemy, certain aspects of Sufism and of monastic Christianity, but often they have fallen into sectarian and acquisitive hands.[13] A consequence of this has been that the bright minds and sensitive hearts in the modern age have shied away from them. As this science of the Spirit is freed from an exclusively sectarian, rationalist, and obscurantist hold, it will be more and more appreciated for its true value in enabling a person to discover and fulfill his unique purpose.

The greatest discovery of modern science is the discovery of its own limitations, and an increasing appreciation of the fact that what we know depends not only on what is out there but also on who we are and how we see. Our knowledge cannot be separated completely from the nature of our being and the quality of our attention. Corresponding to many levels of being within ourselves, from the totally determined to the most free, there are many levels of knowledge. Not all of them are at present included under the rubric of science, but that is not important. What is more important is that there be a practical inquiry into transformation of a human being from being a slave of fear and ambition to becoming a free man. Natural science can help this inquiry but it can also hinder it, depending on what relationship we have with science. But, whatever science may discover, whatever social or political conditions may prevail, the cultivation of inner freedom cannot but be undertaken by an individual, in the arena of his own soul. There he must struggle with those parts of himself which are frightened by the possibility of genuine transformation and which would barter away real freedom for self-importance.

Natural Law as a Foundation for Freedom

All ancient traditions believed in the lawfulness of the universe, and the corresponding bondage imposed on human beings by nature and her laws. From a philosophical and spiritual point of view, there is nothing new about the so-called problem of determinism versus free-will; it has not arisen since the successful application of Newtonian mechanics to the solar system; nor has any radically new light been thrown on it since the development of quantum mechanics. Determinism of the effect from the cause is a notion which is integrally built right into the meaning of law. If there is lawfulness, there is determinism.

But, also, and this needs to be emphasized, precisely because there is lawfulness, there is the possibility of freedom. A law also indicates the payment required for freedom from that law. Space travel would have been impossible without understanding the law of gravitation which keeps us tied to the earth, and without knowing precisely what escape velocity is needed to overcome the effect of that law in a particular situation, and without having the requisite fuel and technology to acquire that velocity. It is only a romantic notion to imagine that we can acquire immortality, salvation or freedom for ourselves without making the requisite payment exacted by the law which keeps us naturally and quite lawfully enslaved. Of course, everywhere in the world some form of religion can be found which will sell some cheap indulgences, physical or doctrinal, to unsuspecting buyers and try to assure those who are gullible that they are specially chosen for grace now and glory in the hereafter.

Returning to an example of natural law, we can look at the law of causality, applicable to all nature, internal and external, and enunciated in many cultures in one form or another for millennia. In India it is expressed as the *Law of Karma*. Confining our attention to human beings alone, we can express the Law of Karma as follows: as one is so one acts; and as one acts so one becomes. It is like the mutually interactive system of spacetime and matter in the theory of General Relativity: matter affects spacetime and spacetime affects matter. In the Law of Karma, being affects action and action affects being. If I am a certain kind of person, I would naturally find myself doing certain sorts of actions. In their turn, these actions which I perform leave grooves of tendencies on my being, altering it so that I become a certain kind of person. Next moment I shall act in accordance with these tendencies of my being, my future action (*karma*) thus being determined by my past action. Major actions leave deep impressions in the psyche, creating knots in it which will affect my future actions for a long time without my being necessarily aware of the knots or their initial causes. As a general principle, the effects of karma are not restricted to only one life time; the law cuts across the boundary of what is ordinarily called life and death. It may be remarked parenthetically that action here does not simply mean bodily activity, but also includes thoughts and feelings and intentions. If I think bad thoughts about any one of you, not only does that reflect the quality of my being but it also further affects this quality.

This is an example of a traditional law of nature, understood in more or less this form by two thirds of mankind now residing in Asia, and in any case by the vast population in Hindu and Buddhist countries. This law is a law of determinism; but it is also a law which makes freedom possible and provides the basis for any spiritual practice. Understood partially, from the point of view of only one level within a human being, the Law of Karma creates a vicious circle from which one cannot escape, and it has quite often been understood in this manner leading to despair and resignation. However, when viewed from the perspective of a whole person, the Law of Karma can indicate to a person willing to undertake the discipline involved in the cleansing of his perceptions precisely what the knots are in his life which compel him to act the way he does, even against the will and understanding of his right mind, and how to resolve and overcome these.

More importantly, a person can depend on the Law of Karma and undertake his striving in the assurance of the knowledge that the universe or the gods do not act capriciously, and that he is not going to be elevated or degraded accidentally. He is responsible for his life—even to the final extent of salvation or perdition—and the dignity of his human existence and action is founded on the solidity of a law working in every part of the cosmos. In correspondence with his own deep-seated spiritual urges, every person has the possibility of making efforts in order to overcome the compulsions of the lawful and natural workings of one's own tendencies, which are based on one's past experiences, knowledge, and impressions. This is the meaning of spiritual striving, a struggle against one's own determined nature, in which the spiritual aspects of the cosmos help the spiritual aspects of man, just as the unintentional and natural parts of the universe aid the unintentional and natural existence of man.

Freedom Not For Oneself But From Oneself

As has been remarked, it is intentional intervention which transforms a human being so that he does not only perform a natural function in the cosmos, but also has the possibility of fulfilling a spiritual purpose. What makes this intentional undertaking possible is attention. This is the reason why in all spiritual teachings, whether represented in the *Yoga Sutras* or in the *Philokalia* or in Zen practice, attention in its various qualities and levels constitutes the main instrument of transformation. Attention freed from egoistic fears and ambitions, which are constantly turning the mind to the past and the future dimensions of time, taking it away from the present moment in which alone the dimension of eternity intersects that of time, is the essence of serious prayer and meditation. These in turn are the ways of connecting with the higher parts of oneself and of the universe, and the corresponding higher laws, rather than being petitions for the suspension of laws in special cases.

Whether the Spirit is discovered or created, it is done with attention founded on a progressive clarity of the mind and the heart. From the grossest level of being to the most subtle, all levels are reflected in the quality of attention and the corresponding degrees of freedom. The creatures most bound are the sleepiest, with only the instinctive attention. At the highest level, the freest attention, or the purest seeing, is what constitutes wakefulness and Spirit. The basic existence of the spiritual self has to do with attention, sensitivity, mindfulness, intention, and insight—the very qualities which make us truly human and truly free. But these are not the qualities which are automatically acquired in nature; they all require effort, education, work, and, in general, a spiritual path involving an enormous struggle with the worldly forces within oneself, fueled by fear, ambition, and egocentricity.

Freedom thus is not an actuality for a vast majority of human beings who have neither the inclination nor the ability to struggle against their own lower natures. However, it remains a potentiality for any man who has cultivated himself properly. An ordinary man is in fact quite determined by his cultural, social, and psychological conditioning, in reaction to which arises his so-called self-will. He who lives wholly from his self-will is completely determined by his past actions and reactions, ricocheting down the corridor of time, without ever being able to engage in a fresh action, in the present moment of eternal now, in which alone there is real freedom. As *Theologia Germanica* (chapter 34) says, "Nothing burneth in hell except self-will." And what is hell if not the prison created by a totally determined ego?

A free man, on the other hand, by no means does 'his own thing.' He realizes that freedom is not in opposition to law or order—that would be just anarchy and chaos—nor even in spite of the law, but because of it. Freedom is grounded in the law; he who does not respect the natural law—both the inner and the outer—cannot be free. Freedom is possible only when a person is internally rightly ordered, so that his own lower and less conscious parts are able to hear and obey the more conscious parts. Certainly in the spiritual context it can be said that perfect freedom arises only from perfect obedience, a complete submission of self-will to the order inherent in the vastness or the Tao. The ultimate payment exacted by the law of freedom is the sacrifice of one's egoistic self, of all the parts which are bound and unconsciously repeat compulsive actions determined by the past, which gives one self-importance and the impression of having a purpose isolated from that of the cosmos. He who can pay the price of self-sacrifice can be free. That was the case of Jesus Christ who thoroughly emptied himself and died to his self-will, so that he could be filled with the being and the will of God, and say on the eve of his death that his joy was now complete.

According to the *Yoga Sutras* a sage comes to final freedom when his insight is by itself in accord with cosmic order, so that his conflict and sorrow are ended. Such a person is not free *for himself*; he is free *from himself*, that part of himself which is willfully isolated from the laws, purposes, and intentions of the vastness. Freed from the burden of himself, and from the regrets about his past and the anxieties about his future, he is able to be present here and now and dance. A dancer is freest when he is naturally in harmony with the tempo and the rhythm of the dance. Then, he belongs to the universe and the universe belongs to him, mutually supporting the fulfillment of each other's purpose.

Notes

1. This and the immediately following quotations are all from Albert Einstein, *Ideas and Opinions* (New York, 1954).
2. We do not have any commonly accepted names for such a science at present: we may use *Numenology* or *Autology* to convey some idea about the sort of inquiry it is. Older labels, such as *Theology* and *Ontology*, although by themselves wholly appropriate, will no longer now do because they have been co-opted by sectarian and exclusively mentalistic enterprises without reference to any objective experience.
3. See R. Ravindra, "Experience and Experiment: A Critique of Modern Scientific Knowing," Chapter 7, this volume.
4. For a non-sectarian interpretation of the whole of the Gospel According to St. John, please see R. Ravindra, *The Yoga of Christ in the Gospel According to St. John* (Shaftesbury, England: Element Books, 1990).
5. See R. Ravindra, *Whispers from the Other Shore: Spiritual Research, East and West* (Wheaton, Illinois: Quest Books, 1984).
6. See A.H. Armstrong and R. Ravindra, "The Dimensions of the Self: *Buddhi* in the *Bhagavad Gita* and *Psyché* in Plotinus," *Religious Studies* 7, 1979, 317–332.
7. In this paper, following more or less the usual custom, supra-personal entities or qualities, such as Spirit and God, are written with an initial capital letter.
8. See R. Ravindra, "In the Beginning is the Dance of Love," Chapter 18, this volume.
9. In an interview contained in M. Planck, *Where is Science Going?* (New York: Norton, 1932), 209.
10. Erwin Schroedinger, *Science, Theory and Man* (New York: Dover, 1935), 307–308.
11. Erwin Schroedinger, *Nature and the Greeks* (Cambridge University Press, 1954), 8.
12. See R. Ravindra, "Perception in Yoga and Physics," Chapter 16, this volume.
13. A similar situation has increasingly threatened the modern natural sciences, especially since the Second World War, in their takeover by national and industrial interests.

PART FIVE:

SCIENCE AND
SPIRITUAL PATHS

TWENTY

The SPIRITUAL QUEST

Ravi Ravindra

The struggle to know who I am, in truth and spirit, is the spiritual quest. The movement in myself from the mask to the face, from the personality to the person, from the performing actor to the King of the inner chamber, is the spiritual journey. To live, work, and suffer on this shore in faithfulness to the whispers from the other shore is spiritual life. To keep the flame of spiritual yearning alive is to be radically open to the present and to refuse to settle for comforting religious dogma, philosophic certainties, and social sanctions.

Who am I? Am I Judas, am I Jesus? Out of fear, out of desire, I betray myself. I am who I am not. I cover my face with many masks, and even become the masks. I am too busy performing who I think I am to know who I really am. I am afraid: I may be nothing other than what I appear to be; there may be no face behind the mask. I decorate and protect my mask, preferring a fanciful something over a real nothing.

I cling to the herd for comfort. Together we weave varied garments to cover our nakedness. We guard the secret of our nothingness with anxious agility lest we should be discovered.

Occasionally, I hear a voice uttered in some dark recess of myself. Sometimes it is the soft sobbing of a lonely child. At other times, the anguished cry of a witnessing conscience. At yet other times, it is the thundering command of a king.

Who are you? I ask. I AM.

What am I asking when I ask Who am I? What sort of answer would be acceptable? Do I want a chart of my genealogical and social relations? A list of my racial and biological characteristics? A catalogue of my psychological features—my likes and dislikes, desires and fears? These are all the things that shape my personality. But whose personality is it? Who wears this mask? In response to a little knock at the door of my consciousness, I ask Who is it? No naming—son of God, Self, Atman, Krishna—is sufficient.

What I seek is to see the face of the one who calls.

Who am I? does not ask for an enumeration of scientific facts: it expresses a certain restlessness, groping, and exploration. It is the beginning of a movement towards light, towards seeing things clearly, as a whole. It is the refusal to remain in the dark—fragmented and on the surface of myself. It is a state of searching for meaning, comprehensiveness, and depth. It is the desire to wake up.

Soon I betray this impulse and am lulled back to sleep by comforting caresses and fairy tales. I sleep, dreaming of great adventures and questing for the hidden treasures. Many journeys, many peaks, and the lions guarding the mountain passes. For a moment I wake up—to find myself a prisoner of what I know and what I am. Even finding the door of my little prison open, I stay in it, afraid to leave, counting and recounting my possessions and my testimonials.

I share many walls with others. With vigor and imagination, I collaborate with others in building the castles of science, philosophy, and religion in which we may rest secure, unmindful of our ignorance of who we are, why are we here, and why we do what we do. The silent witness inside me asks: What do you seek?

Awakening

All spiritual traditions thus diagnose the human condition: man is asleep and his life—ambitions, fears, activities—is governed by vast forces, outside of his will or control. He can, with instruction, grace, and effort, wake up, see his situation as it is, and begin to listen to his inner voice.

Gurdjieff tells an Eastern tale about a very rich and mean magician who had a great many sheep. But he did not want to hire any shepherds, nor erect fences around the pastures where the sheep grazed. Often the sheep wandered away into the forest and were lost, and some of them ran away, for they knew that the magician wanted their flesh and skins. At last the magician thought of a remedy. He hypnotized his sheep and suggested to them that no harm would come to them because they were immortal, that the magician was a good master who would do anything for his flock, and that even if anything were to happen to them it certainly would not be just then and they need not worry about it. Furthermore, the magician suggested to his sheep that they were not sheep at all: to some he suggested that they were lions, to others that they were eagles, to others that they were men, and to some that they were magicians like himself. Under the influence of hypnotism the sheep believed the magician, who could now rest without care and worry. The sheep never ran away again and quietly awaited the time when the magician would require their flesh and skins. Meanwhile, they grazed happily on the prescribed pasture without needing either shepherds or fences.[1]

Thus we quietly wait; telling each other our conjectures about the wonderful past or the glorious future, our free will or immortality, our loving Father or the great Teacher, the nature of the electron or the rotation of the galaxy—all in a hypnotic sleep, rarely recognizing the real terror of our human situation.

We discover the dream nature of our ordinary existence only when a shock momentarily wakes us up. When we come to, we realize we were sleeping; soon the soporific forces lull us to sleep again. Most of our life is lived in dreaming, day-dreaming or wake-dreaming, and we see the world through a glass darkly: this is the Vedantist's experience of the thralldom of illusion or *maya*. It is only by lifting this veil of *maya* that one can become awake, *buddha*. If we open our eyes, we see that in our ordinary existence we are estranged from our real self and that we live in a fallen state. We are sinful because we have missed the mark; we experience suffering, *dukkha*, out of ignorance.

We are not what we truly are; having forgotten ourselves, we have mistaken our identity.

The nineteenth-century Indian saint Ramakrishna told a story about a tigress who attacked a flock of goats. Shot by a hunter just as she sprang on her prey, the tigress gave birth to a cub and died. The cub grew up in the company of the goats. Following their example, he started eating grass and bleating like them, even when he grew to be a big tiger. One day another tiger attacked the flock and was amazed to see a grass-eating tiger in the flock. When the wild tiger caught up to the grass-eating tiger, the latter began to bleat. The wild tiger dragged the other to the water and asked him to look at his face in the water and see that it was identical to his own. He gave a little meat to the bleating tiger, who had difficulty eating it. Gradually, however, the grass-eating tiger got to know the taste of blood, and came to relish the meat. Then the wild tiger said: "Now you see there is no difference between you and me; come along and follow me into the forest."[2]

We can well imagine the jungle-reverberating sound of the two free tigers roaring! We have forgotten our face, our wild roar, and we bleat—as if we were goats. When we remember ourselves, it is like the prodigal son when he came to himself; this our brother was dead and is alive again, was lost and is found. Miserable though man may be, he can come alive; he can reorient himself and undergo a radical transformation. With effort, knowledge, and guidance, he can become what he is: "Son of the Most High," partaker of divine nature, and a child of God.[3]

When one begins to wake up, one realizes the inner conflict between two poles of oneself; darkness and light, lower self and the higher self (Plotinus), the little I (*ahamkar*) and the real I (*Atman*) of the *Upaniṣads*, world and God (St. John), flesh and Spirit (St. Paul). And this battle is waged in the psyche of man; man's mind is the battleground of the *Bhagavad Gita*. As the *Maitri Upaniṣad* (6.34:11) says, "Mind, in truth, is the cause of bondage and of liberation." Upward and downward tendencies take hold of us periodically; in turn we affirm and deny our deeper selves. In this cosmic play of vast forces, we squirm like hooked fish.

Self-knowledge

In one of the dialogues between disciple and master, Jacob Boehme wrote as follows:

> The Disciple said to his Master: How may I come to the super-sensual life, that I may see God and hear him speak? His Master said: When you can throw yourself but for a moment into that where no creature dwells, then you hear what God speaks. Disciple: Is that near at hand or far off? Master: It is within you and if you can for a while but cease from all your thinking and willing, then you shall hear the unspeakable words of God.[4]

In saying "It is within you," Boehme expressed an eternal truth which has been uttered by practically all the great teachers of the past. Christ said, "The Kingdom of God is within you."[5] Self-realization is the main theme of all the *Upaniṣads*. "He who knows that which is set in the secret place of the heart, he here on earth, O beloved, cuts asunder the knot of ignorance."[6]

However, this hidden one is not easily assigned a place. In a deep experience of listening or seeing, what is outside us is also inside. We ourselves are as mysterious as the kingdom and may hold the keys to it. If we can open the doors of the interior castle, the King might come and sit on the throne.

Self-knowledge is a prerequisite to, if not synonymous with, theology. According to Plutarch, the inscription at Delphi, "know thyself," is an injunction addressed by God to all who approach Him.[7] Man sees "the nature of *Brahman* through the nature of his own self, as by a lamp," says a *Upaniṣad*.[8] Plotinus said, "One that seeks to penetrate the nature of the Divine Mind must see deeply into the nature of his own soul, into the Divinest part of himself."[9] In fact, it appears that the only way to God is by self-knowing, dying to one's superficial self, and being born to a deeper self. There are clearly differences in detail and emphasis, but there is no other point on which there is a greater unanimity of principle among the various masters of spiritual becoming. One of the non-canonical sayings of Jesus Christ is: "The Kingdom of heaven is within you and whosoever knoweth himself shall find it. And having found it, ye shall know yourselves that ye are the sons and heirs of the Father, the Almighty, and shall know yourselves that ye are in God, and God in you. And ye are the City of God."[10]

Obviously, there are levels of self-knowledge and corresponding development or deepening of being. Different traditions refer to these levels in many ways: seven-storied mountain, rungs of a ladder, levels of consciousness. Within ourselves at the level of ordinary humanity, where we usually are, there is confusion and chaos. We are like "a troubled sea, a sea that cannot rest, whose troubled waters cast up mud and filth."[11] We have conflicting desires and compulsions in constant flux; there is nothing abiding, nothing that could properly be called self.

As Pascal said, "We are naught but lies, duplicity, contradiction, and we hide and disguise ourselves from ourselves."[12] Only deeper down, is there the possibility of increased understanding, integration, and wholeness. Only in a state of collectedness, composure, openness, and alertness can we know anything objectively. In all other states our perceiving apparatus is out of tune and introduces its own noise arising out of internal or external distractions and afflictions. Nothing that we decipher in these dispersed states is ultimately trustworthy. One of the purposes of the various spiritual schools is to help men repair themselves and gradually to come to a state of preparedness, freed of subjective desires, expectations, and fears. As long as we keep making our little noises, we cannot truly hear. Only when quietened within, may we encounter what is real.

In that purified, integrated state, arrived at after a long and arduous spiritual journey, we can discover our deepest self, which sages call by various names: "the spirit of the soul" (Eckhart), "*acumen mentis*" (Hugh of St. Victor), "center of the soul" (St. Teresa of Avila), "spark of the soul" (St. Jerome), "the divine person who is beyond the beyond" (*Mundaka Upaniṣad*). These are all attempts to name the nameless, but as Eckhart said: "The God who is without a name is inexpressible, and the soul in its ground is equally inexpressible, as He is inexpressible....To gauge the soul we must gauge it with God, for the ground of God and the ground of soul are one and the same."[13] It is of this self of selves that the *Upaniṣads* speak when they declare: "Thou art that"; it is that *Atman* (Self) which is *Brahman*.[14] Only he who speaks from that center can say, "My Father and I are one....I am the way, the truth and the life; no one comes to the Father except by me."[15]

When we thus know ourselves, we no longer know this self or that self; we know the Self, unrestricted by any particularity. This knowledge is possible only when one's my-ness, one's ego is transcended. Strictly speaking, therefore, there is no one who is anyone who knows the Self; the Self knows itself. This is what Plotinus calls "a flight of the Alone to the Alone."[16] Not I, the I that I am, know these things," says Boehme, "but God knows them in me." It is this Self into which we who labor and are heavy laden must go to find rest.[17] If abandoning all else, in this alone we take refuge, we shall be released from evil.[18]

Notes

1. In P.D. Ouspensky, *In Search of the Miraculous—Fragments of an Unknown Teaching* (London: Routledge, Kegan Paul Ltd., 1957), 219.
2. *The Gospel of Shri Ramakrishna*, trans. with an introduction by Swami Nikhilananda (Madras: Mylapore, 1947), 170.
3. Psalms 82:6; II Peter 1:4; I John 3:1–2. Also St. Athanasius, "He became man that we might be made God" (*Athan. Orat. de Incarn Verbi. Tom.* 1, 108).
4. Jacob Boehme, *A Dialogue between a Scholar and His Master Concerning the Supersensual Life*, Dialogue I.
5. *Luke* 17:21.
6. *Mundaka Upanisad* 2.1:10.
7. *Moralia*, 384 D.f.
8. *Shvetashvatara Upanisad* 2:15.
9. *Enneads* V.3.9.
10. Quoted in F.C. Happold, *Mysticism* (Penguin, 1967), 174–75.
11. *Isaiah* 57:20.
12. Pascal's *Pensées*, with an English translation, brief notes, and introduction by H.F. Stewart (New York: The Modern Library, n.d.), 91.
13. J. Ancelet-Eustache, *Master Eckhart and the Rheineland Mystics*, trans. by H. Graef (New York: Harper Torchbook, n.d.), 66; second part quoted in Aldous Huxley, *The Perennial Philosophy* (New York: Fontana Books, 1958), 24.
14. *Chandogya Upanisad* 6:9ff. and *Mandukya Upanisad* 2.
15. *John* 10:30, 14:6.
16. *Enneads* VI.9.11.
17. *Matthew* 11:28.
18. *Bhagavad Gita* 18:66.

TWENTY-ONE

SOME REFLECTIONS On SCIENCE

Richard W. Sharpe

Some Remarks on Pythagoras and the Birth of Science

From far back in time we have the records (none of them first hand) of the Pythagorean Order. Perhaps one can say that modern science was discovered in this Order in the sense that, seemingly for the first time, the decisive role of number in the becoming of the universe was recognized and used. The discovery of the relation between the length and the frequency of a vibrating cord serves as a canonical example of this relationship even down to the present day. In the purely mathematical realm, the discovery of the irrationality of $\sqrt{2}$ is surely a mathematical result of the first order, the simplicity of today's proofs notwithstanding.

How did the great Pythagoras himself view the relationship between science and spirit? We do not know, but presumably it was related to Plato's idea that, yes, the world of mathematical thought is high above the world of ordinary thought, but that the world of the spirit is much farther yet again above the mathematical. Pythagoras did not regard scientific knowledge as essentially public, and scrupulously kept it from the vulgar and the unprepared. And yet there was interaction between the Order and the public sphere. Pythagoras himself is reported to have delivered a series of public talks to the citizens of Croton, not on his scientific discoveries, but on the principles of harmony and brotherhood in society. In these touching talks he exhorts children to have respect for their elders and parents to have respect for their children, advises never to reprimand in anger, and speaks of the evils of luxurious life and the importance of friendship. The first talk, addressed to the women and children of the community, so excited the respect of everyone that he was asked to address the council. Perhaps even more remarkable than the actual advice, which is *a propos* even today after 25 centuries, is the fact that these talks were remembered by the populace as great events, and that they are reported to have had widespread and lasting effects.

One could hear this story of Pythagoras and say merely that he must have been a very charismatic figure. I would like to suggest that that would be to miss the real point, which is that, somehow, Pythagoras had a living contact with the spirit, (which he refers to as harmony); and that all of the aspects of his life and work were infused and formed and governed by this living principle.

Alongside the praise for the scientific work of Pythagoras, one sometimes sees criticism of a superstitious or shamanic element of a primitive order, with its various injunctions, such as "when you have boiled water in fire, do not leave the imprint of the pot in the ashes, but take a stick and stir the ashes" and "On arising from sleep, do not leave the impression of the body in the bed sheets, but straighten them out."[1] One of the tragedies of modern science is that it ignores the Pythagorean superstition "to leave no trace." One sees too much of its imprint on the world, in the dying of the lakes, the vanishing of the ozone layer, the technology of warfare, the mechanization of life. Even taken as literal injunctions to the neophytes of the Order, we can appreciate the beginning of a training of the moral sensibility. Considering this one example further, we may note that one of the most interesting facts about Pythagoreans is that their society was secret, that Pythagoras himself apparently wrote nothing, nor did his close successors. Much of the influence exerted by his brotherhood was indirect, but can be measured by the high regard in which the Pythagoreans were generally held as is seen in the hints which have come down to us as story and legend.

Spiritual Effort and Modern Scientific Effort

In any discussion about modern science and the spirit, a scientist must first recognize with humility that his knowledge in these two domains is not balanced. While he may know a great deal, both theoretically and through his experience about the practice of his science, in general the question of the spirit remains more or less exactly that, a question. And yet perhaps there is some virtue in the attempt to formulate, insofar as that may be possible, what is the relationship between these two great influences.

Perhaps one may say that the common endeavor of all intellectuals is the act of image making. The making of an image is certainly the very atom of scientific activity. The various models of entities, of their inner processes and interactions are images which are found throughout science and the arts. Now, images are very useful in the sense that they focus one's attention in a specific direction. They can help to concentrate one's attention. On the other hand, images form a barrier between one's self and the direct perception of the wide world. Can one say that it is this direct perception which is the atom of the life of the spirit? Such perception appears in the best scientist also, but only momentarily, at that moment when the old image is discarded and before thought crystallizes perception into a new image.

It may even be that one's correspondence with the spirit is healthiest when one's questioning is the most passionate. This statement may have analogues in science, and yet ultimately science is concerned with answers as well as questions. Answers are the death of questions, and the death of the passionate openness which accompanies the wholeness of spiritual questing.

Perhaps one can say that the life of the spirit involves the choice/agony of acquiring the taste for preferring, moment by moment, the unexpected freshness/discomfort of the direct perception to the act of codifying the perception into an image.

From this perspective the role of thought in spiritual life is very much reduced as compared to its role in the life of a scientist or, more generally, of an intellectual. Indeed the second commandment is not to bow down before graven images.

In rural French villages, until recently, even less than a century ago, every stone, every tree had its resident spirit. There was more life in a little path of a few yards than in many modern city blocks. At this spot one had to give an offering; a leaf, a flower. At that place perhaps one had to turn round on the spot, and not wideshins if you please! When this was done mechanically, it was surely bondage, or worse. When it was felt as sacred ritual, it opened the heart to awe and wonder. Now all this has been destroyed in the great fire raging throughout the world. The doors to eternity are few and well hidden these days.

> When science serves the masses, it serves vulgar distraction;
> When science serves the merchants, it accelerates and
>   disharmonizes the tempo of life;
> When science serves the army, it damns what it touches;
> When science serves itself, it serves the illusion of alienation;
> When science serves the spirit, it acquires the possibility of
>   healing the center.

What has science to offer spirituality? It has, for one thing, the idea of the rigorous experimental method. To apply this to the spiritual domain, however, requires a reinterpretation. The way of science is to study phenomena in the outer world. Even psychology aims to study, for the most part, the projection of the inner world on the outer. For a true application of the method of science to the spirit, what is required is to study directly my own inner world. Rigor is demanded here, since the usual supports for rigor in sciences, for example the criticism of one's colleagues, the criterion of repeatability, etc., may not be available. What then is the meaning of rigor in this domain? It certainly must mean that observation needs to be very keen and from every angle. Each assumption, each working hypothesis, needs to be uncovered, seen fully, and tested carefully, tested from all sides, with every aspect of one's self included as tool and as material. What I like, what I do not like must be considered equally, impartially, scientifically. We can be sure that such an inner study, if it is rigorous enough, and broad enough, and sufficiently scientific must yield true knowledge of one's own nature; knowledge written not in journals available to others, not just in the memory available to the mind, but in the being, available to the whole of one's self.

The Present Moment

There is a widespread notion abroad in the land today, having its origin in many traditions, that the present historical moment is one of the ending of an age. René Guénon gives a very interesting description of the disorders of our time that result from inversions in the usual order of things.[2] In the latter stages of Kali Yuga, the connection between the priest and the spirit is severed, so that the priest can no longer perform his true role. Sooner or later the relationship between the priest and the king is cut, and then between the king and the merchants, and finally between the merchants and the workers. It is clear that in the world today, even more so than when Guénon was writing, that we are subject to the rule of the struggle between the merchants and the workers, a chaotic and dangerous time. But the end of the Kali Yuga coincides with the beginning of the Satva Yuga, the golden age of the next Manvantara. How does the Satva Yuga appear out of the present chaos? Perhaps this is one of the deeper meanings of the myth of the Phoenix which dies in flame, but in the ashes there is an egg out of which the new Phoenix will arise. The seeds of the new age must already be present in the flames and ashes of the old world. And the traditional view is that the first link to be reforged is the first that was broken; that is, the connection between the spirit and the priests. Regeneration comes from above, but it needs to find open hearts that will "cooperate" with it.

It seems pointless to expect modern science to reform itself. Modern science is vital now because it serves the masters of the day, the masses, the merchants and their minions the military. The question is not how modern science can serve the spirit, because that is impossible. The momentum of its present fragmented form is too powerful to be fundamentally altered. In a certain sense, it is not interesting. That impulse must live out, eventually to die. The question is how can the *scientist* serve the spirit? Normally the level of the priest is the same at its root as the level of the intellectual; it is at this level that the spirit will attempt to form a bridge. What is interesting is, can there be a higher science, based on entirely new, or rather eternal, principles, which could begin to incarnate? And how might one aid in this new birth?

Notes

1. These are paraphrases. See Kenneth Sylvan Guthrie, comp. and trans., *The Pythagorean Sourcebook and Library* (Grand Rapids, Mich.: Phanes Press, 1987), 159ff., esp. maxims 12 and 34.
2. René Guénon, *The Reign of Quantity* and the *Signs of the Times* (Baltimore, Maryland: Penguin Books Inc., 1972).

TWENTY-TWO

WHERE ARE RELIGION And SCIENCE COMPLEMENTARY?

Ravi Ravindra

Whenever the question of the complementarity of religion and science is discussed, there is an implicit assumption that what we need to discuss is *why religion* and *science* are complementary, or *how* they are complementary. Of course, there are the reverse, but related, considerations about why they are not and cannot be complementary. What I wish to do here is to raise some questions about *where* are religion and science complementary and *when*. I am not asking which aspects of religion are complementary to science or are acceptable to science. What I ask is something quite spatial and temporal. Are religion and science complementary to each other in Heaven or on Earth? Are they complementary in text books or research papers or in human beings? Are they complementary in sequence or simultaneously? Are they complementary in us now?

By raising this question in this form, I intend to suggest that most of our discussion of science and religion, and particularly in academic philosophical circles, has been too abstract, if not misleading. In general, the discussion is conducted or based on two very inadequate models. There is the model of science, usually based on modern Western physics, which assumes that scientific knowledge is the paradigmatic case of rational knowledge. Whereas the relevant history might easily lead to the suggestion that what has actually happened is that we have slowly adopted our view of *rationality* to fit modern science. For us moderns, science is rational *ipso facto*. Faced with case histories of scientific discoveries, we may become a little less sure about the unmitigated rationality of scientific activity, but we remain persuaded about the rationality of scientific knowledge. And, furthermore, since we are convinced that only rational knowledge is to count as knowledge, we conclude that science and knowledge are more or less synonymous—which they are in any case, etymologically. Thus in modern times, the realm of reason and knowledge has been preempted by science.

On the other side, the model of religion is based on Christianity, particularly Protestant Christianity. This is quite understandable since the discussion has been carried on in the Western academic setting, and until quite recently most Western scholars have felt no great need to inform themselves about non-Western religions. So, we could with profit raise the question whether religion and science are complementary in India or in America. But not here now, for I wish to invite you to other considerations at present.

Reverting to the predominant model for religion, namely Protestant Christianity, it is generally the case that the philosophically oriented scholars have tended to view the essence of religion as a set of propositions in which the religiously minded have *faith*. Since faith is taken to be synonymous with belief in some propositions, much philosophical expertise has been devoted to discussing the ground for such belief, and whether these grounds are compatible with those for holding scientific propositions. It is instructive to follow the history of the meaning of the word *belief*, as has been presented brilliantly by Wilfred Cantewell Smith in a recent book,[1] and to note that what has been of late considered by many to be the essence of religion, namely believing, is quite new on the intellectual scene and that the Biblical understanding of this concept is quite different from the modern one. We may then wish to consider the question of complementarity of religion and science from a historical point of view and wonder whether they were more complementary in, say, the thirteenth century than today. However, I shall not pursue this line of inquiry either at present.

Nevertheless, one may remark that this identification of the essence of religion with faith was not something hoisted upon the faithful wholly from the outside. Although the religious people are not likely, unless cornered by philosophers, to equate faith with having belief in some propositions, they themselves seem to have taken their stand in the realm of faith as distinct from the realm of knowledge. Since knowledge, which in the modern West has become more or less synonymous with science, is allied with reason, the relationship of faith with reason has become quite problematic. Faith is not always regarded as opposed to knowledge and reason—although there are some among both opponents of faith as well as among its supporters who think so and correspondingly recommend leaps of reason or leaps of faith, guarding against contamination from one or the other. More often than not, faith and knowledge are considered somewhat tangential to each other.

However, if faith is regarded as having no connection with reason, because it is radically transcendent or superrational, reasonable men tend to become indifferent to it. The sharp duality introduced by Immanuel Kant between *phenomenon* and *noumenon*, one the concern of reason and the other of faith, is an illustration. This attempt to save faith from the onslaught of reason crystallized the separation of the two, gradually resulting in a reason without significance and a faith without foundation. Then followed an inevitable inversion: what was removed from the scrutiny of philosophical analysis by Kant as superrational *noumenon* came in later for psychological analysis by Freud as subrational *neurosis*.

In the last few decades there has been an increasing awareness and appreciation of the sense of commitment and imagination that scientists bring to their work. We have become cognizant of the fact that creative scientists have a deep-seated faith in cosmic order. "Certain it is," said Albert Einstein, "that a conviction, akin to religious feeling, of the rationality or the intelligibility of the world lies behind all scientific work of a higher order."[2] It is possible in fact to view science as one expression of religious aspiration, among many expressions. At least for scientists, and perhaps for the greatest among them, science is a spiritual path.[3] In the Indic and the Hellenic traditions in particular, among the religious traditions of the world, the greatest expression of spiritual yearning is the search for truth and knowledge.[4] The specific form it has taken in the modern world, particularly in the West, is science. One may say with conviction that *modern science is the yoga of the West*. Like all yogas it has its difficulties.

It is no doubt true that at the level of the vast majority of ordinary work-a-day scientists, truth in any comprehensive sense gets quite a short shrift, and that science has been predominately employed in society for economic and military exploits. But this is not very different from what happens for ordinary Christians or Hindus or anybody else. And that religion has been employed for social exploitation or advancement is no news to anybody. An ordinary scientist is as far removed from Newton or Einstein as an ordinary Indian is from the Buddha or Shankara.

To speak about science and religion in a general manner abstracts them from the only thing that brings them alive. Namely, the human being who practices science or religion. And at the level of a single human being, it is hard to see how either a scientific concern or a religious concern can be wholly absent. Does there exist a man who never thinks of this vast cosmos around him—forming him, sustaining him? Is one not struck by the awesome subtlety, majesty, and order of the universe? Does one not wonder about the regularities, laws, and intelligence underlying the fabric of reality? In other words, is there anyone who is not interested in science? I do not mean any specific kind of science or any particular methodology. What I am referring to is the very urge behind science and its whole point: knowledge of our cosmos.

Similarly, is there anyone who is not, at least occasionally, overwhelmed by questions about the meaning and purpose of human existence in general and one's own in particular? Who is not interested in the knowledge of his self—its arising, its calling, and its destiny? Simply, who is not religious?

We can no doubt get too specialized and occupied with a sub-branch of a sub-branch of the scientific adventure and identify ourselves exclusively with a particular methodology, in the process losing the sense of the whole cosmos. And we can become too narrowly sectarian and communal, forgetting the vastness that is spirit. Institutionalization in these matters is usually an obstacle to understanding. Of course, on an individual level not many of us can bring very creative imagination or sustained discipline to bear on whatever engages us—whether it be science or religion. In general, our attention fluctuates. So, it is not only that science and religion are reconciled (or opposed or complementary) in a single human being, but also they are reconciled only in certain states of being within the same person. It is our addiction to abstractions that makes us think that the question of science and religion is capable of primarily a mental solution. There is so much more to each one of us than discursive reason alone that to be merely reasonable is quite unintelligent. It is certainly fragmentary and impoverished—as is single vision when the possibility exists of a fourfold vision. The larger vision must involve reason, no doubt, but it need not be limited by it.

The locus of real reconciliation of science and religion is a single human being—mind, heart, and body. It is the complementarity of scientific and religious aspirations in the same person that needs to be pondered. And this pondering is more than thinking; it involves embodying this reconciliation and in real time. The idea needs to be incorporated in time and space. If religion and science are not reconciled in us now, the ideas about their complementarity are mere mental ghosts feeding upon hollow emptiness. And this inner reconciliation needs some self-knowledge. Now, is that science or religion? Or a demand that we cannot set aside without denying all that makes us human?

Notes

1. *Belief and History* (Charlottesville: University Press of Virginia), 1977.
2. "On Scientific Truth," in *Essays in Science* (New York: Wisdom Library, 1934), 11.
3. See R. Ravindra, "Science as a Spiritual Path," Chapter 24, this volume.
4. A characteristic Indic view is to be found in *Taittirīya Upaniṣad* (2.1.1): "*Brahman* is truth, *Brahman* is knowledge, *Brahman* is infinite." By contrast, for example, the stress in the Hebraic tradition is more on the submission and obedience to the will of God.
5. That is literally what *Brahman* means. According to the Indian mythology, both gods and antigods are born from the same father, Kashyap (Vision). But the mother of the antigods is Diti (Limited), whereas the gods are the children of Aditi (Unlimited, Vast). Thus the products of limited vision are the antigods, the life-denying negativities; the resplendent gods are created by vast vision.

TWENTY-THREE

SCIENCE And SPIRIT

A PHYSICIST'S VIEW

E. C. George Sudarshan

This is undoubtedly the age of science. Not only is more science research undertaken currently compared to any time in history; but most of the scientists ever born are alive today! Such an explosion of a discipline makes it essential for us to see if science today is truly different in character from science in the past: Is there a difference in the spiritual aspect of science?

In our time science is often (mistakenly) identified with science-based technology and as such science appears to the public generally in its role as high-tech enterprises including space-travel, nuclear reactors, and warheads, electronic miracles including computers and the sophisticated weapons of modern warfare, as well as its more benign forms in agricultural research and miracle drugs. All these are associated with science, but they are associated also with commerce and economics and politics.

The one essential quality of science that is often overlooked is its cultural and personal growth potential. Science is primarily an intellectual discipline where vast amounts of human experience is brought under control in a systematic fashion. It is a way of life, a continuing endeavor; science continues to accumulate facts and theories each influencing the other. In the process the human intellect is cultured and skilled in the orderly perception of the world around and within us.

The dazzle of the technological artifacts so blinds many an eye that science as a cultural discipline, science as a fine art is overlooked. Many students in other disciplines when coming across an instructor or a course emphasizing the human cultural aspects of science are astonished at the bad press the hard sciences get. We scientists should share the blame for the distorted perception of science.

I would like to go one step further and point out that science, particularly so physics, enables a person to comprehend complex ideas. The domain of intellectual experience is enlarged. Physics provides a greater number of metaphors that can be used in other domains of human experience.

Science also provides a methodology that may be considered in other walks of life. First of all it deals with correlations, using them as a means of penetrating the world of appearances and arrive at the deeper level of happenings. This is not to say that the observed world is an illusion, just that it is an appearance which can be penetrated. Second, science deals with an economy of ideas; sometimes this gets distorted into reductionism (but not really!), but the overriding idea is to reduce myriad facts into a few theories derived from even fewer principles. The principles themselves may change with time but one principle that seems constant is that the world is an orderly understandable place.

I must hasten to add that science proceeds by a sequence of cycles. From simple observations one proceeds to controlled experiments based on some theoretical framework. The results of the experiments may strengthen that framework or suggest minor or major modifications in that framework. The newly refurbished theory is used to make new testable scientific predictions which in turn inspire new experiments. In these efforts it is only the simple minded that would assert that the theory suggested is in anyway unique. A different perspective may give a new cognition, a new theory. It does not happen too often: we scientists communicate well with each other, and we share our thoughts and make collective critical assessments, until a truly gifted person of independent vision gives a new perspective. But even in such cases it is hardly "revealed knowledge"; rather it is a system painstakingly built up systematically.

The Role of Mathematics

We are all prisoners of our own culture. We find it difficult to think along radically new paths. The very language is beset with thought habits, and model building and reasoning in science are restricted by the concepts of the times. The great liberation from their bondage came with the use of mathematics as a tool and as the language of science. Twentieth-century physical science is so fully in the language of mathematics that the discoveries and theories of science are difficult to describe in ordinary language. The serious person admiring science sees that science enlarges one's concept structure; and that conceptual models of great subtlety can be borrowed from the physical sciences.

The increasing number of scientists, the technological applications of science which often masquerade as science, the detachment of the abstract mathematical language from everyday speech, the great complexity of scientific theories and the many years of apprenticeship in the process of becoming a scientist have made science a profession. Contemplation and reflection, philosophic inquiry and artistic inspiration—these have been de-emphasized and even derided. Philosophy is suspect: we do science, not reflect on it!

In many ways science has taken the place of religion in human affairs. It is a high calling, requires learning, discipline and dedication, is respectable; and scientists like clerics of a bygone era are assured of a reasonable comfortable living. And like the clergy of an organized religion, good scientists do not speculate, deviate from the norm, or rock the boat, but get along within the community. The community of scientists as a whole make changes in the collective wisdom but no visionaries are encouraged. This provides for stability and orderly progress. If the majority of scientists feel that the universe is without design or purpose, so be it: It is only a Freeman Dyson who dares to enter a different view, a design for the universe in his book *Disturbing the Universe* in contrast to Jacque Monod's *Chance and Necessity*, Steven Weinberg's *First Three Minutes*, or E.O. Wilson's *Sociobiology*.

Science and Spirituality: Symbiosis or Predation?

Contemporary twentieth-century science is rich with conceptual gems: creation and destruction (of particles and excitations), symmetries, spontaneous symmetry breaking, non-commutation and consequent Heisenberg principle of uncertainties, Fourier transforms and holograms, hidden symmetrics, black holes, big bang cosmologies, and so on. At the same time there is a philosophic poverty. The spiritual yearning, the search for meaning and the hankering for magic have made many people turn to esoteric philosophies and religions as counterpoints to a scientific world view and a technological civilization.

Is Science a Spiritual Path?

Does science have a spiritual dimension? The answers are personal. Most scientists see no spiritual dimension. Nor do they feel a personal need for a spiritual path of any kind; they believe that it shows hard-nosed realism to have the courage to deny any such need. Some of them genuinely feel so; others feel that these disturbing questions are for the retirement years; and the majority go along since it is better to march with the crowd. There are a small group of people who do believe that a spiritual path is both desirable and necessary; and that science is an aid in this search.

How could science aid a spiritual search? First, science inculcates the work habit of disciplined observation and careful analysis. What is outward-directed to the extent it can be inward-directed becomes a spiritual discipline. Second, science produces more conceptual models in terms of which one's experience can be systematized and comprehended. We must recognize that this use of science is different from the use of scientific metaphors in exposition of spiritual doctrines.

Cognition and assessment of patterns, correlations, and mechanisms is different for different people. One person may feel that the romance of the celestial objects is tarnished by astro-physics and space exploration; yet another may feel his wonder increase the more he knows of their true nature. Knowing how scattering in the atmosphere induces the color of the setting sun or knowing how twilight or the rainbow come to be does not make them any less enchanting. Being enchanted by a sunset or recognizing the magical quality of twilight depends on the nature of the person, not his knowledge of physical science.

Science and the spiritual search share many characteristics: both are experiential, both involve unchartered domains, both involve personal discipline and dedication; and finally both are creative and joyous.

There are many who say that science has made spiritual search unnecessary. They find that the old ways are misleading or irrelevant; and that science provides the sustenance of the spirit. One can but admire such intellectual austerity. But there are others who are not sure: they are not even sure which brand of science is most akin to religion; they then listen to the people who say that contemporary science has rediscovered/resurrected/vindicated esoteric ancient science. Apart from the precarious validity of an ancient doctrine which depends on today's science, one is also struck by the fact that no clues to the future development of science are forthcoming from these quarters. Sober reflection would suggest that it is the scientific path that is an aid to the spiritual path, not scientific facts or theories.

TWENTY-FOUR

SCIENCE As A
SPIRITUAL PATH

Ravi Ravindra

Science is the paradigm of knowledge for us moderns. What does this knowledge tell me about myself? About my place in the cosmos? About the point of my being? About the direction of my knowing or the sense of my doings?

Science leads to, or perhaps presupposes, not only physical cosmology but also psychological and existential cosmology. How is scientific knowledge related to the spiritual? Is it completely tangential? Then why bother with science? With respect to what does science have any significance?

Does science have any spiritual significance? It seems logical to address this question first of all to scientists, and among them the greatest. What motivates them in their searches? Albert Einstein, in an address given in honor of Max Planck, said:

> In the temple of Science are many mansions, and various indeed are they that dwell therein and the motives that have led them thither. Many take to science out of a joyful sense of superior intellectual power; science is their own special sport to which they look for vivid experience and the satisfaction of ambition; many others are to be found in the temple who have offered the products of their brains on this altar for purely utilitarian purposes. Were an angel of the Lord to come and drive all the people belonging to these two categories out of the temple, it would be noticeably emptier, but there would still be some men, of both present and past times, left inside.... If the types we have just expelled were the only types there

were, the temple would never have existed, any more than one can have a wood consisting of nothing but creepers...Now let us have another look at those who found favor with the angel...What has brought them to the temple? That is a difficult question, and no single answer will cover it. To begin with, I believe with Schopenhauer that one of the strongest motives that leads men to art and science is escape from everyday life with its painful crudity and hopeless dreariness, from the fetters of one's own ever-shifting desires. A finely tempered nature longs to escape from personal life into the world of objective perception and thought; this desire may be compared with the townsman's irresistible longing to escape from his noisy, cramped surroundings into the silence of high mountains, where the eye ranges freely through the still, pure air and fondly traces out the restful contours apparently built for eternity....[1]

In these remarks about Planck, Einstein is of course also revealing his own motives for pursuing science: a longing for freedom from merely personal life and a search for the world of objective perception and thought. Towards the close of his life, while writing a brief autobiography (which is remarkable in its paucity of personal material), he said:

Even when I was a fairly precocious young man the nothingness of the hopes and striving which chase most men restlessly through life came to my consciousness with considerable vitality....By the mere existence of his stomach everyone was condemned to participate in that chase. Moreover, it was possible to satisfy the stomach by such participation, but not man in so far as he is a thinking and feeling being. As the first way out there was religion, which is implanted into every child by way of the traditional education-machine. Thus I came...to a deep religiosity, which, however, found an abrupt ending at the age of 12....

It is quite clear to me that the religious paradise of youth, which was thus lost, was a first attempt to free myself from the chains of the 'merely personal,' from an existence which is dominated by wishes, hopes, and primitive feelings. Out yonder there was this huge world, which exists independently of us human beings and which stands before us like a great, eternal riddle, at least partially accessible to our inspection and thinking. The contemplation of this world beckoned like a liberation, and I soon noticed that many a man whom I had learned to esteem and to admire had found inner freedom and security in devoted occupation with it. The mental grasp of this extrapersonal (*ausserpersonlichen*) world within the frame of the given possibilities swam as highest aim half consciously and half unconsciously before my mind's eye.[2]

It is striking to note how words like 'eternity' and 'liberation' enter Einstein's remarks as a matter of course. What he says about some of the characteristics of a serious scientist can be said as truly about a serious aspirant on a spiritual path. The attempt to free oneself from the chains of the merely personal in order to be available to the world of objective perception and thought is central for both. For Einstein, then, an engagement with science was a matter of spiritual vocation, a response to an inner call, a way of freeing oneself from one's egocentricity.

Einstein viewed science on a very large scale. For him it had to concern itself not only with the nature of the physical world, but also with the fate of man, with existence, and with reality. It was not just a workaday occupation but a way to pursue transcendent aspirations, a way through which he sought to understand "the secrets of the Old One." On one occasion he remarked:

> It is, of course, universally agreed that science has to establish connections between the facts of experience, of such a kind that we can predict further occurrences from those already experienced. Indeed, according to the opinion of many positivists the completest possible accomplishment of this task is the only end of science.
>
> I do not believe, however, that so elementary an ideal could do much to kindle the investigator's passion from which really great achievements have arisen. Behind the tireless efforts of an investigator there lurks a stronger, more mysterious drive: it is existence and reality that one wishes to comprehend.[3]

Of Planck he said, "The state of mind that enables a man to do work of this kind is akin to that of the religious worshipper or the lover; the daily work comes from no deliberate intention or programme, but straight from the heart."[4] On another occasion he said, "Certain it is that a conviction, akin to religious feeling, of the rationality or the intelligibility of the world lies behind all scientific work of a higher order."[5] It is clear that Einstein is not using the phrase religious feeling in any churchly sense; he means a feeling of awe, mystery, subtlety, and vastness—a feeling which in another context he called a *cosmic religious feeling*.

If it is true that a great scientist and a great spiritual aspirant both seek objective perceptions in their attempts to comprehend existence and reality, and that both of them are guided by something akin to religious faith in the possibility of such comprehension, then what is it that distinguishes them and marks them on apparently divergent paths? It is my impression that the fundamental distinction lies in the direction in which they look in pursuit of their aims; the attendant means of investigation naturally vary. Traditional spiritual aspirants, such as those who follow the path of Yoga or of Zen, or of the Prayer of the Heart, seek within, whereas scientists seek outside. The methods and procedures for understanding nature[6] inside man are, of course, different from those appropriate for studying nature outside. We cannot here discuss the different procedures relevant to these two directions. It seems worthwhile, however, to remark that in both cases what is involved is a subtle interplay between theory and observation. Both approaches are intellectual as well as empirical; in one case the confirmation of an idea is sought in external experiment, while in the other this confirmation is sought in internal experience.[7] In both cases we get metaphors of truth: either as scientific theories and explanations or as religious symbols and scriptures.

In the external approach of science, only those aspects of reality are likely to receive attention which lend themselves to precise quantitative measurement. The general area of emotions, and more importantly the higher and more inclusive feeling like love, compassion, or the sense of purpose, may become objects of scientific scrutiny, but must be strictly excluded as instruments of that scrutiny. There may be aspects of reality which are perceptible only to the intelligence of the faculty of feelings, which measures quality and value rather than quantity, but science by definition excludes this faculty as an instrument of its method. Without this self-limitation, science could never have arrived at its own particular achievements. The tragedy is that popular awe of science has led to the devaluation of the function of feeling as a means of arriving at any aspect of the truth, and the quality of feeling in the culture has declined as a consequence to the level of the infantile or brutal. The mistaken conviction that those limited aspects of reality which are accessible to science constitute the whole has become so deeply ingrained in us that it maintains its tenacious hold even against reason itself, which proposes to us that the most complete view of reality possible for human beings must be that which includes the perceptions of all the faculties, and all the faculties perfected to the highest possible degree.

With scientific instruments, such as the telescope or the microscope, we see more facts, or new facts, but we see them with our ordinary eyes. Our seeing is extended but not transformed; our organs of perception are enlarged but not cleansed. In science, change of vision comes about through a new, often more general or simpler, theoretical formulation which provides a different point of view so that the same facts are now seen in a different light, or new facts are seen which could not have been suspected before and were therefore not attended to. Scientific theories are ways of channeling attention; a new theory is like a new shaft of light bearing the possibility of revealing hidden facts. This new view is arrived at indirectly, through the agency of reasoning. 'Seeing' in science is basically interpretation. This becomes more and more apparent in contemporary physics, where most of the experimental work is performed using instruments which no longer simultaneously involve the object 'seen' and our eyes. We infer many things indirectly about the object, and have confidence in our inferences owing to a logical consistency in our theories and a postulated consistency in nature, but we by no means always perceive the object directly. Thus not only theory but even experiments and 'observations' are mediated by reason. Reality as revealed by science is not directly experienced by feeling or sensation; it is indirectly conjectured by thought. However, scientific speculation undergoes a remarkable and continual self-correction through the subjection of its inferences to repeated experimental checks.

Self-correction also exists in the realm of the internal approach to reality. Here the inter-subjective verification is more subtle and more qualitative, being based, not upon quantitative measurement or statistics, but upon the recognition of a description of inner experience by another who has passed through the same experience and of the external signs of an inner change of being. The unanimity with which the stages of development of an aspirant are assessed in genuine spiritual disciplines of all times and places suggests that this inter-subjective verification is no less precise than that which exists in the realm of science, though of a different nature.

In the inner approach, theory is verified by direct self-observation and inner experience. Change of vision comes about through the transformation of the investigator himself, and hence of his organs of perception. He himself is both the instrument and the object of scrutiny. In perfecting his instrument, he at the same time extends and deepens his field of observation.

What is needed for objective perception is freedom from oneself. The spiritual aspirant escapes the personal self, not by ignoring it, but by attending to it with total honesty and thus establishing a consciousness which is independent of it and which, unlike the turbid medium of personal consciousness, is capable of becoming directly aware of the presence of the non-personal—or rather both suprapersonal and intra-personal—Self of the self. The instrument, the whole man, undergoes a process of transformation brought about by the suffering entailed in the facing of one's inner contradictions and the subsequent voluntary subordination of the personal self to the greater Self discovered within. The perceptions involved in internal knowing are direct and immediate. Understanding here includes poetic and intuitive insight; far from being opposed to scientific and rational knowledge, it opens up even vaster and richer dimensions of reality, adding significance to science itself.

It seems strange, in the light of what has been said above, that men of good sense should regard the internal and external paths as opposing each other, rather than as mutually supportive and complementary. After all, the domain of nature, by which I simply mean all there is, includes what is inside man as well as what is outside. The spiritual aspirant's concern to know the self—both his own ordinary self and the non-personal Self of all that exists—and the scientist's concern to know the world may be estranged halves of a primordial, unified search for knowledge expressed in the ancient idea that man the microcosm mirrors in principle the macrocosm. How can an individual know himself without recognizing his relatedness with the rest of the cosmos? And what point would there be if he knew all about the stars and yet knew nothing essential about himself directly?

I think that the major cause of the imagined opposition between the two paths lies in the different faculties involved in the change of perception. In both cases there is a firm conviction that reality is not as it appears to our ordinary senses. In the external approach of science the change of vision is brought about primarily through the agency of reason, whereas in the internal approach it is brought about mainly through feeling. Goethe was right in calling mysticism a dialectic of feeling; science, on the other hand, is a dialectic of reason. As Einstein remarked, "In a man of my type the turning-point of the development lies in the fact that gradually the major interest disengages itself to a far-reaching degree from the momentary and the merely personal and turns towards the striving for a mental grasp of things."[8]

Wisdom must consist in a reconciliation of the various parts of a man's soul. An integration of the intellectual and the mystical or of science and religion as Einstein understood them (without meaning thereby anything denominational or institutional) is essential for the healing of our whole culture. It is important to stress, however, that the primary reconciliation that is needed is not of science and religion as abstractions. What is needed is a harmonization of the scientific and religious aspirations in the same person. The locus of reconciliation is within the soul of a single human being. The more an individual is integrated in his various faculties the wiser he is likely to be, in whatever specialty his own particular calling and capacities engage him.

What makes any career a spiritual path are the breadth of view with which one understands its purpose and the motives for which one pursues it. So long as an occupation is primarily motivated by ambition for self-advancement and self-aggrandizement, or by fear and insecurity, or by gratification of personal pleasure and inclinations, it cannot become a spiritual path. Freedom from oneself is a necessary prerequisite for apprehending reality as it is, rather than as we wish it to be.

Freedom from one's personal subjectivity, however, is not obtained by appealing to a collective subjectivity which remains an extension of oneself in a horizontal plane. Real objectivity seems to include an altogether different dimension. When Christ says, "He who would follow me must leave self behind," he is calling for movement along a vertical axis of being. In this connection it is worth recalling a remark of Einstein as well: "The true value of a human being is determined primarily by the measure and the sense in which he has attained liberation from the self."[9]

As far as Einstein is concerned, we can say with confidence that for him science was a spiritual path, whereas on any path—scientific, religious, or artistic—the vast majority are no doubt self-seekers, more or less. Perhaps it cannot be otherwise. But one cannot have a wood consisting of nothing but creepers. "...science can only be created by those who are thoroughly imbued with the aspiration toward truth and understanding. This source of feeling, however, springs from the sphere of religion. To this there also belongs the faith in the possibility that the regulations valid for the world of existence are rational, that is, comprehensible to reason. I cannot conceive of a genuine scientist without that profound faith. The situation may be expressed by an image: Science without religion is lame, religion without science is blind."[10]

Notes

1. "Principles of Research," in Albert Einstein, *Essays in Science* (New York: Philosophical Library, 1934), 1–2.
2. "Autobiographical Notes," in P.A. Schilpp (ed.), *Albert Einstein: Philosopher-Scientist* (New York: Harper and Row, 1959), vol. I, 3–5.
3. Address at Columbia University, New York, January 15, n.d., in *Essays in Science*, 112–113.
4. "Principles of Research," 5.
5. "On Scientific Truth," in *Essays in Science*, 11.
6. Here I am using 'nature' in the sense of all there is, known or unknown, without entertaining a distinction between what is 'natural' and what is 'supernatural.' Spinoza, Goethe, and Einstein understood nature in the sense used here.
7. 'Experience' and 'experiment' are quite different from each other, although philosophers and scientists often use these words interchangeably. In this connection, see R. Ravindra, Chapter 7, this volume.
8. "Autobiographical Notes," *op. cit.*, 7. (Italics mine.)
9. Albert Einstein, *Ideas and Opinions* (New York: Crown Publishers Inc., 1954), 12.
10. "Science and Religion" in *ibid.*, 46.

TWENTY-FIVE

MICHAEL FARADAY'S APPRENTICESHIP

SCIENCE AS A SPIRITUAL PATH

David C. Gooding

Can Science Be a Spiritual Path?

This question links two seemingly incompatible activities and aspirations. Do these well-trodden paths lead in different, if not opposite, directions? Science is active and manipulative (of thoughts as well as things); it analyzes, dissects, selects, and simplifies, working with partial and incomplete models of the world. This means of acquiring natural knowledge sets it apart from the spiritual quest. On the other hand, science has intellectual, aesthetic, practical, and religious dimensions, and it would be presumptuous to suppose that scientific activity has not had, or cannot have, a spiritual dimension. Yet there has never been a great spiritual teacher who was also a scientist. The provenance and purpose of scientific knowledge is change in the *external* world. Insofar as spiritual teachings seek change, they do so through change in the consciousness of individuals. Does the image of diverging paths reflect our preconceptions about science and spirituality, rather than some essential, irreconcilable difference between them?

The suggestion that scientific pursuits are compatible with spiritual aspirations (or even conducive to them) arises because of the lives of a very few scientists. I suspect that an answer to our question has more to do with a quality such people achieved than with the nature or purpose of their activity. This quality is the extent to which they were able to transcend the ego. Einstein saw science as one means of liberation from the temporal self. Faraday conducted his science according to a discipline of self-observation and what he called 'self-abnegation.' In this respect, I shall argue, his science was as much an expression of his spirituality as it was an expression of the intellectual and practical implications of his religious beliefs.

Could a scientist's writings show us that science was, in its own right, a spiritual path? I doubt that they could for two reasons. The first is that it is so easy for us to read spirituality into a scientist's less worldly pronouncements, especially when—as with Einstein—he fits the image of the pure scientist as an unworldly enquirer after truths that are not of the marketplace. This is not to devalue, say, Einstein's expressions of a 'cosmic religious feeling.'[1] But we need to consider whether such words reflect the aspirations of maturity rather than a state of being achieved much earlier and through science. The testimony of friends and colleagues is another source of evidence about a person's spirituality. Faraday insisted—both in private correspondence and in public—on a separation between matters religious and scientific. Yet the physicist John Tyndall still saw that:

> contemplation of Nature, and his own relation to her, produced in Faraday a kind of spiritual exaltation....His religious feeling and his [science] could not be kept apart; there was an habitual overflow of the one into the other.[2]

Tyndall, whose materialist metaphysics were incompatible with Faraday's own beliefs, also perceived that the spiritual strength Faraday received on Sundays sustained him throughout the week. Tyndall's testimony suggests that Faraday's scientific work benefited from the strength of his religious commitments.[3] Personal qualities cited by friends and colleagues may well indicate a transcendence of self and of worldly values. But this may have owed little or nothing to science. This sort of testimony shows at best that a scientific mode of knowing has coexisted with a spiritual one, not that Faraday's spirituality was somehow enabled by his life's work. We need to ask a further question: Where science was a spiritual path, was this work an expression of a spirituality achieved by other means?[4]

To approach these questions it is as important to convey a little of the quality of Faraday's scientific activity as it is to develop Faraday's articulate and public views on science and religion.[5] It seems to me that as far as spirituality is concerned, a person is not made special by the fact that he or she is a scientist: scientists' pronouncements about themselves should be read in the light of how they actually did their work, how they lived, and how they affected people around them.

In this paper I can convey only a little of the quality of Faraday's work.[6] Before doing so I want to explain my caveat about the interpretation of scientists' religious and spiritual utterances. This is needed because the Western intellectual tradition defines knowledge as an intellectual (linguistic) category, separating knowledge from value and, more fundamentally, divorcing knowing from being. The focus on manipulable beliefs means that most of the considerable literature on the interaction of Western science with religion and with theology tends to deal only with the intellectual dimension, that is, with systems of *beliefs*, which are construed in terms of the assent of individuals to certain propositions. Important and interesting though it is, this sort of history does not address spiritual awareness as something which may inform attitudes, shape practices, and inspire scientific activity.[7] Can the spirituality of a scientist be discussed on an intellectual plane? In considering whether science and spirituality are merely compatible or are sometimes one and the same path, we should be prepared for the possibility that the harmony of science and spirit cannot be captured fully in a web of words. Knowing and being may not be related in the ways that historical explanations require.

Faraday's life provides a contrast to the traditional approach to 'science and religion' as distinct but interacting systems of belief. As we'll see, certain of Faraday's religious beliefs—acquired in childhood but renewed by his conversion to Sandemanianism in 1821—would make it seem *less* likely that he should have made so great a contribution to natural science. Sandemanianism was a demanding version of Christianity which required that he practice his faith in the smallest details of life as well as the greatest. That is to say, it emphasized the implementation of Christ's teachings in everyday life and conduct.[8] The Sandemanians or Glasites were a dissenting sect who believed that the truth of the Bible was to be recovered by as literal a reading as possible.[9] Having no clergy to guide and instruct them made the Bible all-important to the conduct of their lives and their worship. I believe that Sandemanian views on the fallibility of theology encouraged Faraday to adopt an experimental path in science. They colored his attitude to theorizing in science, reinforcing his distrust of theoretical (and, especially, mathematical) interpretations of nature.[10] As a Sandemanian, Faraday would not have accepted that the book of nature is written in a language so removed from experience as is the language of mathematics.[11] His often playful enjoyment of the imaginings of the mind—fiction, poetry, science, and (presumably) theology—was bounded by a deep awareness of the aspirations of theories and theologies to comprehend the world through intellectual ordering.[12] Theories were to be admired and used, but they were more 'tinged with humanity' than with the divine, for our humanity enters alike into the construction of natural theology and mathematical natural philosophy. Both may come between the observer and the Book of Nature.

Because their humanity engenders a power to promote and preserve illusion—or as he called it—'error,' theologies no less than philosophies should be held 'at arms length.' Their humanity makes all people including scientists 'active promoters of error.' Nonetheless, Faraday believed it is possible to learn something of God's creation. He devoted much of his energy towards doing just that, with results that have won him a place among the very best experimentalists of Western science. In the process Faraday came to realize that science requires a form of knowledge traditionally excluded by the methodologies of scientists, namely, self-knowledge. I will examine his arguments about the relationship between self-knowledge and public forms of knowledge (such as science) in a later section.

A Brief Life History

Faraday's ambivalent attitude to intellect makes him an unusual companion for the greatest of Western scientists. A brief look at his life may help us to understand this peculiarity. Faraday was born in September of 1791 the third son of James Faraday, a blacksmith living in Stoke Newington, then on the outskirts of London.[13] Faraday was raised in circumstances that hardly foretold a life in science. He had little public education until he was 13 and of course none at all in any of the sciences. Becoming apprenticed to a bookbinder in 1805 gave him access to works such as the *Encyclopaedia Britannica*, and he was able occasionally to attend courses of lectures given, for example by Jack Tatum and by Humphry Davy. This self-education convinced Faraday that he wanted to become a chemical philosopher. By 1813 he had become a journeyman printer but was released from this when Davy was persuaded to employ Faraday as his assistant. Though Faraday's position was at first a lowly one, it placed him in a leading laboratory with Davy and W. T. Brande, two very able and experienced experimentalists. His tour of Europe from 1813 to 1815 as Davy's amanuensis was an excellent introduction to the leading edge of continental science. Faraday learned quickly and was soon contributing to the analytical work of the Royal Institution's laboratory. By 1821 he had begun to eclipse his teacher and mentor, with the discovery of electromagnetic rotations in 1821, soon followed by the discovery of hydrocarbons (including benzene) in 1825 and work on stainless steels and optical glass, commissioned by the Royal Society.[14] Faraday became "Assistant and Superintendent" of the laboratory in 1815 when he was given lodgings within the institution and Superintendent of the house of the Royal Institution in 1821 and Director of the Laboratory in 1825. He lived at the Royal Institution with his wife Sarah until he retired to Hampton Court in 1862. He carried a considerable responsibility for the running of the Royal Institution, which housed Britain's foremost working laboratory. The great lecture theatre was the focal point of metropolitan science for much of the nineteenth century.[15]

Much of his time in the 1820s and the early 1830s was devoted to applied science, particularly consulting work ('professional business,' as he called it).[16] The time available for research was limited, but enormously productive. Following on from the discovery of electromagnetic induction in 1831, Faraday investigated and enunciated two laws of electrochemistry in 1833–4 (his electrochemical nomenclature is still in use) and self-induction in 1834. A thorough experimental investigation of electrostatic phenomena lead to the invention of the Faraday cage, an experimental proof that inductive capacitance is specific, a direct challenge to the established distinction between conductors and insulators and to the extension of his model of lines of induction to electrostatics.[17] The magnetic analogue to electric capacity eluded his experiments until 1845, when he showed that light is affected by magnetism. This, the magneto-optic effect (or Faraday-effect) led directly to his demonstration, between 1845 and 1848, of the magnetic susceptibility of all matter. By 1848 he had included crystalline forces and proven the magnetic susceptibility of gases.[18] He had nearly completed a comprehensive, unified theory of electricity and magnetism that promised to incorporate optical phenomena as well. During the 1850s Faraday was largely concerned to develop and defend this theory of lines of electric and magnetic force.

Mental Education

I remarked earlier that, although he believed that their humanity makes scientists 'active promoters of error,' Faraday thought that natural philosophers could learn something of God's creation. This requires a form of knowledge—self knowledge—that is excluded by the scientific method, which is meant to winnow out the objective, natural phenomenon from the personal, or 'observer-effects.' Faraday introduced this point in a lecture that he gave in May of 1854.[19] At first sight this lecture had little to say about a spiritual dimension to science or anything else, for his declared purpose was to remedy the credulity and gullibility of a public willing to misuse scientific opinion in support of unsubstantiated and even physically impossible claims. Faraday had himself been misused in connection with a controversy about the creation of living organisms with electric currents in 1836. Then, some had claimed that he endorsed experiments by Andrew Crosse which created living mites from inert matter by electrical means.[20] During a later craze for spiritualism and table turning, others had invoked Faraday's name in similar ways. By mid-century Faraday was one of Britain's best-known scientists and, when he chose to be, a very public figure. As the greatest experimentalist of his day, he was expected to apply scientific method to determine whether material objects had indeed been moved by natural or by supernatural influences.

Faraday responded at first in the way you might expect an established expert to respond. He asserted the authority of established scientific laws and experimental practices against the claims of the para-normal.[21] He also drew another boundary, asserting the independence of religious and spiritual certainties from the 'exertion of [our] mental powers.' This is one source of the mistaken view that Faraday kept his science and religion apart.[22] Much of the lecture dealt with conventional problems of observation and errors of perceptual judgment resulting from lack of education and training—and he offered equally conventional remedies ('mental' discipline). Although to disprove spiritualism was the overt agenda, it was not his main concern. For those who could hear it, this lecture carried a more radical message. In tracing the problem to the poor 'mental condition' of man, Faraday challenged the accepted view of scientific knowledge itself. This in turn placed a very different interpretation on his opening remarks about the separation of his science from his religion.

Faraday set his discussion of mental education in the context of a 'distinction...of the utmost importance:'

> High as man is placed above the creatures around him, there is a higher and far more exalted position within his view; and the ways are infinite in which he occupies his thoughts about the fears, or hopes or expectations of a future life. I believe that the truth of that future cannot be brought to his knowledge by any exertion of his mental powers...that it is made known to him by other teaching than his own, and is received through simple belief of the testimony given.[23]

Here he introduced an 'absolute distinction' between religious and ordinary belief:

> ...let no one suppose for a moment that the self-education I am
> about to commend in respect of the things of this life extends to any
> considerations of the hope set before us, as if man by reasoning could
> find out God.[24]

Thus, in a well-known passage, he says he is 'content to bear the reproach' that he is being weak in 'refusing to apply those mental operations which I think good in respect of high things to the very highest.' This refusal reflects his understanding of the sort of motivations that affect and limit the application of ordinary 'mental operations' to matters of faith and the spirit. In other words, this passage is about the state of enlightenment (or level of being) of those who would reason from Nature to God, not about our powers of reasoning.[25] He goes on to say, paraphrasing *Romans* 1, v.20, that:

> even in earthly matters, I believe that the invisible things of Him
> from the creation of the world are clearly seen, being understood by
> the things that are made, even His eternal power and Godhead....[26]

Why does he claim to be using only the 'ordinary faculties of the mind in ordinary things'? This looks like a conventional expression of humility. It probably was intended to discourage his audience from drawing theological conclusions from science. I think that Faraday was also preparing his audience for a less palatable, more radical message.

Elspeth Crawford has drawn attention to one aspect of this: that is Faraday's claim for a need for self-awareness with regard to the disturbing influence of emotions.[27] Objectivity in science requires that the observer be just as aware of his emotions and desires and their effect on what he is doing, as he is of external experience. Internal observation is essential to observation of the external world, unless we are to be satisfied with mere projections of our own hopes and fears. This remedy for the misunderstanding and misuse of scientific knowledge goes far beyond the issues of credulity versus authority, or the policing of boundaries between science, pseudo-science, and religion. It is very different from the usual notion of scientific objectivity, to be achieved through the elimination of subjective aspects of experience. Moreover, it is unusual for a scientist to make this sort of claim in public, especially from an established *scientific* platform. This lecture was given in the famous lecture theatre of the Royal Institution in the presence of Prince Albert. It would have been easy for Faraday to use this august occasion to present science in terms more acceptable to his public, say, as a moral and intellectual discipline, and to promote its importance to general education. He chose instead to attack— albeit obliquely—a false view of knowledge implicit in the conventional methodology of science.

Since the seventeenth century the methodologies of scientists and philosophers of science use nature (tried in experiment) as an objective means of discriminating between the natural (taken to be external) and the merely personal (internal), in order to eliminate the latter.[28] Faraday knew that there is a created, natural order, but he did not believe that nature can be observed in the way that empiricists assume. Lack of self-knowledge is an obstacle to having knowledge of *any* kind. Thus, he notes the following:

> Among those points of self-education which take up the form of *mental discipline*, there is one of great importance, and, moreover, difficult to deal with, because it involves an internal conflict, and equally touches *our vanity and our ease*.[29]

The conflict consists in our "tendency to deceive ourselves regarding all we wish for, and the necessity of resistance to these desires." Faraday had given over thirty years of his life to the attempt to read the book of Nature. The Sandemanianism in his Christianity promised that like the Bible, this book could be open to anyone who sought to read it *without prejudice*.

Is prejudice merely personal bias, which can be removed by the adherence to scientific method? In practice the scientific method commits scientists to a degree of intellectual honesty, to submit to the critical appraisal of their colleagues, and so on. One of the fundamental *differences* between scientific methods and spiritual ones is that the former seek to remove the personal aspects of experience while the latter depend upon self-observation to transcend the ego. What Faraday has in mind resembles scientific method less than it does a spiritual discipline. Referring to his own experience, he explains that:

> it is impossible for anyone who has not been constrained, by the course of his occupation and thoughts, to a habit of continual self-correction, to be aware of the amount of error in relation to judgment arising from this tendency [to deceive ourselves].[30]

As I show elsewhere,[31] Faraday's letters and his laboratory *Diary* support his testimony that he had found, time and again, that 'The force of the temptation which urges us to seek for such evidence and appearances as are in favor of our desires, and to disregard those which oppose them, is wonderfully great.'[32] By our nature *'we are all, more or less active promoters of error'* because we fail to practice 'wholesome self-abnegation.'[33] Self-education 'consists in teaching the mind to resist its desires and inclinations....' This is *'the most important of all, not only in things of natural philosophy, but in every department of daily life.'*[34]

This last phrase removes the distinction between science and other aspects of life that Faraday had erected at the beginning of his lecture. Faraday knew that human fallibility is not confined to non-scientific matters. Similarly, failures of judgment in scientific matters reflect, and will be carried 'into other matters of life' because 'proof of deficient judgment in one department shows the habit of mind, and the general want, in relation to others.'[35] This is why Faraday had insisted in a letter of 1844 that 'there is no philosophy [i.e. science] in my religion' and why he insisted on this occasion that man cannot find out God's nature by reasoning. Obviously we cannot infer from this sort of statement that there was no religion in his science.

The first remedy he proposes for failures of judgment is 'nature's school': 'all persons may find in natural things an admirable school for self-instruction.'[36] This could be read as an appeal to contemporary expectations that science, the study of God's created order, could provide for moral uplift and self-improvement. However, Faraday's own experience showed that such instruction would be worthless without the second remedy: disciplined self-observation. This comes to terms with the very humanity of the would-be student of nature. Although the overt message of this lecture is a moral one, 'mental education' is more than a moral or psychological discipline. It is needed in every area of life. Science, too, must involve an attempt to purify one's perception of the influence of ego.[37]

Insofar as he was able to practice it according to the spiritual disciplines of Sandemanian Christianity, Faraday's science challenges the traditional separation of personal experience from objective knowledge.

Tinged with Humanity

This lecture shows that towards the end of his career Faraday had come to practice science by trying to free himself of prejudice by freeing himself of its sources, so that a little of God's truth might be revealed. It was not a means of producing knowledge according to certain prescriptions and conventions. There can be little doubt that Faraday sometimes achieved a state of openness to unresolved experience, setting aside the demand of intellect for order and meaning, so as to accept a play of experiential possibilities. Some of his most original work involved describing these experiential possibilities, and this required that he avoid premature judgments about just how they should look or what they might mean.[38] Many scientists are capable of this 'creative uncertainty,' but Faraday seems to have had an unusual ability to stay with something even if it made no sense or was upsetting to his 'favorite notions.' The ability to suspend judgment may be likened to what the poet John Keats (rather unpoetically) called 'negative capability,' a state of 'being in uncertainties, mysteries, doubts, without any irritable reaching after fact and reason.'[39] Occasionally his laboratory *Diary* shows Faraday trying to record his uncertainty about just how to see (resolve) some phenomenon, or setting out his mental preferences explicitly, so as to be reminded of their influence on perceptual judgments and on subsequent interpretation of resolved experience. After all, these notions expressed mere human aspirations for order.

When read in the context of his Sandemanian Christianity, Faraday's lecture on mental education helps us to understand why he did this. Had he always lived, worked, and thought in this way? A letter of 1826 shows that he already believed that the most important limitation of the human condition is the partiality and fallibility of ordinary knowing:

> However strong and certain the appearances [of natural phenomena] are to me, if I venture an internal judgment, I am always

wrong in something; and the only conclusion that I can come to is, that the end is as beneficial as the means of its attainment are beautiful. So it is in life....[40]

The possibility of acting in, and upon, the world depended upon his awareness and acceptance of his limited and fallible judgment:

The point is this: in all kinds of knowledge I perceive that my views are insufficient, and my judgement imperfect. In experiments I come to conclusions which, if partly right, are sure to be in part wrong; if I correct by other experiments, I advance a step, my old error is in part diminished, but is always left with a tinge of humanity, evidenced by its imperfection.[41]

Christian teaching emphasizes the finitude and imperfection of human endeavor. Faraday's acceptance of this was reinforced by his Sandemanianism, and he was a Sandemanian before he became a scientist.

Nature's Apprentice

These passages show that the lecture on mental education, given when Faraday was 62, describe a way that Faraday had tried to follow since the 1820s, if not before. Besides a 'placidity' and readiness of mind, his faith assured Faraday that the value of his endeavors was not tied to the opinions of men; there was no need to triumph over the views of others. This is why, by contrast to many of his contemporaries, he was not concerned to establish views as his own, or to establish his views as scientific doctrine. Nor did he ensure the continuation of his work by building up a school of 'Faradayan' students, he made no attempt to win influential office and declined one of most prestigious—the presidency of the Royal Society—when pressed to stand for it. As Pearce Williams points out—'When one basks every week in the glow of eternity, years, decades, even centuries seem trivial.'[42]

This is shown in the quality of his daily working, as well as by his verbal and pictorial expression of that work. Isaac Newton once described his life's work as having been playing with pebbles whilst the whole ocean of truth lay undiscovered before him. In Faraday's *Diary* a narrow and often very practical focus informs and interacts with a larger, intellectual, and holistic vision in which each entity or phenomenon owes its existence, meaning, and purpose to the whole. There is a painstaking attention to every aspect of a phenomenon and an attempt to follow where nature may lead. Here the human timescale seems unimportant: Faraday could spend months, for example, exploring the details of the behavior of reagents near the surface of an electrode, just to establish whether secondary chemical actions would interfere with measurements he was making to establish laws of electrochemical action. How much he could discover was unimportant, provided that it was as free as possible of prejudice and error.

In his dealings with others, it is striking that Faraday avoided controversy and that his response to criticism was usually to clarify his position, always drawing attention to the dangers of reading more into the language of human experience than nature had shown. It is as though he regarded himself as a means of disclosing or conveying natural knowledge, which he thought scientists have a duty to do.[43] Of course, Faraday invested enormous amounts of time and energy in the construction and defense of a unified field theory. This explained material properties such as inertial mass—traditionally treated as essential to (or inherent in) individual discrete bits of matter—relationally, that is, as properties an entity may have in virtue of being part of a larger whole, which Faraday called the 'great field of nature.'[44] Yet, even after forty years, Faraday was able to set aside this investment of himself just in case he had been mistaken. For example, in 1856, close to the end of his scientific career, he re-opened a line of inquiry about the relationship between aether and matter, taking up a research project that obliged him to re-evaluate views he had developed many years earlier.[45]

In this respect Faraday remained *apprenticed* to Nature: unaffected by public acclaim for his mastery of experimental skills. He never allowed himself to assume the status of a Master theorist. Faraday could do this because he had long ago discovered something of greater importance: a unity of activity and purpose that few people achieve in any walk of life. He practiced science in an enlightened way. Although his science was not a spiritual path in its own right—any more than spinning was for Gandhi—it became an expression of Faraday's spirituality.

Notes

1. Quoted in R. Ravindra, "Science as a Spiritual Path," Chapter 24, this volume.
2. J. Tyndall, *Faraday as a Discoverer* (London, 4th ed. 1868), 178.
3. See also H. Bence-Jones, *The Life and Letters of Faraday* (2 vols.) (London, 1870) and G. N. Cantor, "Reading the Book of Nature: the Relation between Faraday's Religion and His Science," in D. Gooding and F. James, eds., *Faraday Rediscovered* (London and New York: Macmillan/Stockton, 1985), 69–81.
4. This seems likely, given the different sorts of knowledge acquired by the sciences and by spiritual disciplines. Moreover, all spiritual traditions emphasize the personal nature of spirituality, whereas science seeks a collective, publicly certified knowledge.
5. I develop this theme in a forthcoming biography of Faraday, *Nature's Apprentice*.
6. Tyndall attempted to do this (*op. cit.* note 2). See also T. Martin, ed., *Faraday's Diary, Being the Various Philosophical Notes of Experimental Investigation Made by Michael Faraday...1820–1862* (7 vols. + index) (London: Bell, 1932–36). And for studies of Faraday's experiments based on his diary, see: D. Gooding, "Final steps to the Field theory: Faraday's study of magnetic phenomena, 1845–50," *Historical Studies in the Physical Sciences* 11, 231–75 and *Experiment and the Making of Meaning: Human Agency in Scientific Observation and Experiment* (Dordrecht and Boston: Kluwer/Nijhoff, 1990), especially chapters 2 and 5.
7. See, e.g. R. Hooykas, *Religion and the Rise of Modern Science* (Edinburgh: Scottish Academic Press, 1973).
8. Sandemanianism is named after Robert Sandeman, who married the daughter of one John Glas, a dissenting minister of the Scottish Presbytery who led a sect that had broken away from the established church in 1730. A similar sect, founded by Benjamin Ingham in Yorkshire ten years later, joined the Glasite communion in 1760. Robert Sandeman subsequently provided a unifying theology for the small but growing group. For the origins of the Sandemanian Church see: J.F. Riley, *The Hammer and the Anvil: A Background to Michael Faraday* (Clapham, Yorkshire, 1954); Bence Jones (*op. cit.* note 2); and L. P. Williams, *Michael Faraday: A Biography* (London: Chapman and Hall, 1965).

9. For John Glas' position on this, see Cantor, *op. cit.* note 3, 73ff. The implication is that theology—as a construction of human intellect—comes between the individual and the word of God as revealed in the Bible. The Sandemanians dispensed with theologians and ministers in favor of an eldership for each church.

10. Soon after his discovery of electromagnetic induction, Faraday explained to a friend that he would call his researches 'experimental' to express their difference from the work of 'high mathematicians' who anticipate nature rather than observe it. See D. Gooding, "A Convergence of Opinion on the Divergence of Lines: Faraday and Thomson's Discussion of Diamagnetism," *Notes and Records of the Royal Society of London* 36, 1982, 243–59, at 246–8.

11. Faraday's preoccupation with plain, descriptive language was partly due to the influence of Lockean ideas which he absorbed through the writings of Isaac Watts, particularly *The Improvement of the Mind* (London, 1811). His assiduous application of their precepts owes a great deal to attitudes shaped by Sandemanianism. On this see my forthcoming biography of Faraday, *Nature's Apprentice*, and Cantor (*op. cit.* note 3, 70ff.) who argues that the Sandemanians did not treat the Bible as a basis for developing a natural theology. The sect produced little in the way of theological or philosophical writings. Intellectual disputation may even have been discouraged.

12. Faraday's work was of course influenced by theoretical, metaphysical, and epistemological precepts. The most general and fundamental are those of a Christian worldview, e.g., a teleological understanding of certain laws of motion and of the conservation of force. Their role i to create a general framework of possibilities (within which Faraday constructed explanations of natural phenomenal rather than a platform of axioms upon which a theory of nature is constructed). See D. Gooding, "Metaphysics versus Measurement: the Conversion and Conservation of Force in Faraday's Physics," *Annals of Science*, 1980, 37:1–29 and "Empiricism in Practice: Teleology, Economy, and Observation in Faraday's Physics," *Isis*, 1982, 73:46–67.

13. See Tyndall *op. cit.* note 2. Bence-Jones, *op. cit.* note 3. Williams, *op. cit.* note 8, and S. Forgan, "Faraday—from Servant to Savant: the Institutional Context," in Gooding and James, *op. cit.* note 3, 51–67.

14. For Faraday's and Davy's changing relationship see D. M. Knight, "Davy and Faraday: Fathers and Sons," in Gooding and James, eds., *op. cit.* note 3, 33–49.

15. The Friday Evening Discourses, which Faraday established in 1825, continue to this day. Between 1825 and 1861 he gave over a hundred of these. For the importance of the Royal Institution, its laboratory and lecture theatre in the nineteenth century, see Williams, *op. cit.* note 8, M. Berman, *Social Change and Scientific Organization: the Royal Institution, 1799–1844* (London: Heinemann, 1978). Forgan, *op. cit.*

note 13, and essays in I. Inkster and J. Morrell, eds., *Metropolis and Province: Science in British Culture 1780–1850* (London: Hutchinson, 1983).

16. Tyndall, *op. cit.* note 2, 181. Besides his superintendence of the house of the Royal Institution and his lectures and analytical work there, Faraday taught chemistry at the military academies at Woolwich and at Addiscombe.

17. See D. Gooding, "Conceptual and Experimental Bases of Faraday's Denial of Electrostatic Action at a Distance," *Studies in History and Philosophy of Science* 9, 1978, 117–49 and "In Nature's School: Faraday as an Experimentalist," in Gooding and James, eds., *op. cit.* note 3, 105–135.

18. See Gooding, "Final Steps," *op. cit.* note 6.

19. "Observations on Mental Education," reprinted in M. Faraday, *Experimental Researches in Chemistry and Physics* (London, 1859), 463–491.

20. See J. Secord, "Extraordinary Experiment: Electricity and the Creation of Life in Victorian England," in D. Gooding, T. Pinch, and S. Schaffer (eds.), *The Uses of Experiment* (Cambridge: Cambridge University Press, 1989), 337–383. Faraday alludes to this episode in *op. cit.* note 19 at 487.

21. *Op. cit.* note 19, 466–72.

22. Despite some good discussions such as Williams, *op. cit.* note 8 and Cantor, *op. cit.* note 3, the idea persists that Faraday consciously kept religion and science apart. See J. Polkinghorne, *One World: the Interaction of Science and Theology* (London: SPCK, 1986), 97. Faraday did say in a letter to Maria Edgeworth, that "there is no [science] in my religion" and as we see below he distinguished religious knowledge from every other kind. Such comments need careful interpretation because, aside from them, nothing else in Faraday's life supports the view that he did keep the two apart. Like Tyndall (cited earlier), I am doubtful that he could have done so in any case.

23. *Op. cit.* note 19, 464.

24. *Ibid.*

25. This is why he makes it clear that there is [more] than mere 'compatibility' between "those things of man which can be known by the spirit of man which is within him, and those high things concerning his future, which he cannot know by that spirit." *Ibid.*, 465.

26. *Ibid.*

27. In "Learning from Experience," in Gooding and James, *op. cit.* note 3, 211–227.

28. For the distinction between external and internal knowledge see R. Ravindra, "Experience and Experiment: A Critique of Modern Scientific Knowing," Chapter 7, this volume.

29. *Op. cit.*, 475.

30. *Ibid.*

31. In *Nature's Apprentice*.
32. *Op. cit.*, 475.
33. Thus he remarks, "...I believe that a very large proportion of the errors we make in judgment is a simple and direct result of our perfectly unconscious state," *ibid.*, 465. To Faraday it was self-evident that "no man can examine himself in the most common things, having any reference to him personally, or to any person, thought or matter related to him, without being soon made aware of *the temptation* and the difficulty of opposing it. I could give you many illustrations personal to myself, about atmospheric magnetism, lines of force...etc." *Ibid.*, 477.
34. *Ibid.*, Faraday's emphasis.
35. *Ibid.*
36. *Ibid.*, 473.
37. Notice that Faraday *does not* suggest that emotions should be eliminated or suppressed—only that their effects should be observed and understood. For Faraday's use of anger, see Tyndall, *op. cit.* note 2, 43–44.
38. See D. Gooding, "Thought in Action: Making Sense of Uncertainty in the Laboratory," in M. Shortland and A. Warwick, eds., *Teaching the History of Science* (Oxford: Blackwell/BSHS), 126–141.
39. Cited in Crawford, *op. cit.* note, 218–219.
40. Faraday to E. Barnard, 23 July 1826, quoted in Williams, *op. cit.* note 8, 105–106.
41. *Ibid.*
42. *Ibid.*, 104. See also the epilogue to C. A. Russell, *Crosscurrents: Interactions between Science and Faith* (Leicester: Intervarsity Press, 1985).
43. In 1858, for example, he argued that the purpose of a scientific education is to enable "the mind to apply the natural power[s] through law[s] of nature" and so "conveys the gifts of God to man," "On Wheatstone's Electric Telegraph in Relation to Science," *Proceedings of the Royal Institution* 2, 1854–58, 555–560.
44. This vision became the classical theory of the electromagnetic field. For its development see D. Gooding, "Magnetic Curves and the Magnetic Field: Experimentation and Representation in the History of a Theory," Gooding *et al.*, *op. cit.* note 20, 182–223.
45. See Williams, *op. cit.* note 8, 471–474.

CONTRIBUTORS

R. Balasubramanian is the Director of the Radhakrishnan Institute for Advanced Study in Philosophy, University of Madras in India. His field of specialization has been Vedanta and he has published many papers and books.

Osman B. Bakar is at present an associate professor in History and Philosophy of Science in the University of Malaya, Kuala Lumpur, Malaysia. He obtained his B.Sc. and M.Sc. in Mathematics from the University of London and a Ph.D. in Islamic Philosophy from Temple University, Philadelphia. He is a founding member and the current President of the Islamic Academy of Science of Malaysia. He is the author of several books and numerous articles on Islamic science and philosophy. Among his books are *Classification of Knowledge in Islam* and *Studies in Islamic Science and Philosophy*.

Ruth Tiffany Barnhouse, M.D., Th.M., is Professor Emerita of Psychiatry and Pastoral Care, Southern Methodist University. She is a Life Fellow of the American Psychiatric Association and a member of The American Academy of Psychoanalysis. She is an Episcopal priest, an Assistant Editor of *The Anglican Theological Review*, and a Past President of the Conference of Anglican Theologians. She is President of the Isthmus Institute and President of Peacemakers, Inc.

M. W. Padmasiri de Silva is Professor and Chairman of the Department of Philosophy and Psychology, University of Peradeniya, Sri Lanka. He received his Ph.D. in Comparative Philosophy from the University of Hawaii. His main interest is in the field of Philosophical Psychology. Among his many papers and books is an *Introduction to Buddhist Psychology*.

Manuel B. Dy, Jr. is a professor in the Chinese Studies Programme in the Ateneo de Manila University in the Philippines. He is interested in the history of ideas and the impact of modernization on traditional cultures.

Tor Ragnar Gerholm received a Ph.D. in physics from the University of Uppsala in Sweden. He is Professor of Physics and Head of the Department at the University of Stockholm where he is also the Dean of the Faculty of Science. He is the author of more than a hundred scientific publications and of four books on science and technology. He earned the Swedish Authors' Association Literary Prize in 1962, the Riddare of Nordstierne Orden in 1975, and the Natur Och Kultur's Cultural Prize in 1978.

David C. Gooding received his Ph.D. in the History and Philosophy of Science from Oxford University. He is a specialist on the life and work of Michael Faraday. He is at present a Professor of Philosophy at the University of Bath in England.

Alfredo V. Lagmay is Professor of Philosophy and Psychology at the University of the Philippines. He received his Ph.D. in Experimental Psychology from Harvard University. He has written numerous papers and books and has been given many awards for his distinguished scholarship and service in psychology. Recently the title and rank of 'National Scientist of the Republic' was conferred on him by the President of the Philippines.

Priscilla Murray is an educator with teaching experience in high schools and in universities in England and Canada. She has an M.A. in philosophy and is now a doctoral candidate in the School of Education at Dalhousie University, Halifax, Canada. She is the Associate Director of the Institute for the Integration of Spirit and Mind. Her major interests at present are moral education and the interface between science and spirituality.

Francis G. Nagasaka received a Ph.D. in physics from the University of Notre Dame, U.S.A. He is presently a Professor in the Department of British-American Studies, Nanzan University in Japan. He is interested in Japanese traditional thought and in philosophy of science, as well as in theoretical nuclear physics. He has translated into Japanese Carl Hempel's *Aspects of Scientific Explanation*, and he is the author of *System: Its Science and Its Philosophy* (with others), and *Life Science and Religion*, both in Japanese.

Philip C. Novak is Associate Professor and Chairman of the Department of Philosophy and Religious Studies, Dominican College, San Rafael, California. He received his Ph.D. in Religious Studies from Syracuse University. He is the author of several papers dealing with mysticism and consciousness. He received the Graves Award for outstanding accomplishment in the teaching of the Humanities in 1987.

Ravi Ravindra has master's degrees in technology, physics, and philosophy; he has a Ph.D. in physics from the University of Toronto. He was the Founding Director of the Threshold Award for Integrative Knowledge. He is currently Adjunct Professor of Physics and Professor & Chair of Comparative Religion at Dalhousie University, Halifax, Canada. He has published many papers in the areas of physics, philosophy, and religion. His books include *Theory of Seismic Head Waves* (co-authored with V. Cerveny), *Whispers from the Other Shore: Spiritual Search—East and West*, and *The Yoga of the Christ in the Gospel of St. John*.

Richard W. Sharpe received his Ph.D. in mathematics at Yale University. He has taught at Princeton and at Columbia and is at present Professor of Mathematics at the University of Toronto. His mathematical researches have spanned diverse areas including topology, differential geometry, algebra, and ergodic theory, and have appeared in journals in North America and abroad. He has long been a student of the spiritual life and has read widely in this area.

E. C. George Sudarshan is the Director of the Indian Institute of Mathematics in Madras, and of the Particle Research Center in the University of Texas at Austin. He is a distinguished theoretical physicist and has been nominated for the Nobel Prize in physics. He has published very widely and has received numerous awards for his work.

Index